fMRI Neurofeedback

fMRI Neurofeedback

Edited by

Michelle Hampson

Associate Professor, Department of Radiology and Biomedical Imaging,
Psychiatry, Biomedical Engineering and the Child Study Center,
Yale University School of Medicine, New Haven, CT, United States

ELSEVIER

ACADEMIC PRESS

An imprint of Elsevier

Academic Press
125 London Wall, London EC2Y 5AS, United Kingdom
525 B Street, Suite 1650, San Diego, CA 92101, United States
50 Hampshire Street, 5th Floor, Cambridge, MA 02139, United States
The Boulevard, Langford Lane, Kidlington, Oxford OX5 1GB, United Kingdom

Notices
Knowledge and best practice in this field are constantly changing. As new research and experience broaden our understanding, changes in research methods, professional practices, or medical treatment may become necessary.

Practitioners and researchers must always rely on their own experience and knowledge in evaluating and using any information, methods, compounds, or experiments described herein. In using such information or methods they should be mindful of their own safety and the safety of others, including parties for whom they have a professional responsibility.

To the fullest extent of the law, neither the Publisher nor the authors, contributors, or editors, assume any liability for any injury and/or damage to persons or property as a matter of products liability, negligence or otherwise, or from any use or operation

of any methods, products, instructions, or ideas contained in the material herein.

Library of Congress Cataloging-in-Publication Data
A catalog record for this book is available from the Library of Congress

British Library Cataloguing-in-Publication Data
A catalogue record for this book is available from the British Library

ISBN: 978-0-12-822421-2

For information on all Academic Press publications
visit our website at https://www.elsevier.com/books-and-journals

Publisher: Mara Conner
Acquisitions Editor: Tim Pitts
Editorial Project Manager: Susan Ikeda
Production Project Manager: Manju Thirumalaivasan
Cover Designer: Miles Hitchen

Typeset by STRAIVE, India

Contents

Contents

Contributors

R. Alison Adcock   Department of Psychiatry & Behavioral Sciences; Department of Psychology & Neuroscience; Department of Neurobiology, Center for Cognitive Neuroscience, Duke University, Durham, NC, United States

Mouslim Cherkaoui   Department of Psychology, University of California, Los Angeles (UCLA), Los Angeles, CA, United States

Toshinori Chiba   Advanced Telecommunications Research Institute International (ATR), Kyoto, Japan

Kathryn C. Dickerson   Department of Psychiatry & Behavioral Sciences, Center for Cognitive Neuroscience, Duke University, Durham, NC, United States

Naomi Fine   School of Psychological Sciences, Tel Aviv University, Tel Aviv, Israel

Rainer Goebel   Department of Cognitive Neuroscience, Faculty of Psychology and Neuroscience, Maastricht University; Brain Innovation B.V., Maastricht, Netherlands

Michelle Hampson   Department of Radiology and Biomedical Imaging, Yale University School of Medicine, New Haven, CT, United States

Talma Hendler   Department of Psychiatry and Neuroscience, Sagol School of Neuroscience; School of Psychological Sciences; Faculty of Medicine; Tel Aviv University; Sagol Brain Institute, Imaging Section, Tel Aviv Sourasky Medical Center (Ichilov), Tel Aviv, Israel

Itamar Jalon   School of Psychological Sciences, Tel Aviv University; Sagol Brain Institute, Tel Aviv Sourasky Medical Center, Tel Aviv, Israel

Mitsuo Kawato   Department of Decoded Neurofeedback, Computational Neuroscience Laboratories, Advanced Telecommunications Research Institute International (ATR), Kyoto; RIKEN Center for Advanced Intelligence Project (AIP), Tokyo, Japan

Ai Koizumi   Department of Decoded Neurofeedback, Computational Neuroscience Laboratories, Advanced Telecommunications Research Institute International (ATR), Kyoto; Sony Computer Science Laboratories, Inc., Tokyo; Graduate School of Media and Governance, Keio University, Minato City, Japan

Hakwan Lau   Department of Psychology, University of California, Los Angeles (UCLA), Los Angeles, CA, United States; State Key Laboratory of Brain and Cognitive Sciences, The University of Hong Kong, Hong Kong

Qi Lin   Department of Psychology, Yale University, New Haven, CT, United States

David Linden   School for Mental Health and Neuroscience, Faculty of Health, Medicine and Life Sciences, Maastricht University, Maastricht, Netherlands

Tomokazu Motegi   Advanced Telecommunications Research Institute International (ATR), Kyoto, Japan

Kenneth A. Norman   Department of Psychology, Princeton University, Princeton, NJ, United States

Jesse Rissman   Department of Psychology, University of California, Los Angeles (UCLA), Los Angeles, CA, United States

Emma Romaker   Department of Radiology and Biomedical Imaging, Yale University School of Medicine, New Haven, CT, United States

Yuka Sasaki   Department of Cognitive, Linguistic, and Psychological Sciences, Brown University, Providence, RI, United States

Kazuhisa Shibata   Lab for Human Cognition and Learning, Center for Brain Science, RIKEN, Wako, Saitama, Japan

James S. Sulzer   Department of Mechanical Engineering, University of Texas at Austin, Austin, TX, United States

Jessica Elizabeth Taylor   Advanced Telecommunications Research Institute International (ATR), Kyoto, Japan

Nicholas B. Turk-Browne   Department of Psychology, Yale University, New Haven, CT, United States

Jeffrey D. Wammes   Department of Psychology, Queen's University, Kingston, ON, Canada; Department of Psychology, Yale University, New Haven, CT, United States

Zhiyan Wang   Department of Cognitive, Linguistic, and Psychological Sciences, Brown University, Providence, RI, United States

Takeo Watanabe   Department of Cognitive, Linguistic, and Psychological Sciences, Brown University, Providence, RI, United States

Nikolaus Weiskopf   Department of Neurophysics, Max Planck Institute for Human Cognitive and Brain Sciences; Felix Bloch Institute for Solid State Physics, Faculty of Physics and Earth Sciences, Leipzig University, Leipzig, Germany

Kymberly Young   Department of Psychiatry, University of Pittsburgh, Pittsburgh, PA, United States

Zhiying Zhao   Department of Radiology and Biomedical Imaging, Yale University School of Medicine, New Haven, CT, United States

Introduction

Michelle Hampson

Associate Professor, Department of Radiology and Biomedical Imaging, Psychiatry, Biomedical Engineering and the Child Study Center, Yale University School of Medicine, New Haven, CT, United States

The analysis of functional magnetic resonance imaging (fMRI) data in real time, that is, during the scan in which it is collected, has enabled a new form of neurofeedback known as real-time fMRI neurofeedback or more simply as fMRI neurofeedback. This form of neurofeedback can target any aspect of brain function that can be measured in real time via fMRI, including (but not limited to) activity in specific brain loci, spatially distributed patterns of brain activity, or connectivity patterns in the brain. The feedback provided can act as a training signal for feedback learning that enables participants to gain control over their brain patterns. As described throughout this book, researchers around the world have found that fMRI neurofeedback can be used to successfully train various aspects of brain function and that such training can induce targeted changes in perception, cognition, and emotion. Thus fMRI neurofeedback is emerging as a new tool for human neuroscience that offers an unparalleled opportunity for noninvasive, flexible, and precisely targeted modulation of human brain function.

For this reason, fMRI neurofeedback draws researchers from a wide array of backgrounds. Neuroscientists and psychologists are attracted to its potential as a technique for testing brain-behavior relationships: it allows specific aspects of brain function to be altered and downstream effects on cognition, perception, and emotion can then be examined. Clinical researchers excited by its therapeutic potential are developing paradigms for treating and studying neuropsychiatric disorders—these typically involve training patients to control their symptom-relevant brain patterns and examining the effects of that training on their brain activity patterns, mental function, and clinical condition. Imaging analysis experts and software engineers are addressing technical challenges and advancing existing capabilities for real-time imaging. This includes developing software for targeting new types of biomarkers of brain function and optimizing analytic techniques to maximize the signal-to-noise ratio of the feedback. All these individuals with their varied backgrounds converge to create a rich mélange of expertise. However, as with all interdisciplinary work, individuals from one background are challenged with knowledge gaps as they cross disciplines into other research domains. For example, technical researchers may be unaware of expectations and concerns relevant to clinical trial research, while researchers from nontechnical backgrounds may struggle to make real-time imaging analysis choices. *fMRI Neurofeedback* is intended to address these challenges.

More specifically, the book is designed to provide a didactic reference and basic introduction to the field for individuals from various backgrounds. World leaders in the field of fMRI neurofeedback have contributed, ensuring the material is imbued with their deep expertise and a rich array of perspectives. Critically, however, the chapters are not snapshots of work conducted in individual labs. Each chapter aims to provide comprehensive knowledge of the relevant topic area written in a jargon-free manner accessible to all researchers. The chapter topics were selected to cover the foundational material needed for researchers who are new to the field.

This work is organized into a textbook format. It opens with a review of the history of fMRI neurofeedback research that describes the progress of the field from early proof-of-concept studies to multisite trials. Following the history chapter, the book is structured into three multichapter sections. Each section has an introduction that gives an overview of the topic and the chapters within. The first section is on neurofeedback methods. This section, introduced by Rainer Goebel, covers real-time imaging and data analysis as well as protocol design. It incorporates numerous illustrations to clarify methodological concepts. The methods section is followed by a section discussing basic science applications, introduced by Nicholas Turk-Browne, that describes the work done to date demonstrating how fMRI neurofeedback can alter mental function in a targeted manner and discussing the potential of real-time imaging protocols for human neuroscience. The last and largest section, introduced by David Linden, covers clinical applications. This section provides background on clinical intervention development and reviews the literature on clinical fMRI neurofeedback research in a didactic manner that encourages an examination of design decisions and highlights future directions of interest. Several chapters covering topics that were not specific to a section are then included at the end of the book. First, Chapter 13 addresses questions regarding the mechanisms underlying fMRI neurofeedback learning. For example, does fMRI neurofeedback induce plasticity directly in the target region, or does it rewire the broader circuitry so that the target region is modulated differently by its connected regions? And how is it possible that a few sessions of training using a feedback signal with relatively low spatial resolution can still enable effective learning of specific neural activity patterns? Data of relevance to these questions are discussed and a theoretical model of neurofeedback learning is proposed. Following this chapter, there is a chapter on the ethics of fMRI neurofeedback. Any intervention used to modulate human mental function raises ethical issues, and these are amplified for fMRI neurofeedback by the demonstrated efficacy of implicit training paradigms that can alter mental function in a targeted manner without participant awareness of what is being trained, or even that training is occurring. Humane and socially responsible development of fMRI neurofeedback thus requires active engagement of the research community and this chapter provides an introduction to many of the complex ethical issues involved. Finally, in the last chapter, a list of resources for fMRI neurofeedback research is provided as a practical reference for readers.

In summary, this book is intended as an educational resource for those interested in joining the interdisciplinary community of researchers who use real-time fMRI neurofeedback to treat and study the human brain. However, the book may also be of interest to a broader audience of educated readers, including those who are simply curious about neuroscience and brain-computer interfaces. Hopefully, readers of disparate backgrounds will find the material accessible and will enjoy learning about fMRI neurofeedback and its promise for advancing our understanding of the human brain.

CHAPTER 1

A brief history of real-time fMRI neurofeedback*

David Linden[a], Rainer Goebel[b,c], and Nikolaus Weiskopf[d,e]
[a]School for Mental Health and Neuroscience, Faculty of Health, Medicine and Life Sciences, Maastricht University, Maastricht, Netherlands, [b]Department of Cognitive Neuroscience, Faculty of Psychology and Neuroscience, Maastricht University, Maastricht, Netherlands, [c]Brain Innovation B.V., Maastricht, Netherlands, [d]Department of Neurophysics, Max Planck Institute for Human Cognitive and Brain Sciences, Leipzig, Germany, [e]Felix Bloch Institute for Solid State Physics, Faculty of Physics and Earth Sciences, Leipzig University, Leipzig, Germany

1 From inception of rtfMRI neurofeedback to clinical trials in 15 years

Functional magnetic resonance imaging (fMRI) has revolutionized the study of the human brain, since it allows high-resolution noninvasive recordings of the blood oxygen level-dependent (BOLD) response as an indirect measure of neuroelectric activity (Rosen and Savoy, 2012). Typically, results of fMRI studies become accessible with several hours or days delay after data acquisition. Real-time fMRI (rtfMRI) systems were developed (Cox et al., 1995) shortly after the inception of fMRI, which processed the data as quickly as it was acquired. Their potential for quality assurance, functional localizers, intraoperative studies, and teaching was recognized (for reviews, see Cohen, 2001; Weiskopf et al., 2007). However, their uptake was rather slow and restricted to a few specialized neuroimaging sites.

This has changed over the last 20 years as new types of real-time experiments have been developed with designs and stimuli that adapt to the participants' measured brain activity. These include—but are not limited to—biofeedback of neuronal responses, i.e., neurofeedback (for reviews, see LaConte, 2011; Sitaram et al., 2017; Weiskopf, 2012; Weiskopf et al., 2007). In neurofeedback, which is the object of this text book, participants learn to control their brain activity using real-time feedback they receive about their brain activity (Fig. 1).

This chapter will provide a brief view of the history of rtfMRI neurofeedback, which is a rapidly evolving field that has gone from pilot experiments to clinical trials in less than 15 years. We will cover the motivation for this work and important technical and scientific developments, and will place these developments in the context of the growth of the scientific

---

* Parts of the chapter were adapted from Weiskopf (2012), Copyright Elsevier.

fMRI Neurofeedback. https://doi.org/10.1016/B978-0-12-822421-2.00005-3

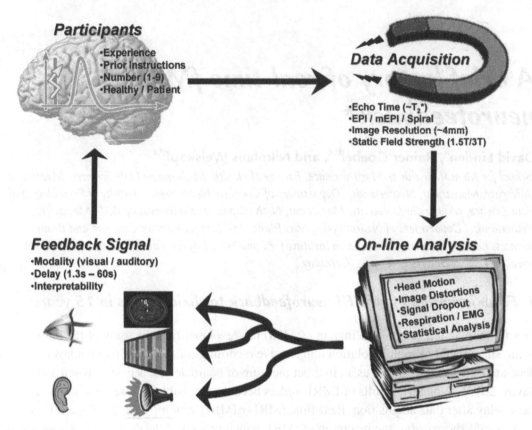

Fig. 1

Setup of an rtfMRI neurofeedback experiment and flow of data in neurofeedback experiments as conceptualized in Weiskopf et al. (2004b). The concepts and distributed acquisition and computation approach were widely adopted from these early studies. *Reprinted with permission from Weiskopf, N., Scharnowski, F., Veit, R., Goebel, R., Birbaumer, N., Mathiak, K., 2004b. Self-regulation of local brain activity using real-time functional magnetic resonance imaging (fMRI). J. Physiol.-Paris 98, 357–373. https://doi:10.1016/j.jphysparis.2005.09.019.*

field and its community. This chapter will not systematically review the field of rtfMRI neurofeedback and may be steered by the perspectives of the authors to varying degrees, who contributed to the different phases of development from the early pioneering experiments to the first clinical trials.

We identify three main phases in the development of rtfMRI neurofeedback with fuzzy transitions. In the first phase less than a handful of groups developed acquisition methods, processing methods, and foundations of experimental designs, while testing them in proof-of-concept studies. In the second transition phase new groups entered the field and explored new potential applications—especially the behavioral effects of physiological self-regulation.

In the third phase we saw a substantial increase in the size of the field and its consolidation, which included clinical trials, large multisite consortia, and regular specialized conferences. Of course, the development of rtfMRI neurofeedback did not take place in isolation from major developments in the broader field of human functional neuroimaging. For example, the impact of machine learning methods, multivariate analysis, and open science practices can also be recognized in its history.

2 The first steps: Early exploration

One of the driving forces behind the development of rtfMRI neurofeedback was EEG neurofeedback, which had shown significant promise in neuroscientific and clinical applications (Birbaumer et al., 1999; Kotchoubey et al., 2001; Rockstroh et al., 1990), but suffered from major limitations. The precise localization of neuronal sources with EEG is difficult due to the ill-posed inference from the measured scalp potentials. This problem becomes even less tractable for multiple neuroelectric sources as typically found in neuronal network activity. Furthermore, the sensitivity to neuronal sources varies substantially across the brain. These issues hamper the precise measurement of brain activity in deep brain areas and of network activity in general. RtfMRI neurofeedback promised to overcome these limitations and allow for feedback from precisely defined brain areas and network activity, which play a major role in cognitive and affective processes. The earliest rtfMRI neurofeedback studies already attempted to find out what areas are accessible to neurofeedback, how self-regulation is mediated, how self-regulation can be learned, what kinds of behavioral effects can be induced, and how specific the effects are. As it turned out, these are all still important questions today despite significant advances in neurofeedback.

2.1 Challenges of fast and reliable rtfMRI neurofeedback

The first studies aimed to establish neurofeedback using rtfMRI with a variety of methodological and experimental approaches (Posse et al., 2003; Weiskopf et al., 2004a; Weiskopf et al., 2003; Yoo and Jolesz, 2002). Although methods for real-time processing were available at the time (Cohen, 2001; Cox et al., 1995; Goebel, 2001; Posse et al., 2001; Smyser et al., 2001; Voyvodic, 1999), they only provided a partial solution and significant challenges remained. Since feedback needs to be accurate and fast for effective learning, the fMRI data acquisition had to be considered carefully to balance trade-offs in speed, spatial resolution, and functional sensitivity. This led to acquisitions with partial brain coverage and moderate voxel sizes (ca. $50\,mm^3$) and the use of advanced MRI pulse sequences such as multiecho EPI (Weiskopf et al., 2004b, 2005).

Fast and reliable access to image data in real time was another major challenge on clinical MRI systems, which are relatively closed systems due to their medical device status. This required developing specialized image reconstruction and real-time export and analysis methods, which flexibly supported different types of acquisition methods, and different feedback and stimulus presentation modes, resulting in different distributed computing approaches (Fig. 1; Hollmann et al., 2008; Johnston et al., 2010; LaConte, 2011; Sorger et al., 2009; Weiskopf et al., 2004a, 2005; Yoo and Jolesz, 2002). With the advent of various robust—even commercially available—solutions and the constant increase in computational power these challenges have become less pressing. Furthermore, tools are now provided by many scanner manufacturers including streamlined data export. However, in the early days of rtfMRI, neurofeedback robustness was a real issue, since many components had to work together perfectly. For example, a simple calculation shows that if five independent components work with a failure rate of 5% each and all of them have to work at the same time, then the assembled system will have a failure rate of ca. 25%. Unfortunately, this comes close to what the authors experienced at the time.

2.2 Challenges of designing neurofeedback experiments from scratch

The challenges in designing rtfMRI neurofeedback experiments were surely on par with the technical challenges for several reasons. The characteristics of the rtfMRI signal were rather different from previously employed neurofeedback measurements. For example, EEG-feedback designs usually worked with short trials of a few seconds with immediate feedback, which are not amenable to rtfMRI due to its lower temporal resolution and the sluggish BOLD response. On the other hand, rtfMRI could provide a much more precise spatial localization and more precise regional training. Therefore the majority of rtfMRI neurofeedback used longer trials consisting of ca. 30–40 s long blocks (Weiskopf et al., 2003, 2004a) with only few exceptions such as BrainPong (Goebel et al., 2004). In this variant of the classic electronic game Pong, two players compete on a virtual tennis court controlling their rackets by the level of instantaneous BOLD activity, i.e., with a high temporal resolution of a couple seconds (Fig. 2 and Video 1 in the online version at https://doi.org/10.1016/B978-0-12-822421-2.00005-3). The BrainPong study required participants to change their target brain patterns dynamically and achieve many different levels of BOLD activity, and thus paved the way for *gradual* fMRI neurofeedback (e.g., Sorger et al., 2018) targeting specific BOLD signal levels at specific times, and brain-computer interfaces for communication (e.g., Sorger et al., 2012).

To satisfy the need for fast feedback to facilitate learning, we used a minimal delay of a couple of seconds between changes in BOLD activity and its feedback by providing continuous and immediate feedback of the mean BOLD activity from a region of interest. Continuous online feedback of the BOLD activity became the most widely adopted approach in early rtfMRI neurofeedback (Fig. 2; e.g., deCharms et al., 2004, 2005; Caria et al., 2007; Rota et al., 2009; Ruiz et al., 2013), although intermittent feedback was also investigated as an alternative (Johnston et al., 2010; Sarkheil et al., 2011), and has become increasingly popular.

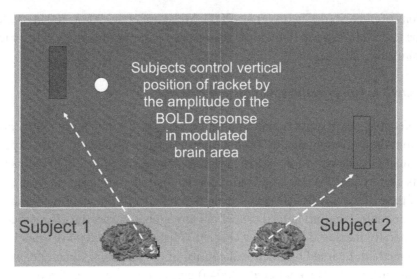

Fig. 2

Principle of the BOLD Brain Pong experiment. In this hyperscanning experiment (Goebel et al., 2004), two simultaneously scanned participants looked at a screen depicting a simple version of the classical computer game "Pong." The task of the subjects was to move their racket up and down to hit the approaching ball and to gain as many hit points as possible. Instead of using a joystick, participants learned to move the racket solely by regulating the amplitude of the BOLD signal within a participant-specific ROI selected in a localizer session. A video showing a live recording of the display as seen by two playing participants during scanning can be inspected here: Video 1 in the online version at https://doi.org/10.1016/B978-0-12-822421-2.00005-3.

In addition to the unknown optimal timing of neurofeedback designs, it was not clear how the feedback itself would be best presented. Visual feedback was chosen over auditory or other types of feedback, since studies demonstrated that visual feedback outperformed auditory feedback in EEG feedback (Hinterberger et al., 2004). Moreover, it was not clear either what type of visual feedback would work best, e.g., a graph, map, or virtual reality presentation. To reduce the cognitive load, our early studies used a simple scrolling graph of the mean BOLD signal (Fig. 3; Weiskopf et al., 2003, 2004a, b). Later studies followed similar strategies by presenting feedback as a temperature on a schematic mercury thermometer or a scrolling graph (Caria et al., 2007, 2010; deCharms et al., 2004; Scharnowski et al., 2010). However, feedback was also presented as a simplified virtual reality depicting a fire of different extent (deCharms et al., 2005), activation maps (Yoo and Jolesz, 2002), an emotional face for social reinforcement (Mathiak et al., 2010), or as a numerical character (Sarkheil et al., 2011).

Similarly, it was not clear what physiological targets would be most amenable to feedback learning. For example, would feedback from a single region of interest, a brain network, or connectivity work best? Thus early studies mainly focused on the mean BOLD signal of one or two regions of interest (deCharms et al., 2004; Weiskopf et al., 2003, 2004a). Later studies extended the target of feedback to multiple regions and patterns of activity (LaConte et al., 2007; Sitaram et al., 2011a).

2.3 The search for an effective and efficient control

Since neurofeedback experiments entail multiple layers of often lengthy interventions, it was clear from the beginning that designing the appropriate efficient control experiments would be a major challenge. Motivated by internal controls used in EEG feedback experiments, differential feedback and bidirectional control were used early on. Here, feedback of the differential BOLD signal from two regions of interest (or one active and one larger control region) helped cancel out any global unspecific effects due to, for example, generally increased blood flow (Fig. 3; Weiskopf et al., 2004a)—this is now a widely used method. Learned bidirectional control of the feedback signal, i.e., up- and down-regulation (Fig. 2; Weiskopf et al., 2004a) ensured that general effects due to the regulation task demands, e.g., arousal and attention, could not influence the feedback signal. The up- and down-regulation of activity demonstrates two mutually exclusive physiological responses, which act as a further internal control as proposed in early animal experiments on neurofeedback (Fox and Rudell, 1968). Other early studies included sham feedback control groups being presented with pseudofeedback and/or combinations thereof (deCharms et al., 2004, 2005).

For the first studies we chose the anterior cingulate cortex, supplementary motor area (SMA), and parahippocampal place area (PPA) as target regions, since particularly ACC and PPA could not simply be activated by overt movements (Scharnowski et al., 2004, 2015; Weiskopf et al., 2004a). Thus the successful regulation observed could not be explained simply by straightforward motor output and strategies, corroborating the importance of feedback for learning.

3 The second phase: Evaluating the potential for modifying human behavior, cognition, and affect

The use of rtfMRI neurofeedback for basic neuroscientific studies on physiological self-regulation investigates the relationship between self-regulated brain activity and behavior. Conventional neuroimaging studies examine the physiological response in the brain, such as the BOLD response, to external stimuli, overt behavior, or measures of peripheral physiology. That is, the neuronal response is regarded as the dependent and the behavior as the independent variable. The neurofeedback approach can be used to swap this dependence, since the effect of the self-regulated neuronal activity on behavior can be studied. Thus neuronal activity can be regarded as the independent and behavior as the dependent variable.

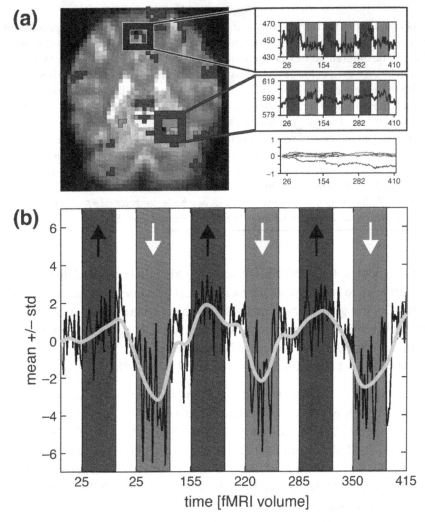

Fig. 3

Example for differential rtfMRI neurofeedback training bidirectional self-regulation (from Weiskopf et al., 2004a; Weiskopf, 2012). The subject should increase and decrease the differential feedback signal of supplementary motor area and parahippocampal place area (SMA minus PPA) according to the block design. (A) Display presented to the experimenter. On the left panel a statistical map was superimposed over one echo-planar image. Dark spots indicated areas which were activated during up-regulation blocks, and gray spots indicated areas which were activated during down-regulation blocks. Regions of interest were marked as rectangles which approximated the SMA (black rectangle with white outline) and PPA (black rectangle). On the right upper and middle panel time courses of SMA and PPA, respectively, were plotted as curves superimposed over the experimental block design which was represented by white (baseline), black (up-regulation), and gray (down-regulation) stripes. The right lower panel displayed the estimated and corrected head

(Continued)

Fig. 3, cont'd

motion (units equal 1 mm for translations and 1° for rotations). Statistical maps and time courses were continuously updated within 1.3 s after image acquisition. (B) Feedback screen presented to the subject. The differential BOLD signal of SMA minus PPA was presented as a continuously updated black curve on a color-coded background (transformed to gray scale in this printed figure). The tasks were presented as stripes: white indicates the baseline, during black blocks subjects had to raise the curve (up-regulation), and during gray blocks subjects had to decrease the curve (down-regulation). The gray curve is the low-pass filtered time-series. The arrows and filtered curve are for visual guidance and were not presented during the feedback experiment. Mean and standard deviation were estimated from the first baseline block. Note that colors were changed to gray scales for the print version. A color version of the figure can be found in to online or Weiskopf et al. (2004a). *Modified with permission from Weiskopf, N., Mathiak, K., Bock, S.W., Scharnowski, F., Veit, R., Grodd, W., Goebel, R., Birbaumer, N., 2004a. Principles of a brain-computer interface (BCI) based on real-time functional magnetic resonance imaging (fMRI). IEEE Trans. Biomed. Eng. 51, 966–970. © 2004 by IEEE.*

Exploiting the higher resolution of rtfMRI, several studies demonstrated that healthy volunteers could learn to self-regulate the *local* BOLD response with the help of rtfMRI neurofeedback. Control groups or internal within-subject controls were used to demonstrate the importance of the feedback for learning self-regulation that goes beyond what could be achieved by the sole use of conscious cognitive strategies (e.g., Caria et al., 2007; deCharms et al., 2004, 2005; Rota et al., 2009; Scharnowski et al., 2012; Shibata et al., 2011).

Brain regions studied by rtfMRI neurofeedback in the first and second phase of developments included motor areas (Bray et al., 2007; deCharms et al., 2004; LaConte et al., 2007; Sitaram et al., 2011b; Weiskopf et al., 2004a; Yoo et al., 2004; Yoo and Jolesz, 2002), somatosensory cortex (Bray et al., 2007; deCharms et al., 2004; Yoo et al., 2004; Yoo and Jolesz, 2002), ACC (deCharms et al., 2005; Hamilton et al., 2011; Weiskopf et al., 2003), amygdala (Johnston et al., 2010; Posse et al., 2003), inferior frontal gyrus (Rota et al., 2009), insula (Caria et al., 2007, 2010), rostrolateral prefrontal cortex (McCaig et al., 2011), parahippocampus (Scharnowski et al., 2015; Weiskopf et al., 2004a), visual areas (Scharnowski et al., 2012), and auditory cortex (Haller et al., 2010; Yoo et al., 2006, 2007). These different brain areas mediate a wide range of functions such as motor, sensory, visual, emotional, or cognitive processing.

Importantly, the studies demonstrated that specific behavioral effects correlated with regulation of particular brain areas, indicating the specificity of the training. For example, ratings of emotional pictures changed under insula regulation (Caria et al., 2010), reaction time changed with regulation of motor areas (Bray et al., 2007; Scharnowski et al., 2015), memory performance varied with regulation of the PPA (Scharnowski et al., 2015), linguistic processing changed with activation of the inferior frontal gyrus (Rota et al., 2009), pain ratings depended on ACC activity (deCharms et al., 2005), and visual detection thresholds covaried with retinotopic specific activity in visual cortex (Scharnowski et al., 2012). Other studies showed changes in mood related to changes in amygdala activity (Posse et al., 2003) or a wider network for emotional processing (Johnston et al., 2010), although the effect of mental strategies could not be unequivocally separated from the self-regulation. However, significant behavioral effects were not observed in all studies. For example, Johnston et al. (2011) did not find an increased positive mood in relation to self-regulation, which might have been due to the short training and aversive reaction to the scanning environment.

The second phase also saw the emergence of rtfMRI neurofeedback aimed at behavioral modulation in pathology. Although larger controlled clinical studies were still outstanding, the positive results of smaller studies suggested the promise for novel noninvasive treatment of clinical disorders. Investigations targeted chronic pain (deCharms et al., 2005), tinnitus (Haller et al., 2010), depression (Habes et al., 2010), schizophrenia (Ruiz et al., 2013), psychopathy (Veit, 2009), and stroke (Sitaram et al., 2011b). Additionally, although the studies on regulating brain areas relevant for emotion processing were performed on healthy volunteers, they suggested that rtfMRI neurofeedback may be applicable to disorders of emotion regulation and depression (Caria et al., 2010; Hamilton et al., 2011; Johnston et al., 2010, 2011; Posse et al., 2003; Sarkheil et al., 2011; Weiskopf et al., 2003). In short, although preliminary, these early data suggested rtfMRI neurofeedback had promise as a potential intervention.

Furthermore, the specific behavioral effects observed in patients and healthy volunteers suggested high specificity in the effects of neurofeedback interventions, making adverse effects less likely compared to pharmaceutical treatments. As a case in point, a study on 114 chronic pain patients did not find a significant increase of adverse events in fMRI and rtfMRI neurofeedback research scan sessions compared to baseline nonscanning sessions (Hawkinson et al., 2012).

4 Toward an international research community

4.1 The first four international conferences

Up until 2012 research groups working in the field were largely working on their own, developing protocols and analysis pipelines for real-time fMRI data analysis and conducting pilot studies on the feasibility, cognitive, and clinical effects of neurofeedback. One landmark event to change this was the first international rtfMRI Neurofeedback Conference at ETH Zurich, organized by James Sulzer and Roger Gassert (see Fig. 4). At this 2-day conference, more than 100 researchers discussed methodological developments and potential clinical applications, for example in the management of chronic pain, Parkinson's disease, or depression.

Based on discussions at this conference, several neurofeedback researchers with interest in psychiatric applications (including the authors of this chapter) formed the "BRAINTRAIN" consortium, which was funded by the European Commission for the development and

Day 1: 16.02.2012

10:30 Registration and Coffee

11:00 **Prof. Dr. Roger Gassert (ETH):** Welcome greeting

11:15 **Prof. Dr. Rainer Goebel (University of Maastricht):** Real-time fMRI neurofeedback and brain computer interfaces: Methods and applications

12:00 **Dr. Christopher DeCharms (Omneuron):** Real Time fMRI: Clinical Trial Results and a Current Appraisal

12:45 Lunch

14:00 **Dr. med Sergio Ruiz (University of Tuebingen):** Neurofeedback based on real-time fMRI: Applications in schizophrenia and direct brain connectivity enhancement

14:15 **Dr. med Annette Bruehl (Psychiatric University Hospital Zurich):** Training to regulate the amygdala by means of real-time fMRI neurofeedback

14:30 **Prof. Dr. David Linden (Cardiff University):** Clinical applications of fMRI-neurofeedback in neuropsychiatry

15:15 Coffee

15:30 **Dr. med Leonardo Cohen (National Institutes of Health):** Parietofrontal integrity determines neural modulation associated with grasping imagery after stroke

16:15 **Dr. Maria Laura Blefari (ETH):** Real-time fMRI neurofeedback as a tool to investigate motor performance

16:30 **Dr. Amanda Kaas (University of Maastricht):** Online decoding of finger activations using fMRI

16:45 **Dr. med Maurice Hollman (Max Planck Institute Leipzig):** Learned regulation of activity in posterior insular cortex using real-time fMRI neurofeedback

17:45 Depart from main entrance (Raemistrasse) of main building to Restaurant Linde Oberstrass

18:00 Dinner at Linde Oberstrass

Day 2: 17.02.2012

8:30 Coffee and Registration

9:00 **Prof. Dr. Niels Birbaumer (University of Tuebingen):** Brain Computer Interfaces (BCI) in paralysis and psychological disorders

9:45 **Dr. Nikolaus Weiskopf (University College London): Real-Time fMRI: From MR Physics to Neurofeedback**

10:30 Coffee

11:00 **Prof. Dr. Ranganatha Sitaram (University of Tuebingen, University of Florida)**

11:45 **Dr. Frank Scharnowski (University of Geneva):** Improving visual perception through neurofeedback

12:00 **Dr. James Sulzer (ETH):** Neurofeedback-mediated Self-Regulation of Substantia Nigra

12:15 **Sebastian Baecke (Otto-von-Guericke University in Magdeburg):** Social interaction in real-time with hyperscan fMRI

12:30 Lunch

13:30 **Prof. Dr. Stephen LaConte (Virginia Tech University)**

14:15 **Dr. med Sven Haller (University of Geneva):** Dynamical reconfiguration of human brain functional networks during self-regulation in real-time fMRI

14:30 **Dr. Yury Koush (Aachen University):** BOLD neurofeedback at high and ultra-high magnetic field: real-time Bayesian signal processing, functional MR imaging and spectroscopy

14:45 **Balint Varkuti (University of Tuebingen):** Real-time regulation of perfusion in the brain using ASL

15:00 Coffee

15:30 **Roundtable Discussion**

17:00 Closing

17

Fig. 4
Program of Zurich meeting. *Courtesy of Dr. James Sulzer.*

evaluation of fMRI-NF protocols in autism, alcohol dependence, eating disorders, posttraumatic stress disorder, and childhood anxiety. Although each clinical research group developed their own neurofeedback paradigm and trials were conducted in single centers this was the first fMRI-neurofeedback consortium to develop recommendations for standardization and trials methodology specifically for this field (Cox et al., 2016; Randell et al., 2018). Also around this time (in July 2013) Edith Evans and Luke Stoeckel organized a meeting titled: "Optimizing real-time fMRI for neurotherapeutic discovery and development" that was held at the Radcliffe Institute for Advanced Study, Harvard University and drew speakers from across North America. Many attendees at the meeting collaborated on one of the first review papers of clinical fMRI-neurofeedback (Stoeckel et al., 2014). In parallel, Mitsuo Kawato's group set up the DecNef (decoded neurofeedback, see Chapter 2) consortium with funding from the Japan Agency for Medical Research and Development (AMED) as part of the Japanese Strategic Research Program for the Promotion of Brain Science (SRPBS). This consortium (https://bicr.atr.jp/decnefpro/) comprises neuroscientists, neuropsychiatrists, engineers, computational scientists with interest in big data applications, machine-learning algorithms, and novel fMRI neurofeedback methods, and their application in multiple psychiatric disorders (see Fig. 5). From 2018 onward, this consortium was expanded into Brain/MINDS Beyond (https://brainminds-beyond.jp/) with support from AMED.

The second international conference was organized by Ranganatha Sitaram at the University of Florida in Gainesville in 2015. Novel topics at this meeting included the combination of fMRI and EEG neurofeedback and the use of functional connectivity patterns as neurofeedback targets. The increasing number of attendees, close to 200, attested to the growing international interest in the field. This was also evident from a growing number of review papers in neuroimaging, psychiatry, and neurology journals and regular training courses at the large international neuroimaging conferences such as the Annual Meeting of the Organisation for Human Brain Mapping (OHBM). Some of these resources are available for educational use, for example the slides from a workshop organized by Rainer Goebel at the 2016 OHBM Meeting in Geneva (https://www.pathlms.com/ohbm/courses/2658/sections/4358).

The 3rd International Conference, organized by the DECNEF group in Nara, Japan, saw another increase in delegates, up to almost 300. The conference moved to a 3-day program with an additional 2-day satellite symposium at the Advanced Telecommunications Research Institute in Kyoto. Highlights of this conference were reports on a number of randomized clinical trials of neurofeedback with promising results, new methodological developments in multivariate neurofeedback, and links with Brain-Computer-Interface (BCI) research using hemodynamic (fMRI, fNIRS) or electrophysiological (EEG, MEG, invasive recordings) signals.

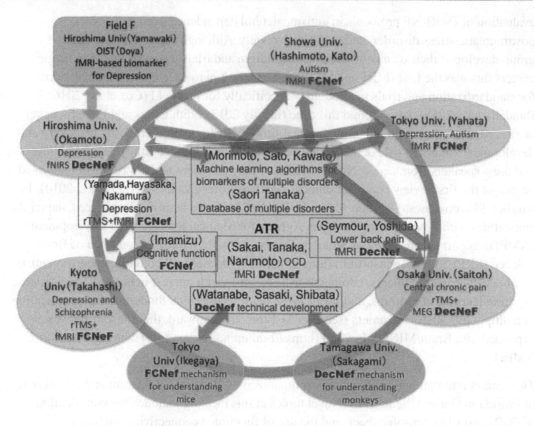

Fig. 5

Structure and topics of the Japanese DECNEF consortium. *With kind permission of Prof. Mitsuo Kawato.*

In 2019 it was the turn of the BRAINTRAIN group to organize the 4th International Conference. We teamed up with Klaus Mathiak's group to organize another two-city event, in Aachen, Germany and Maastricht, Netherlands. The keynote lectures, which are publicly available (https://www.rtfin2019.org/107020/wiki/484037/keynote-speakers), reflect the community's ongoing interests in clinical applications in psychiatry and neurorehabilitation, multivariate methods, and links with computational psychiatry and consciousness research.

Planning for the 5th International Conference, which was due to be held at Yale University and organized by Michelle Hampson and Nick Turk-Browne in 2021 or 2022, is currently on hold because of the COVID-19 crisis.

4.2 Links with research communities in related fields

Compared with the fMRI-NF community, the EEG-NF community has a much longer history and also a tighter professional organization, partly because it comprises a considerable number of clinical practitioners in need of accreditation. Although many of the underlying principles of learning theories are the same across the different types of neurofeedback, and some of the pioneers of fMRI-NF, notably Niels Birbaumer, had a background in EEG-NF research, the initial development of fMRI-NF was rather separate from the EEG-NF community. Over the last few years there has been considerable convergence, though, both through the development of joint EEG-fMRI neurofeedback protocols and through collaborations in joint conferences. For example, the NExT (Neurofeedback Evaluation & Training) section of the French Association of Biological Psychiatry and Neuropsychopharmacology (AFPBN) has been organizing annual national neurofeedback training days since 2016 (https://www.afpbn.org/sections/next/), which always consider all available neurofeedback modalities. Another scientific community with considerable overlap is the BCI community. BCIs, which use brain signals for the control of computers or other external devices, in general either use neurofeedback training or neuromimetic architectures.

For a neuromimetic BCI, only the algorithm needs to be trained (the participant just engages in "natural" cognitive activity, such as inner speech or mental calculation (Sorger et al., 2009)). For a neurofeedback BCI, the participant needs to train to obtain a particular brain state, for example a particular activation pattern in the motor cortex, which will then be read out for binary (or more complex) communication devices. As a consequence, many BCI researchers use principles of neurofeedback, and these communities have become more tightly intertwined, also because they largely use the same analysis pipelines and software packages. One example of the closer integration is the increasing interest in fMRI-NF at the Society of Applied Neuroscience, which is one of the main bodies representing both EEG-NF and BCI research.

4.3 Increasing publication activity

The time around 2011/2012 was also a watershed for fMRI-NF because publication activity suddenly jumped from single- to double-digit numbers (Fig. 6). In 2020 there were over 100 peer-reviewed publications, of which roughly a quarter were review papers. The community has also made steps toward standardization of experimental protocols and reporting practices (Ros et al., 2020), which is generally considered a step toward maturity of a research area (and a precondition for broader clinical applications).

The publication activity has certainly been fostered by a number of recent special issues, which are collections of peer-reviewed papers on a particular topic put together by a journal. These include the Research Topic "Towards Expanded Utility of Real Time fMRI Neurofeedback in Clinical Applications" in Frontiers in Human Neuroscience edited by Reza Momenan, Michal Ramot, and Javier Gonzalez-Castillo; the Special Issue on Neurofeedback in Neuroimage edited by Michelle Hampson, Junichi Ushiba, and Sergio Ruiz; and the Special Issue on Clinical applications of imaging-based neurofeedback in Neuroimage Clinical edited by Kymberly Young and Heidi Johansen-Berg. Of course, the present textbook

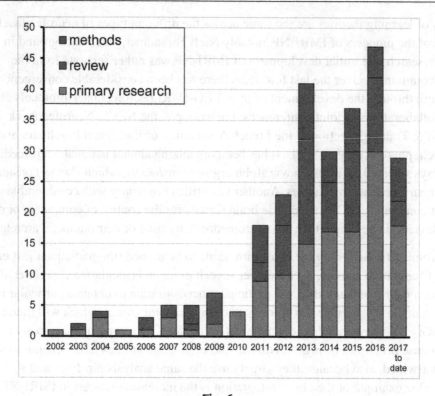

Fig. 6

Publication activity in fMRI-NF until 2017 (5). *From Thibault, R.T., MacPherson, A., Lifshitz, M., Roth, R.R., Raz, A., 2018. Neurofeedback with fMRI: a critical systematic review. NeuroImage 172, 786–807. https://doi.org/10.1016/j.neuroimage.2017.12.071.*

can also be regarded as part of this increasing publication activity and sign of the widening interest in the field.

Another interesting feature of the publication activities in neurofeedback, as in many other areas of science, has been the increasing use of open science tools. Many researchers now publish their papers on preprint servers such as PsyArXiv before submitting it to a traditional journal for peer review. Another option is to use the Open Science Framework (OSF) for the preregistration of whole study protocols, and also to share educational material and presentations with the scientific community.

4.4 Expansion of clinical trials and critique

One of the most remarkable features of the recent history of fMRI-NF has been the expansion of clinical trial activities. Although individual trials are still relatively small—mostly with sample sizes in the low teens, their number and geographic spread are certainly increasing. The trial registration website clinicaltrials.gov currently (November 2020) lists around 50 completed or ongoing clinical trials, and this list is not complete because trials may also be listed in other registers. Over 80% of these trials are located in the USA and Europe and, thus, expanding the geographic range even further is one of the challenges of the field. Of course, availability of MRI systems remains a limiting factor for the general take-up of real-time fMRI methodologies, but transfer technologies that can mimic or complement fMRI-NF such as fMRI-inspired EEG or fNIRS (see Chapter 12) may help increase the dissemination of hemodynamic neurofeedback particularly into a wider range of clinical research settings.

With the increasing interest in clinical applications of neurofeedback has also come increasing scrutiny of trial methodology and claims made about its efficacy. Although this critique has focused on the field of EEG neurofeedback (Thibault et al., 2017), recent studies have also scrutinized the methodology of fMRI-neurofeedback trials and commented on the small sample sizes and limited power of the clinical studies conducted thus far (Thibault et al., 2018; Tursic et al., 2020). Although small sample sizes are to be expected for such early stage research, this will be an important issue to address as the field develops.

5 Conclusion

Neurofeedback based on rtfMRI has gone through a rapid development from the first pilot experiments in a handful of labs to a broad research field pursued by a diverse international community within less than two decades. Major advances were achieved and the field has matured significantly and started reflecting critically on itself. Although there are many challenges especially in the standardization and clinical development of neurofeedback protocols, we believe that rtfMRI-neurofeedback will lead to more discoveries in basic neuroscience and clinical neuroscience and establish itself as a tool for noninvasive manipulation of brain activity and brain-computer interfacing. The present chapter will certainly not be the last history chapter of a neurofeedback textbook.

Potential conflicts of interest

The Max Planck Institute for Human Cognitive and Brain Sciences has an institutional research agreement with Siemens Healthcare. NW was a speaker at an event organized by Siemens Healthcare and was reimbursed for the travel expenses.

Acknowledgments

NW would like to thank his former colleagues at the University of Tuebingen (Germany) and long-term collaborators including RG for their strong support, making the early rtfMRI neurofeedback projects successful; particularly, his PhD supervisor Niels Birbaumer and PhD cosupervisors Klaus Mathiak and Uwe Klose. The authors' research was supported by the European Commission under the Health Cooperation Work Programme of the 7th Framework Programme (Grant agreement n° 602186) as part of the BRAINTRAIN European research network (Collaborative Project).

References

Birbaumer, N., Ghanayim, N., Hinterberger, T., Iversen, I., Kotchoubey, B., Kubler, A., Perelmouter, J., Taub, E., Flor, H., 1999. A spelling device for the paralysed. Nature 398, 297–298.

Bray, S., Shimojo, S., O'Doherty, J.P., 2007. Direct instrumental conditioning of neural activity using functional magnetic resonance imaging-derived reward feedback. J. Neurosci. 27, 7498–7507.

Caria, A., Sitaram, R., Veit, R., Begliomini, C., Birbaumer, N., 2010. Volitional control of anterior insula activity modulates the response to aversive stimuli. A real-time functional magnetic resonance imaging study. Biol. Psychiatry 68, 425–432. https://doi.org/10.1016/j.biopsych.2010.04.020.

Caria, A., Veit, R., Sitaram, R., Lotze, M., Weiskopf, N., Grodd, W., Birbaumer, N., 2007. Regulation of anterior insular cortex activity using real-time fMRI. NeuroImage 35, 1238–1246.

Cohen, M.S., 2001. Real-time functional magnetic resonance imaging. Methods 25, 201–220.

Cox, R.W., Jesmanowicz, A., Hyde, J.S., 1995. Real-time functional magnetic resonance imaging. Magn. Reson. 33, 230–236.

Cox, W.M., Subramanian, L., Linden, D.E.J., Lührs, M., McNamara, R., Playle, R., Hood, K., Watson, G., Whittaker, J.R., Sakhuja, R., Ihssen, N., 2016. Neurofeedback training for alcohol dependence versus treatment as usual: study protocol for a randomized controlled trial. Trials 17, 480. https://doi.org/10.1186/s13063-016-1607-7.

deCharms, R.C., Christoff, K., Glover, G.H., Pauly, J.M., Whitfield, S., Gabrieli, J.D., 2004. Learned regulation of spatially localized brain activation using real-time fMRI. NeuroImage 21, 436–443.

deCharms, R.C., Maeda, F., Glover, G.H., Ludlow, D., Pauly, J.M., Soneji, D., Gabrieli, J.D., Mackey, S.C., 2005. Control over brain activation and pain learned by using real-time functional MRI. Proc. Natl. Acad. Sci. U. S. A. 102, 18626–18631.

Fox, S.S., Rudell, A.P., 1968. Operant controlled neural event: formal and systematic approach to electrical coding of behavior in brain. Science, New Series 162, 1299–1302.

Goebel, R., 2001. Cortex-based real-time fMRI. NeuroImage 13, S129.

Goebel, R., Sorger, B., Kaiser, J., Birbaumer, N., Weiskopf, N., 2004. BOLD brain pong: self-regulation of local brain activity during synchronously scanned, interacting subjects. Abstr. Vieweritinerary Plan. Soc. Neurosci. Wash. DC.

Habes, I., Johnston, S.J., Tatineni, R., Boehm, S.G., Linden, S.C., Sorger, B., Healy, D., Goebel, R., Linden, D.E.J., 2010. Functional Magnetic Resonance (fMRI)-Based Neurofeedback as a Potential Treatment Method for Depression. FENS Abstr., vol. 5, 01715.

Haller, S., Birbaumer, N., Veit, R., 2010. Real-time fMRI feedback training may improve chronic tinnitus. Eur. Radiol. 20, 696–703. https://doi.org/10.1007/s00330-009-1595-z.

Hamilton, J.P., Glover, G.H., Hsu, J.-J., Johnson, R.F., Gotlib, I.H., 2011. Modulation of subgenual anterior cingulate cortex activity with real-time neurofeedback. Hum. Brain Mapp. 32, 22–31. https://doi.org/10.1002/hbm.20997.

Hawkinson, J.E., Ross, A.J., Parthasarathy, S., Scott, D.J., Laramee, E.A., Posecion, L.J., Rekshan, W.R., Sheau, K.E., Njaka, N.D., Bayley, P.J., deCharms, R.C., 2012. Quantification of adverse events associated with functional MRI scanning and with real-time fMRI-based training. Int. J. Behav. Med. 19, 372–381. https://doi.org/10.1007/s12529-011-9165-6.

Hinterberger, T., Neumann, N., Pham, M., Kubler, A., Grether, A., Hofmayer, N., Wilhelm, B., Flor, H., Birbaumer, N., 2004. A multimodal brain-based feedback and communication system. Exp. Brain Res. 154, 521–526.

Hollmann, M., Monch, T., Mulla-Osman, S., Tempelmann, C., Stadler, J., Bernarding, J., 2008. A new concept of a unified parameter management, experiment control, and data analysis in fMRI: application to real-time fMRI at 3T and 7T. J. Neurosci. Methods 175, 154–162. S0165-0270(08)00490-1 [pii] https://doi.org/10.1016/j.jneumeth.2008.08.013.

Johnston, S., Linden, D.E.J., Healy, D., Goebel, R., Habes, I., Boehm, S.G., 2011. Upregulation of emotion areas through neurofeedback with a focus on positive mood. Cogn. Affect. Behav. Neurosci. 11, 44–51. https://doi.org/10.3758/s13415-010-0010-1.

Johnston, S.J., Boehm, S.G., Healy, D., Goebel, R., Linden, D.E.J., 2010. Neurofeedback: a promising tool for the self-regulation of emotion networks. NeuroImage 49, 1066–1072. https://doi.org/10.1016/j.neuroimage.2009.07.056.

Kotchoubey, B., Strehl, U., Uhlmann, C., Holzapfel, S., Konig, M., Froscher, W., Blankenhorn, V., Birbaumer, N., 2001. Modification of slow cortical potentials in patients with refractory epilepsy: a controlled outcome study. Epilepsia 42, 406–416.

LaConte, S.M., 2011. Decoding fMRI brain states in real-time. NeuroImage 56, 440–454. https://doi.org/10.1016/j.neuroimage.2010.06.052.

LaConte, S.M., Peltier, S.J., Hu, X.P., 2007. Real-time fMRI using brain-state classification. Hum. Brain Mapp. 28, 1033–1044. https://doi.org/10.1002/hbm.20326.

Mathiak, K.A., Koush, Y., Dyck, M., Gaber, T.J., Alawi, E., Zepf, F.D., Zvyagintsev, M., Mathiak, K., 2010. Social reinforcement can regulate localized brain activity. Eur. Arch. Psychiatry Clin. Neurosci. 260 (Suppl. 2), S132–S136. https://doi.org/10.1007/s00406-010-0135-9.

McCaig, R.G., Dixon, M., Keramatian, K., Liu, I., Christoff, K., 2011. Improved modulation of rostrolateral prefrontal cortex using real-time fMRI training and meta-cognitive awareness. NeuroImage 55, 1298–1305. https://doi.org/10.1016/j.neuroimage.2010.12.016.

Posse, S., Binkofski, F., Schneider, F., Gembris, D., Frings, W., Habel, U., Salloum, J.B., Mathiak, K., Wiese, S., Kiselev, V., Graf, T., Elghahwagi, B., Grosse-Ruyken, M.L., Eickermann, T., 2001. A new approach to measure single-event related brain activity using real-time fMRI: feasibility of sensory, motor, and higher cognitive tasks. Hum. Brain Mapp. 12, 25–41.

Posse, S., Fitzgerald, D., Gao, K., Habel, U., Rosenberg, D., Moore, G.J., Schneider, F., 2003. Real-time fMRI of temporolimbic regions detects amygdala activation during single-trial self-induced sadness. NeuroImage 18, 760–768.

Randell, E., McNamara, R., Subramanian, L., Hood, K., Linden, D., 2018. Current practices in clinical neurofeedback with functional MRI-analysis of a survey using the TIDieR checklist. Eur. Psychiatry J. Assoc. Eur. Psychiatr. 50, 28–33. https://doi.org/10.1016/j.eurpsy.2017.10.011.

Rockstroh, B., Elbert, T., Birbaumer, N., Lutzenberger, W., 1990. Biofeedback-produced hemispheric asymmetry of slow cortical potentials and its behavioural effects. Int. J. Psychophysiol. 9, 151–165.

Ros, T., Enriquez-Geppert, S., Zotev, V., Young, K.D., Wood, G., Whitfield-Gabrieli, S., Wan, F., Vuilleumier, P., Vialatte, F., Van De Ville, D., Todder, D., Surmeli, T., Sulzer, J.S., Strehl, U., Sterman, M.B., Steiner, N.J., Sorger, B., Soekadar, S.R., Sitaram, R., Sherlin, L.H., Schönenberg, M., Scharnowski, F., Schabus, M., Rubia, K., Rosa, A., Reiner, M., Pineda, J.A., Paret, C., Ossadtchi, A., Nicholson, A.A., Nan, W., Minguez, J., Micoulaud-Franchi, J.-A., Mehler, D.M.A., Lührs, M., Lubar, J., Lotte, F., Linden, D.E.J., Lewis-Peacock, J.A., Lebedev, M.A., Lanius, R.A., Kübler, A., Kranczioch, C., Koush, Y., Konicar, L., Kohl, S.H., Kober, S.E., Klados, M.A., Jeunet, C., Janssen, T.W.P., Huster, R.J., Hoedlmoser, K., Hirshberg, L.M., Heunis, S., Hendler, T., Hampson, M., Guggisberg, A.G., Guggenberger, R., Gruzelier, J.H., Göbel, R.W., Gninenko, N., Gharabaghi, A., Frewen, P., Fovet, T., Fernández, T., Escolano, C., Ehlis, A.-C., Drechsler, R., deCharms, R.C., Debener, S., De Ridder, D., Davelaar, E.J., Congedo, M., Cavazza, M., Breteler, M.H.M., Brandeis, D., Bodurka, J., Birbaumer, N., Bazanova, O.M., Barth, B., Bamidis, P.D., Auer, T., Arns, M., Thibault, R.T., 2020. Consensus on the reporting and experimental design of clinical and cognitive-behavioural neurofeedback studies (CRED-nf checklist). Brain 143, 1674–1685. https://doi.org/10.1093/brain/awaa009.

Rosen, B.R., Savoy, R.L., 2012. fMRI at 20: has it changed the world? NeuroImage 62, 1316–1324. https://doi.org/10.1016/j.neuroimage.2012.03.004.

Rota, G., Sitaram, R., Veit, R., Erb, M., Weiskopf, N., Dogil, G., Birbaumer, N., 2009. Self-regulation of regional cortical activity using real-time fMRI: the right inferior frontal gyrus and linguistic processing. Hum. Brain Mapp. 30, 1605–1614. https://doi.org/10.1002/hbm.20621.

Ruiz, S., Lee, S., Soekadar, S.R., Caria, A., Veit, R., Kircher, T., Birbaumer, N., Sitaram, R., 2013. Acquired self-control of insula cortex modulates emotion recognition and brain network connectivity in schizophrenia. Hum. Brain Mapp. 34, 200–212. https://doi.org/10.1002/hbm.21427.

Sarkheil, P., Zilverstand, A., Kilian-Huetten, N., Schneider, F., Mathiak, K., Goebel, R., 2011. Application of real-time fMRI-neurofeedback in treatment of emotional disorders. In: Abstr. 17th Annu. Meet. OHBM Quebec City Can.

Scharnowski, F., Hutton, C., Josephs, O., Weiskopf, N., Rees, G., 2012. Improving visual perception through neurofeedback. J. Neurosci. 32, 17830–17841. https://doi.org/10.1523/JNEUROSCI.6334-11.2012.

Scharnowski, F., Hutton, C., Josephs, O., Weiskopf, N., Rees, G., 2010. Manipulating visual perception with real-time fMRI-based neurofeedback. In: Abstr. 16th Annu. Meet. OHBM Barc. Spain.

Scharnowski, F., Veit, R., Zopf, R., Studer, P., Bock, S., Diedrichsen, J., Goebel, R., Mathiak, K., Birbaumer, N., Weiskopf, N., 2015. Manipulating motor performance and memory through real-time fMRI neurofeedback. Biol. Psychol. 108, 85–97. https://doi.org/10.1016/j.biopsycho.2015.03.009.

Scharnowski, F., Weiskopf, N., Mathiak, K., Zopf, R., Studer, P., Bock, S.W., Grodd, W., Goebel, R., Birbaumer, N., 2004. Self-regulation of the BOLD signal of supplementary motor area (SMA) and parahippocampal place area (PPA): fMRI-neurofeedback and its behavioral consequences. In: Abstr. 10th Annu. Meet. OHBM Bp. Hung.

Shibata, K., Watanabe, T., Sasaki, Y., Kawato, M., 2011. Perceptual learning incepted by decoded fMRI neurofeedback without stimulus presentation. Science 334, 1413–1415. https://doi.org/10.1126/science.1212003.

Sitaram, R., Lee, S., Ruiz, S., Rana, M., Veit, R., Birbaumer, N., 2011a. Real-time support vector classification and feedback of multiple emotional brain states. NeuroImage 56, 753–765. https://doi.org/10.1016/j.neuroimage.2010.08.007.

Sitaram, R., Ros, T., Stoeckel, L., Haller, S., Scharnowski, F., Lewis-Peacock, J., Weiskopf, N., Blefari, M.L., Rana, M., Oblak, E., Birbaumer, N., Sulzer, J., 2017. Closed-loop brain training: the science of neurofeedback. Nat. Rev. Neurosci. 18, 86–100. https://doi.org/10.1038/nrn.2016.164.

Sitaram, R., Veit, R., Stevens, B., Caria, A., Gerloff, C., Birbaumer, N., Hummel, F., 2011b. Acquired control of ventral premotor cortex activity by feedback training: an exploratory real-time fMRI and TMS study. Neurorehabil. Neural Repair. https://doi.org/10.1177/1545968311418345.

Smyser, C., Grabowski, T.J., Frank, R.J., Haller, J.W., Bolinger, L., 2001. Real-time multiple linear regression for fMRI supported by time-aware acquisition and processing. Magn. Reson. 45, 289–298.

Sorger, B., Dahmen, B., Reithler, J., Gosseries, O., Maudoux, A., Laureys, S., Goebel, R., 2009. Another kind of "BOLD Response": answering multiple-choice questions via online decoded single-trial brain signals. Prog. Brain Res. 177, 275–292.

Sorger, B., Kamp, T., Weiskopf, N., Peters, J.C., Goebel, R., 2018. When the brain takes 'BOLD' steps: real-time fMRI neurofeedback can further enhance the ability to gradually self-regulate regional brain activation. Neuroscience 378, 71–88. https://doi.org/10.1016/j.neuroscience.2016.09.026.

Sorger, B., Reithler, J., Dahmen, B., Goebel, R., 2012. A real-time fMRI-based spelling device immediately enabling robust motor-independent communication. Curr. Biol. CB 22, 1333–1338. https://doi.org/10.1016/j.cub.2012.05.022.

Stoeckel, L.E., Garrison, K.A., Ghosh, S., Wighton, P., Hanlon, C.A., Gilman, J.M., Greer, S., Turk-Browne, N.B., deBettencourt, M.T., Scheinost, D., Craddock, C., Thompson, T., Calderon, V., Bauer, C.C., George, M., Breiter, H.C., Whitfield-Gabrieli, S., Gabrieli, J.D., LaConte, S.M., Hirshberg, L., Brewer, J.A., Hampson, M., Van Der Kouwe, A., Mackey, S., Evins, A.E., 2014. Optimizing real time fMRI neurofeedback for therapeutic discovery and development. NeuroImage Clin. 5, 245–255. https://doi.org/10.1016/j.nicl.2014.07.002.

Thibault, R.T., Lifshitz, M., Raz, A., 2017. Neurofeedback or neuroplacebo? Brain 140, 862–864. https://doi.org/10.1093/brain/awx033.

Thibault, R.T., MacPherson, A., Lifshitz, M., Roth, R.R., Raz, A., 2018. Neurofeedback with fMRI: a critical systematic review. NeuroImage 172, 786–807. https://doi.org/10.1016/j.neuroimage.2017.12.071.

Tursic, A., Eck, J., Lührs, M., Linden, D.E.J., Goebel, R., 2020. A systematic review of fMRI neurofeedback reporting and effects in clinical populations. NeuroImage Clin. 102496. https://doi.org/10.1016/j.nicl.2020.102496.

Veit, R., 2009. Echtzeit-fMRT und Therapie, in: Neurobiologie Forensisch Relevanter Stoerungen. Kohlhammer, Stuttgart.

Voyvodic, J.T., 1999. Real-time fMRI paradigm control, physiology, and behavior combined with near real-time statistical analysis. NeuroImage 10, 91–106.

Weiskopf, N., 2012. Real-time fMRI and its application to neurofeedback. NeuroImage 62, 682–692. https://doi.org/10.1016/j.neuroimage.2011.10.009.

Weiskopf, N., Klose, U., Birbaumer, N., Mathiak, K., 2005. Single-shot compensation of image distortions and BOLD contrast optimization using multi-echo EPI for real-time fMRI. NeuroImage 24, 1068–1079. https://doi.org/10.1016/j.neuroimage.2004.10.012.

Weiskopf, N., Mathiak, K., Bock, S.W., Scharnowski, F., Veit, R., Grodd, W., Goebel, R., Birbaumer, N., 2004a. Principles of a brain-computer interface (BCI) based on real-time functional magnetic resonance imaging (fMRI). IEEE Trans. Biomed. Eng. 51, 966–970.

Weiskopf, N., Scharnowski, F., Veit, R., Goebel, R., Birbaumer, N., Mathiak, K., 2004b. Self-regulation of local brain activity using real-time functional magnetic resonance imaging (fMRI). J. Physiol.-Paris 98, 357–373. https://doi.org/10.1016/j.jphysparis.2005.09.019.

Weiskopf, N., Sitaram, R., Josephs, O., Veit, R., Scharnowski, F., Goebel, R., Birbaumer, N., Deichmann, R., Mathiak, K., 2007. Real-time functional magnetic resonance imaging: methods and applications. Magn. Reson. Imaging 25, 989–1003. https://doi.org/10.1016/j.mri.2007.02.007.

Weiskopf, N., Veit, R., Erb, M., Mathiak, K., Grodd, W., Goebel, R., Birbaumer, N., 2003. Physiological self-regulation of regional brain activity using real-time functional magnetic resonance imaging (fMRI): methodology and exemplary data. NeuroImage 19, 577–586.

Yoo, S.S., Fairneny, T., Chen, N.K., Choo, S.E., Panych, L.P., Park, H., Lee, S.Y., Jolesz, F.A., 2004. Brain-computer interface using fMRI: spatial navigation by thoughts. Neuroreport 15, 1591–1595.

Yoo, S.S., Jolesz, F.A., 2002. Functional MRI for neurofeedback: feasibility study on a hand motor task. Neuroreport 13, 1377–1381.

Yoo, S.-S., Lee, J.-H., O'Leary, H., Lee, V., Choo, S.-E., Jolesz, F.A., 2007. Functional magnetic resonance imaging-mediated learning of increased activity in auditory areas. Neuroreport 18, 1915–1920. https://doi.org/10.1097/WNR.0b013e3282f202ac.

Yoo, S.S., O'leary, H.M., Fairneny, T., Chen, N.K., Panych, L.P., Park, H., Jolesz, F.A., 2006. Increasing cortical activity in auditory areas through neurofeedback functional magnetic resonance imaging. Neuroreport 17, 1273–1278.

Introduction to methods section

Rainer Goebel[a,b]

[a]*Department of Cognitive Neuroscience, Faculty of Psychology and Neuroscience, Maastricht University, Maastricht, Netherlands,* [b]*Brain Innovation B.V., Maastricht, Netherlands*

Learning to control brain activity using real-time fMRI neurofeedback offers exciting possibilities for innovative research about the relationship of mind and brain as well as for novel treatment options of patients suffering from psychiatric and neurological diseases. Setting up and running (clinical) fMRI neurofeedback studies is, however, still a nontrivial enterprise involving technical and methodological challenges. In order to conduct compelling neurofeedback studies, it is important that the entire chain of technological and methodological components is operating at an optimal level—if only one hardware or software component is malfunctioning or working suboptimally, the entire neurofeedback study is at risk. As an example, issues with prolonged variable delays during moment-to-moment neurofeedback could be, in some cases, traced back to unreliable data transmission in the scanner network. By simply excluding computers from the local network that are not necessary for the rt-fMRI experiment such transmission delays could be minimized.

Designing real-time fMRI neurofeedback experiments provides its own challenges, including decisions about the training paradigm, selection of regions or networks from which activation data are extracted, the type of controls to include, the number of training sessions, the type of provided feedback, and many more. Designing NF studies for new applications, for example, as a therapy for a hitherto unexplored disease, is particularly challenging since it is not clear whether extracted brain signals provide enough information to support explicit or implicit feedback-driven learning. As opposed to extensive trial or block averaging in the context of conventional offline analysis, the real-time nature of fMRI neurofeedback requires *meaningful single-trial results* to enable learning from moment-to-moment or block-to-block feedback information. Consider, for example, a binary multivoxel pattern classifier: For offline analysis, an average accuracy of 55% is often significant and interpreted in a way that the brain region from which the patterns are extracted contains differential information about the underlying condition-specific representations. For real-time neurofeedback (or BCI) applications, an accuracy level of 55% would likely be insufficient to trigger learning because provided single-trial feedback would be too close to chance level.

In the first chapter of this section, *Analysis Methods for Real-Time fMRI Neurofeedback*, I describe how activation feedback values are incrementally calculated from real-time measured fMRI data in a way that is directly usable as analog feedback such as the filling level of thermometer-like displays. Methods supporting multirun, multisession NF training are described, including across-run motion correction and across-session alignment of regions of interest. The chapter then describes approaches that are used to improve the quality of the raw fMRI data emphasizing the role of the general linear model (GLM) to remove low-frequency drifts and other global confounds from voxel time courses. Methods improving the signal quality are important since they affect the quality of the calculated feedback. The chapter concludes with a short overview of more recently proposed neurofeedback approaches, including connectivity feedback, decoded neurofeedback, and semantic neurofeedback.

In the second chapter, *Protocol Design in fMRI Neurofeedback Studies*, Michelle Hampson and David Linden provide useful concepts and practical guidance to meet the challenges arising when developing new applications of rt-fMRI neurofeedback. Considering the rather idiosyncratic designs of previous fMRI NF studies, they stress that neurofeedback is far from a standardized intervention. Besides the NF approach that needs to be chosen (activation-, connectivity-, or multivoxel pattern based), they discuss important aspects of NF training, including specificity of provided instructions, explicit versus implicit feedback, continuous versus intermittent feedback, various forms of feedback presentations as well as training schedules. The challenging issue of controlling for nonspecific effects is presented with a detailed explanation of advantages and disadvantages of 6 different types of control conditions. The last topic discusses different ways that are available to assess outcomes of NF training, including comparison of feedback vs no-feedback runs, monitoring of adverse events, verifying whether participant blinding was maintained, and assessment of long-term effects.

CHAPTER 2

Analysis methods for real-time fMRI neurofeedback

Rainer Goebel[a,b]

[a]*Department of Cognitive Neuroscience, Faculty of Psychology and Neuroscience, Maastricht University, Maastricht, Netherlands,* [b]*Brain Innovation B.V., Maastricht, Netherlands*

1 Real-time versus offline analysis

In order to enable neurofeedback applications, the measured fMRI data needs to be processed *online*, i.e., during functional scanning; data analysis should preferentially operate in *real time*, requiring that analysis for a newly measured functional volume has been completed before the next functional volume becomes available (Sorger and Goebel, 2020). Real-time processing (as opposed to *near* real-time fMRI), thus, restricts processing time to a maximum duration that is defined by the temporal interval between successive functional volumes. This volume sampling interval is usually indicated by the volume *repetition time* (TR), which typically assumes values between 1 and 3 s for whole-brain fMRI studies. With modern multiband (also referred to as simultaneous multislice, SMS) sequences, subsecond TRs are possible. The requirement for incremental analysis in limited computational time windows contrasts with conventional *offline* fMRI data analyses, where data processing is performed after the entire functional dataset has been recorded without specific restrictions on the calculation time. For real-time moment-to-moment analysis and neurofeedback, the time to handle a new data point (next incoming functional volume) needs to be constant over time, otherwise one might risk that the data can no longer be processed in real time. If one includes, for example, a conventional whole-brain general linear model (GLM) analysis at each time point in the analysis pipeline, processing time will increase over time since the conventional GLM implementation needs to process the entire (growing) past voxel time courses. The requirement of *constant volume-by-volume calculation time* is probably the most essential requirement of real-time fMRI and requires special implementations of some basic processing algorithms such as incremental GLM analysis (see later) instead of conventional implementations.

Another basic prerequisite of real-time fMRI (rt-fMRI) analysis is that images are reconstructed from k-space to image space in real time during the scan. Image reconstruction

fMRI Neurofeedback. https://doi.org/10.1016/B978-0-12-822421-2.00015-6

is usually performed by fast image reconstruction computers of the scanner manufacturer. It must be ensured that recorded data is reconstructed incrementally during real-time fMRI and that the data is stored to disk volume by volume (or slice by slice) in image space. The data should be stored in a known format (usually DICOM) and be accessible to real-time analysis software. Besides image reconstruction, most scanner manufacturers provide basic real-time analysis tools, which are sufficient for simple applications such as quality assurance. For advanced real-time applications such as neurofeedback, specialized software packages are usually employed that provide comprehensive processing options such as motion correction and drift removal, advanced statistical and machine learning tools, manual or automatic definition of regions-of-interest (ROIs), and support for various NF approaches, e.g., activity-, connectivity-, and multivoxel pattern-based NF. Data acquisition techniques and analysis software have been considerably improved since the introduction of real-time fMRI (Cox et al., 1995). The first real-time fMRI setups provided limited processing capabilities, lacking e.g., motion correction or advanced moment-to-moment statistical analysis. Recent real-time fMRI studies employ analysis pipelines that include almost all preprocessing and analysis steps used in conventional offline analysis. In this chapter we provide a short overview of typical analysis tools; more detailed reviews are provided, among others, by Weiskopf et al. (2004a), Goebel et al. (2010), LaConte (2011), Caria et al. (2012), Weiskopf (2012), Watanabe et al. (2017), and Heunis et al. (2020).

2 Technical setup

Fig. 1 illustrates a typical technical setup for a neurofeedback experiment. The technical requirements include direct access to the reconstructed images from the analysis PC, software that processes the incoming data in real time and computes incremental feedback as well as software presenting information to the participant in the scanner, usually including neurofeedback data converted into sensory stimulation (e.g., visual, auditory, tactile). A major challenge to establish real-time fMRI in a scanner lab is to provide access to the image data in real time and to integrate the real-time analysis computer and the stimulus/feedback presentation computer in the existing scanner network.

The relevant setup and workflows have been successfully established with systems from all major MRI scanner manufacturers, and several custom-made and commercial software tools have been developed for online preprocessing, statistical analysis, as well as calculation and display of neurofeedback signals.

3 Univariate activation neurofeedback

In activity-based neurofeedback experiments, NF blocks are usually alternated with baseline ("rest") blocks. It is assumed that engaging in mental activities (e.g., motor imagery, mental calculation, inner speech, emotion regulation) during neurofeedback modulates the mean

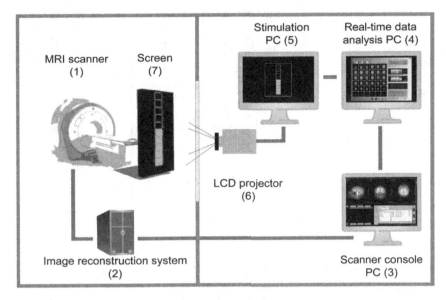

Fig. 1

Technical setup and data flow of a typical real-time fMRI neurofeedback experiment. A participant observes feedback information via a presentation screen (7) while functional images are being acquired and reconstructed incrementally (2). The images are sent to the scanner console (3). The PC performing real-time data analysis (4) needs to have immediate access to the reconstructed images in the scanner network. The real-time data analysis PC (4) sends neurofeedback information to the stimulation PC (5), which generates the stimulus containing the neurofeedback information (here a simple visual thermometer display). The feedback information is presented via the projector (6) on the presentation screen (7).

signal time course extracted from a *target* ROI. When engaging in a mental task during neurofeedback blocks, one usually expects an increase of activity in the target ROI with respect to the previous baseline ("rest") condition. The modulation of activity (e.g., motor imagery) in the selected target region (e.g., supplementary motor area, SMA) during neurofeedback blocks is fed back to the participant, for example, as the filling level of a visually presented thermometer (see Figs. 1 and 2). With the help of provided instructions that can be specific ("imagine finger tapping") or more general ("increase the level of the thermometer"), the participant aims to find or modify a mental task in a way that the level of activity in the target ROI increases over time. In some variants, the participant is asked to regulate the activity in the target region to reach different target levels that are cued at the start or during neurofeedback blocks, which requires adjustments in the intensity or variant of employed mental task (Sorger et al., 2018). After some practice over one or more training sessions, participants usually get increasingly skilled at modulating the activity in the selected target region. The learned *self-regulation of brain activity* offers the possibility to use neurofeedback training as a tool to unveil detailed information about the functional specificity

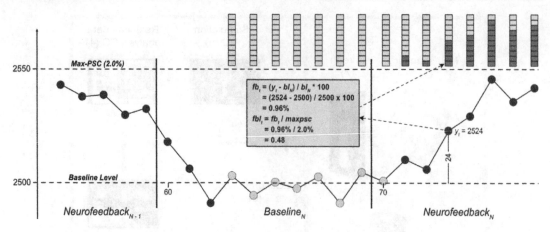

Fig. 2

Basic approach to calculate moment-to-moment feedback values. The value of a point y_t inside neurofeedback block N is converted in a percent signal change *feedback* value fb_t with respect to the value of the preceding *baseline* bl_N (see box for calculation). The baseline value is the mean of the values in the baseline interval adjusted for the hemodynamic delay (orange data points—light gray data points in print version, see text for details). To convert the percent signal change value to a *feedback level* value fbl_t for the participant, the percent signal change value is usually related to a *max*imum *p*ercent *s*ignal *c*hange value *maxpsc* that may be specified based on previous neurofeedback or localizer runs. The resulting feedback level value expressed in the baseline to maxpsc range (e.g., 0.48 for the selected point in the example) can be mapped to any feedback modality, for example, as the level of filled elements in a visually displayed thermometer (see plots at top).

of targeted brain areas. Furthermore, the neurofeedback training is often accompanied by behaviorally measurable effects. This link to behavior has not only been investigated in many scientific applications (see Chapters 4–6) but also stimulated clinical applications of fMRI neurofeedback (see Chapters 7–12). Some of these applications used stimuli to evoke activity in target regions during neurofeedback and instructed participants to learn to *decrease* activity. In a neurofeedback study aimed to prevent relapse in alcohol dependence (Subramanian et al., 2021), participants learned to *downregulate* activation in the salience network in the presence of alcohol stimuli. Instead of a thermometer, neurofeedback was provided by scaling the size of the displayed pictures according to the mean extracted ROI signal. This approach has the advantage to integrate the visual stimuli with the feedback information. In case that visual stimuli are shown but a direct integration of feedback is not possible, the additional display of moment-to-moment feedback might be interfering with the task-related stimulus presentation. To avoid such interference, feedback information may be provided delayed, e.g., as a summary signal at the end of each neurofeedback block. Providing feedback after neurofeedback blocks is also referred to as *intermittent feedback* as opposed to moment-to-moment or *continuous feedback*.

3.1 ROI selection

The ROI used to extract relevant functional information from the participant's brain is usually selected based on neuroscientific knowledge. For a motor imagery task, for example, the SMA might be selected, whereas for inner speech, regions in the language network of the dominant hemisphere might be used. In the context of clinical applications, areas or networks are usually selected as target regions that are known to be related to a disorder with the rationale that self-regulation training of disease-related regions may lead to positive outcome effects. Another rationale would be to train brain regions that enhance cognitive and emotional abilities more generally. Note that specification of an ROI does not imply that it corresponds to exactly one contiguous region; the term ROI is used here in a flexible way to refer to any set of selected voxels. An ROI can thus reflect several contiguous regions as well as all voxels of a task-related or resting state network, or even all (gray matter) brain voxels.

After having decided which target area to use for neurofeedback, different methods are available to find that region in an individual brain. The easiest way to locate a selected target region in an individual brain is to use a generic definition of its location in one of the available *anatomical brain atlases* (e.g., Eickhoff et al., 2005; Rosenke et al., 2018), which are usually normalized in MNI (based on the Montreal Neurological Institute or MNI template) or Talairach (based on the classical atlas by Jean Talairach) space. If one wants, for example, to provide feedback from Broca's area during inner speech NF blocks, one can project the location of Brodmann Area 44/45 from the atlas brain to the space of the participant's functional data. This approach requires only standard brain alignment methods such as MNI or Talairach normalization of a participant's 3D anatomical dataset to the atlas; the obtained forward spatial transformation can then be used backward to bring the target area in the atlas in the anatomical space of the participant. After coregistration of functional data and (same session) anatomical data at the start of each NF run, the target region can be further transformed to corresponding regions in the functional data.

Another approach to locate selected target areas in individual brains is to perform one or more *functional localizer runs* before starting the main neurofeedback runs. The employed localizer runs need, of course, to consist of tasks or stimuli that are known to activate the desired brain region(s) or network(s). In an emotion regulation experiment, for example, the localizer run may consist of blocks with emotional pictures inducing, e.g., positive versus neutral emotional states in the participant. A statistical analysis contrasting positive versus neutral emotion will then help to find participant-specific regions that can be selected as neurofeedback target regions. Active voxels in relevant regions can be selected manually or automatically to define the ROI (Lührs et al., 2017). The averaged signal time course from a functionally defined ROI usually provides higher signal modulation values and lower noise fluctuations than when using anatomical atlas-based ROIs because it includes only voxels that are detected as related to the task in an individualized manner. Using atlas-based region definitions has, however, the advantage that no extra time is required for localizer runs, which leaves more time in a scanning session for neurofeedback training. Another approach combining the advantages of the anatomical atlas and functional localizer method to some extent is to use a *probabilistic functional atlas* if available for the desired (localizer) task. Instead of anatomically defined regions, a probabilistic functional atlas is based on functional measurements in a larger group of participants and it offers the possibility to select only those voxels in a common space that were activated by a certain proportion of individuals (e.g., 50% or higher). Like anatomical brain atlases, the probabilistic functional maps approach does not require separate localizer runs; furthermore, regions in probabilistic functional atlases are usually defined using advanced brain alignment schemes (e.g., Rosenke et al., 2021) and will likely provide better suited target ROIs for a new individual than an anatomically defined region.

3.2 Neurofeedback calculation

While real-time data analysis usually includes many useful methods improving data quality (see Section 4), the basic approach to calculate moment-to-moment neurofeedback values is rather simple, relating measured BOLD responses during a neurofeedback block N to the average measured response in a preceding baseline block bl_N (see Fig. 2). Baseline and neurofeedback blocks typically last for about 10–30 s. Using a rather short time window containing only the current neurofeedback (mental task) block and the preceding baseline ("rest") period has the advantage that slow drifts have minor impact on the neurofeedback signal since all relevant time points are in close temporal proximity (but see Section 4.2). Given a mean baseline level bl_N, the feedback value for subsequent time points t during the neurofeedback block N can be calculated from the measured values y_t simply as:

$$fb_t = (y_t - bl_N)/bl_N \times 100\%$$

The feedback value fb_t expresses activity changes with respect to the baseline level as a percent signal change value. Because of the sluggishness of the BOLD response, the data points defined as baseline should take the hemodynamic delay into account at the start and the end of the baseline interval. To "protect" the baseline from high signal values from a decaying BOLD response from a previous neurofeedback block $N - 1$, some data points at the beginning of the baseline condition should be excluded (see Fig. 2). The number of points to exclude should account for about 6 s, which is long enough to reach a signal level close to baseline. If, for example, the TR value is 2.0 s, the number of excluded time points at the beginning of the previous baseline would be 6/2 = 3 time points. In a similar way one can also extend the used baseline interval into the subsequent NF block since it takes some time until the BOLD signal rises after engaging in a mental task. Since it is expected from standard hemodynamic responses that the signal starts to rise already after about 2–3 s, the number of time points included into the baseline should be smaller than those excluded at the start of the baseline condition. A value covering 2 s may be useful, which corresponds to one time point in the case of a TR value of 2 s (see Fig. 2). Following these considerations and assuming a TR of 2 s, a baseline defined in the experimental protocol in the interval 60–69 would lead to an effective baseline using the data values in the interval 63–70; the signal values of the identified baseline data points (8 in the example) are averaged to obtain the baseline level *bl* for the subsequent neurofeedback block.

3.2.1 Displaying feedback

The calculated neurofeedback signal can be visualized in various ways to the participant in the scanner, e.g., as the filling level in a thermometer display (see Fig. 1). To convert the calculated percent signal change value into a corresponding feedback level *fbl* in a normalized 0.0–1.0 range (e.g., empty to fully filled thermometer), the percent value is usually related to an expected *maximum modulation value* or *maxpsc* as:

$$fbl_t = fb_t / maxpsc$$

If, for example, the calculated feedback value at time point t is: $fb_t = 1.2\%$, and the maximum percent signal change value has been set to $maxpsc = 2.0\%$, the normalized feedback level at time point t will be: $fbl_t = 1.2\%/2.0\% = 0.6$. When using a thermometer for feedback display, it would, thus, be shown in a 60% filled state to the participant (see Fig. 2 for feedback calculation and visualization). The expected maximum modulation value is either specified based on general experience with BOLD signal amplitudes in selected target brain regions or it is derived from measured responses in the same individual using data from prior localizer or neurofeedback runs. In case that activation increases beyond the *maxpsc* value, the provided feedback is usually the same as when reaching the maximum value (e.g., a fully filled thermometer). To reduce noise fluctuations to some degree, the feedback level values can be further discretized. In a thermometer with 10 levels, for example, each level may be shown either filled or empty (see Fig. 2), which can be achieved by assigning each discrete fill state to a range of values; levels 1–5 in a thermometer would be filled, for example, if the feedback level value would fall in the half-open interval [0.45–0.55), or equivalent: $0.45 \leq fbl < 0.55$. Another common approach to reduce noise fluctuations is to average the values of the last N time points (temporal smoothing) instead of only using the current one. The number of averaged values should be, however, small, otherwise time lags (in addition to hemodynamics and the processing pipeline) will be introduced (see also Section 4.5).

This described visualization approach assumes that only increases of activation relative to the baseline level are considered. In case one wants to also visualize deactivations below baseline, the feedback information (e.g., thermometer display) needs to be extended for negative values accordingly. Besides simple activation displays (thermometer, continuous scrolling time course, numerical value, e.g., Krause et al., 2017), more expressive visualizations have been used in the past such as images of a virtual fire that increased in size with increasing activation levels (deCharms et al., 2005), level of a racket in a "brain pong" computer game (Goebel et al., 2004, see also Chapter 1), virtual reality (e.g., Sitaram et al., 2005), and socially rewarding facial expressions (Mathiak et al., 2015). Direito et al. (2019), for example, morphed the face of an avatar toward happy (or sad) facial expression depending on the amount of activation in a carefully localized subpart of the posterior superior temporal sulcus (pSTS) responding to dynamic facial expressions. Besides the visual modality, feedback may also be provided via haptic (e.g., Young et al., 2020) or auditory (e.g., Direito et al., 2019) stimuli but most neurofeedback studies have employed continuous or intermittent visual feedback. While simple feedback representations may be generated directly from the used real-time analysis software (data analysis PC in Fig. 1), more complex feedback presentations are usually generated by custom-made software running on a dedicated computer (stimulation PC in Fig. 1) that accesses the feedback signals (or ROI time courses) produced by the real-time data analysis PC. Note that it is also possible to present feedback from multiple areas simultaneously. In a spider phobia study (Zilverstand et al., 2015), for example, two thermometer displays were used as intermittent feedback after regulation blocks with one thermometer representing activity in the dorsolateral prefrontal cortex (supposed to reflect engagement in regulation) while the other thermometer represented activity in the insula (supposed to reflect sustained anxious emotion).

3.2.2 Removing drifts

Whereas drifts are unlikely in short temporal windows (baseline + NF block), it is possible to remove local drifts in the baseline period that can then be eliminated from subsequent neurofeedback time points by extrapolation. Linear and nonlinear drifts in the time window or the entire past time course of all voxels can, for example, be regressed out with a general linear model (GLM). Using a GLM also opens the possibility to use the estimated baseline level (beta value of the constant predictor) fitted by a GLM as an alternative to the mean activation level of the previous baseline condition. The GLM baseline can include the full past time course, which might lead to a more stable baseline estimation than using only the (few) data points from a single baseline before the current neurofeedback block. More generally, one can use the GLM to incrementally calculate *detrended* voxel or ROI time courses that can be used as input for neurofeedback calculations resulting in improved feedback quality (Hinds et al., 2011). For further details on how to remove drifts using the GLM, see Section 4.2.

3.3 Multisession neurofeedback training

Since neurofeedback training studies may include multiple sessions, it is often desired to reuse the same individual ROIs across sessions. Although time consuming, the best approach is arguably to run a functional localizer at the start of each separate neurofeedback session. Detected active regions should be similar if the localizer induces robust stimulus-evoked responses. In case that the localizer involves mental tasks, results might be more variable, which could be, at least to some extent, the result of NF training in previous sessions. Adjusting a participant's ROI to a potentially changing mental strategy might be optimal for individualized training but it makes it more challenging to quantify and interpret learning progress when comparing, for example, achieved modulation amplitudes or *t* values in different target regions across sessions. A less flexible but more consistent strategy is to stick to the participant's ROI as defined in the first session. Since slice positions might differ across sessions, transferring functional ROIs of a participant from one session to the next can be achieved conveniently and precisely with the help of anatomical datasets recorded in each session: (1) after functional-to-anatomical coregistration, a participant's functional ROI is projected on the corresponding location of the anatomical dataset of the first session; (2) the anatomical dataset of the first session is aligned to the anatomical dataset of the subsequent session; this across-session anatomical alignment is used to transform the original ROI coordinates in the anatomical space of the subsequent session; (3) the ROI is finally projected on the corresponding location of the functional data of the subsequent session using anatomical-to-functional coregistration. One can further minimize differences in recording across sessions by placing the head of a participant in a similar position and orientation inside the head coil. Furthermore, it is recommended to adjust the position and orientation of the functional slices relative to the participant's brain in the same way in all sessions manually or by using software provided by scanner manufacturers (e.g., the "AutoAlign" tool on SIEMENS scanners).

Across-session alignment as well as reporting of neurofeedback target locations is facilitated by normalizing the brain of a participant to a standard (e.g., Talairach or MNI) space in each session. If brain normalization has been performed prior to neurofeedback runs, ROIs and real-time data such as statistical maps can be visualized in Talairach or MNI space during scanning, which may help interpreting the location of observed activation foci as compared to visualizing activations on the measured functional slices. If a high-quality anatomical dataset is available prior to functional scanning, it is even possible to visualize results, such as dynamic statistical maps, on reconstructed, inflated, or flattened cortex mesh representations using fast automated 3D segmentation and cortex reconstruction methods (Goebel, 2001).

4 Methods to improve signal quality

To improve the quality of the voxel time courses used for neurofeedback calculations as well as the overall data, the recorded fMRI data is incrementally processed with a variety of methods (Heunis et al., 2020). Most of these additional methods are also routinely performed in standard offline fMRI data preprocessing, but some of them need to be adapted to the incremental processing requirements of real-time fMRI analysis. Two of the most often employed methods are motion correction (Section 4.1) and drift removal (Section 4.2). While motion correction can be performed volume-by-volume with (fast implementations of) the same routines used for offline analysis, drift removal requires special considerations in a real-time context. Further important methods to increase signal quality are related to global signal fluctuations (Section 4.3) and physiological noise caused by respiration and pulsation (Section 4.4). Besides these major signal quality improvement methods, spatial and temporal smoothing (Section 4.5) might be added to suppress high-frequency noise. In case of low sampling rates such as volume TRs of more than 1–2 s, the correction of slice scan timing (not discussed here) may also be considered.

4.1 Motion correction within and across runs

Most real-time processing pipelines include 3D rigid body motion correction that detects and corrects head movements in the same way as used in offline analysis. To allow motion correction from the second time point onward, the first functional volume is used as the reference to which subsequent functional volumes are aligned (see Fig. 3). According to the rigid body model, 6 parameters (3 translations and 3 rotations) are estimated. In order

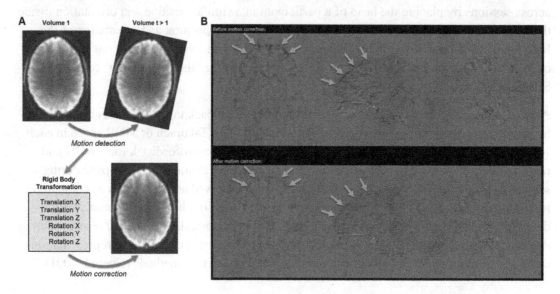

Fig. 3

Incremental correction of head motion. (A) Because of incremental analysis, the first volume of the run needs to serve as the reference (volume 1). Parameters of rigid body displacement (3 translations and 3 rotations) are calculated as soon as a new volume at time point $t > 1$ is available. The estimated parameters are applied to the volume to correct the detected motion. (B) Effect of motion correction. Subtracting the first (reference volume) from a volume at a later time point ($t > 1$) can be used as a measure of motion artifacts and success of volume realignment when comparing the difference image before (top) and after (bottom) motion correction. The arrows in the upper panel show that in this example largest displacements occur in frontal brain regions, which can be explained by a nodding movement ("chin moves downwards"). Arrows at corresponding positions in the lower panel indicate smaller differences between the two volumes after rigid body realignment.

to find the parameters that minimize the sum of squared differences between the adjusted and reference volume, a standard iterative optimization method is used (e.g., Levenberg-Marquardt algorithm). To reduce calculation time, realignment of images to the reference volume is usually performed using trilinear interpolation but more accurate methods such as windowed sinc interpolation are nowadays also possible for real-time analysis. Efficient parallel implementations of motion correction (e.g., Scheinost et al., 2013) benefit from the increasing availability of general-purpose graphics processing units (GP-GPUs). Since motion often accumulates gradually over time, it is useful to provide the parameters estimated for the current volume as starting values for the parameter estimates of the next volume, which usually reduces the number of required iterations to find the (local) minimum of the objective function.

To correct for head movements across runs of the same session, motion correction can be performed to a reference volume of a previous run. If, for example, a neurofeedback run uses an ROI defined on the functional data of a localizer run, the localizer run can be specified as the motion correction target of the neurofeedback run; the volumes of all subsequent neurofeedback runs are then realigned to the same space as the volumes of the localizer run ensuring validity of ROIs across runs. Fig. 4 shows detected motion parameters across 3 runs where the first volume of the first run serves as the target volume for motion correction. Realigning all subsequent functional volumes to the same volume is especially important for

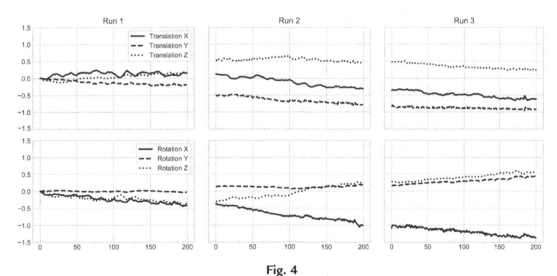

Fig. 4

Example of calculated motion parameters (translations at top, rotations at bottom, see plot legends) within and across runs. The functional volumes of all three runs are aligned to the first volume of the first run. Note that while detected motion values continue across runs, they are not always exactly at the same level at the start of a run as compared to the end of the previous run; this seems to be caused partly by gradient heating effects and head movements in the periods between runs. Note that (*z* normalized) motion parameters can be added incrementally as confound predictors when running a general linear model.

neurofeedback based on multivoxel pattern analysis (MVPA) (see Sections 5.2–5.4) since it is critical to establish good correspondence of voxels for fine-grained distributed patterns between training and testing (neurofeedback) runs.

It is important to note that minimizing head motion best starts already in the scanner. It has been shown that visual or tactile feedback may substantially reduce motion of participants. A strip of medical tape applied from one side of the magnetic resonance head coil, via the participant's forehead, to the other side, provides already useful feedback for participants resulting in substantially reduced head motion (Krause et al., 2019). Another approach to minimize motion artifacts is to detect and correct motion online during scanning. This technique is referred to as *prospective motion correction*. After detecting motion parameters during acquisition using recorded images (Thesen et al., 2000) or external optical tracking (Zaitsev et al., 2006), pulse sequence parameters are updated in real time in such a way that the imaging volume "follows" the moving head of the participant (Maclaren et al., 2012). While prospective motion correction techniques are arguably the best possible solution, errors during motion detection may lead to wrong adjustments that in the worst case might even introduce motion artifacts. Such techniques need thus to be carefully evaluated and used with care.

4.2 Removing drifts using incremental GLM analysis

Voxel time courses often rise or fall slowly even after motion correction has been performed (see examples in Figs. 6 and 7). Such slowly varying signal changes are called *drifts* that are caused by physical and physiological noise sources. If the signal in a voxel rises or falls with a constant slope from start to end of a run, it is called a *linear trend*. Linear trends can be removed rather easily by fitting a straight line through the time course and then subtracting the values of the fitted line from the original data points. If the signal level slowly varies over time with a nonconstant slope, the drift is called a *nonlinear trend*—they are more difficult to remove during real-time analysis (see later). In offline analysis, drifts are typically removed in a separate preprocessing step by applying a (time or frequency domain) high-pass filter to the entire time course of each voxel. Since this is not possible in incremental real-time analysis, drift removal is usually incorporated in a GLM analysis. While there are other tools to incrementally remove drifts (e.g., the exponential moving average algorithm), the (windowed) incremental GLM has been demonstrated to outperform other online algorithms achieving detrending performance that is as good as that of offline procedures (Kopel et al., 2019). A GLM fits a set of predictor time courses to the time course of a voxel or ROI. The set of predictors forms the *design matrix* of the GLM. An important feature of the GLM is that it will find a weight (called beta) value for each predictor that scales the respective predictor time course. These predictor beta values indicate how strong a certain predictor explains part of the fluctuations of the voxel time course on top of what other included predictors explain. Most importantly for the present topic, contributions of specific predictors to explain the data can be removed ("regressed out") from the time course. This property of the GLM can be used to remove signal drifts by adding slowly varying (low-frequency) time courses as confounds (predictors of no interest) to the GLM's design matrix next to condition-related main predictors. The box "Incremental General Linear Model (GLM)" provides more details about how the GLM works and how it can be calculated efficiently in real time (Box 1).

Although basic moment-to-moment neurofeedback calculation uses a small temporal window (see Section 3.2), removal of drifts is important for neurofeedback studies to ensure that analyzed and visualized increases or decreases of activation are related to mental tasks and are not the result of unrelated signal drifts. A GLM can be applied to the time course extracted for neurofeedback from the target ROI but it is common to run an incremental GLM for all voxel time courses of the brain. Such a whole-brain GLM is useful for the experimenter who might be interested in task-related activity not only in the target ROI during neurofeedback but also in other brain regions. A whole-brain GLM is also useful to remove drifts from all voxel time courses in case that large ROIs up to the entire brain are used as the source for neurofeedback calculations, for example when using whole-brain multivariate classifiers (see Section 5.2).

Box 1   Incremental general linear model (GLM).

The GLM has become the core tool for fMRI data analysis since its introduction into the neuroimaging community by Friston and colleagues (Friston et al., 1995). For a comprehensive treatment of the GLM in the standard statistical literature, see, for example, Draper and Smith (1998) and Kutner et al. (2005). From the perspective of multiple regression analysis, the GLM aims to "explain" or "predict" the variation of a dependent variable in terms of a *linear combination* (weighted sum) of several reference functions. The dependent variable corresponds to the observed fMRI time course of a voxel and the reference functions correspond to time courses of expected (noise-free) fMRI responses for different conditions of the experimental paradigm (see Fig. Box 1). The reference functions are also called *predictors, regressors, explanatory variables, covariates,* or *basis functions.* A set of specified predictors forms the *design matrix,* also called the *model.* A predictor time course is typically obtained by convolution of a "box-car" (square-wave) time course with a standard hemodynamic response function. The box-car (square-wave) time course is assumed to reflect neuronal timing, i.e., responses are considered to occur immediately after stimulus onset in the context of the low temporal resolution of fMRI; the stimulus time course is therefore usually defined by setting predictor values to 1 at time points at which the modeled condition is specified as "on" (e.g., stimulus is shown, mental task is performed) and 0 at all other time points (see red and green boxes in task predictors of Fig. Box 1). The time courses actually used to define the predictors of the GLM (see white curves in task predictors of Fig. Box 1) are obtained by convolution of the square-wave functions with a hemodynamic response function (Friston et al., 1998).

Continued

Box 1   Incremental general linear model (GLM).—cont'd

estimate!

$\beta_0 \times$ $\beta_1 \times$ $\beta_2 \times$

fMRI signal
= *data*

design matrix
= *model*

residuals
= *error*

Fig. Box 1

Graphical depiction of a general linear model (GLM). The white curve in the panel on the left side is the voxel (or region) time course that will be "explained" by the sum of predictors each weighted by a separate beta weight. Green and red sections—light and middle gray sections in print version represent stimulus blocks from two conditions (one block per condition). All predictors together (modeling task-related effects and confounds such as drifts) form the design matrix (here only the constant and two task predictors are shown). Time courses of predictors (generated by convolution of task square wave functions with a hemodynamic response function) are shown both as curves (white lines) and as image cells (see column at right side of predictors; black to white intensities → low to high values). Signal fluctuations in the data time course that cannot be explained by the sum of optimally weighted predictors form the error or residuals (panel on right side). Running ("fitting") a GLM will find optimal beta weights so that the weighted sum of predictors results in a predicted time course that is as similar as possible to the data time course; the weights are optimal in the sense that there are no other beta values leading to a smaller sum of squared residuals.

Each predictor time course X_i gets an associated coefficient or *beta weight* b_i that quantifies the contribution of a predictor in explaining variance in the voxel time course y. The voxel time course y is modeled as the sum of the defined predictors, each multiplied with the associated beta weight b. Since this linear combination will not perfectly explain the data due to noise fluctuations, an error value e is added to the GLM system of equations with n data points and p predictors. The GLM system of equations may be expressed elegantly using matrix notation.

Box 1   Incremental general linear model (GLM).—cont'd

For this purpose, the voxel time course, the beta values, and the residuals are represented as vectors, and the set of predictors as a matrix:

$$
\begin{bmatrix} y_1 \\ \vdots \\ \vdots \\ y_n \end{bmatrix} = \begin{bmatrix} 1 & X_{11} & \cdots & \cdots & x_{1p} \\ \vdots & \vdots & \vdots & \vdots & \vdots \\ \vdots & \vdots & \vdots & \vdots & \vdots \\ 1 & X_{n1} & \cdots & \cdots & X_{np} \end{bmatrix} \begin{bmatrix} b_0 \\ b_1 \\ \vdots \\ b_p \end{bmatrix} + \begin{bmatrix} e_1 \\ e_2 \\ \vdots \\ e_n \end{bmatrix}
$$

Representing the indicated vectors and matrix with single letters, we obtain this simple form of the GLM system of equations:

$$\mathbf{y} = \mathbf{Xb} + \mathbf{e}$$

In this notation, the matrix **X** represents the *design matrix* containing the predictor time courses as column vectors. The beta values now appear in a separate vector **b**. The term **Xb** indicates matrix-vector multiplication. Fig. Box 1 shows a graphical representation of the GLM. Time courses of the signal, predictors, and residuals have been arranged in column form with time running from top to bottom.

Given the data **y** and the design matrix **X**, the GLM fitting procedure must find a set of beta values explaining the data as well as possible. It can be shown that the optimal beta weights minimizing the squared error values (the "least squares estimate") are obtained noniteratively by the following equation:

$$\mathbf{b} = (\mathbf{X'X})^{-1} \mathbf{X'y}$$

The described standard GLM can, unfortunately, not be used for real-time fMRI since it does not fulfill the constant computation time requirement. To fit beta values at each time point, the standard GLM needs the full past time course and calculation times will grow with each new time point. In order to guarantee constant (and fast) processing time, the GLM can, fortunately, be calculated recursively: Estimated statistical parameters are not calculated from scratch but are updated by the information arriving with the next available functional volume (Goebel, 2001; Smyser et al., 2001; Bagarinao et al., 2003; Weiskopf et al., 2004a; Bagarinao et al., 2006; Hinds et al., 2011). The recursive (incremental) implementation ensures constant calculation time per data point (volume) and enables real-time processing even for very long functional scans. While the equations to obtain the beta weights are mathematically more complex than standard GLM computations, the recursive GLM calculations have the desired property of constant calculation time from volume-to-volume while providing results at any time point that are usually identical to those that would be obtained by running a full (standard) GLM using the entire time course from the begin to the current time point. The recursive GLM calculations may, however, fail in case that predictors are highly correlated. See Section 4.2 for strategies to prevent such issues when removing drifts from voxel time courses.

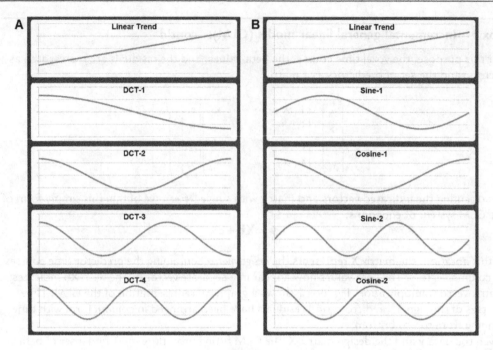

Fig. 5

Drift predictors defined over the expected duration (time points) of a real-time fMRI run can be added to the design matrix of a GLM to model (and thereby remove) low-frequency drifts. (A) Discrete cosine transform (DCT) basis set. In addition to a linear trend predictor, 4 DCT predictors are shown that are often used for low-frequency drift modeling. (B) Fourier basis set. In addition to a linear trend predictor, 2 Sine/Cosine pairs are shown. Both sets can be extended with higher frequencies. Note that for incremental real-time analysis, predictors are highly correlated at the start of the run requiring special treatment (see text for details).

Fig. 5 shows example sets of popular drift-removal confound predictors, the discrete cosine transform (DCT, Fig. 5A) and Fourier (Fig. 5B) basis functions. These slowly varying time courses can be added to the design matrix of a GLM to model low-frequency drifts that will then be removed from the data time course. The displayed confound predictors implement a temporal *high-pass filter* with a *cutoff frequency* of two cycles since drifts going up to two times up and down can be modeled and removed. If the next two DCT or Fourier basis functions would be added, the cutoff frequency would be three cycles per time course. The term "high-pass" indicates that fast fluctuations beyond the cutoff frequency pass through (are retained), while lower-frequency fluctuations up to the cutoff frequency are filtered out (in practice the transition from removed to retained frequencies is not sharp but happens gradually). The retained higher frequencies will include fluctuations related to task-related activation as well as various other noise sources (see Sections 4.3 and 4.4). Although more basis functions can be added to filter out higher frequencies, it is important that the frequencies implemented in the experimental paradigm are not affected. For example, if a run contains five neurofeedback blocks that are interspersed with equal length rest blocks, the cutoff frequency should be lower than five cycles (eight or fewer DCT/Fourier basis functions), otherwise task-related increases and decreases might be modeled by the drift confound predictors and thus filtered out from the time course!

Note that the drift-related confound predictors are defined over the whole expected time course leading to highly correlated predictors at the start of real-time processing when only a few (less than about 15%) data points are available, which may lead to unstable GLM fits. One way to handle this issue is to incrementally add predictors over time starting with the linear trend confound predictor at the begin of a run and adding more drift predictors over time when enough time points are available . Another approach is to convert the predictor time courses into orthogonal functions using the Gram-Schmidt orthogonalization procedure, which will ensure stable performance of incremental GLM fitting (Bagarinao et al., 2003).

Fig. 6 shows an application of GLM-based drift removal. The partial time courses in the left column show that the nonlinear drift visible in the original time course (top panels) has been successfully removed incrementally using a design matrix with a linear trend predictor and 2 DCT basis functions (plus a constant). To obtain (incremental) detrended time courses (right column), the beta values of the task predictor(s) are set to zero, which results in a predicted "drift" time course (top right panel) as the sum of all confound predictors weighted by their respective estimated beta values. Subtracting this drift time course from the original time course results in a detrended stationary time course that can be used for visualization as well as for neurofeedback calculations.

4.2.1 Motion predictors

In offline analysis, time courses with detected motion parameters for translation and rotation (and their derivatives) are often added to the design matrix to capture residual motion effects. Since motion parameters become incrementally available during real-time analysis, they can be added volume-by-volume to the design matrix and, thus, used during incremental GLM calculation. Using detected motion parameters as confound predictors is one possibility to remove drifts and noise from voxel time courses. Fig. 7 shows a time course exhibiting a (mainly) linear trend that remains in the data despite performed incremental motion correction (upper left panel). When including the 6 motion predictors (3 translation and 3 rotation parameter time courses) as confounds, the drift is removed although no further low-frequency predictors were included (see detrended residuals time course). When using instead explicit low-frequency drift predictors without motion parameters, the estimated drift and detrended time course look similar (right column in Fig. 7). Since (some) motion parameters usually exhibit a linear increase or decrease, motion parameters seem to be sufficient to remove linear (and modest nonlinear) drifts as an alternative to adding explicit low-frequency confound predictors. Furthermore, motion parameters may remove additional (higher frequency) noise sources.

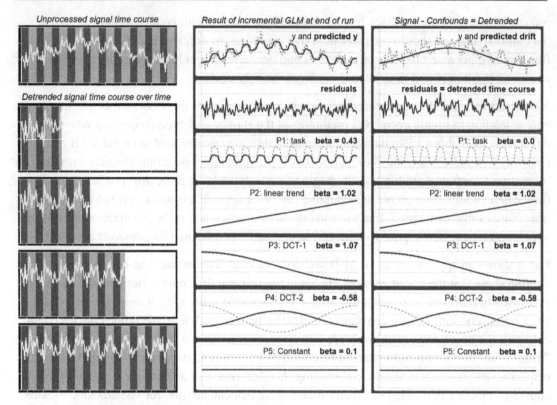

Fig. 6

Incremental drift removal using a linear trend (P2) and two DCT confound predictors (P3, P4) that are added in addition to a task (P1) and constant (P5) predictor. Top panels show a voxel time course exhibiting a low-frequency drift moving upward roughly over the first half of the run and moving downward afterward. The panels on the left side show the detrended time course over time as used for neurofeedback and visualization. The middle column shows the predictors P1–P5 forming the design matrix of the GLM (stippled lines) as well as the time course after multiplication with the fitted beta weights (solid thick lines). The top panel shows the data time course (stippled line) and the fitted time course (solid thick line). The panel below the data time course shows the residuals time course. In the right column, the task predictor has been removed (beta set to 0.0) resulting in a predicted time course which is the sum of all confound predictors shown as the solid thick line in the top panel. Since the residuals time course is the difference of the data time course and the predicted (now drift) time course, the residuals time course now contains the desired detrended time course that can be used for visualization and as input for neurofeedback calculation.

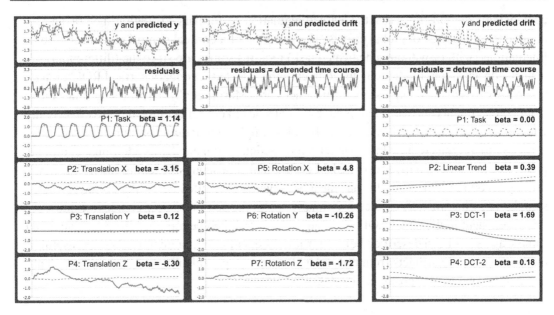

Fig. 7

Adding motion parameters as confound predictors to the design matrix removes drifts from voxel time courses in a similar way as low-frequency drift predictors. Left column and lower part of second column show (fitted) data time course (top left panel) with a design matrix consisting of a task predictor (P1), constant (not shown), and 6 motion parameters (P2–P7). The upper middle panel shows that the (mainly linear) drift in the time course is fitted well by the combined 6 motion predictors (task predictor removed by setting its beta to 0.0). The result is similar as the one obtained when using a set of low-frequency drift predictors (right panel).

Slightly better results will be obtained when adding both motion and low-frequency confound predictor sets but if one wants to keep the number of confound predictors low either nonlinear (DCT) time courses or motion parameters should be added as a minimum.

4.3 Removing global signal fluctuations

Besides low-frequency drifts, higher frequency global intensity fluctuations are observed in fMRI data that may be related to various noise sources including respiration- and pulsation-induced artifacts (see Section 4.4). One strategy to reduce the impact of such global signal fluctuations is to subtract the time course of another ROI from the target ROI. The other ROI may be chosen to reflect noise sources only, e.g., white matter, or as another cortical ROI also used for neurofeedback with a different task (Weiskopf et al., 2004a; deCharms et al., 2004). In the study by Weiskopf et al. (2004b), for example, the difference signal of the SMA and the parahippocampal place area (PPA) was presented as the neurofeedback signal (see Fig. 3 in Chapter 1): the signal went up when participants activated SMA and it went below baseline when participants activated PPA. If successful, this form of *differential neurofeedback* convincingly demonstrates that the learned regulation performance is region specific and not due to modulation of global effects. The selection of a cortical control region for global fluctuations (with or without a dedicated task) requires some care since the (differential) neurofeedback signal might be reduced in case the selected secondary cortical ROI belongs to the same coactivated large-scale cortical network (Marins et al., 2015). Using time courses from compartments such as white matter or ventricles likely reflect global noise effects only with no or little task-specific activation. Besides simple subtraction, confound time courses from control regions (e.g., white matter) can be added incrementally as additional confound predictors to the design matrix of a GLM during real-time analysis (next to low-frequency drift and motion predictors); this has the advantage that the fitted beta value for the global signal (e.g., white matter) predictor optimally scales the confound time course to capture this component in the target ROI time course and it can then be removed from the data in the same way as has been described before for low-frequency drift predictors. Another useful method to separate artifacts from task-related activity is provided by real-time independent component analysis (Esposito et al., 2003).

4.4 Physiological noise correction

Denoising physiological confounds has been approached in a variety of ways in rt-fMRI neurofeedback research, even though most studies do not report any correction for physiological noise (Heunis et al., 2020). The differential feedback or white matter subtraction approach described in the previous section is most often used as a potential correction method for global effects assumed to be caused by respiration and pulsation. More specifically, one can reduce physiology-related variance by using a GLM as described above to regress out the spatial averaged time course of compartments like white matter and the ventricles from the voxel time courses of the whole brain or only from the ROI time course used for neurofeedback. Yamashita et al. (2017), for example, included averaged signals from white matter, gray matter, and CSF as confound time courses in a real-time regression analysis. Spetter et al. (2017) calculated partial correlation of areas of interest with white matter and used these results to regress out unwanted fluctuations before the neurofeedback signal was calculated.

More advanced model-based approaches use concurrent recordings of the participant's breathing and heart rate. These recordings can be converted into confound regressors using methods like retrospective image correction (RETROICOR, Glover et al., 2000), respiratory volume per time (RVT, Birn et al., 2006), and heart rate variability (HRV, Chang et al., 2009). To be suitable for neurofeedback, these tools—originally developed for offline analysis—need to be adjusted for real-time processing. Misaki et al. (2015), for example, implemented a real-time version of RETROICOR and RVT and used a GPU to regress out physiological confounds in 100,000 voxels in under 300ms per volume.

4.5 Spatial and temporal smoothing

To enhance the signal-to-noise ratio, functional volumes are often spatially smoothed by convolution with a 3D Gaussian kernel. In this process, each voxel is replaced by a weighted average value calculated across neighboring voxels. The weighting is often specified using a Gaussian shape around a voxel; the width of the Gaussian shape determines the amount of smoothing—the broader the Gaussian, the more neighboring values influence the newly calculated value of a voxel. Since a Gaussian shape drops with increasing distance to the center, voxels further apart from the center will contribute less to the weighted average than voxels close to the center of the considered voxel. The amount of smoothing is usually expressed in terms of the full-width-at-half-maximum (FWHM) value of the Gaussian kernel, i.e., the width in millimeter when the values drop to half the peak value of the Gaussian (see Fig. 8). Since neurofeedback experiments operate on individual data, large smoothing kernels (8 mm or more) are not needed but modest smoothing in the order of 4 mm seems to be beneficial. While spatial smoothing suppresses noise, it reduces the spatial resolution of the data and should be therefore applied with care. According to the matched filter theorem, spatial smoothing increases sensitivity to effects of similar (or larger) scale to the kernel but decreases sensitivity to smaller scales. When calculating feedback using MVPA (see later),

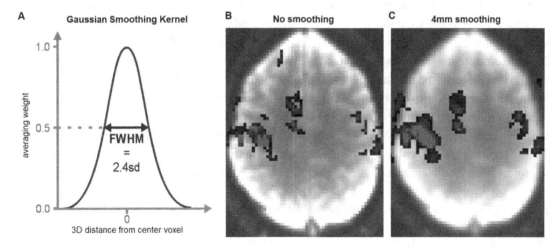

Fig. 8

Spatial Gaussian smoothing. (A) The width of the Gaussian bell shape determines how far smoothing extends into the voxel neighborhood, which is expressed as the full-width-at-half-maximum (FWHM) value (about 2.4 times the value of the standard deviation (sd), which is also often used). (B) A functional slice (voxel size = 2 mm × 2 mm × 3 mm) with overlaid statistical map (finger tapping > baseline, yellow to red colors—black to dark-gray colors in print version); no spatial smoothing has been applied. (C) After modest spatial smoothing (FWHM = 4 mm), the functional slice appears more blurred and the overlaid statistical map appears more "blobby." The same threshold (*t* = 3.0) has been used for map overlays in B and C.

spatial smoothing is usually avoided or used with very small kernels on the order of the voxel size since differential effects in neighboring voxels may contribute to separating patterns from each other, which would be reduced when performing spatial smoothing.

Less common than spatial smoothing is temporal smoothing of voxel time courses in neurofeedback studies. The same Gaussian shape as for spatial smoothing is often used (Fig. 8A) but the width of the Gaussian now extends along the one-dimensional time axis of a voxel time course. Temporal smoothing increases signal-to-noise since it acts as a low-pass filter removing high-frequency signal fluctuations, which are considered as noise. Because of incremental data processing, standard Gaussian temporal smoothing can, however, not be used in real-time analysis since only past data is available when the next data point arrives. To provide a neurofeedback signal to the participant that is less noisy, temporal (weighted) averaging of the last N data points can be applied. In case of moment-to-moment feedback this, however, introduces additional delays (beyond hemodynamics and processing time), and it is thus recommended to keep the number of averaged past time points low, such as 2–3 points when using a TR of 1–2 s.

5 Other neurofeedback methods

Regional univariate activation-based feedback was the first investigated NF approach (see Chapter 1). While still used in most (clinical) studies, other approaches have been explored such as connectivity feedback and multivoxel pattern classifier feedback (Watanabe et al., 2017). Connectivity feedback also extracts activity time courses from ROIs, but the feedback signal is based on some measure of functional or effective connectivity between two or more ROI time courses. Multivoxel pattern classification (or multivoxel pattern regression) feedback is based on machine learning determining optimal weights for the activity of individual voxels to calculate summary values that maximally differentiate brain states from each other. This section concludes with two recently introduced neurofeedback approaches, decoded neurofeedback (DecNef) and semantic neurofeedback, which are both based on MVPA.

5.1 Functional or effective connectivity feedback

Functional connectivity feedback has been used to target brain networks and their correlation rather than isolated activity in specific ROIs (Ruiz et al., 2013). In its simplest case, time courses from two ROIs are extracted and a correlation value is calculated in a sliding time window. The calculated functional correlation value may be used directly as a feedback signal, e.g., in a thermometer display. An increasing (decreasing) feedback signal would then reflect a stronger (weaker) *coupling* between brain areas instead of (only) reflecting the mean activation level of the involved areas, especially when using activity intervals that exclude task onset and offset phases (Zilverstand et al., 2014). Various connectivity measures can be used as a basis for the neurofeedback signal, including Pearson's (Partial) Correlation (Zilverstand et al., 2014) and dynamic causal modeling (DCM) (Koush et al., 2013). When using connectivity feedback, it is important to model and remove global signal fluctuations (see Sections 4.2–4.4) because such fluctuations will artificially increase the calculated connectivity measure biasing the provided feedback signal (Power et al., 2012; Van Dijk et al., 2012).

Online estimation of functional or effective connectivity between two or more brain areas requires the use of sufficiently long sliding windows to compute robust "instantaneous" values of coupling strength or to fit the connectivity parameters of DCM. In an offline analyzed study, it has been shown that time windows of about 20–30 s with a TR of 1–2 s are sufficient to calculate robust (partial) correlation coefficients in the context of various uni- and bimanual motor tasks (Zilverstand et al., 2014). Furthermore, this study showed that instantaneous functional correlations may indeed provide relevant and unique information regarding ongoing brain processes that are not captured equally well by standard activation level-based neurofeedback measures. Functional connectivity feedback will also benefit from technical advances including the multiband accelerated imaging pulse sequences mentioned earlier (Feinberg and Yacoub, 2012) as well as new imaging approaches such as MR-Encephalography (Lührs et al., 2019) that allow a substantial increase in the number of collected data points per time unit.

Functional connectivity feedback seems especially relevant for future clinical neurofeedback studies since research indicates that fMRI functional connectivity network measures may belong to the most robust indicators of pathological brain processes that may be "normalized" by feedback training. Ramot et al. (2017), for example, used neurofeedback to train three brain nodes in participants with autism spectrum disorder (ASD) based on the assumption that ASD is associated with abnormal connectivity patterns between resting state networks. More specifically, aberrant connectivity correlated with symptom severity in the investigated participants. Desired network connectivity patterns were reinforced in real time by revealing part of a hidden picture (plus an upbeat sound) whenever connections between the resting state networks changed toward the target ("healthy") pattern. The neurofeedback training produced large, significant long-term changes in correlations at the network level. Moreover, observed changes in ASD resting state connectivity following the training were correlated to changes in behavior, suggesting that neurofeedback can be used to change complex, clinically relevant network connectivity patterns.

5.2 Multivoxel pattern analysis feedback

As for offline analysis, MVPA has gained increasing interest also for real-time fMRI studies starting with whole-brain state classifiers (LaConte et al., 2007) and more regional approaches (e.g., Sorger et al., 2010) in the context of brain-computer interface applications (Sorger and Goebel, 2020). One reason for the popularity of MVPA is its potential to detect differences between neural correlates of mental states with higher sensitivity than conventional univariate statistical analysis since responses from voxels are *jointly* analyzed (see Fig. 9) to decode specific mental states or representational content. After performing a

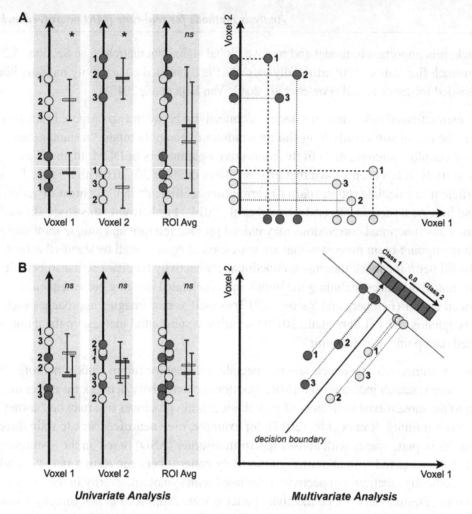

Fig. 9

Schematic comparison of univariate and multivariate analysis (MVPA) for the simple case of two voxels responding to three trials of two conditions, class 1 (orange disks—dark-gray disks in print version) and class 2 (blue disks—light-gray disks in print version). (A) Voxel 1 and 2 respond significantly differently to the two conditions (indicated by asterisk) but in opposite direction. When these voxels are averaged in a two-voxel ROI (see ROI Avg), their opposite preferences cancel out leading to a weak nonsignificant (*ns*) difference. In multivariate analysis, the responses of the voxels are *jointly* analyzed: each point in the panel on the right represents one distributed activity pattern (a pattern from N voxels is represented as a point in *N*-dimensional space); the location of a point (pattern) is determined by the joint activation of voxel 1 (*X* axis component) and voxel 2 (*Y* axis component). (B) Same explanations as in A but now the two voxels differentiate the two conditions only weakly leading to nonsignificant single-voxel and ROI averaging results. Using multivariate analysis, the two conditions can still be separated by finding an appropriate separation line (or plane in higher-dimensional space), called *decision boundary*. This boundary is determined during the training phase by assigning weights to each voxel in a way that patterns of the two classes will be maximally discriminated. The output value of the (linear) classifier is the projection of a data point on the solid line orthogonal to the decision boundary for any new incoming pattern. This value can be used to calculate a neurofeedback signal as indicated by the thermometer display.

training phase, the decoding phase requires little computational load and it is, thus, suitable for real-time applications. In real-time fMRI, MVPA is typically implemented using the *support vector machine* (SVM) learning algorithm producing particularly good generalization performance with small training datasets as compared to other approaches. The SVM classifier is trained on data from one or more training runs in a real-time session to learn to associate distributed brain patterns with different conditions (called classes or *labels* in machine learning) and to determine decision boundaries optimally discriminating exemplars of classes. In a *binary classifier*, one class could be condition (or task) A, and the other "rest"; in a *multiclass classifier*, brain patterns are associated with more than two conditions. To obtain distributed patterns for different classes during training and testing, response values are estimated for each individual trial at each voxel (called *feature* in machine learning). Estimated single-trial responses across voxels then form the *feature vectors* used to train and later apply (test) the classifier. After the training phase, online classification (decoding) is enabled in neurofeedback runs producing prediction values for evoked patterns based on the estimated classifier weights. The predicted value can be converted into a neurofeedback value indicating the likelihood that the current distributed activity pattern belongs to a given class (Fig. 9B).

Standard ROI averaging can be viewed in this context as a *nonadaptive* multivoxel approach with voxel weights set to $1/N$ with N the number of voxels; because of fixed equal weights opposing preferences of voxels will cancel out (see Fig. 9). Adaptive classifiers on the other hand may assign opposing (positive vs. negative) weights to voxels with opposing preferences increasing instead of decreasing the discriminative power of a classifier; furthermore, voxels that do not help to discriminate patterns will receive a weight value close to zero. The higher sensitivity of MVPA to differentiate brain states as compared to simple voxel averaging in ROI activation approaches may enable more effective neurofeedback training. In a MVPA-SVM neurofeedback application, for example, volunteers achieved successful control of emotion-related activation patterns (Sitaram et al., 2011). MVPA may also serve as a smart method to localize brain regions for subsequent neurofeedback examination as an alternative to the use of univariate GLM statistical analysis; as opposed to focal ROIs, MVPA may be especially useful to identify complex (noncontiguous and even interdigitated) regions in the whole brain as targets for neurofeedback (LaConte, 2011; LaConte et al., 2007). In the context of fMRI neurofeedback patient studies, MVPA may also be used as a means for participants to learn to "mimic desired brain states or mimicking the brain states of others" (deCharms, 2008). In this scenario, the feedback signal provided to a patient would reflect how much the currently evoked activity pattern resembles a desired target pattern. This approach (see also Section 5.3) requires more fundamental research in cognitive and affective neuroscience to explore whether it will be possible to define desirable brain states for specific patients as described before for connectivity feedback (Ramot et al., 2017). Since this would likely involve a transfer of desirable neural activation states obtained in a training group of individuals to other participants, advanced brain normalization schemes, such as cortex-based alignment (Fischl et al., 1999; Goebel et al., 2006) or hyperalignment (Haxby et al., 2011, see also next section), may be useful to relate corresponding brain regions across participants' brains as well as possible.

5.3 Decoded neurofeedback

DecNef is a form of multivoxel pattern feedback focusing on unconscious reinforcement learning, usually with monetary reward (Watanabe et al., 2017; Shibata et al., 2019; Taschereau-Dumouchel et al., 2020). While the experimental setup and analysis methods are similar to MVPA neurofeedback as described in the previous section, and although reinforcement learning can be employed also in the context of other types of NF (e.g., Ramot et al., 2017), DecNef can be viewed as a unique NF category because of several strategic decisions that will be described briefly in this section. As opposed to conventional *explicit neurofeedback* where participants engage consciously in instructed mental tasks during neurofeedback training, DecNef is based on an *implicit approach* that does not require conscious knowledge of participants about what they are supposed to do or to learn (Watanabe et al., 2017; Shibata et al., 2019; Taschereau-Dumouchel et al., 2020). Explicit neurofeedback is replaced with *associative learning* by pairing multivoxel patterns with *online reward* (or online punishment or another stimulus). To relate to a specific brain process, it is, however, necessary to train a multivariate predictive model (decoder) in a training session (called the *decoder construction session*) in the same way as described for MVPA NF in the previous section. For instance, to design an experiment to train selective visual attention, brain data needs to be acquired when the participant is attending or not attending to visual stimuli, and the classifier is trained to discriminate low versus high attention states (likelihood output of binary classifier) or to predict the level of attention (output of multivariate regression). During neurofeedback runs, the brain pattern generated by a participant during *induction* blocks is "decoded" by applying the trained classifier in a similar way as described for MVPA NF. The main difference is that the participant does not obtain instructions about a specific mental strategy but only gets the general instruction to "manipulate brain activity in order to maximize reward." Monetary reward is provided intermittently (after the induction block) depending on the decoded outcome of the classifier. Since decoded NF studies do not provide explicit task instructions, they allow researchers to conduct double-blind studies and to control for placebo effects more easily as compared to conventional explicit neurofeedback training. Without explicit instructions participants nonetheless learn over time to induce the "ideal" multivoxel pattern (corresponding, e.g., to a high attentional state) of neural activation thereby maximizing reward. A study by Shibata et al. (2011) has, for example, shown that decoded feedback leads to orientation-specific visual perceptual learning without presentation of an actual stimulus during the induction phase and without awareness of the participants regarding what they were supposed to learn. In a variant called *associative* DecNef, (visual) stimuli are shown during the induction phase with the rationale of providing the possibility to create a new unconscious association between the (visual) stimuli and the target pattern trained (e.g., Amano et al., 2016). A recent decoded NF application (Taschereau-Dumouchel et al., 2018) used hyperalignment of higher-level visual cortex to transfer trained patterns representing naturally feared animal categories (e.g., snakes and spiders) from surrogate participants to new individuals. The surrogate participants were exposed to fear-inducing as well as nonthreatening animal categories. While hyperalignment needs functional data also from a new participant, correspondence between brains can be established based on data from exposure to nonthreatening animal categories only. This offers the exciting possibility to untrain fear responses unconsciously during reinforcement (MVPA NF) runs in participants with high levels of fear (e.g., to spiders) without exposing them to feared stimuli during classifier training runs. A puzzling aspect of this (and other) DecNef studies is that participants learn to produce brain patterns that are "recognized" by the classifier as the target stimulus (e.g., "snake" in the described study) without becoming consciously aware of that stimulus as is evident from participant's reports about what they think they are doing during the induction phase.

5.4 Semantic neurofeedback

In most previous activation-, connectivity-, and MVPA-based neurofeedback studies, feedback is provided as a single summary signal, often presented over time in a one-dimensional analog display such as the filling level of a thermometer or the expansion of a disk. The main idea of semantic neurofeedback (Goebel, 2019; Russo et al., 2021) is to provide rich information to participants by relating the current mental state to multiple other relevant "anchor" mental states visualized in a two-dimensional semantic map. Related brain states in such a map are characterized by a small distance while unrelated states are located further apart. The semantic map is calculated in preparatory (localizer) runs and provided to participants together with a marked location as explicit feedback indicating the distance of the current mental state to the states evoked in the localizer run(s). This novel representation enables participants to navigate to desired mental states in the semantic map. Fig. 10 illustrates schematically how semantic feedback is displayed to participants during NF runs.

To calculate the similarity between evoked distributed patterns, representational similarity analysis (RSA) (Kriegeskorte et al., 2008) has been adapted for incremental real-time analysis (rt-RSA). RSA assumes that, in a time window of observation, the spatial activity pattern across voxels encodes the neural representation of contents, e.g., of an image, a sound, or a mental state. The combination of different patterns of neuronal activity defines a multidimensional space where the dimensions are the number of voxels and a single point in this space is a pattern. For semantic neurofeedback, a set of relevant mental states are evoked in participants and the representational space of the underlying distributed activity patterns is determined using RSA by estimating their mutual (dis)similarities (see Fig. 11). The most

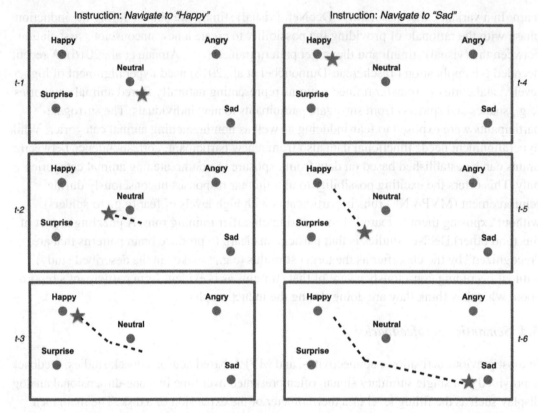

Fig. 10

Illustration of the type of feedback presented to participants in the context of emotional semantic neurofeedback. Disks indicate mental states mapped in localizer run(s). The participant starts in a rather neutral state (red asterisk = current mental state— dark gray asterisk in print version) in first displayed semantic map ($t - 1$). Via headphones, the participant receives instruction to navigate to the "happy" state. Feedback displays at time points $t - 2$ and $t - 3$ indicate that participant successfully moved to the "happy" state. At $t - 4$, the participant gets the new instruction to navigate to "sad" state. Feedback displays at $t - 5$ and $t - 6$ indicate that the participant successfully moves to the "sad" state.

common measure to compute the dissimilarities between two brain patterns is the correlation distance (i.e., one minus the linear correlation). The pairwise pattern dissimilarity values are usually summarized in a representational dissimilarity matrix (RDM) (Fig. 11B).

While the RDM with all pairwise (dis)similarities captures the similarity relationships of the total stimulus space, it is not suited directly as feedback information since its contents would not be easily interpretable by participants. To create a visualization that is suited for neurofeedback, the calculated RDM is converted into a 2-dimensional map using multidimensional scaling (MDS), which is a standard dimensionality reduction method to visualize the similarity structure of high-dimensional data in a low (2 or 3) dimensional

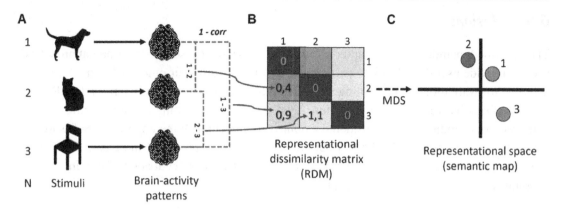

Fig. 11

Illustration of representational similarity analysis and semantic map creation using *N* = 3 visual stimuli as an example. (A) The presented or imagined *N* = 3 stimuli evoke *N* distributed activity patterns. For the subset of voxels in a selected ROI (e.g., in ventral visual cortex), the N patterns are compared pairwise, usually by calculating a linear correlation value. (B) Correlations are converted into dissimilarity values (1 – correlation) to fill the respective cells in the representational dissimilarity matrix (RDM). Besides numerical values, the RDM cells are often visualized using a color scale (e.g., dark blue cells—dark cells in print version → low dissimilarity, light blue/orange cells—bright cells in print version → high dissimilarity). (C) Using multidimensional scaling (MDS), the similarity information in the RDM can be projected onto a two-dimensional representational space also referred to as the semantic map.

space (e.g., Borg and Groenen, 2005). The calculated and visualized 2D map is referred to as *representational space* or as the *semantic map* (Fig. 11C). In the 2D semantic map, the mutual Euclidean distances among points reflect the dissimilarities among the high-dimensional response patterns as faithfully as possible. During neurofeedback runs, the similarity between the current mental state pattern of the participant and the mental state patterns used in the localizer run is calculated and projected in the semantic 2D map as a moving point indicating its semantic distance to the other mental states that are represented as fixed landmark points in the semantic map. To enhance the sensitivity to capture fine-grained pattern information, first studies have been conducted using 7 Tesla fMRI (Russo et al., 2021).

Semantic neurofeedback has been only recently proposed and needs to be evaluated and tested further in the future. It offers the potential to provide a more transparent neurofeedback experience for both the experimenter and the participant, which may lead to more specific and effective training results. In an emotion paradigm, for example, the transparent semantic feedback display would reveal if a patient instructed to move to a positive emotion would move instead to a negative emotion, which would likely go unnoticed when using a conventional mean activity (thermometer) display since positive and negative emotions are represented largely in the same network (Habes et al., 2013; Chikazoe et al., 2014).

6 Conclusions

The described methods in this chapter provide an overview of essential tools and approaches used to provide useful feedback to participants extracted from their ongoing brain activity. Software tools implementing such methods are available in many labs and fMRI neurofeedback has reached a rather mature level. Nonetheless, setting up and running fMRI neurofeedback studies is still considered a nontrivial and challenging enterprise. Software products are, thus, needed that largely automatize established pipelines and create intuitive user interfaces for specific goals to help establishing fMRI neurofeedback training in hospitals as an innovative treatment option for patients.

Acknowledgments

I would like to thank Michelle Hampson, Michael Lührs, and David Linden for helpful comments.

References

Amano, K., Shibata, K., Kawato, M., Sasaki, Y., Watanabe, T., 2016. Learning to associate orientation with color in early visual areas by associative decoded fMRI neurofeedback. Curr. Biol. 26, 1861–1866.

Bagarinao, E., Matsuo, K., Nakai, T., Sato, S., 2003. Estimation of general linear model coefficients for real-time application. NeuroImage 19, 422–429.

Bagarinao, E., Nakai, T., Tanaka, Y., 2006. Real-time functional MRI: development and emerging applications. Magn. Reson. Med. Sci. 5, 157–165.

Birn, R.M., Diamond, J.B., Smith, M.A., Bandettini, P.A., 2006. Separating respiratory-variation-related fluctuations from neuronal-activity-related fluctuations in fMRI. NeuroImage 31, 1536–1548.

Borg, I., Groenen, P.J.F., 2005. Modern Multidimensional Scaling: Theory and Applications, second ed. Springer Series in Statistics, Springer-Verlag, New York, https://doi.org/10.1007/0-387-28981-X.

Caria, A., Sitaram, R., Birbaumer, N., 2012. Real-time fMRI: a tool for local brain regulation. Neuroscientist 18 (5), 487–501.

Chang, C., Cunningham, J.P., Glover, G.H., 2009. Influence of heart rate on the BOLD signal: the cardiac response function. NeuroImage 44, 857–869.

Chikazoe, J., Lee, D.H., Kriegeskorte, N., Anderson, A.K., 2014. Population coding of affect across stimuli, modalities and individuals. Nat. Neurosci. 17 (8), 1114–1122.

Cox, R.W., Jesmanowicz, A., Hyde, J.S., 1995. Real-time functional magnetic resonance imaging. Magn. Reson. Med. 33 (2), 230–236.

deCharms, R.C., 2008. Applications of real-time fMRI. Nat. Rev. Neurosci. 9, 720–729.

deCharms, R., Christoff, K., Glover, G., Pauly, J., Whitfield, S., Gabrieli, J., 2004. Learned regulation of spatially localized brain activation using real-time fMRI. NeuroImage 21 (1), 436–443.

deCharms, R.C., Maeda, F., Glover, G.H., Ludlow, D., Pauly, J.M., Soneji, D., Gabrieli, J.D., Mackey, S.C., 2005. Control over brain activation and pain learned by using real-time functional MRI. Proc. Natl. Acad. Sci. U. S. A. 102, 18626–18631.

Direito, B., Lima, J., Simões, M., Sayal, A., Sousa, T., Lührs, M., Ferreira, C., Castelo-Branco, M., 2019. Targeting dynamic facial processing mechanisms in superior temporal sulcus using a novel fMRI neurofeedback target. Neuroscience 406, 97–108.

Draper, N.R., Smith, H., 1998. Applied Regression Analysis, third ed. John Wiley & Sons, New York.

Eickhoff, S.B., Stephan, K.E., Mohlberg, H., Grefkes, C., Fink, G.R., Amunts, K., Zilles, K., 2005. A new SPM toolbox for combining probabilistic cytoarchitectonic maps and functional imaging data. NeuroImage 25, 1325–1335.

Esposito, F., Seifritz, E., Formisano, E., Morrone, R., Scarabino, T., Tedeschi, G., Cirillo, S., Goebel, R., Di Salle, F., 2003. Real-time independent component analysis of fMRI time-series. NeuroImage 20, 2209–2224.

Feinberg, D.A., Yacoub, E., 2012. The rapid development of high speed, resolution and precision in fMRI. NeuroImage 62 (2), 720–725.

Fischl, B., Sereno, M.I., Tootell, R.B.H., Dale, A.M., 1999. High-resolution inter-subject averaging and a coordinate system for the cortical surface. Hum. Brain Mapp. 8, 272–284.

Friston, K.J., Holmes, A.P., Worsley, K.J., Poline, J.P., Frith, C.D., Frackowiak, R.S.J., 1995. Statistical parametric maps in functional imaging: a general linear approach. Hum. Brain Mapp. 2, 189–210.

Friston, K.J., Fletcher, P., Josephs, O., Holmes, A., Rugg, M.D., Turner, R., 1998. Event-related fMRI: characterizing differential responses. NeuroImage 7, 30–40.

Glover, G.H., Li, T.-Q., Ress, D., 2000. Image-based method for retrospective correction of physiological motion effects in fMRI: RETROICOR. Magn. Reson. Med. 44, 162–167.

Goebel, R., 2001. Cortex-based real-time fMRI. NeuroImage 13, S129.

Goebel, R., 2019. What's in the thermometer? Towards semantic neurofeedback at 7 Tesla. In: Talk in Chair Symposium of Real-Time Functional Imaging and Neurofeedback Conference (rtFIN), Maastricht, NL, Dec 9.

Goebel, R., Sorger, B., Kaiser, J., Birbaumer, N., Weiskopf, N., 2004. BOLD brain pong: self regulation of local brain activity during synchronously scanned, interacting subjects. In: Presented at: 34th Annual Meeting of the Society for Neuroscience, CA, USA.

Goebel, R., Esposito, F., Formisano, E., 2006. Analysis of functional image analysis contest (FIAC) data with brainvoyager QX: from single-subject to cortically aligned group general linear model analysis and self-organizing group independent component analysis. Hum. Brain Mapp. 27 (5), 392–401.

Goebel, R., Zilverstand, A., Sorger, B., 2010. Real-time fMRI-based brain computer interfacing for neurofeedback therapy and compensation of lost motor functions. Imaging Med. 2, 407–415.

Habes, I., Krall, S.C., Johnston, S.J., Yuen, K.S., Healy, D., Goebel, R., Sorger, B., Linden, D.E., 2013. Pattern classification of valence in depression. Neuroimage Clin. 2, 675–683.

Haxby, J.V., Guntupalli, J.S., Connolly, A.C., Halchenko, Y.O., Conroy, B.R., Gobbini, M.I., Hanke, M., Ramadge, P.J., 2011. A common, high-dimensional model of the representational space in human ventral temporal cortex. Neuron 72 (2), 404–416.

Heunis, S., Lamerichs, R., Zinger, S., Caballero-Gaudes, C., Jansen, J., Aldenkamp, B., Breeuwer, M., 2020. Quality and denoising in real-time functional magnetic resonance imaging neurofeedback: a methods review. Hum. Brain Mapp. 41 (12), 3439–3467.

Hinds, O., Ghosh, S., Thompson, T.W., Yoo, J.J., Whitfield-Gabrieli, S., Triantafyllou, C., Gabrieli, J.D.E., 2011. Computing moment-to-moment BOLD activation for real-time neurofeedback. NeuroImage 54, 361–368.

Kopel, R., Sladky, R., Laub, P., Koush, Y., Robineau, F., Hutton, C., Weiskopf, N., Vuilleumier, P., Van De Ville, D., Scharnowski, F., 2019. No time for drifting: Comparing performance and applicability of signal detrending algorithms for real-time fMRI. NeuroImage 191, 421–429.

Koush, Y., Rosa, M.J., Robineau, F., Heinen, K., Rieger, S., Weiskopf, N., Vuilleumier, P., Van De Ville, D., Scharnowski, F., 2013. Connectivity-based neurofeedback: dynamic causal modeling for real-time fMRI. NeuroImage 81, 422–430.

Krause, F., Benjamins, C., Lührs, M., Eck, J., Noirhomme, Q., Rosenke, M., Brunheim, S., Sorger, B., Goebel, R., 2017. Real-time fMRI-based self-regulation of brain activation across different visual feedback presentations. Brain-Comput. Interfaces 4, 87–101.

Krause, F., Benjamins, C., Eck, J., Lührs, M., van Hoof, R., Goebel, R., 2019. Active head motion reduction in magnetic resonance imaging using tactile feedback. Hum. Brain Mapp. 40 (14), 4026–4037.

Kriegeskorte, N., Mur, M., Bandettini, P., 2008. Representational similarity analysis connecting the branches of systems neuroscience. Front. Syst. Neurosci. 2, 4.

Kutner, M.H., Nachtsheim, C.J., Neter, J., Li, W., 2005. Applied Linear Statistical Models, fifth ed. McGraw-Hill, Boston.

LaConte, S.M., 2011. Decoding fMRI brain states in real-time. NeuroImage 56, 440–454.

LaConte, S.M., Peltier, S.J., Hu, X.P., 2007. Real-time fMRI using brain-state classification. Hum. Brain Mapp. 28, 1033–1044.

Lührs, M., Sorger, B., Goebel, R., Esposito, F., 2017. Automated selection of brain regions for real-time fMRI brain-computer interfaces. J. Neural Eng. 14 (1), 016004.

Lührs, M., Riemenschneider, B., Eck, J., Andonegui, A.B., Poser, B.A., Heinecke, A., Krause, F., Esposito, F., Sorger, B., Hennig, J., Goebel, R., 2019. The potential of MR-encephalography for BCI/neurofeedback applications with high temporal resolution. NeuroImage 194, 228–243.

Maclaren, J., Herbst, M., Speck, O., Zaitsev, M., 2012. Prospective motion correction in brain imaging: A review. Magn. Reson. Med. 69, 621–636.

Marins, T.F., Rodrigues, E.C., Engel, A., Hoefle, S., Basílio, R., Lent, R., Moll, J., Tovar-Moll, F., 2015. Enhancing motor network activity using real-time functional MRI neurofeedback of left premotor cortex. Front. Behav. Neurosci. 9.

Mathiak, K.A., Alawi, E.M., Koush, Y., Dyck, M., Cordes, J.S., Gaber, T.J., Zepf, F.D., Palomero-Gallagher, N., Sarkheil, P., Bergert, S., Zvyagintsev, M., Mathiak, K., 2015. Social reward improves the voluntary control over localized brain activity in fMRI-based neurofeedback training. Front. Behav. Neurosci. 9, 136.

Misaki, M., Barzigar, N., Zotev, V., Phillips, R., Cheng, S., Bodurka, J., 2015. Real-time fMRI processing with physiological noise correction—comparison with off-line analysis. J. Neurosci. Methods 256, 117–121.

Power, J.D., Barnes, K.A., Snyder, A.Z., Schlaggar, B.L., Petersen, S.E., 2012. Spurious but systematic correlations in functional connectivity MRI networks arise from subject motion. NeuroImage 59, 2142–2154.

Ramot, M., Kimmich, S., Gonzalez-Castillo, J., et al., 2017. Direct modulation of aberrant brain network connectivity through real-time NeuroFeedback. elife 6, e28974.

Rosenke, M., Weiner, K.S., Barnett, M.A., Zilles, K., Amunts, K., Goebel, R., Grill-Spector, K., 2018. A cross-validated cytoarchitectonic atlas of the human ventral visual stream. NeuroImage 170, 257–270.

Rosenke, M., van Hoof, R., van den Hurk, J., Grill-Spector, K., Goebel, R., 2021. A probabilistic functional atlas of human occipito-temporal visual cortex. Cerebral Cortex (New York, N.Y.: 1991) 31 (1), 603–619.

Ruiz, S., Lee, S., Soekadar, S.R., Caria, A., Veit, R., Kircher, T., Birbaumer, N., Sitaram, R., 2013. Acquired self-control of insula cortex modulates emotion recognition and brain network connectivity in schizophrenia. Hum. Brain Mapp. 34, 200–212.

Russo, A.G., Lührs, M., Di Salle, F., Esposito, F., Goebel, R., 2021. Towards semantic fMRI neurofeedback: navigating among mental states using real-time representational similarity analysis. J. Neural Eng. Online ahead of print.

Scheinost, D., Hampson, M., Qiu, M., Bhawnani, J., Constable, R.T., Papademetris, X., 2013. A graphics processing unit accelerated motion correction algorithm and modular system for real-time fMRI. Neuroinformatics 11, 291–300.

Shibata, K., Watanabe, T., Sasaki, Y., Kawato, M., 2011. Perceptual learning incepted by decoded fMRI neurofeedback without stimulus presentation. Science 334 (6061), 1413–1415.

Shibata, K., Lisi, G., Cortese, A., Watanabe, T., Sasaki, Y., Kawato, M., 2019. Toward a comprehensive understanding of the neural mechanisms of decoded neurofeedback. NeuroImage 188, 539–556.

Sitaram, R., Caria, A., Veit, R., Gaber, T., Kuebler, A., Birbaumer, N., 2005. Real-time fMRI based brain-computer interface enhanced by interactive virtual worlds. In: 45th Annual Meeting Society for Psychophysiological Research, Lisbon, Portugal.

Sitaram, R., Lee, S., Ruiz, S., Rana, M., Veit, R., Birbaumer, N., 2011. Real-time support vector classification and feedback of multiple emotional brain states. NeuroImage 56 (2), 753–765.

Smyser, C., Grabowski, T.J., Frank, R.J., Haller, J.W., Bolinger, L., 2001. Real-time multiple linear regression for fMRI supported by time-aware acquisition and processing. Magn. Reson. Med. 45, 289–298.

Sorger, B., Goebel, R., 2020. Real-time fMRI for brain-computer interfacing. Handb. Clin. Neurol. 168, 289–302.

Sorger, B., Peters, J., van den Boomen, C., Zilverstand, A., Reithler, R., Goebel, R., 2010. Real-time decoding the locus of visuospatial attention using multi-voxel pattern classification. In: Human Brain Mapping Conference, 16th edition, Barcelona, Spain.

Sorger, B., Kamp, T., Weiskopf, N., Peters, J.C., Goebel, R., 2018. When the brain takes 'BOLD' steps: real-time fMRI neurofeedback can further enhance the ability to gradually self-regulate regional brain activation. Neuroscience 378, 71–88.

Spetter, M.S., Malekshahi, R., Birbaumer, N., Lührs, M., van der Veer, A.H., Scheffler, K., Spuckti, S., Preissl, H., Veit, R., Hallschmid, M., 2017. Volitional regulation of brain responses to food stimuli in overweight and obese subjects: a real-time fMRI feedback study. Appetite 112, 188–195.

Subramanian, L., Skottnik, L., Cox, W.M., Lührs, M., McNamara, R., Hood, K., Watson, G., Whittaker, J.R., Williams, A.N., Sakhuja, R., Ihssen, N., Goebel, R., Playle, R., Linden, D.E.J., 2021. Neurofeedback training versus treatment as usual for alcohol dependence: results of an early phase randomized controlled trial and neuroimaging correlates. Eur. Addict. Res., 1–14 (online ahead of print).

Taschereau-Dumouchel, V., Cortese, A., Chiba, T., Knotts, J.D., Kawato, M., Lau, H., 2018. Towards an unconscious neural reinforcement intervention for common fears. Proc. Natl. Acad. Sci. U. S. A. 115 (13), 3470–3475.

Taschereau-Dumouchel, V., Cortese, A., Lau, H., Kawato, M., 2020. Conducting decoded neurofeedback studies. In: Social Cognitive and Affective Neuroscience. Advance Online Publication.

Thesen, S., Heid, O., Mueller, E., Schad, L.R., 2000. Prospective acquisition correction for head motion with image-based tracking for real-time fMRI. Magn. Reson. Med. 44 (3), 457–465.

Van Dijk, K.R.A., Sabuncu, M.R., Buckner, R.L., 2012. The influence of head motion on intrinsic functional connectivity MRI. NeuroImage 59, 431–438.

Watanabe, T., Sasaki, Y., Shibata, K., Kawato, M., 2017. Advances in fMRI Real-Time Neurofeedback. Trends Cogn. Sci. 21, 997–1010.

Weiskopf, N., 2012. Real-time fMRI and its application to neurofeedback. NeuroImage 62, 682–692.

Weiskopf, N., Scharnowski, F., Veit, R., Goebel, R., Birbaumer, N., Mathiak, K., 2004a. Self-regulation of local brain activity using real-time functional magnetic resonance imaging (fMRI). J. Physiol. Paris 98, 357–373.

Weiskopf, N., Mathiak, K., Bock, S., et al., 2004b. Principles of a brain-computer interface (BCI) based on real-time functional magnetic resonance imaging (fMRI). IEEE Trans. Biomed. Eng. 51 (6), 966–970.

Yamashita, A., Hayasaka, S., Kawato, M., Imamizu, H., 2017. Connectivity neurofeedback training can differentially change functional connectivity and cognitive performance. Cereb. Cortex 27, 4960–4970.

Young, K.D., Prause, N., Lazzaro, S., Siegle, G.J., 2020. Low cost MR compatible haptic stimulation with application to fMRI neurofeedback. Brain Sci. 10 (11), 790.

Zaitsev, M., Dold, C., Sakas, G., Hennig, J., Speck, O., 2006. Magnetic resonance imaging of freely moving objects: prospective real-time motion correction using an external optical motion tracking system. NeuroImage 31 (3), 1038–1050.

Zilverstand, A., Sorger, B., Zimmermann, J., Kaas, A., Goebel, R., 2014. Windowed correlation: a suitable tool for providing dynamic fMRI-based functional connectivity neurofeedback on task difficulty. PLoS One 9 (1), e85929.

Zilverstand, A., Sorger, B., Sarkheil, P., Goebel, R., 2015. fMRI neurofeedback facilitates anxiety regulation in females with spider phobia. Front. Behav. Neurosci. 9, 148.

CHAPTER 3

Protocol design in fMRI neurofeedback studies

Michelle Hampson[a] and David Linden[b]

[a]Department of Radiology and Biomedical Imaging, Yale University School of Medicine, New Haven, CT, United States, [b]School for Mental Health and Neuroscience, Faculty of Health, Medicine and Life Sciences, Maastricht University, Maastricht, Netherlands

An acute reader of the fMRI neurofeedback research literature will quickly realize how difficult it is to make direct comparisons across neurofeedback studies due to the idiosyncratic nature of each training protocol. Two studies trying to influence the same aspects of behavior may differ on the brain pattern targeted, the type of feedback used, the instructions given to participants, the amount of training provided, and even how success in improving brain regulation is measured (see Box 1). Any one of these differences could contribute to differences in reported results. Even when results are superficially similar, a close read will often reveal that the studies have completely different implications due to differences in what was trained, how the training was conducted, and how results were evaluated. In short, although there are some guidelines for good practices in neurofeedback studies that can be helpful to consider (Ros et al., 2020), neurofeedback is far from a standardized intervention. In some respects, this is positive as there is room for creative designs and flexibility of application. However, it can be challenging for researchers entering the field.

Here we address many of the questions that arise when a new training protocol is being developed, beginning with the most fundamental decision to be made: what to target?

1 What to target?

In theory, it is possible to target any aspect of brain function that can be measured via fMRI in a matter of seconds or tens of seconds. The simplest and most common type of neurofeedback study trains up or down the average activity in a single region of the brain (e.g., deCharms et al., 2004; Yoo et al., 2006). The region can be defined anatomically (e.g., Mathiak et al., 2015; Young et al., 2017) or can be functionally localized in each

fMRI Neurofeedback. https://doi.org/10.1016/B978-0-12-822421-2.00012-0

BOX 1 Example of the diversity of protocols used in fMRI neurofeedback studies: two studies training sustained attention

Sustained attention refers to the ability to maintain mental focus over a period of time. There have been a number of fMRI neurofeedback studies training sustained attention (deBettencourt et al., 2015; Alegria et al., 2017; Zilverstand et al., 2017; Scheinost et al., 2020) and the diversity of approaches used in these studies is striking. To illustrate this we directly compare the work of deBettencourt et al. (2015) and Alegria et al. (2017) in Table 1.

Although the two studies compared in Table 1 were both attempting to upregulate sustained attention, they used completely different training paradigms. They targeted different types of brain biomarkers in different populations. The training contexts were different in terms of tasks assigned during regulation periods, feedback interfaces used, and the training schedule adopted. Different types of control comparison groups were used, and different outcome measures were examined. In short, other than providing neurofeedback via a visual modality in an ongoing manner during regulation periods, the training approaches used in these studies had almost nothing in common. Furthermore, both studies found that the training improved control over brain function more in the experimental than the control group, but these findings were based on different forms of data. Alegria and colleagues found group differences in activation of the target region in transfer runs collected after the training. In contrast, deBettencourt and colleagues found increased discriminability between brain patterns associated with different attentional states as assessed in "stable" (nonneurofeedback) blocks of training runs late in the training relative to early in the training, and these changes were greater in the experimental than the control group. Clearly, comparison of results from these studies is difficult, given the multifaceted differences in approach they used and differences in how their outcome measures were defined.

Table 1: Comparison of training protocol characteristics for two sustained attention studies.

	deBettencourt et al. (2015)	Alegria et al. (2017)
Neural target trained	Whole brain multivoxel pattern associated with task relevant stimuli	Activity in the right inferior frontal gyrus
Task performed during brain regulation (other than regulation itself)	Continuous performance visual category decision (go-no go) task	None
Feedback modality	Visual	Visual
Feedback interface	Closed-loop feedback, with task difficulty inversely related to expression of target brain pattern	Direct feedback regarding target activation in the form of movement of a rocket
Monetary reward associated with regulation performance	No	Yes
Feedback type (continuous/intermittent)	Continuous	Continuous
Number of training sessions	1	4
Mental practice assigned between sessions	No	Yes
Control group	Yoked sham	Trained on a different brain area
Population	Healthy young adults	Adolescent boys with attention deficit disorder
Information and instructions given to participants	Explicit training with task instructions	Explicit training but minimal instructions
Primary outcome measure	Improvement in performance on the no-go no task after training relative to baseline	ADHD rating scale

subject to optimize its relevance to whatever aspect of mental function is of interest (e.g., Subramanian et al., 2011; Scheinost et al., 2013). Variants of this approach include training more than one brain area at a time by providing multiple feedback signals (Zilverstand et al., 2015) or training the relative activity across two or more brain areas, for example, by providing feedback on the difference in activity levels across the regions (Scharnowski et al., 2015; Habes et al., 2016).

A more sophisticated approach that has proven very successful is to train participants toward specific multivariate patterns of activity either in a given area of the brain (Shibata et al., 2011, 2016; Amano et al., 2016; Koizumi et al., 2016), or across the brain as a whole (LaConte et al., 2007; deBettencourt et al., 2015). These patterns are often defined in a manner specific to the individual. That is, the brain pattern associated with a particular aspect of mental function for each individual is first identified and then trained up or down in that participant.

It is also possible to train connectivity patterns. This includes functional connectivity training that focuses on a single connection (Megumi et al., 2015; Tinaz et al., 2018), as well as training on more complicated patterns of functional connectivity, including networks of interest identified in the whole brain functional connectome (Ramot et al., 2017; Scheinost et al., 2020). While functional connectivity is by nature correlational, causal relationships between brain areas can be estimated via models of effective connectivity and provided as feedback. For example, software is available for neurofeedback of effective connectivity computed based on dynamic causal modeling (Koush et al., 2013, 2017). It is important to note that all forms of connectivity training require longer time windows of data over which the feedback signal is computed than activity-based feedback, due to the fact that connectivity calculations require multiple volumes of imaging data. For this reason, many connectivity training paradigms adopt an intermittent feedback approach in which participants try to regulate their connectivity patterns for a block of time (generally tens of seconds) after which they are given feedback on their success for the whole block (Megumi et al., 2015; Tinaz et al., 2018). This is in contrast to so-called continuous feedback (more accurately termed "moment-to-moment" feedback) in which feedback is provided as each volume is collected. Intermittent feedback is not the only way to deal with the time window of data required for connectivity feedback. Two other options include: (1) a sliding window approach—with this approach consecutive feedback signals will be highly correlated due to the overlapping data window they are computed from, and (2) an approach introduced by Ramot et al. (2017) that estimates connectivity using a two-volume time window.

The various types of training protocols described before (see Fig. 1 for illustration) provide a sense of the diverse types of brain biomarkers that can be trained via fMRI neurofeedback,

---

[a] The term "aspect of mental function" is used here in a broad sense to an aspect of perception, emotion, or cognition.

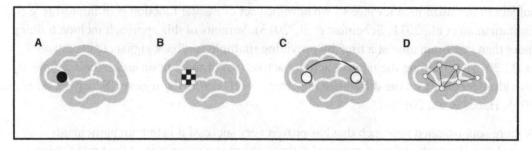

Fig. 1
Illustration of various types of biomarkers that can be targeted using fMRI neurofeedback.
(A) Mean activity in a specific brain area. (B) A multivariate pattern of activity in a specific brain
area. (C) Functional connectivity between two different brain areas. (D) A pattern of network
connectivity across multiple brain areas.

but this is by no means a comprehensive summary. In the coming years, training paradigms targeting other measures (such as network properties) are likely to emerge. In short, fMRI neurofeedback is highly flexible in terms of what can be targeted.

For researchers wishing to use neurofeedback to alter a specific aspect of mental function, decisions regarding what to target are typically influenced by both theoretical and practical considerations. Theoretical considerations are based on the existing scientific literature and our understanding of the functional brain substrates that underlie the mental function of interest. For example, in clinical studies, biomarkers identified as relevant to a specific disorder via functional neuroimaging are a common target. One key consideration when reading the literature and considering different options for biomarkers of relevance is the effect size of the brain-behavior relationship reported. It is important to remember that a relationship can be statistically significant while still having a small effect size (this is particularly likely in studies with large sample sizes that are powered to detect small effects). In such a case, successfully altering the brain pattern via neurofeedback may not have an appreciable effect on the mental function of interest, because the two are only weakly related. In contrast, targeting a biomarker that is tightly coupled to the mental function of interest will ensure that any success in improving brain regulation will be likely to yield a corresponding success in altering mental function, assuming a causal relationship exists in which the brain function drives the behavior and not, for example, the reverse.

Practical considerations for neurofeedback researchers are related to the real-time imaging system they have access to, and the options available in the software installed on their system. For technically oriented researchers, it is always possible to develop new software tailored to the needs of a given application, or to install another software package that has the desired functionality, but of course, the task of developing (or even installing and testing existing software developed at other sites) can be time consuming. At present, this is an issue for many research sites that have developed software for real-time imaging to track certain aspects of brain function and not others, but as the field becomes more established, the breadth of functionality available at most sites will likely improve.

2 How to train?

This question covers a number of design issues including what information and instructions are given to subjects, the type of feedback interface used, and the training schedule adopted.

2.1 Providing strategies/instructions to subjects

The information provided to participants in neurofeedback studies can range from extremely limited to quite extensive. On one end of this continuum are studies that do not even inform participants that they are being trained with neurofeedback. An example of this is a study in which healthy participants were told they would receive monetary benefit each time they heard a positive sound and would be monetarily penalized each time they heard a negative sound (Ramot et al., 2016). They were led to believe that the study was intended to examine reward processing in the brain and were not informed that the auditory signals were actually based on brain activity patterns. On the other end of the spectrum are many clinical trial neurofeedback studies in which patients are told the study involves neurofeedback that is designed to help them learn to control their symptom-related brain activity and the patients are provided with evidence-based cognitive-behavioral strategies that they have the option of using (e.g., Scheinost et al., 2013; Mehler et al., 2018; Sukhodolsky et al., 2020). In some of these cases, the mental strategies are not presented as optional, and instead a mental task is assigned to the participants to be performed during the feedback session that is believed to engage the network of interest. For example, in a study of depression, patients were instructed to think about positive autobiographical memories while attempting to upregulate their amygdala activity during neurofeedback (Young et al., 2017). Training paradigms where participants are not informed regarding what is being trained (or even that training is occurring) are often referred to as "implicit" training, while those where subjects are given information regarding what is being trained are referred to as "explicit" training. Which of these is optimal for a given application depends on the purpose of the study.

For studies that are designed primarily to test hypothesized brain-behavior relationships, implicit studies have the important advantage that they avoid confounds such as placebo effects (the tendency for participants to experience changes in health or mental function consistent with their expectations) and demand bias (the tendency for patients to report changes consistent with what they think experimenters want), because participants have no specific expectations and no understanding of the goals of the experiment. Therefore implicit studies can be a great option for basic science studies testing hypotheses regarding the neural substrates of specific aspects of mental function. However, the lack of disclosure inherent in these studies raises ethical challenges that must be considered carefully (see Chapter 14 for further discussion).

How about for studies where the primary aim is to change mental function? There is some debate whether implicit or explicit neurofeedback is more powerful for this purpose. Implicit neurofeedback relies on implicit learning, while explicit neurofeedback can potentially engage both implicit learning, and consciously mediated learning. On the one hand, engaging additional conscious learning mechanisms has potential to amplify the overall learning. On the other hand, it has also been suggested that engagement of the conscious learning system could potentially interfere with subconscious learning processes and thus decrease the overall efficacy of the intervention (Sepulveda et al., 2016).

Regardless of which approach is more effective at inducing learning, explicit neurofeedback is often preferable in clinical studies for several reasons. First, from a practical perspective, it can be easier to recruit patients for explicit neurofeedback studies as many patients are interested in participating in research that has some potential to improve their symptoms. Second, it can be challenging to fully blind patients to the purpose of the study—if they are aware that they were recruited because of their clinical condition, and are aware they are receiving neurofeedback, they may suspect the goal is to influence their symptoms, even if they are not told anything about what is being trained. Third, and most importantly, there is the ethical aspect. Symptoms are an important part of a person's life and identity and thus any intervention designed to change those symptoms should not be administered without an informed consent process that ensures the participant has agreed to participate in an intervention that could potentially reduce their symptoms. This can be done while preserving some aspects of implicit training, for example, subjects may be told that the training may affect their symptoms without disclosing what is targeted at a neural level and without providing any conscious strategies to the participants. However, fully implicit training, that is, when participants have no knowledge of the purpose of the training, is not generally suitable for clinical application.

Another question related to the amount of information shared with participants is whether participants should be assigned a mental task to do during the neurofeedback that is likely to engage the relevant circuitry. One feature of this approach is that it can reduce variability in regulation performance driven by task switching between effective and ineffective tasks, and can thereby improve power for detecting regulation success or improvements in regulation ability. However, a counterargument (that is grounded in humility regarding our understanding of brain function) is that providing a specific mental strategy will constrain the learning space and could therefore prevent participants from learning to regulate their brain circuitry in a manner very different from the way their brains function during the task.

In essence, the concern from this perspective is that constraining participants to perform a specific task may prevent them from adopting the necessary brain state for optimal learning. In addition to these practical and theoretical considerations, for some applications, there may also be relevant ethical concerns. For example, given that the amygdala activates for both positive and negative affect processing, studies that train patients to regulate the region may want to ensure that the context for the regulation is therapeutic. For example, depressed patients who were trained to upregulate the amygdala in a recent study were instructed to do so in the context of positive autobiographical memory recall (Young et al., 2017). This explicit instruction was important for preventing patients from ruminating on negative thoughts to activate their amygdala, which could be an effective upregulation strategy, but would likely be unhealthy and possibly even dangerous in patients with depression.

Researchers may also choose not to assign a task to participants, but to still provide the participants with suggested strategies that they have the option of trying during the neurofeedback (Scheinost et al., 2013; Mehler et al., 2018; Sukhodolsky et al., 2020). This may be particularly appealing when there are evidence-based techniques for controlling the mental function of interest (such as cognitive-behavioral therapy techniques that have been demonstrated effective for controlling specific types of symptoms) that a subset of the participant population is likely to be familiar with. Providing an introduction to these techniques for all participants can ensure they enter the training with same toolkit of strategies to try, while presenting the strategies as optional leaves open the possibility that participants can learn to regulate using neural mechanisms very different from those relevant to the strategies discussed. However, when tasks or strategies are involved in a training paradigm, even if they are optional, it is important to be aware that these alone could potentially drive learning. This concern is typically managed by comparison with a control group that is given similar strategies and instructions.

In short, the information and instructions given to subjects will depend on goals of the study and whether the researchers believe that performance of a mental task can induce a neural context that is optimal, or nearly optimal, for inducing the desired learning. It is also important to consider the existing knowledge base of the population trained and to carefully examine ethical issues in the context of the specific application.

2.2 Feedback interface

The majority of studies to date have used so-called continuous feedback in which the feedback is updated frequently, typically providing a new feedback signal after each brain volume is processed (Fig. 2A). An alternative approach is the use of intermittent feedback, where subjects try to regulate for blocks of time and receive feedback signals after each regulation block (Fig. 2B). As noted earlier, intermittent feedback is a good option when providing feedback on a measure that requires a time window for computation, such as

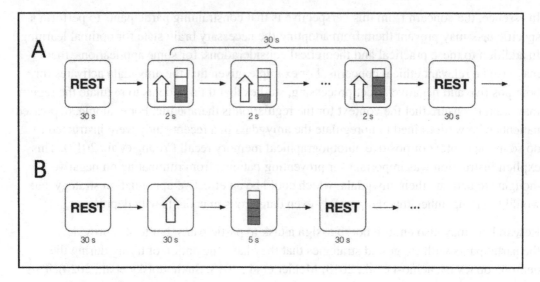

Fig. 2
Continuous versus intermittent feedback. Panel A illustrates a continuous feedback paradigm
(although not strictly speaking continuous, this is the common terminology in the field). Here
participants are cued, via the *arrow*, to upregulate their biomarker and feedback is provided with
a thermometer to the right of the *arrow*. In this example, volumes are collected every 2 s, and the
feedback is updated for each new volume. Panel B illustrates an intermittent feedback paradigm in
which participants are cued to upregulate for a block of time with no feedback, and then receive
feedback summarizing how well they performed after the regulation block.

functional connectivity. It also has the advantage of reducing cognitive load, both because
participants do not need to process the feedback signal at the same time that they are trying
to regulate, and because there is no need for them to mentally adjust for the hemodynamic
delay. On the other hand, it provides more limited information to participants and may be less
engaging.

A number of studies have compared the efficacy of intermittent with continuous feedback.
These studies have generally found both forms of feedback to be effective and, although
qualitatively better results have been found for one or the other in different contexts, no
significant differences in efficacy have been reported between the two approaches (Johnson
et al., 2012; Emmert et al., 2017; Hellrung et al., 2018). Thus it seems that either type of
feedback can reasonably be used, as needed for a given application. For example, in studies
in populations with attentional deficits, continuous feedback may be preferable in order
to maintain engagement. In contrast, for studies trying to downregulate reward circuitry,
intermittent feedback may be preferable to prevent feedback of success during the regulation
block from activating the very circuitry that participants are struggling to control (Greer
et al., 2014).

Most fMRI neurofeedback studies to date have used a simple form of visual feedback, such as a line graph (Scheinost et al., 2013; Scharnowski et al., 2015; Sukhodolsky et al., 2020), a thermometer (Linden et al., 2012; Paret et al., 2016a,b), or a circle of varying diameter (Shibata et al., 2011; Cortese et al., 2016), although a few have used auditory feedback (Banca et al., 2015; Ramot et al., 2016). In order to induce specific mental contexts during training, stimuli designed to provoke that brain state are often presented on the screen at the same time as the feedback in a dual display format (Scheinost et al., 2013; Paret et al., 2016a,b). An interesting variant of this is to adaptively update the provocative stimuli based on brain state, rather than providing a separate feedback signal. This has been referred to as "closed-loop feedback" (deBettencourt et al., 2015) or "motivational feedback" (Ihssen et al., 2016) and is illustrated in Fig. 3. For example, in a study training brain activity responses to appetitive stimuli, images of food became larger when subjects showed greater brain

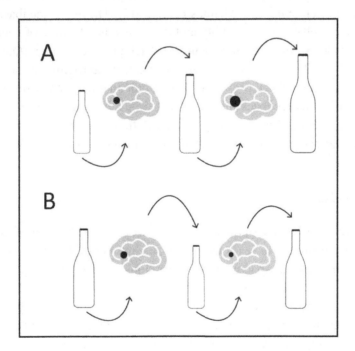

Fig. 3
Closed-loop neurofeedback protocols. Here, a symptom-related cue (perhaps a drink in a study training alcohol urges) changes in size, and thus salience, in a manner that depends on activity in the target brain area. In Panel A, the more active the target region becomes, the more salient the stimulus. In Panel B, this relationship is reversed, so that lower activation yields a more salient stimulus. The participant sees only the drink as it grows or shrinks, and tries to control their desire for the drink, so the task difficulty is varied depending on activity in the target region. If activity in the target region is associated with craving, the task in Panel A will become harder when they are doing poorly, thus amplifying lapses of focus, as previous studies have done.

responses in appetitive circuitry and smaller when they successfully regulated those responses (Ihssen et al., 2016). Similarly, a study of sustained attention used an approach in which the stimuli presented made it more difficult to perform an attention task when regulation waned, amplifying lapses in attention and thus encouraging participants to maintain a consistent focus (deBettencourt et al., 2015). In addition to ensuring salience of the feedback signal, these approaches have the advantage over dual displays of reducing the cognitive demand on participants by removing their need to monitor two different types of stimuli at one time. However, the changing intensity of the stimuli, and its relationship to regulation success, can confound attempts to tease apart brain patterns related to positive/negative feedback from those related to the intensity of provocation, so this approach may not be a good choice if a major goal of the study is to explore feedback learning processes in the brain.

A few recent studies have explored the use of more ecologically valid interfaces. One study compared feedback using smiling avatars (designed to engage social reward learning) to feedback provided via a moving bar (Mathiak et al., 2015). The avatar feedback interface was found to increase self-regulation ability and improve generalization of neurofeedback learning to other contexts. More recently, neurofeedback provided via a virtual reality interface that simulated fluctuating levels of unrest in a waiting room was shown to amplify learning relative to neurofeedback provided via a graphic thermometer (Cohen et al., 2016). Thus the adoption of richer feedback interfaces that simulate natural learning scenarios has potential to improve the efficacy of neurofeedback training. Of course, more complex interfaces may require more resources to develop and this must also be considered during application development.

2.3 Training schedule

Very little is known regarding the optimal training schedule for fMRI neurofeedback. Data are needed on how the number of sessions (that is, the number of days that participants are brought in for training) and the spacing between sessions affect the efficacy of the training and the persistence of the learning induced. The number of sessions typically used in fMRI neurofeedback is very small compared to EEG neurofeedback: while an EEG neurofeedback protocol typically involves 15–40 sessions, most fMRI neurofeedback studies have involved only a few sessions. Notably, successful training with fMRI neurofeedback has been reported with three (Amano et al., 2016; Subramanian et al., 2016), two (Scheinost et al., 2013; Young et al., 2017), or even a single session of neurofeedback (Harmelech et al., 2013; deBettencourt et al., 2015), although fMRI neurofeedback studies have used as many as ten sessions (Shibata et al., 2011). The spacing between sessions has generally varied from a few days (Sukhodolsky et al., 2020) to a week (Mehler et al., 2018), and is often not rigidly adhered to, given the difficulties inherent in scheduling MR scan sessions. Thus although there are some typical scheduling parameters that many successful studies have followed, these are not based on data from optimization studies. Unfortunately, optimization studies are expensive, in terms of both time and money, so until the funding agencies support such work, the optimal parameters are unlikely to be known.

2.4 Performance-based pay

Some research groups pay participants based on their success in controlling the brain pattern trained during neurofeedback with the aim of maximizing motivation and reward-based learning. Whether this increases training efficacy is an open question, but a small study examining the issue did suggest it can be helpful (Sepulveda et al., 2016). However, one challenge raised by this approach is how to create a fair and reward-matched reimbursement scheme for control participants, particularly in studies that have yoked sham or no-feedback control conditions.

3 Controlling for nonspecific effects

3.1 Types of control conditions

What type of control condition should be used to control for nonspecific effects of the intervention? This is an important decision when planning an fMRI neurofeedback study. All of the options have advantages and disadvantages, and none is perfect. Ideally, multiple control conditions would be used for each study, but in reality, properly powering a study with multiple control conditions is not feasible for most groups due to the high cost involved, in terms of both time and money. The pros and cons of the various types of control conditions used for fMRI neurofeedback studies have been discussed in detail at recent real-time Functional Imaging and Neurofeedback meetings (rtFIN: keynote lectures of most recent meeting can be seen at www.rtfin2019.org) and have been addressed in a recent review paper (Sorger et al., 2019). Here we briefly summarize the features and shortcomings of the most common types of control conditions used.

1. *No control condition*: Having no control condition is an affordable and popular option for early stage, feasibility and proof-of-concept studies. However, it cannot control for natural remission, placebo effects, practice effects of any tasks performed during the feedback training, or effects of exposure to any symptom-provoking stimuli used during the training.
2. *Waitlist control*: This controls for natural remission but none of the other earlier listed confounds and is substantially more demanding in terms of recruitment than having no control condition. A popular approach used in clinical studies that could be considered a variant of the waitlist control occurs when both groups also receive "treatment as usual," or TAU. In this scenario, NF + TAU is compared to TAU alone. The aim in such studies is not to demonstrate that neurofeedback has specific effects above and beyond the

nonspecific effects of the intervention (such as placebo), but rather to demonstrate that the neurofeedback intervention as a whole, including both specific and nonspecific effects, can augment standard treatment and result in improved patient outcomes.

3. *A "no feedback" control:* The control group gets scanned and does the same tasks during the scanning session as the experimental group, but does not receive feedback. This does not control for how engaging the neurofeedback is or allow for participant blinding, but does control for practice effects of the task, exposure to the stimuli, and participation in a "high tech" study.

4. *Training the brain pattern in the opposite direction*: This is a popular control in basic science studies that can potentially double the effect size if the two groups show effects in opposite directions. However, in clinical populations, training a group in the opposite direction to what is believed to be healthy is generally not an ethical option.

5. *Training a different aspect of brain function (we will term this the control biomarker) that is believed to be unrelated to what is targeted in the experimental group (we will term this the experimental biomarker).* The first step in designing a study with this type of control is identifying a truly unrelated aspect of brain function to use as the control biomarker. Given the complex, networked nature of the brain and our limited understanding of it, this can already be a challenge. If the control biomarker is not independent, this can undermine power (in the case that the control and experimental biomarkers tend to activate together) or can even potentially be unhealthy for control participants in clinical studies (if the control biomarker inhibits the experimental one). A second issue of concern is that the control biomarker may be easier or more difficult to modulate than the experimental biomarker. If so, the control group will likely be more or less successful during training than the experimental group, and receive a different level of feedback indicating their success, which can impact their affect, motivation, and expectation as well as the magnitude of their placebo effects. Finally, if the training occurs in the context of a task or stimulation paradigm that is expected to be associated with activity in the experimental biomarker and the control biomarker is truly independent of the experimental biomarker, then the control biomarker is unlikely to show the expected effects of the task or stimulation. For example, if participants are told they are trying to control symptom relevant brain patterns and they are shown symptom-provoking images but the feedback signal does not show any response to the provocative imagery, this could provide a clue to control participants that they are not receiving the experimental feedback, essentially damaging the blind. For this reason, collecting data from subjects at the end of the study on which intervention they believed they received (experimental versus control) is important for checking whether the blind was effectively maintained. Recent fMRI neurofeedback studies using this form of control condition when training depressed patients illustrate some of these challenges. One study found both groups (the experimental and control group) were regulating the experimental biomarker during training (Mehler et al., 2018, see Fig. 4) and another showed differential levels of regulation success during feedback in the two groups (Young et al., 2017, see Fig. 1),

resulting in different levels of positive feedback received during training. On the positive side, this approach has potential for successful participant blinding, and can control for practice and stimulation effects, natural remission, and the highly motivating nature of neurofeedback. It also has the interesting feature that both groups are being trained to control brain activity patterns. If this in itself is therapeutic, this type of control is unique among the various options in controlling for that nonspecific training effect, which may be a key feature to control for, or may be unduly conservative, depending on the study aims. For further discussion of the different types of nonspecific effects, see Chapter 7 (on the design of clinical neurofeedback studies).

6. *Yoked sham*: In this scenario, the control participants are typically matched one-to-one to the experimental participants and shown exactly the same feedback their matched experimental participant received. By design, this approach matches across groups how much the feedback signal indicates success or failure to the subjects. It also ensures that the feedback signal shows a similar response across groups to any symptom-provocative images or tasks performed during different periods of the feedback runs, thus reducing one possible source of unblinding. However, it has the drawback that the control feedback may not match what the subjects are thinking or feeling during the feedback sessions. Self-aware control participants may recognize this incongruency and may therefore suspect they are receiving the control intervention. Thus for this type of control it is also important to collect data at the end of the study on which intervention participants believed they received (experimental versus control), in order to check if the blind was maintained. On the positive side, this approach has the potential for successful participant blinding, and can control for amount of positive feedback, practice and stimulation effects, natural remission, and the highly motivating nature of neurofeedback training.

Over the course of developing an intervention, a series of studies is generally run. This provides an opportunity for research groups to test the intervention against more than one type of control condition. For example, an intervention that yielded differences between the experimental group and a yoked sham control in an early phase study may be compared to a control group trained on a different brain pattern in the next phase of development. This approach can minimize the chance that positive findings are idiosyncratic to the contrast with a specific control condition, and provide a stronger argument (if subsequent studies also show promising results) that there is a specific effect of the experimental intervention.

3.2 Assignment of participants to control conditions

The gold standard for assigning participants to groups in large clinical trials is randomization. In randomized studies, an individual should be assigned to a group only after it has been decided that they meet all inclusion criteria for the study, and their assignment should be based on a randomization list (or program) created prior to the start of the study. In some cases, if it is important to ensure the groups do not end up differing on a critical variable (or variables), stratified randomization can be used. In this scenario, subjects will first be categorized based on the critical variable (or variables), and a different randomization list will be used for each category of subjects. For example, a study may choose to stratify based on baseline symptom severity and assign incoming participants to either a high symptom severity category or a low symptom severity category. Two different randomization lists would then be used, one for the high symptom severity participants and one for the low symptom severity participants. In this way, the study can ensure that similar numbers of high and low symptom severity participants get randomized to the experimental and control groups. Another way of balancing patients for critical variables in randomized studies is minimization, which aims to keep group differences low on a number of parameters. However, these types of approaches have also been criticized for violating the principles of pure randomization (Senn, 2013), and entail the need to control for stratification/minimization variables in the analysis of outcome measures (for example, in an Analysis of Covariance, ANCOVA) (Raab et al., 2000).

For yoked sham feedback studies with one-to-one matching of participants across groups, it is necessary that every time a participant is randomized to receive sham feedback, that there exists a previous participant who received the experimental intervention, and who has not been matched with a sham subject already, that the new sham subject can be matched to. This creates some challenges for randomization, as illustrated and discussed in Fig. 4. To address this issue, our randomization lists for yoked sham studies are created subject to the constraint that at any point on the list there are at least as many experimental as control subjects. Furthermore, when an experimental subject withdraws after randomization in a yoked sham study, this can create problems later for the sham subject that would normally be matched to that subject. Our approach to addressing this is to reuse randomization slots of participants who withdraw from the study midway. Although this is not the gold-standard approach to randomization in drug trials, it is a practical approach that deals with some difficulties using randomization in a yoked sham context. Other groups may choose a different approach. For example, yoked sham without one-to-one matching may be used. However, this approach risks losing one of the key advantages of yoked sham: the matching across groups in terms of positive feedback provided to the participants. For example, if all sham participants are matched to the first experimental subject, then the two groups will be unlikely to be matched in terms of total positive feedback, or in terms of the increase in positive feedback across runs during training, because the first experimental subject is unlikely to fall exactly at the mean of the experimental group on these two variables. In summary, if a randomized trial with a yoked sham control group is planned, we recommend that the research group develop a plan prior to study initiation outlining how randomization will work in the context of their yoked sham design.

Randomization also has limitations for small sample studies. The sample sizes of current fMRI neurofeedback studies are often quite small. This is to be expected, given the early stage of fMRI neurofeedback research, as the huge investment required for a large sample size study is not warranted until some data have been collected demonstrating that the

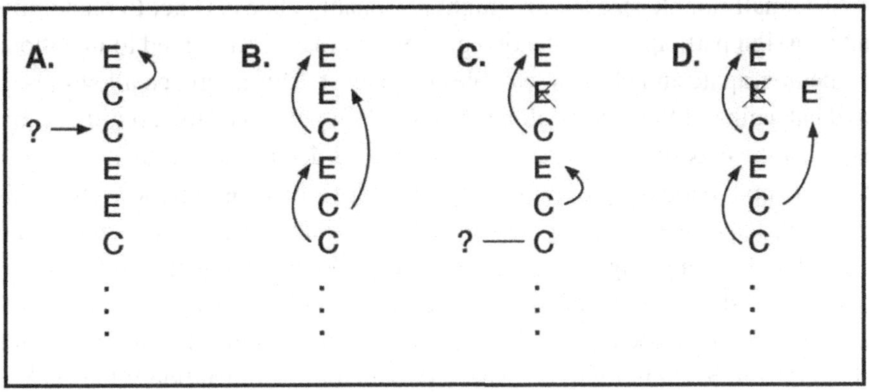

Fig. 4

Randomization issues associated with a yoked sham control group when one-to-one matching between groups is desired. Each panel shows a randomization list in column format, where E denotes an experimental subject and C denotes a control subject. Every control subject must be matched to a preceding experimental subject (whose feedback will be used during their training). Panel A shows a problematic randomization sequence: although the first control subject can be matched to the first experimental subject (indicated by the *curved arrow* connecting these), the second control subject cannot be matched to any preceding experimental subject. Panel B shows a randomization sequence created subject to the constraint that at all points in the randomization list there are at least as many experimental as control subjects. This ensures each new control subject has a unique experimental subject they can be matched to. However, even this becomes problematic when experimental participants drop out prior to completion of their training, as a control subject cannot be properly matched to an incomplete experimental subject (the feedback time courses for all runs will not be available if the experimental subject dropped out midway). Panel C illustrates this problem. If the second experimental subject randomized into the study does not complete their training, there will be no experimental subject to match the third control subject to. Panel D shows how our group addresses this problem: essentially, we reuse the randomization slots of dropout subjects, so the very next subject recruited will have the same group assignment and will "take" the dropout slot. By doing this, we ensure that the study always has as many completed experimental subjects as there are control subjects randomized, so that every control subject has an experimental subject who completed the training that they can be matched with.

intervention shows some promise. However, a problem with using randomization for small sample size studies is that the experimental and control groups can, by chance, end up very unbalanced along certain critical dimensions, such as age, gender, symptom severity, comorbid conditions, current pharmaceutical use, etc. In large samples, the randomization tends to even these variables out, but in small samples, this cannot be relied on. Stratification, as addressed before, can be helpful in medium-sized studies, but is problematic in small samples as it relies upon balancing experimental and control subjects across multiple categories of participants each of which is a fraction of the original sample size. One alternative that small sample size studies might reasonably choose is not to randomize, and instead to assign participants to the two groups in a manner designed to intentionally balance the demographic and clinical variables of interest. This approach allows participant blinding and balancing of the groups along important dimensions. However, it is subject to the criticism that the experimenter's subjective judgment determines group assignment which can bias the outcome. For example, if the experimenter tends to assign more enthusiastic participants to the experimental group, this is itself could drive a group difference in response. Concern regarding bias in group assignment is why randomization is the preferred approach for large scale, later stage clinical trials. However, this is not a critical issue in small, early stage clinical trials that are focused on demonstrating some promise for the intervention. Later (and larger) future studies will be expected to adopt randomization if the early data for the intervention are promising.

4 Assessing outcomes

4.1 Different ways of assessing control over brain patterns

The ability to control brain activity is monitored in fMRI neurofeedback studies by two different types of MR imaging runs. First, the feedback runs themselves, during which subjects are being trained, can be used to evaluate regulation success. In addition, some studies also use what are referred to as control task (CT), or transfer runs, to evaluate the ability to regulate brain activity in the absence of feedback. These CT runs are generally identical to the feedback runs except that no feedback is provided. These two types of runs are illustrated in Fig. 5. Some studies include CT runs only at the end of the feedback training, while others include them both prior to and after feedback training.

The data from these two types of runs can be analyzed in a number of different ways to assess whether neurofeedback training improves control over the targeted brain activity patterns. For example, in a study that collects CT runs both before and after a two session neurofeedback training protocol, and that includes a sham control group for comparison, the following findings could all be reasonably considered evidence that the training was effective in improving brain regulation.

In the feedback runs:

1. A significant group difference in the overall level of regulation success (assessed as the average level of control across all feedback runs) between the experimental and control group, with the experimental group having greater regulation success.
2. A significant improvement in regulation success from the first to the second day of training within the experimental group.
3. A significant group difference in the increase in regulation success from the first to the second day of training between the experimental and control group, with the experimental group improving more.

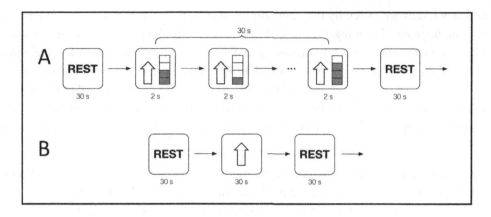

Fig. 5

The two types of runs typically used to assess control over brain activity. Panel A shows the
neurofeedback runs themselves. In this example, participants are cued to upregulate their brain
activity by the *arrow* on the left, and feedback is provided by a thermometer on the right that is
updated as each volume is collected (every 2 s). Panel B illustrates a control task run where the
same task is performed in regulation blocks for the same period of time (30 s), but no feedback is
provided.

4. A significant positive slope of change in regulation success within each training day in
   the experimental group, based on best fit lines computed within session.
5. A significantly greater improvement in the experimental than the control group in
   regulation success within each training day.

In the control task runs:

1. A significant group difference in regulation success in the post-intervention control task
   run between experimental and control groups, with the experimental group having greater
   success.
2. A significant improvement in regulation success in the experimental group from
   the pre-intervention control task (CTpre) run to the post-intervention control task
   (CTpost) run.
3. A significant group difference in the improvement in regulation success from CTpre to
   CTpost, with the experimental group showing greater improvement.

These are just a subset of the possible ways to demonstrate an improvement in control over
brain activity patterns. In addition, there may be multiple ways to extract a measure of
regulation success from each FB or CT run. For example, in studies that have upregulate,
downregulate, and rest blocks, a contrast in signal level between any two of the three blocks
could be used as the measure of regulation success that is entered into the group-level
analyses. In short, in many neurofeedback studies, there are a multitude of possible ways to
evaluate how well the intervention improves control over brain activity.

Two different issues are raised by the many different possible ways a study can evaluate how well training improved brain regulation. The first is related to the potential for false positives if multiple measures are examined without clear disclosure of, and correction for, the number of statistical tests run. The best approach to addressing this issue is to have the planned outcome measures of the study registered publicly a priori with enough detail to specify exactly how training efficacy will be measured. Additional (unregistered) measures can also be examined and reported, but these should be clearly identified as exploratory analyses when reported.

A second problem arising from the many different ways regulation success can be evaluated is the challenge it creates for integrating the literature as a whole. Over the last two decades, the technique of meta-analysis has assumed a central role in the evaluation of new interventions, enabling analysis of effects across multiple studies and thereby minimizing biases arising from the settings of any individual study. However, meta-analysis depends on a minimum of standardization across interventions and outcome measures, and is therefore challenging to apply meaningfully to (fMRI-)neurofeedback studies, although some work on this front is beginning to emerge (e.g., Dudek and Dodell-Feder, 2021).

4.2 Monitoring adverse events

Monitoring adverse events is expected for clinical trials, as outlined in the CONSORT guidelines (http://www.consort-statement.org/), and many clinical neurofeedback studies to date have collected and reported adverse event information (Hawkinson et al., 2012; Mehler et al., 2018; Sukhodolsky et al., 2020). However, many basic science neurofeedback studies and early stage clinically oriented studies have not monitored and reported adverse events. We recommend going forward that all neurofeedback studies include adverse event monitoring: it is not burdensome to collect and is critical for informing our understanding of the safety profile of neurofeedback in different groups, including healthy populations.

How should a research group query their participants regarding adverse events? The goal is to ask questions that are broad enough to cover unforeseen and unexpected problems, while being specific enough that participants are prompted to report relevant events. Generally, a brief questionnaire is given to participants at each visit (including follow-up visits) that asks them a series of questions probing about negative life experiences of various kinds that may have arisen since the last visit. If the participant indicates that any of these problems have occurred, more detailed, follow-up questioning is initiated to fully characterize the nature and severity of the event and to explore the probability that it was related in any way to the research intervention. The questionnaire used may be modified as needed to probe for adverse events that may be of concern in a specific application. For example, a basic science study training people to rewire their motor circuitry may include additional questions probing about difficulties with balance or coordination.

The monitoring of adverse events is closely coupled with the provision of appropriate clinical cover. This is standard in clinical research settings but because many researchers in neurofeedback have a nonclinical background it may be worth discussing this issue in this design chapter. It is important that researchers have a protocol for access to clinical support in case this is needed. This will generally be required by the ethics committees/ Institutional Review Boards for patient studies but may also be needed for studies in healthy volunteers, especially if potentially distressing stimuli are used or novel neurofeedback protocols are employed. It is important to remember that neurofeedback, by definition, involves participants exploring and learning to use new strategies to attain a particular neural target, and there is always a theoretical possibility of distressing experiences. Participants should therefore be asked about adverse experiences after each neurofeedback session, and support should be available in case it is needed. This could entail neutralization procedures (for example positive mood induction), or a consultation with a duty psychiatrist, clinical psychologist, or counselor who could determine whether additional clinical support or follow-up is needed. These safety measures also apply to the collection of outcome measures that include information about immediate danger to the participant or others. For example the frequently used Beck Depression Inventory, a questionnaire about depressive symptoms, probes suicidal ideation which, if present, needs to be followed up by a clinician or appropriately trained investigator following the study protocol.

The widespread adoption of adverse event monitoring in the field of fMRI neurofeedback will enable the field to identify any risks at an early stage thus mitigating their impact, and will provide confidence going forward regarding the safety of neurofeedback, not just in clinical interventions, but for use in the general population. This will ultimately facilitate the translation of findings to applications beyond the research context.

4.3 Collecting data on whether the participant blinding was maintained

As noted earlier in the discussion of different types of control groups, the possibility that participants assigned to the control group may suspect their group assignment is an important concern, particularly in explicit neurofeedback studies where this expectation can influence placebo effects and create group differences unrelated to the training per se. Given that most studies with participant blinding are required to unblind and debrief participants at the very end of the study, a simple approach to addressing this issue is to query participants regarding which group they believe they were in prior to unblinding them in this final debriefing session. Having participants provide a rating that indicates the confidence level of their belief (e.g. using a Likert scale response) is likely to provide a more sensitive measure than requesting a binary response.

4.4 *Following up subjects*

Characterization of the long-term effect of fMRI neurofeedback is critical for understanding both the potential benefits and the potential risks of neurofeedback interventions. A number of studies have reported effects of fMRI neurofeedback that persisted for weeks to months to years after the intervention was completed (Yoo et al., 2007, 2008; Megumi et al., 2015; Amano et al., 2016; Robineau et al., 2017). Not only does it appear that fMRI neurofeedback effects can persist, but a number of studies have reported effects that continued to grow in the days to weeks after the neurofeedback training was completed (Harmelech et al., 2013; Mehler et al., 2018; Rance et al., 2018). This has important implications for the design of fMRI neurofeedback studies as discussed in detail by Rance et al. (2018). Most critically, a study that does not follow-up participants may be missing the time point of greatest effect.

Typically, the investment of time and money required to run a participant through fMRI neurofeedback is much greater than the investment required to collect follow-up data on participants monitoring the behavioral or clinical effects of the intervention over the weeks to months after the intervention is completed. Thus for a small increase in the effort invested, a study can include follow-up assessments that maximize the chance of sampling the time point of greatest effect. This is important not only for optimizing the power of studies to demonstrate that they can induce the desired training effects, but also for ensuring that any negative impacts that are slow to unfold are identified at an early stage of development of the intervention. In short, the inclusion of follow-up assessments to measure how the desired training effects unfold over time and to monitor for adverse events is an inexpensive yet valuable addition to a research protocol.

5 *Conclusion*

fMRI neurofeedback is a versatile tool that can target many different aspects of brain function. The studies that have reported success in modulating brain function to date have helped clarify some training parameters that are generally *sufficient* for inducing learning (e.g., three or fewer sessions have proven effective in many studies), but the *optimal* parameters are still unknown. Furthermore, it is unknown whether optimal parameters for one application will tend to translate to optimal (or nearly optimal) training in other contexts. In short, we are very far from having a clear and complete set of principles guiding the optimization of fMRI neurofeedback protocols.

Thus this chapter is not a summary of known principles for the design of effective neurofeedback protocols. Instead, it discusses considerations of relevance to a number of important design decisions. These include decisions regarding how much information to give subjects, what kinds of comparison condition should be used to control for nonspecific effects of the intervention, and how to assess the efficacy of the training. The best approach for any given application will depend on the goals of the study and the nature of the participant population: a study probing brain-behavior relationships will need a different design than a study aiming to provide clinical benefits to patients. However, all studies must carefully consider the ethical implications of each design decision and most studies will benefit from following up participants to monitor for both desired training effects and potential adverse events. As the field of fMRI neurofeedback advances, standard approaches may emerge, but at present, fMRI neurofeedback study design remains a creative endeavor.

Acknowledgments

M. Hampson was supported by the National Institute of Mental Health (R01 MH100068 and R61 MH115110), and the American Endowment Foundation (project titled "A neurofeedback booster for emotion regulation therapy"). We are grateful to Peggy Bisschoff, communication officer at the School for Mental Health and Neuroscience at Maastricht University, for the illustrations for this chapter.

References

Alegria, A.A., Wulff, M., 2017. Real-time fMRI neurofeedback in adolescents with attention deficit hyperactivity disorder. Hum. Brain Mapp. 38 (6), 3190–3209.

Amano, K., Shibata, K., 2016. Learning to associate orientation with color in early visual areas by associative decoded fMRI neurofeedback. Curr. Biol. 26 (14), 1861–1866.

Banca, P., Sousa, T., 2015. Visual motion imagery neurofeedback based on the hMT+/V5 complex: evidence for a feedback-specific neural circuit involving neocortical and cerebellar regions. J. Neural Eng. 12 (6), 066003.

Cohen, A., Keynan, J.N., et al., 2016. Multi-modal virtual scenario enhances neurofeedback learning. Front. Robot. Ai 3, 52.

Cortese, A., Amano, K., 2016. Multivoxel neurofeedback selectively modulates confidence without changing perceptual performance. Nat. Commun. 7, 13669.

deBettencourt, M.T., Cohen, J.D., 2015. Closed-loop training of attention with real-time brain imaging. Nat. Neurosci. 18 (3), 470–475.

deCharms, R.C., Christoff, K., 2004. Learned regulation of spatially localized brain activation using real-time fMRI. NeuroImage 21, 436–443.

Dudek, E., Dodell-Feder, D., 2021. The efficacy of real-time functional magnetic resonance imaging neurofeedback for psychiatric illness: a meta-analysis of brain and behavioral outcomes. Neurosci. Biobehav. Rev. 121, 291–306.

Emmert, K., Kopel, R., 2017. Continuous vs. intermittent neurofeedback to regulate auditory cortex activity of tinnitus patients using real-time fMRI—a pilot study. Neuroimage Clin. 14, 97–104.

Greer, S.M., Trujillo, A.J., 2014. Control of nucleus accumbens activity with neurofeedback. NeuroImage 96, 237–244.

Habes, I., Rushton, S., 2016. fMRI neurofeedback of higher visual areas and perceptual biases. Neuropsychologia 85, 208–215.

Harmelech, T., Preminger, S., 2013. The day-after effect: long term, Hebbian-like restructuring of resting-state fMRI patterns induced by a single epoch of cortical activation. J. Neurosci. 33 (22), 9488–9497.

Hawkinson, J.E., Ross, A.J., 2012. Quantification of adverse events associated with functional MRI scanning and with real-time fMRI-based training. Int. J. Behav. Med. 19 (3), 372–381.

Hellrung, L., Dietrich, A., 2018. Intermittent compared to continuous real-time fMRI neurofeedback boosts control over amygdala activation. NeuroImage 166, 198–208.

Ihssen, N., Sokunbi, M.O., 2016. Neurofeedback of visual food cue reactivity: a potential avenue to alter incentive sensitization and craving. Brain Imaging Behav. 11 (3), 915–924.

Johnson, K.A., Hartwell, K., 2012. Intermittent "real-time" fMRI feedback is superior to continuous presentation for a motor imagery task: a pilot study. J. Neuroimaging 22 (1), 58–66.

Koush, Y., Rosa, M.J., 2013. Connectivity-based neurofeedback: dynamic causal modeling for real-time fMRI. NeuroImage 81, 422–430.

Koizumi, A., Amano, K., et al., 2016. Fear reduction without fear through reinforcement of neural activity that bypasses conscious exposure. Nat. Hum. Behav. 1, 0006.

Koush, Y., Meskaldji, D.E., 2017. Learning control over emotion networks through connectivity-based neurofeedback. Cereb. Cortex 27 (2), 1193–1202.

LaConte, S.M., Peltier, S.J., 2007. Real-time fMRI using brain-state classification. Hum. Brain Mapp. 28 (10), 1033–1044.

Linden, D.E., Habes, I., 2012. Real-time self-regulation of emotion networks in patients with depression. PLoS One 7 (6), e38115.

Mathiak, K.A., Alawi, E.M., 2015. Social reward improves the voluntary control over localized brain activity in fMRI-based neurofeedback training. Front. Behav. Neurosci. 9, 136.

Megumi, F., Yamashita, A., 2015. Functional MRI neurofeedback training on connectivity between two regions induces long-lasting changes in intrinsic functional network. Front. Hum. Neurosci. 9, 160.

Mehler, D.M.A., Sokunbi, M.O., 2018. Targeting the affective brain-a randomized controlled trial of real-time fMRI neurofeedback in patients with depression. Neuropsychopharmacology 43 (13), 2578–2585.

Paret, C., Kluetsch, R., 2016a. Alterations of amygdala-prefrontal connectivity with real-time fMRI neurofeedback in BPD patients. Soc. Cogn. Affect. Neurosci. 11 (6), 952–960.

Paret, C., Ruf, M., 2016b. fMRI neurofeedback of amygdala response to aversive stimuli enhances prefrontal-limbic brain connectivity. NeuroImage 125, 182–188.

Raab, G.M., Day, S., 2000. How to select covariates to include in the analysis of a clinical trial. Control. Clin. Trials 21 (4), 330–342.

Ramot, M., Grossman, S., 2016. Covert neurofeedback without awareness shapes cortical network spontaneous connectivity. Proc. Natl. Acad. Sci. USA 113 (17), E2413–E2420.

Ramot, M., Kimmich, S., et al., 2017. Direct modulation of aberrant brain network connectivity through real-time neurofeedback. Elife 6, e28974.

Rance, M., Walsh, C., 2018. Time course of clinical change following neurofeedback. NeuroImage 181, 807–813.

Robineau, F., Meskaldji, D.E., 2017. Maintenance of voluntary self-regulation learned through real-time fMRI neurofeedback. Front. Hum. Neurosci. 11, 131.

Ros, T., Enriquez-Geppert, S., 2020. Consensus on the reporting and experimental design of clinical and cognitive-behavioural neurofeedback studies (CRED-nf checklist). Brain 143 (6), 1674–1685.

Scharnowski, F., Veit, R., 2015. Manipulating motor performance and memory through real-time fMRI neurofeedback. Biol. Psychol. 108, 85–97.

Scheinost, D., Stoica, T., 2013. Orbitofrontal cortex neurofeedback produces lasting changes in contamination anxiety and resting-state connectivity. Transl. Psychiatry 3, e250.

Scheinost, D., Hsu, T.W., 2020. Connectome-based neurofeedback: a pilot study to improve sustained attention. NeuroImage 212, 116684.

Senn, S., 2013. Seven myths of randomisation in clinical trials. Stat. Med. 32 (9), 1439–1450.

Sepulveda, P., Sitaram, R., 2016. How feedback, motor imagery, and reward influence brain self-regulation using real-time fMRI. Hum. Brain Mapp. 37 (9), 3153–3171.

Shibata, K., Watanabe, T., 2011. Perceptual learning incepted by decoded fMRI neurofeedback without stimulus presentation. Science 334 (6061), 1413–1415.

Shibata, K., Watanabe, T., 2016. Differential activation patterns in the same brain region led to opposite emotional states. PLoS Biol. 14 (9), e1002546.

Sorger, B., Scharnowski, F., 2019. Control freaks: towards optimal selection of control conditions for fMRI neurofeedback studies. NeuroImage 186, 256–265.

Subramanian, L., Hindle, J.V., 2011. Real-time functional magnetic resonance imaging neurofeedback for treatment of Parkinson's disease. J. Neurosci. 31 (45), 16309–16317.

Subramanian, L., Morris, M.B., 2016. Functional magnetic resonance imaging neurofeedback-guided motor imagery training and motor training for Parkinson's disease: randomized trial. Front. Behav. Neurosci. 10, 111.

Sukhodolsky, D.G., Walsh, C., et al., 2020. Randomized, sham-controlled trial of real-time functional magnetic resonance imaging neurofeedback for tics in adolescents with Tourette syndrome. Biol Psychiatry 87 (12), 1063–1070.

Tinaz, S., Para, K., 2018. Insula as the interface between body awareness and movement: a neurofeedback-guided kinesthetic motor imagery study in Parkinson's disease. Front. Hum. Neurosci. 12, 496.

Yoo, S.S., O'Leary, H.M., 2006. Increasing cortical activity in auditory areas through neurofeedback functional magnetic resonance imaging. Neuroreport 17 (12), 1273–1278.

Yoo, S.S., Lee, J.H., 2007. Functional magnetic resonance imaging-mediated learning of increased activity in auditory areas. Neuroreport 18 (18), 1915–1920.

Yoo, S.S., Lee, J.H., 2008. Neurofeedback fMRI-mediated learning and consolidation of regional brain activation during motor imagery. Int. J. Imaging Syst. Technol. 18 (1), 69–78.

Young, K.D., Siegle, G.J., 2017. Randomized clinical trial of real-time fMRI amygdala neurofeedback for major depressive disorder: effects on symptoms and autobiographical memory recall. Am. J. Psychiatry 174 (8), 748–755.

Zilverstand, A., Sorger, B., 2015. fMRI neurofeedback facilitates anxiety regulation in females with spider phobia. Front. Behav. Neurosci. 9, 148.

Zilverstand, A., Sorger, B., 2017. fMRI neurofeedback training for increasing anterior cingulate cortex activation in adult attention deficit hyperactivity disorder. An exploratory randomized, single-blinded study. PLoS One 12 (1), e0170795.

Introduction to basic science section

Nicholas B. Turk-Browne

Department of Psychology, Yale University, New Haven, CT, United States

The vast majority of fMRI studies in cognitive neuroscience are the opposite of real time. Data are collected from each participant and then transferred to a server at the end of the session. After some number of participants, the resulting group is analyzed as a batch over a period of weeks, months, or even years. Because the results arrive so long after data collection, there can be no impact of the findings on the experimental design. Rather, the design is fixed in advance and then repeated mostly identically across participants (perhaps with some counterbalancing of timing or stimuli). The logic of such experiments is that one or more aspects of the task are manipulated as the independent variable(s) and the brain activity evoked by these events is measured as the dependent variable. This approach has dominated cognitive neuroscience since inception, fruitfully allowing tasks, the cognitive processes they invoke, and the behaviors they generate, to be mapped to regions, patterns, or networks in the brain. However, because brain activity is an observation, there is no way to conclude from such studies alone that this activity plays a necessary role in task performance and behavior.

There are several differences in fMRI studies employing real-time neurofeedback. The most obvious is that the data are analyzed immediately upon collection. This creates the possibility of using the results of the analysis to modify and personalize the task. There are three ways of introducing these task changes. The first is a conventional neurofeedback approach in which brain activity is visualized as a scale or gauge that the participant needs to control. The second is a triggering approach in which brain activity is used as a switch to initiate a trial or condition. The third is an adaptive approach in which brain activity is used to modify the parameters (e.g., difficulty, stimuli) of an ongoing cognitive task. The experimental logic of all three designs is flipped on its head relative to standard cognitive neuroscience studies. Brain activity (quantified by the average level in a region, or the spatial pattern or temporal correlation across regions) serves as an independent variable, controlling what happens in the task and when. Although how the brain responds to these task changes is often a dependent variable, almost always the key dependent variable is some change or difference in behavior, either concurrently or from before to after a training protocol. Such experiments afford an interesting and different causal inference, whereby the brain region, pattern, or network being manipulated can be said to play a pseudo-causal role in the behavioral effect.

This ability to use real-time neurofeedback to manipulate the brain clearly has translational value, as discussed in the clinical section of this book. However, it also has tremendous value for basic science, given that the options for intervention in the human brain are highly limited. Whereas lesions, optogenetics, designer drugs, and other invasive techniques can be used to selectively manipulate the brains of animal models, such experiments are limited technically and ethically in humans. Instead, cognitive neuroscience often relies upon interventions that compromise precision for safety, including external brain stimulation such as transcranial magnetic stimulation that is restricted to the cortical surface and hard to target, or pharmacology that tends to have nonspecific effects throughout the brain. Real-time neurofeedback offers the potential for noninvasive but selective disruption or strengthening of brain activity to test causal, mechanistic hypotheses about the neuroscience of cognition.

The chapters in this section of the book adopt this innovative perspective and review what has been learned from real-time fMRI neurofeedback in three areas of cognitive neuroscience. In *fMRI Neurofeedback for Perception and Attention*, Wang, Watanabe, and Sasaki describe some of the earliest and most impressive examples of how real-time fMRI can enhance cognitive abilities. These studies of visual and auditory perception and attention raise fascinating questions about consciousness and learning, and they lead to the surprising conclusion that early sensory areas may show as much or more plasticity during neurofeedback training than later areas. In *Studying Episodic Memory Using Real-time fMRI*, Wammes, Lin, Norman, and I describe an emerging and exciting literature using real-time fMRI to investigate memory encoding, consolidation, and retrieval. With an eye to the future, we explain how real-time fMRI could be used to decisively test competing theories of long-term memory and to enhance a range of learning and memory abilities. In *Using fMRI Neurofeedback to Interrogate Emotion, Motivation, and Social Neurocognition*, Dickerson and Adcock elevate the discussion to how real-time fMRI not only helps understand individual cognition, but also how we interface with each other socially through motivation, emotion, and empathy. They chart a course for the future of real-time fMRI in social and affective neuroscience, including exciting ideas about the neuromodulatory systems that regulate many of these processes.

This is a smaller subfield than clinical applications of real-time neurofeedback. Although the translational impact may be less proximal, these chapters highlight the outstanding progress and potential for answering fundamental questions about the mind and brain. Indeed, several lines of research that began by addressing basic science questions about cognition in healthy individuals (e.g., fear conditioning: Koizumi et al., 2017; sustained attention: deBettencourt et al., 2015) produced discoveries and techniques that shortly thereafter found clinical application (e.g., phobia: Taschereau-Dumouchel et al., 2018; depression: Mennen et al., 2021). By boosting learning and memory, and by changing expertise in the brain, another mostly unexplored application of these approaches could be to pedagogy and education. Ultimately, the purpose of school is to change the brains of students so they carry knowledge and skills forward, so why not build into this process the real-time capability to track whether and how well this information is being registered. As more portable brain imaging technologies and more accessible computing platforms become available, the technical barriers that have limited uptake of real-time neurofeedback for basic science will diminish. We therefore see this section as a promissory note about the incredible potential of real-time neurofeedback as a unique and powerful approach to fMRI that might provide convincing clarity about the brain mechanisms of behavior.

References

deBettencourt, M.T., Cohen, J.D., Lee, R.F., Norman, K.A., Turk-Browne, N.B., 2015. Closed-loop training of attention with real-time brain imaging. Nat. Neurosci. 18, 470–475.

Koizumi, A., et al., 2017. Fear reduction without fear through reinforcement of neural activity that bypasses conscious exposure. Nat. Hum. Behav. 1, 6.

Mennen, A.C., et al., 2021. Cloud-based fMRI neurofeedback to reduce the negative attentional bias in depression: a proof-of-concept study. Biol. Psychiatry: Cogn. Neurosci. Neuroimaging. 6, 490–497.

Taschereau-Dumouchel, V., Cortese, A., Chiba, T., Knotts, J.D., Kawato, M., Lau, H., 2018. Towards an unconscious neural reinforcement intervention for common fears. Proc. Natl. Acad. Sci. 115, 3470–3475.

fMRI neurofeedback for perception and attention

Zhiyan Wang, Takeo Watanabe, and Yuka Sasaki
Department of Cognitive, Linguistic, and Psychological Sciences, Brown University, Providence, RI, United States

In the past decade, a multitude of studies have demonstrated that functional magnetic resonance imaging (fMRI) neurofeedback is effective in changing perception and attention. For example, fMRI neurofeedback induced changes in visual perception in association with primary visual areas (Shibata et al., 2011; Scharnowski et al., 2012; Amano et al., 2016) and higher visual areas (Ramot et al., 2016; Ekanayake et al., 2019). Successful attempts to change auditory perception have also been reported (Emmert et al., 2017; Haller et al., 2010). Furthermore, it has been found that sustained attention (deBettencourt et al., 2015) is improved through fMRI neurofeedback.

This chapter focuses on how fMRI neurofeedback has been implemented to change brain processing related to perception and attention. Specifically, we address the following three questions: (1) What are the evolving approaches for performing fMRI neurofeedback training? (2) What behavioral outcomes in perception and attention can be achieved by fMRI neurofeedback? (3) How does fMRI neurofeedback allow us to explore causal relationships between brain activity and behavior?

1 What approaches for fMRI neurofeedback training modulate perception and attention?

FMRI neurofeedback methods have been significantly advanced in multiple ways relevant to studying perception and attention, including the delivery of explicit vs implicit feedback and the quantification of target representations (e.g., univariate and multivariate approaches to activation and connectivity). Here, we discuss these different methods and their potential as optimal ways to perform neurofeedback training.

1.1 Explicit vs implicit feedback

Explicit feedback has conventionally been used in neurofeedback studies. This involves providing participants with feedback about a neural state while they consciously attempt

fMRI Neurofeedback. https://doi.org/10.1016/B978-0-12-822421-2.00010-7

to regulate certain areas of their brain to change desired perception outcomes (deCharms et al., 2005). Implicit feedback has been developed more recently. This involves providing participants with feedback about a neural state without verbally informing of the purpose of the experiment or training.

An example of implicit neurofeedback is presented in Shibata et al. (2011). During training, a green disk represented the feedback score, roughly reflecting the degree of similarity between the current activation in a targeted brain area and predetermined brain activation in the area corresponding to a certain perceptual state. Participants were instructed to make the disk as large as possible without being informed of what the disk size actually indicated. By making the disk larger, participants were trained to approximate the predetermined perceptual state without explicitly knowing what changed the disk size.

A benefit of implicit feedback is that it rules out the possibility that the changes in behavior and brain activation are a consequence of intentional effort to change certain brain regions (Watanabe et al., 2017; Shibata et al., 2019). Intentional effort is not favorable in neurofeedback because it does not rule out the possibility that the behavioral changes are not directly related to the neural representation change but influenced by the participants' cognitive bias during training procedures. Implicit feedback reduces such possibility.

Both implicit and explicit feedback have been employed in the process of neurofeedback training for perception and attention. While it seems that both types of feedback work in many cases, future studies are necessary to compare the effect of both types using procedures that are otherwise the same.

1.2 Neural representations of targets

Recent fMRI neurofeedback studies have been conducted based on knowledge about the functions of a local brain region. Prior to neurofeedback training, experimenters select target brain regions for modulation. Perception and attention are optimal functions to be changed by fMRI neurofeedback because the relationship between processing in brain regions and their corresponding behavioral outcomes has been extensively studied and established by previous studies. For example, based on physiological knowledge that the V1 and V2 regions play an important role in processing orientation, fMRI neurofeedback of an activity pattern from V1 and V2 was able to alter orientation perception (Amano et al., 2016).

Researchers have used various types of neural representations of targets as the basis of modulation from fMRI neurofeedback. First, in the earliest phase of fMRI neurofeedback studies, the average blood-oxygen-level-dependent (BOLD) signal across voxels within a region of interest (ROI), known as univariate activation, was taken as a neural correlate of an attentional or perceptual function. In most of these studies, the ROI was selected as the target based on knowledge of how average BOLD signals in the region correlated with a behavioral function (deCharms et al., 2005; Scharnowski et al., 2012; Robineau et al., 2014; Ekanayake et al., 2019). Neurofeedback based on ROI univariate activation has been used to change some behavioral functions, including simple visual detection, object-specific perception, auditory perception, and pain perception (deCharms et al., 2005; Haller et al., 2010; Scharnowski et al., 2012; Emmert et al., 2017; Ekanayake et al., 2019).

Second, BOLD signal analyses have become significantly more sophisticated in the past decade. Instead of using the average BOLD signal within an ROI, the pattern of BOLD signals across voxels in the ROI, known as multivariate pattern analysis, has been used to investigate the content of the information represented in brain regions (Haxby et al., 2001, 2014; Kamitani and Tong, 2005; Shibata et al., 2016). Following the shift from univariate to multivariate analyses for standard fMRI studies, a number of recent fMRI neurofeedback studies have used multivariate pattern analysis in an ROI to modulate brain activity (LaConte et al., 2007; Shibata et al., 2011; deBettencourt et al., 2015). The use of multivariate decoding signals enables neurofeedback to influence the processing of complex representations in the brain. For instance, neurofeedback training based on univariate activation is not sufficient to learn to better discriminate between visual features (e.g., orientations) or to establish associations between features (e.g., color and orientation). This is because the average BOLD signals between different visual features (e.g., orientations) can be indistinguishable within an ROI. In contrast, multivariate signals for different visual features (e.g., orientations) are distinguishable (Kamitani and Tong, 2005). A representative protocol for such training is Decoded Neurofeedback (DecNef) (Shibata et al., 2011; Amano et al., 2016), in which a decoded pattern in an ROI is repetitively induced with real-time implicit feedback to the targeted brain area.

Finally, more recent fMRI neurofeedback studies have attempted to induce changes in functional connectivity across the whole brain (Ramot et al., 2017; Scheinost et al., 2020), rather than using the activation or pattern within one region. Functional connectivity reflects a statistical correlation between the time courses of activation in two or more brain regions. Previous fMRI studies have suggested that certain behaviors or functions are coordinated by interactions between a number of brain regions across the whole brain, shown as the strength of complex functional networks spanning the brain (Rosenberg et al., 2016; Yahata et al., 2016). A new type of fMRI neurofeedback, connectome-based fMRI neurofeedback, aims to modulate such whole-brain complex functional networks. For example, Scheinost et al. (2020) proposed an fMRI neurofeedback method that utilized the connectome-based connectivity underlying sustained attention. However, it is unclear whether connectome-based neurofeedback is more effective than activation-based (univariate and multivariate BOLD) neurofeedback in modulating attention and perception because the number of studies that have investigated perception and attention with connectome-based neurofeedback is still limited.

2 What behavioral outcomes for perception and attention can be achieved by fMRI neurofeedback?

Following we review advances and behavioral outcomes achieved by fMRI neurofeedback in studies of visual and auditory perception as well as attention.

2.1 Visual perception

It has been demonstrated that fMRI neurofeedback is a powerful tool for inducing changes in visual perception. We first discuss studies in which neurofeedback was applied to early visual areas, including the primary visual area (V1), and then those in higher-level cortical areas.

2.1.1 Early visual areas

First, we review a study by Scharnowski et al. (2012) in which explicit neurofeedback was used to modulate the average BOLD signal in early visual areas. Scharnowski et al. (2012) explicitly asked participants to try to voluntarily increase the activity in functionally defined ROIs in early visual cortical areas (V1, V2, and V3) and successfully increased visual sensitivity for detecting visual stimuli. In early visual areas, one hemisphere was functionally localized as the target area for neurofeedback.

The participants were explicitly asked to attempt to regulate their visual activity through real-time feedback. Experimenters also instructed participants to utilize strategies such as visual imagery with high-resolution details or changes in stimulus features (brightness, color, etc.) in the spatial location corresponding to the target ROI. The explicit fMRI neurofeedback training consisted of two components: baseline periods and regulation periods. During baseline periods, participants maintained stable brain activity by counting backward from 99 in steps of 7. During the explicit regulation periods, they were instructed to upregulate activity in the visual areas to enhance the activation in the target ROI compared to the activity at baseline. The brain activation of participants measured in real time was shown as a thermometer. The participants were instructed to increase activity to the predetermined target thermometer level, while their brain activations were calculated online and feedback to the participants was represented as a change in the value displayed on the thermometer.

After several days of fMRI neurofeedback training, participants successfully increased the activity in the targeted visual areas compared to the baseline period. Participants then performed a "transfer" run in which they tried to upregulate the target ROI as they had in the neurofeedback training sessions but without receiving visual thermometer feedback. The participants who learned during neurofeedback training were able to maintain their self-regulation without feedback in the transfer run. Next, to test the effect of self-regulation on behavior, participants performed a detection task of a near-threshold grating that might occur in different visual locations while simultaneously self-regulating brain activity in the target ROI as they had in neurofeedback training. Behavioral performance was shown as changes in visual sensitivity measured as d' between the "regulation" period and the "baseline" period.

Visual sensitivity in detecting a grating in the contralateral visual field of the target ROI improved in participants who successfully learned to modulate activation in the target areas during the neurofeedback training. No significant difference in visual sensitivity was observed for the participants who did not show successful neurofeedback modulation and for the control group that did not participate in neurofeedback training. Importantly, performance improvement was specific to the detection task, which was paired with self-regulation neurofeedback training. Before and after such training, perceptual contrast thresholds for detecting gratings were measured behaviorally for each individual without self-regulation. However, no change in contrast threshold was observed. Thus neurofeedback training led to a specific performance improvement, accompanied by the upregulation strategies each participant developed, not a general perceptual improvement of detection.

Although the results of this study were very interesting, two issues prohibited a conclusion that neurofeedback was successful. First, how the behavioral changes were linked with neural changes achieved by fMRI neurofeedback is unclear. Neurofeedback in this study was based on univariate activation. Although it is possible that the overall activity of early visual areas changed and visual processing was modified on a global scale, it may be difficult to interpret how the overall change led to finer-grained signal processing, such as increased sensitivity to a particular orientation. Second, we cannot rule out the possibility that the participants developed a cognitive bias toward a particular visual location during feedback training because of the explicit feedback. In that case, the conclusion that changes in behavioral performance are driven by neurofeedback might be confounded by the possibility of developing cognitive bias.

DecNef is a more recent fMRI neurofeedback protocol that can prevail over these potential shortcomings. First, DecNef makes use of multivariate signals (Haxby et al., 2001; Kamitani and Tong, 2005) in the targeted brain region, including early visual areas. This allows fine-grained orientation information to be manipulated in early visual areas. Second, neurofeedback training is implicit: participants are given feedback by changing the size of a disk that reflects a similarity between the targeted activation patterns and those measured in real time, without any other information provided. Because multivariate signals contain finer information about visual signals than univariate signals, more detailed and precise changes in visual representation can be obtained by DecNef.

Shibata et al. (2011) demonstrated that training with implicit feedback for multivariate signals of a target orientation resulted in selective enhancement in the detection of the target orientation. The experiment consisted of several different phases: pretest, decoder construction, neurofeedback training by DecNef, and posttest. In the pretest and posttest, the participants performed an orientation discrimination task. The participants were asked to report which one of three possible orientations (tilted 10°, 70°, and 130° from the horizontal axis, shown in Fig. 1) had been presented in a grating stimulus with various noise levels.

In the decoder construction phase, which occurred prior to neurofeedback training, the brain activation patterns in association with each oriented grating (10°, 70°, and 130°) were measured in the target region—early visual areas (V1 and V2). A decoder, which is a statistical classifier, was constructed based on the activation patterns for each grating in the target area. During 10 days of neurofeedback training sessions, the participants were instructed to make a green disk as large as possible. A brain activation pattern in the target area was measured on a real-time trial basis and then entered into the decoder. The decoder indicated the likelihood of each of the three orientations, including the target orientation. The disk size was changed to reflect the likelihood of the target orientation calculated by the decoder. The disk size corresponded to the similarity between the current brain activation pattern and that of the target orientation in V1/V2. The participants were not informed of the relationship between disk size and brain activation and were not trained to improve orientation detectability. Unwittingly, participants were inducing the target brain activation patterns and attempting to align their brain activation patterns to be more similar to the target patterns. During the posttest, participants successfully enhanced their behavioral performance on the targeted orientation but not on the other two orientations that were not trained by DecNef. Moreover, in an interview after the experiment, none of the participants reported that they had any visual imagery related to orientations and gratings during training. They were at chance level when asked which of the three orientations they had learned. Together, these findings show that sensitivity to the orientation trained by DecNef was enhanced without any actual stimulus presentation during training or awareness of the purpose of the training in this study (Shibata et al., 2011). This was the first study to show that the activation of specific visual patterns in early visual areas led to improved visual performance.

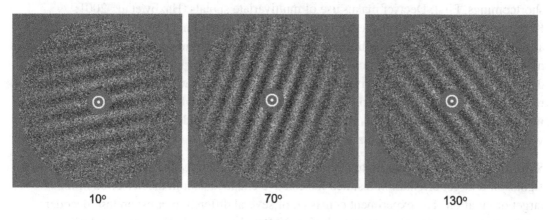

| 10° | 70° | 130° |

Fig. 1
Illustration of grating stimuli with different orientations.

Did DecNef selectively modulate the target V1/V2 area alone, or were other brain regions modulated in addition to the target area? To this end, the following control test was performed. Shibata et al. put the activation pattern in each of the control brain regions (V3, V4, the intraparietal sulcus, and the lateral prefrontal cortex) into the decoder to measure the similarity between the activation pattern in the control regions and that of the target area. If DecNef modulated the control areas in addition to the target area, the similarity between the target area and these control areas should have been statistically different than zero during DecNef. However, they found that the similarities between the target area and the control areas were very low and not significantly different from zero. This suggested that the activation pattern in the target area did not "leak" into brain regions other than V1/V2, that is, outside the target area.

A third study tested whether DecNef selectively changes processing in the target area or in regions beyond the target area (Wang et al., 2018). The study used a Sekuler-type motion display, which consists of dots moving randomly within a certain motion direction range, as shown in Fig. 2. This motion display induces not only the perception of locally moving dots but also the perception of the global motion whose direction corresponds to the spatiotemporal average of all of the local motion vectors (Williams and Sekuler, 1984).

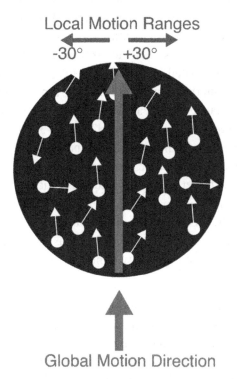

Fig. 2
Illustration of a global motion stimulus with ± 30° local motion ranges. The *arrows* pointing outside the local motion ranges represent a small percentage of randomly moving dots added as noise.

Importantly, this display activates two different visual areas: brain imaging studies found that fMRI signals in human V1 were activated by local dot motion, whereas in MT + and/or V3A were activated in response to global motion (Salzman et al., 1992; Rees et al., 2000; Braddick et al., 2001; Koyama et al., 2005). In other words, local motion signals in lower visual areas such as V1/V2 may be averaged and output to higher visual areas such as MT +/ V3A. Taking advantage of these properties of Sekuler-type motion to test the specificity of training effects, Wang et al. (2018) examined whether training the V1/V2 region implicated in local motion improved perception of global motion. The authors hypothesized that if DecNef training within V1/V2 influenced processing in higher visual areas, perception should improve not only in the local motion directions but also in the global motion direction.

Multivariate BOLD signals across voxels in the target area (V1/V2) in response to the Sekuler-type motion display were used to provide neurofeedback. DecNef was used to train participants so that the activation in the target area approximated the activation pattern evoked by local motion directions. To evaluate training effects, sensitivity to several motion directions was measured before and after training using a coherent motion discrimination task. Importantly, approximately half of the coherent motion directions corresponded to the local motion directions trained by DecNef, within the range of the Sekuler-type motion (that is, $-30°$ to $+30°$ of the global motion), whereas the other half of the measured coherent motion directions corresponded to control location motion directions untrained by DecNef, outside the Sekuler-type motion (that is, $-30°$ to $-60°$ and $+30°$ to $+60°$ of the global motion). If DecNef training modulated only the target area, increased sensitivity should be found for local motion within the range of the Sekuler-type motion. This is because the trained region V1/V2 is associated with local motion directions but not with the global motion direction. Global motion perception involves the MT + or V3A regions, which are outside the V1/V2 region. Moreover, increased sensitivity should be demonstrated in the trained motion directions, not in the untrained motion directions, as shown in Fig. 3A. If DecNef training modulated regions outside the target area, increased sensitivity should occur in the global motion direction, as shown in Fig. 3B or C. Fig. 3B reflects the prediction that increased sensitivity is shown only in the global motion direction. Fig. 3C reflects the increased sensitivity in both global and local motions. If DecNef was ineffective, perceptual learning would not be observed, as shown in Fig. 3D, with no increased sensitivity for any motion direction.

Participants showed increased sensitivity to motion directions in the local motion range, as predicted in Fig. 3A. These results are in accordance with the hypothesis that DecNef induced changes in target representations only in the target area, and did not significantly influence nontarget areas. Interestingly, the same pattern of sensitivity increase occurred as a result of mere exposure to a real Sekuler-type display (Watanabe et al., 2002). This further suggests that DecNef may induce learning in a similar way to passive exposure to a real stimulus.

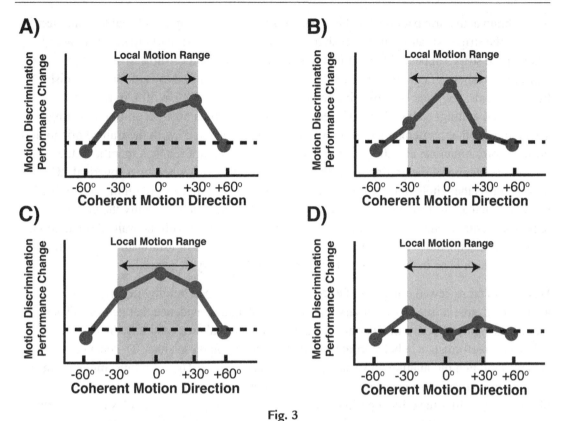

Fig. 3

Hypothetical behavior results after neurofeedback training. The *X* axis shows several coherent motion directions tested in the pretest and posttest. The *Y* axis shows the improvement in each motion direction in the motion discrimination task. *Shaded areas* indicate the local motion direction range. 0° indicates the global motion direction. (A) Only local motion directions are improved. (B) Only the global motion direction is improved. (C) Both local motion and global motion directions are improved. (D) No learning occurred. *Dashed lines* indicate no performance improvement on motion discrimination tasks.

A fourth study established associative learning by DecNef (Amano et al., 2016). The aforementioned studies focused on changes to one specific visual feature, location, or orientation. What about associations between two or more stimuli?

Amano et al. (2016) tested the hypothesis that associations between orientation and color can be established in early visual areas through neurofeedback. During neurofeedback training, the brain activation pattern that corresponded to a specific color (red, in this case) was repetitively induced in the V1/V2 region, while participants were presented with a black-and-white grating with a particular orientation. After DecNef training, the researchers tested whether the association between color and orientation had been formed. In a posttest, the participants were presented with a grating with the same orientation as that in the grating whose brain activation patterns had been used for DecNef training. From trial to trial, the color of the stripes varied from greenish to reddish in the posttest. Participants were asked whether the stripes appeared to be tinted red or green. The point of subjective equality where participant response rates for "red" and "green" were equal shifted toward more greenish. In other words, the point of subjective equality changed from 50% to 50% in red- and green-tinted gratings to less than 50% red-tinted and more than 50% green-tinted gratings. This indicates that participants were more likely to perceive "red" with the trained orientation. Furthermore, Amano et al. (2016) found that such a shift toward red was specific to the trained orientation of the grating. A further searchlight analysis, whereby a spherical ROI was moved across the whole brain, confirmed that the relevant changes were highly constrained in early visual areas during neurofeedback training. This indicates that only the target region was correlated with the reddish perception in association with the trained orientation. This result demonstrates that neurofeedback training is capable of establishing associative learning, which is an important aspect of learning and memory in general.

We have so far reviewed critical studies on fMRI neurofeedback training in early visual areas. The degree of success is remarkable. There is abundant evidence that neurofeedback training is highly effective in inducing changes in early visual areas and influencing behavioral performance in behavioral tasks that depend upon these areas. The changes were achieved through modulating univariate or multivariate signals. These findings might seem counterintuitive, because visual cortex in human adults is generally assumed to exhibit less plasticity, long after the critical period in which the visual cortex is highly plastic and acquires important visual functions (Hensch, 2005a,b). However, contrary to dogma—that the visual cortex is hardwired and stable after the critical period—a large number of visual perceptual learning studies have demonstrated that long-term performance changes in perception can be acquired after visual experiences even in adulthood (Watanabe and Sasaki, 2015; Li, 2016; Dosher and Lu, 2017). Nonhuman primate studies have also shown that tuning functions in the primary visual cortex can be sharpened with visual training (Schoups et al., 2001).

Moreover, fMRI neurofeedback experiments have demonstrated a key answer to a controversy in the field of visual perceptual learning. The controversy concerns which brain region is most responsible for visual perceptual learning. FMRI neurofeedback studies (Shibata et al., 2011; Amano et al., 2016; Wang et al., 2018) have shown that in humans, changes in visual abilities are not a result of changes in decision-making or higher-level processing but rather a consequence of changes in plasticity that occur in early visual areas. In other words, early visual areas are plastic enough to be modulated by neural representation induced through fMRI neurofeedback.

2.1.2 Higher-order visual areas

It has been widely recognized that human visual processing consists of two hierarchical pathways with functional and anatomical divisions—the "what" and the "where" pathway

(Mishkin et al., 1983). Along the "what" pathway, also referred to as the ventral pathway, visual signals related to form and color predominantly go from the V1 region, through the V2 and V4 regions, and to the inferior temporal region. On the other hand, visual signals for functions, including location, motion, and guided movement, are predominantly processed along the "where" pathway, also known as the dorsal pathway, which starts in the V1 region and then proceeds dorsally through the MT/V5 region to the posterior parietal cortex.

A number of studies have applied neurofeedback to change higher-level visual processing, including motion perception in the dorsal pathway and object recognition with houses and faces in the ventral pathway. Here we review four such neurofeedback studies that targeted changes in higher visual areas.

The first study functionally localized the human hMT +/V5 region to test the feasibility of applying neurofeedback to train participants to recruit the hMT +/V5 region with visual motion imagery strategies (Banca et al., 2015). The authors used an explicit neurofeedback strategy. During neurofeedback training, participants were asked to use visual motion imagery strategies to regulate their brain activity to a target level during the "regulation" periods compared to the "baseline" periods. The target level and the baseline level were displayed as a thermometer, as was done in a previous study (Scharnowski et al., 2012), but only to the experimenter outside the scanner. The thermometer was not shown to the participants to avoid any potential visual interference from the thermometer display. Then, the experimenter provided audio feedback for the target level and brain activation level of the participants through the communication system of the MRI in a range of 0 (no activation-baseline) to 5 (maximum activation). The participants showed successful regulation of hMT +/V5 to enhance activity during "regulation" periods compared to during "baseline" periods in neurofeedback blocks. Although no behavioral tests were performed, the study identified a possible network that might be related to motion imagery. While the activation of hMT +/V5 was successfully elevated during neurofeedback training, there were also simultaneous activations in the middle cerebellum, the putamen, and the putative V6 region. This might indicate a direct functional connection between the hMT +/V5 region and the cerebellum in the generation of motion imagery.

The second study examined how the difference between activation in the fusiform face area (FFA) and parahippocampal place area (PPA) of the human brain could be modulated with explicit neurofeedback and how the behavior would be changed accordingly in binocular rivalry (Ekanayake et al., 2019). Binocular rivalry is a well-studied perceptual phenomenon (Blake, 1989; Taya and Mogi, 2005; Tong et al., 2006). In binocular rivalry, two conflicting monocular visual images are presented simultaneously to a viewer, one to each eye. In this case, the two images compete for perceptual dominance, while the viewer experiences spontaneous alternations of dominance of one of the two images (Blake, 1989; Taya and Mogi, 2005). Traditional approaches such as mental imagery could bias perception in binocular rivalry on a trial-to-trial basis (Pearson et al., 2008). However, the magnitude of bias from trial-to-trial modulation did not increase due to training (Rademaker and Pearson, 2012). Thus binocular rivalry is considered to be a phenomenon resulting from a hardwired neural network and is difficult to modify. In the study, one eye of participants was presented with a face image and the other eye was presented with a house image to render binocular rivalry. Binocular rivalry performance was measured as the length of time participants perceived a house or a face. Neurofeedback training was performed while participants attempted to modulate the differential BOLD signals predominantly processed in FFA and PPA. FFA responds best to faces, not to nonfacial objects. Conversely, PPA responds best to houses and places, not to faces. The binocular rivalry performance was evaluated before and after neurofeedback training.

Participants were classified into two groups: "Face" and "House" groups. Through neurofeedback training, the Face group aimed to have a higher FFA activation level than that of the PPA. Conversely, the "House" group aimed to have a higher PPA activation level than that in the FFA. The participants were instructed to use mental imagery and were encouraged to use given potential strategies that might work. For instance, an instruction was "think about celebrity faces" or "think about your house or a building." The neurofeedback training procedure was similar to that used in a previous study (Scharnowski et al., 2012) in which the participants used explicit strategies of their own to achieve a certain degree of difference in activation between the two regions, which was shown as degrees on a thermometer. However, the participants were not aware of the relationship that the feedback signal had with both the FFA and the PPA. The participants successfully modulated the differential signals during the regulation period. This was achieved by showing lower activation in the opposite ROI for the assigned Face or House group while maintaining constant activation in the relevant region. For instance, the "Face" group increased the average BOLD difference between the FFA and the PPA by decreasing activity in the PPA while maintaining activity in the FFA, and vice versa for the "House" group. Behavioral effects were also observed. First, the unrelated perception during binocular rivalry decreased. For instance, the duration of house perception was significantly decreased in the "Face" group, whereas that of faces was significantly reduced in the "House" group. Second, the duration of mixed perception significantly increased. Surprisingly, the perception change was not consistent with the instructed strategies such that the duration of face perception in the Face group and the duration of house perception in the House group did not change. In this study, neurofeedback training modulated binocular rivalry, which was once considered to be stable, by suppressing the perception of one category and increasing the mixed perception in two categories.

These results have several interesting implications. While simple imagery, which was the instructed strategy in the neurofeedback experiment, might have worked to upregulate the relevant regions, the effect of imagery is inhibitory to the untrained category. The reason that imagery did not lead to increased activation in the trained category is unclear. However, these results seem to be consistent with the model by Levelt (1966), which predicted that the duration of the dominance of the stimulus in one eye is dependent upon the strength of the stimulus in the other eye. The Ekanayake et al. (2019) study showed that the increases in activity in the trained region (for instance, the FFA) resulted in decreased perception of the untrained category (for instance, the PPA). Thus a longer perception of the trained category was associated with the changes in the difference between the two monocular stimuli. After neurofeedback training, there was reduction in the signal strength of the untrained category and enhanced stable perception of mixed categories, thus resulting in an enhanced mean duration of the relevant category.

The third study also trained participants to upregulate activity in the PPA compared to the FFA over single-session neurofeedback training with explicit strategies (Habes et al., 2016). Although the BOLD signal was enhanced for the PPA compared to the FFA, no behavior effects in scene perception were observed. The difference from Ekanayake et al. (2019), in which there were behavioral effects on rivalry, lies in the length of the training session, indicating the possible necessity of several training sessions and/or an effect of sleep between sessions.

The fourth study again changed the balance between the FFA and the PPA, but now with implicit feedback (Ramot et al., 2016). The general procedure was the same as Ekanayake et al. (2019) except that participants were not aware of the purpose of the feedback and thought the positive/negative feedback signals were given randomly. The results indicated that the balance between the FFA and the PPA can be significantly modulated through implicit fMRI neurofeedback. However, no behavioral tests were reported.

As shown before, fMRI neurofeedback can be an effective tool for regulating brain activation in higher-order visual areas. Compared to the results of early visual areas, less consistent results between neurofeedback training and corresponding behavioral outcomes were obtained in the studies involving higher-order visual areas. Overall, fMRI neurofeedback may help address controversies with regard to neural mechanisms for higher-level visual perception, including those of binocular rivalry and motion imagery.

2.1.3 Comparisons between neurofeedback in early and higher visual areas

As we reviewed before, neurofeedback training is possible for both the ventral and dorsal pathways, including early and higher visual areas. However, it seems that the most robust results have been observed with neural changes in early visual areas. These include changes in BOLD activation (Scharnowski et al., 2012) and enhancement in representation based on multivariate patterns (Shibata et al., 2011; Amano et al., 2016). These neural changes in early visual areas are accompanied by behavioral changes (Shibata et al., 2011; Scharnowski et al., 2012; Amano et al., 2016), for example, with improved ability to detect and discriminate the target orientation of a grating (Shibata et al., 2011; Scharnowski et al., 2012). Moreover, the association between orientation and color was also effectively modified (Amano et al., 2016). Although activations in higher-order visual areas were modulated by neurofeedback (Banca et al., 2015; Habes et al., 2016; Ramot et al., 2016; Ekanayake et al., 2019), the associated behavioral effects were not consistent. More work is necessary to clarify the relationship between neurofeedback in these areas and behavioral outcomes. In general, we observed more consistent behavioral results when neurofeedback was applied to early visual areas rather than higher visual regions. Why we see more consistent behavioral effects for early visual areas need to be investigated in future studies. However, this might be due to the fact that primitive visual features, including orientation, are more robustly represented in early visual areas in a retinotopic fashion than higher visual areas.

2.2 *Auditory perception*

In contrast to the large number of fMRI neurofeedback studies in visual perception, there are only a limited number of fMRI neurofeedback studies of auditory perception. Most have explored the possibility of reducing hyperactivity in auditory perception in tinnitus patients. In one study (Haller et al., 2010), researchers functionally identified a region in the bilateral primary auditory cortices as the target ROI and used a region posterior and inferior to the primary auditory area as the control ROI. The control ROI showed no activation during the auditory localization session and that was not involved in tinnitus processing. The difference in brain activation between the target and control ROIs was the basis of a downregulation neurofeedback training protocol. Using an explicit strategy, participants were shown the thermometer bar as a visual feedback and successfully reduced activation in the auditory cortices. Two weeks after neurofeedback training, two out of six participants reported mild improvement in tinnitus symptoms.

Moreover, neurofeedback training reduced activity in the default mode network (DMN), which includes the prefrontal cortex, the precuneus, and the inferior parietal lobe. The DMN is active during resting states and gets deactivated during cognitively demanding tasks (Raichle, 2015). The involvement of the DMN suggests that the DMN plays a role in downregulating cortical activities or diverting attention. Simultaneous increased activations were found in the insula and the bilateral ventrolateral prefrontal cortex (VLPFC) and the right dorsolateral prefrontal cortex (DLPFC) during the training sessions.

A follow-up study (Emmert et al., 2017) used a similar procedure except that the primary auditory cortex and part of the secondary auditory cortex were localized as the target ROI, and the study compared the efficacy of different explicit feedback methods. The participants were divided into a continuous feedback group and an intermittent feedback group. The participants were asked to downregulate the activity of the ROI by attempting to make a green moving bar as high as possible. The height of the bar was the inverse of the amount of activity in the ROI. The continuous feedback group showed stronger deactivation in the target ROI, in particular the secondary auditory cortex. Moreover, the continuous feedback group showed a longer lasting effect, while the intermittent feedback group showed a stronger effect during the first day of training. There was a tendency in the continuous feedback group for the tinnitus to decrease, although it was not significant. Thus the difference in feedback methods may not have a significant impact in decreasing tinnitus.

FMRI neurofeedback for auditory perception has a certain limitation due to interference caused by noise coming from the MRI scans. Nevertheless, promising results have demonstrated that fMRI neurofeedback successfully decreased activations in the auditory cortex. Continuous feedback seems to be more effective in obtaining a long-lasting training effect, whereas intermittent feedback may be more effective in obtaining immediate results.

2.3 Attention

Attention is the selective processing of relevant information. The first study trained spatial attention (Robineau et al., 2014). Imbalance between the left and right visual hemispheres is a key aspect that has been related to hemispheric neglect and attentional neglect in patients with right hemisphere lesions (Corbetta et al., 2005). If the balance between left and right visual hemispheres can be modulated by fMRI neurofeedback, this might be potentially beneficial for these patients.

In the Robineau et al. (2014) study, the goal for neurofeedback was to modulate the difference in BOLD signals between the left and right early visual areas. Participants were provided with recommended strategies such as covertly diverting their visual attention to the relevant (left or right) visual hemifield to regulate their brain activity to a targeted level, shown as degrees on a thermometer. Participants performed a bilateral visual detection task and a line bisection task before, during, and after each of the three neurofeedback training sessions. In the bilateral visual detection task, a Gabor grating at the participant threshold was presented either in the left visual hemifield, the right visual hemifield, both visual hemifields, or not at all. Performance was measured as a visual extinction index for each visual field, which was defined by the subtraction of the number of failures (misses) to detect the stimuli in the unilateral trials from the number of misses in the bilateral trials, normalized by the number of trials in both conditions. For the line bisection task, the participants were instructed to decide whether a marker was presented at the exact center of the horizontal line when the marker was presented on different eccentricities from the objective center.

Eight out of 14 participants successfully modulated the differential BOLD signals between the two visual hemispheres by upregulating BOLD activity in the target early visual area while maintaining a rather stable level of activation on the opposite side of the early visual area. Only the neurofeedback learners showed a decrease in the extinction rate within each neurofeedback training session in both the target visual field and the opposite visual field.

However, the participants showed no difference in their behavioral performance on the line bisection task. The result that only the target ROI was upregulated while the contralateral visual ROI was not downregulated might be related to an explicit strategy in association with the target ROI only, as the participant was instructed to pay attention to the target visual hemifield. However, it remains to be clarified whether the behavior effect in the detection task was directly related to neurofeedback training, since performance enhancement was observed for both the target visual field and the opposite visual field in which the brain activity remained stable during neurofeedback training.

Sustained attention is defined as the ability to maintain a focus on something (activity or stimuli) over a long period of time and is a necessary function for performing tasks. However, the ability to exert sustained attention is limited in humans. Loss or lapses of sustained attention can cause significantly degraded brain processing and functions. Recently, it has been found that fMRI neurofeedback training is effective in training participants to maintain sustained attention. Here, we review several studies on neurofeedback to modulate attention.

The second study adopted multivariate pattern analysis (MVPA) and explicit real-time fMRI neurofeedback to train participants to maintain sustained attention (deBettencourt et al., 2015). Sustained attention was measured before and after neurofeedback training as follows: For each testing block, the participants were cued to selectively attend to a task-relevant category (e.g., scene) and ignore a task-irrelevant category (e.g., face) in a composite stimulus of a face and a scene. The participants were then required to respond in the "go" subcategory (such as an indoor scene) and withhold responses for another "no-go" subcategory (such as an outdoor scene). In 90% of the trials, the "go" subcategory was presented in the composite image. In the remaining 10% of the trials, the "no-go" subcategory was presented in the composite image. Sustained attention ability was assessed by the false alarm rate (a response when the "go" subcategory was absent), which was 31% on average, measured in a pretraining session.

During neurofeedback training, an image set composed of 50% faces and 50% scenes was first presented. Activation patterns in the whole brain were measured and used to construct an MVPA classifier that distinguished between the two categories. Then, the whole-brain classifier was applied to the real-time fMRI brain activation to decode the category that participants gave their attention to when viewing composite scene-face images on a trial-by-trial basis. The output from the classifier was transformed using a sigmoid function into a new composite image with a different mixture of the face and scene, to be shown on the next trial. If less attention was allocated to the relevant category (for instance, a scene), the percentage of the scene in the next composite scene-face image was decreased proportionally. The purpose of decreasing the proportion of the relevant category stimulus in the composite image was to warn participants that their attention was lapsing and to discourage this by making their task more difficult (they still had to judge the subcategory of the scene that was now less visible). The hypothesis was that this timely and informative feedback would make participants more vigilant to their lapses of attention. In this study, participants were only aware of the fact that feedback was related to their attention to the relevant category. The participants were not aware of how or where the feedback was calculated, unlike in other explicit neurofeedback studies. From before to after neurofeedback training, performance on the sustained attention task improved. The control group underwent a similar procedure except that they received feedback that was inappropriate to their brain state. Specifically, they were given yoked feedback from the attentional state of a different participant. The participants in the control group did not show similar behavioral improvements.

deBettencourt et al. (2015) found that category-specific networks such as the FFA and the PPA were recruited for sustained attention during training. Similarly, the occipitotemporal cortex involved in the perceptual system and the frontoparietal region involved in the attentional system were activated during training. However, only the decoding accuracy in the attentional system was correlated with the behavior improvement. The results demonstrated that neurofeedback training was highly specific in enhancing sustained attention.

The third study adopted a connectivity-based neurofeedback paradigm, or connectome-based neurofeedback, to modulate sustained attention (Scheinost et al., 2020). This study was based on a previous study, which identified the complex functional networks spanning the whole brain that predicted an individual's performance in sustained attention (Rosenberg et al., 2016). Sustained attention ability was measured by the gradual-onset continuous performance task (gradCPT), a test of sustained attention and inhibition similar to the task from deBettencourt et al. (2015). In the gradCPT, an image transitioned gradually from one image to the next in 800 ms with linear pixel-by-pixel interpolation. Participants responded when they detected a city scene but withheld their response when they detected a mountain scene. Pairwise functional connectivity was measured between hundreds of nodes used to evaluate the whole brain while participants were performing the task. The network was built by selecting the connectivity edges (regions) that predicted the participants' sustained attention performance.

During neurofeedback, real-time functional connectivity in the whole brain was measured in 3 min blocks. Connectivity was evaluated within the predefined network to acquire a score for the current attentional state. The score was provided as explicit feedback during neurofeedback training. A control group was recruited with a similar procedure but with yoked feedback as used in deBettencourt et al. (2015), based on the brain states of other participants. In the experimental group, the online neurofeedback score correlated with the offline activation of the predefined attentional network. The correlation did not exist in the control group. However, no significant behavioral effects were observed in association with neurofeedback training. The results indicate that the predictive attentional network could be tracked by neurofeedback in real time. The lack of behavioral outcomes may reflect the need for more than one session of training. More work is necessary to select a more behaviorally relevant network of attention and to clarify the effectiveness of connectome-based fMRI neurofeedback to influence attention.

3 How does fMRI neurofeedback allow us to explore causal relationships between brain activity and behavior?

A causal relationship between brain activities and behavior is usually measured with direct stimulation (such as TMS) in humans. The studies before demonstrated that with fMRI neurofeedback we can induce changes directly to the brain activity (BOLD activity, multivariate pattern, and connectivity). Moreover, in most cases, we observe a corresponding behavior change consistent with the brain activity change. This shows that fMRI neurofeedback may be able to explore a causal relationship without direct stimulation, which may generate discomfort and raise concern about safety issues when applied for a longer period of time. Is a certain type of neurofeedback more favorable for exploration of a causal relationship? Because experimenters provide participants with a strategy about how to change their brain activation in explicit feedback tasks, it may be difficult to rule out the possibility that behavioral changes are caused by the cognitive biases of participants, or that participants change their behaviors in response to experimenter expectations. In implicit feedback procedures, participants are to some extent "blind" to the expected results, so it is less likely that cognitive biases played a major role in the observed behavior changes. Interestingly, implicit fMRI neurofeedback successfully changed participants' behaviors (Shibata et al., 2011; Amano et al., 2016) as well as modulated brain activation (Ramot et al., 2016), even when participants did not know the expected behavioral results. Moreover, the behavior change was highly correlated with neural changes by fMRI neurofeedback (Shibata et al., 2011). Thus implicit neurofeedback may reflect a causal relationship between neural changes and behavioral changes in humans.

4 Summary

Real-time fMRI neurofeedback is effective in changing perception and attention. The recent development of methods of neurofeedback based on a multivariate pattern analysis has made it possible to induce finer-grained attentional and perceptual changes than conventional methods of neurofeedback based on univariate signal analysis. Moreover, implicit neurofeedback has great potential to help us explore possible causal links between brain activation changes in target brain regions and the consequent changes in attention and perception phenomenology and behavior.

fMRI neurofeedback has shown remarkable success in changing perception and attention, especially in the visual domain, through its influence on neural representations. The following concepts have been elucidated: (1) real-time fMRI neurofeedback has a robust influence across different levels of processing to induce behavioral changes from lower level simple visual features (e.g., orientation) to higher-level object recognition and attention; (2) real-time fMRI neurofeedback is capable of inducing a highly precise change on a wide range of representations of perception. For instance, DecNef can selectively change the representation of a particular orientation and specific orientation-color pairing, as well as selectively modify the processing of primitive local motion features in early visual areas without influencing processing in other regions of the brain.

The power and precision of fMRI neurofeedback demonstrate its strong potential to become a useful tool in influencing perception and attention, as well as in investigating causal relationships between processing in brain regions and behavioral outcomes.

Conflict of Interest

T. Watanabe and Y. Sasaki are part of team of inventors of the patents associated with DecNef, although they do not own the rights to it.

References

Amano, K., Shibata, K., Kawato, M., Sasaki, Y., Watanabe, T., 2016. Learning to associate orientation with color in early visual areas by associative decoded fMRI neurofeedback. Curr. Biol. 26, 1861–1866.

Banca, P., Sousa, T., Duarte, I.C., Castelo-Branco, M., 2015. Visual motion imagery neurofeedback based on the hMT+/V5 complex: evidence for a feedback-specific neural circuit involving neocortical and cerebellar regions. J. Neural Eng. 12, 066003.

Blake, R., 1989. A neural theory of binocular rivalry. Psychol. Rev. 96, 145–167.

Braddick, O.J., O'Brien, J.M., Wattam-Bell, J., Atkinson, J., Hartley, T., Turner, R., 2001. Brain areas sensitive to coherent visual motion. Perception 30, 61–72.

Corbetta, M., Kincade, M.J., Lewis, C., Snyder, A.Z., Sapir, A., 2005. Neural basis and recovery of spatial attention deficits in spatial neglect. Nat. Neurosci. 8, 1603–1610.

deBettencourt, M.T., Cohen, J.D., Lee, R.F., Norman, K.A., Turk-Browne, N.B., 2015. Closed-loop training of attention with real-time brain imaging. Nat. Neurosci. 18, 470–475.

deCharms, R.C., Maeda, F., Glover, G.H., Ludlow, D., Pauly, J.M., Soneji, D., Gabrieli, J.D., Mackey, S.C., 2005. Control over brain activation and pain learned by using real-time functional MRI. Proc. Natl. Acad. Sci. USA 102, 18626–18631.

Dosher, B., Lu, Z.-L., 2017. Visual perceptual learning and models. Ann. Rev. Vis. Sci. 3, 343–363.

Ekanayake, J., Ridgway, G.R., Winston, J.S., Feredoes, E., Razi, A., Koush, Y., Scharnowski, F., Weiskopf, N., Rees, G., 2019. Volitional modulation of higher-order visual cortex alters human perception. NeuroImage 188, 291–301.

Emmert, K., Kopel, R., Koush, Y., Maire, R., Senn, P., Van De Ville, D., Haller, S., 2017. Continuous vs. intermittent neurofeedback to regulate auditory cortex activity of tinnitus patients using real-time fMRI—a pilot study. Neuroimage Clin. 14, 97–104.

Habes, I., Rushton, S., Johnston, S.J., Sokunbi, M.O., Barawi, K., Brosnan, M., Daly, T., Ihssen, N., Linden, D.E., 2016. fMRI neurofeedback of higher visual areas and perceptual biases. Neuropsychologia 85, 208–215.

Haller, S., Birbaumer, N., Veit, R., 2010. Real-time fMRI feedback training may improve chronic tinnitus. Eur. Radiol. 20, 696–703.

Haxby, J.V., Gobbini, M.I., Furey, M.L., Ishai, A., Schouten, J.L., Pietrini, P., 2001. Distributed and overlapping representations of faces and objects in ventral temporal cortex. Science 293 (5539), 2425–2430.

Haxby, J.V., Connolly, A.C., Guntupalli, J.S., 2014. Decoding neural representational spaces using multivariate pattern analysis. Annu. Rev. Neurosci. 37, 435–456.

Hensch, T.K., 2005a. Critical period mechanisms in developing visual cortex. Curr. Top. Dev. Biol. 69, 215–237.

Hensch, T.K., 2005b. Critical period plasticity in local cortical circuits. Nat. Rev. Neurosci. 6, 877–888.

Kamitani, Y., Tong, F., 2005. Decoding the visual and subjective contents of the human brain. Nat. Neurosci. 8, 679–685.

Koyama, S., Sasaki, Y., Andersen, G.J., Tootell, R.B.H., Matsuura, M., Watanabe, T., 2005. Separate processing of different global-motion structures in visual cortex is revealed by fMRI. Curr. Biol. 15, 2027–2032.

LaConte, S.M., Peltier, S.J., Hu, X.P., 2007. Real-time fMRI using brain-state classification. Hum. Brain Mapp. 28, 1033–1044.

Levelt, W.J.M., 1966. The attention process in binocular rivalry. Br. J. Psychol. 57, 225–238.

Li, W., 2016. Perceptual learning: use-dependent cortical plasticity. Ann. Rev. Vis. Sci. 2, 109–130.

Mishkin, M., Ungerleider, L.G., Macko, K.A., 1983. Object vision and spatial vision: two cortical pathways. Trends Neurosci. 6, 414–417.

Pearson, J., Clifford, C.W., Tong, F., 2008. The functional impact of mental imagery on conscious perception. Curr. Biol. 18, 982–986.

Rademaker, R.L., Pearson, J., 2012. Training visual imagery: improvements of metacognition, but not imagery strength. Front. Psychol. 3, 224.

Raichle, M.E., 2015. The brain's default mode network. Annu. Rev. Neurosci. 38, 433–447.

Ramot, M., Grossman, S., Friedman, D., Malach, R., 2016. Covert neurofeedback without awareness shapes cortical network spontaneous connectivity. Proc. Natl. Acad. Sci. USA 113, E2413–E2420.

Ramot, M., Kimmich, S., Gonzalez-Castillo, J., Roopchansingh, V., Popal, H., White, E., Gotts, S.J., Martin, A., 2017. Direct modulation of aberrant brain network connectivity through real-time NeuroFeedback. eLife 6, e28974.

Rees, G., Friston, K., Koch, C., 2000. A direct quantitative relationship between the functional properties of human and macaque V5. Nat. Neurosci. 3, 716–723.

Robineau, F., Rieger, S.W., Mermoud, C., Pichon, S., Koush, Y., Van De Ville, D., Vuilleumier, P., Scharnowski, F., 2014. Self-regulation of inter-hemispheric visual cortex balance through real-time fMRI neurofeedback training. NeuroImage 100, 1–14.

Rosenberg, M.D., Finn, E.S., Scheinost, D., Papademetris, X., Shen, X., Constable, R.T., Chun, M.M., 2016. A neuromarker of sustained attention from whole-brain functional connectivity. Nat. Neurosci. 19, 165–171.

Salzman, C.D., Murasugi, C.M., Britten, K.H., Newsome, W.T., 1992. Microstimulation in visual area MT: effects on direction discrimination performance. J. Neurosci. 12, 2331–2355.

Scharnowski, F., Hutton, C., Josephs, O., Weiskopf, N., Rees, G., 2012. Improving visual perception through neurofeedback. J. Neurosci. 32, 17830–17841.

Scheinost, D., Hsu, T.W., Avery, E.W., Hampson, M., Constable, R.T., Chun, M.M., Rosenberg, M.D., 2020. Connectome-based neurofeedback: a pilot study to improve sustained attention. NeuroImage 212, 116684.

Shibata, K., Watanabe, T., Sasaki, Y., Kawato, M., 2011. Perceptual learning incepted by decoded fMRI neurofeedback without stimulus presentation. Science 334, 1413–1415.

Shibata, K., Sasaki, Y., Kawato, M., Watanabe, T., 2016. Neuroimaging evidence for 2 types of plasticity in association with visual perceptual learning. Cereb. Cortex 26, 3681–3689.

Schoups, A., Vogels, R., Qian, N., Orban, G., 2001. Practising orientation identification improves orientation coding in V1 neurons. Nature 412 (6846), 549–553.

Shibata, K., Lisi, G., Cortese, A., Watanabe, T., Sasaki, Y., Kawato, M., 2019. Toward a comprehensive understanding of the neural mechanisms of decoded neurofeedback. NeuroImage 188, 539–556.

Taya, F., Mogi, K., 2005. Spatio-temporal dynamics of the visual system revealed in binocular rivalry. Neurosci. Lett. 381, 63–68.

Tong, F., Meng, M., Blake, R., 2006. Neural bases of binocular rivalry. Trends Cogn. Sci. 10, 502–511.

Wang, Z., Tamaki, M., Shibata, K., Worden, M., Sasaki, Y., Watanabe, T., 2018. Feature-based plasticity revealed by decoded fMRI neural feedback (DecNef). J. Vis. 18, 759.

Watanabe, T., Sasaki, Y., 2015. Perceptual learning: toward a comprehensive theory. Annu. Rev. Psychol. 66, 197–221.

Watanabe, T., Náñez, J.E., Koyama, S., Mukai, I., Liederman, J., Sasaki, Y., 2002. Greater plasticity in lower-level than higher-level visual motion processing in a passive perceptual learning task. Nat. Neurosci. 5, 1003–1009.

Watanabe, T., Sasaki, Y., Shibata, K., Kawato, M., 2017. Advances in fMRI real-time neurofeedback. Trends Cogn. Sci. 21, 997–1010.

Williams, D.F., Sekuler, R., 1984. Coherent global motion percepts from stochastic local motions. Vis. Res. 24 (1), 55–62.

Yahata, N., Morimoto, J., Hashimoto, R., Lisi, G., Shibata, K., Kawakubo, Y., Kuwabara, H., Kuroda, M., Yamada, T., Megumi, F., Imamizu, H., Náñez Sr., J.E., Takahashi, H., Okamoto, Y., Kasai, K., Kato, N., Sasaki, Y., Watanabe, T., Kawato, M., 2016. A small number of abnormal brain connections predicts adult autism spectrum disorder. Nat. Commun. 7, 11254.

CHAPTER 5

Studying episodic memory using real-time fMRI

Jeffrey D. Wammes[a,b], Qi Lin[b], Kenneth A. Norman[c], and Nicholas B. Turk-Browne[b]

[a]Department of Psychology, Queen's University, Kingston, ON, Canada, [b]Department of Psychology, Yale University, New Haven, CT, United States, [c]Department of Psychology, Princeton University, Princeton, NJ, United States

1 Introduction

Memory is absolutely critical to our functioning in the world—it allows us to acquire new knowledge, make generalizations, develop expertise, adapt to changes in our world, and to allow prior experience to shape our future behavior. Here, we focus on episodic memory: the ability to form lasting memories of individual experiences (i.e., episodes) that support cued recall of details from those experiences—for example, being able to recall the particular dish that you have ordered when you visited a restaurant on a particular day. Understanding the complex brain states that support episodic memory has been a popular research objective. Many of these studies use functional magnetic resonance imaging (fMRI) as a noninvasive technique that is able to record from deep-brain structures important for episodic memory (e.g., the hippocampus) and that provides the spatial resolution needed to understand how memories are represented in the brain. In most fMRI studies of episodic memory, participants learn some new information in the laboratory and their memory for this information is later tested. This takes place while brain images are being collected every few seconds. Following the experiment, the brain images are compiled, preprocessed, and analyzed. The conclusions of such studies are often correlational: better memory in condition A is associated with the presence of brain state P, or conditions B and C can be distinguished based on memory-related information carried in brain region Q. Such analyses provide important insights about how the human brain supports memory, but without directly speaking to the causal role of brain states or regions.

In contrast, real-time fMRI (rtfMRI) can be considered an intervention, affording researchers the unprecedented ability to monitor, perturb, and even instantiate brain states noninvasively in healthy, normally functioning humans. Using this approach,

fMRI Neurofeedback. https://doi.org/10.1016/B978-0-12-822421-2.00011-9

the experiment can be turned on its head: in a conventional fMRI design, the tasks or stimuli are predetermined and brain activity is treated as a dependent variable; in an rtfMRI design, brain activity controls the tasks or stimuli and thus serves as more of an independent variable. This can be accomplished in two ways: in a *triggering* design, brain activity determines the timing of a task or stimulus. For example, a stimulus appears when the brain enters into a desired state. In a *neurofeedback* design, brain activity determines the content of the task or stimulus. For example, the activity of a brain region might be conveyed as explicit feedback via a visual display. In both cases, the impact of rtfMRI is usually measured in terms of changes in subsequent behavior and brain activity. Conclusions drawn using rtfMRI are not entirely causal, because controlling activity in a brain region and observing a change in subsequent behavior does not rule out additional links in the causal chain (e.g., an intermediate region or an explicit strategy). Nevertheless, the relationships established with rtfMRI are closer to establishing causation than conventional fMRI approaches because an intervention is applied to perturb brain states, as opposed to simply observing how the brain responds to a task manipulation.

Causal approaches have long been possible in nonhuman animals, but are generally more invasive than is feasible or ethical for humans (e.g., lesion, pharmacology, optogenetics). Some noninvasive approaches used in humans, including electroencephalography (EEG) neurofeedback or transcranial magnetic stimulation (TMS), have supported causal inferences (e.g., Antony et al., 2018; Tambini et al., 2018; Wang et al., 2019). However, these approaches have limitations when studying the mechanisms underlying memory, related to the fact that memories are distributed within and across brain regions (Johnson et al., 2009; Kuhl et al., 2011, 2012; Polyn et al., 2005; Xue et al., 2010; Ward et al., 2013). Measuring and manipulating distributed representations require a technique with: (1) high spatial resolution, (2) the ability to record simultaneously from multiple regions, and (3) access to deep-brain structures central to memory (e.g., hippocampus). EEG and TMS do not satisfy these prerequisites. EEG has high temporal resolution and measures simultaneously across multiple channels, but has low spatial resolution and is most sensitive to brain structures on the cortical surface. TMS can achieve higher spatial specificity (Hanlon, 2017), but is still an order of magnitude coarser than fMRI. TMS is also typically only applied to one or a small number of sites, and there is no direct access to deep-brain structures (though indirect access may be possible: Tambini et al., 2018; Wang et al., 2014; Hermiller et al., 2020).

Invasive methods for studying memory in humans, such as intracranial EEG (iEEG) and direct electrical stimulation (DES), can be highly precise, allow for direct measurement and manipulation of multiple sites, and provide access to deep-brain structures. However, an obvious limitation to this approach is that such procedures are only possible when clinically indicated, for example, in patients with intractable epilepsy. Not only is the pool of such patients limited, but electrodes are generally implanted in brain regions because of the potential role of these regions in the disease. This may restrict the generalizability of the results to the healthy brain. Because the placement of electrodes is entirely determined by clinical need, there is also no experimenter control in which brain regions are measured or manipulated. Many electrodes are typically implanted, but the resulting coverage is still far from spanning the whole brain.

fMRI represents a desirable alternative to EEG, TMS, and iEEG/DES for studying the distributed brain states subserving memory. It provides simultaneous measurement of the whole brain, including deep-brain structures, with relatively high spatial resolution. When analyzed in real time, fMRI can be used for online monitoring and perturbation of the brain in healthy, normally functioning humans. rtfMRI studies build on a strong foundation from conventional fMRI and other techniques, which have identified clear signatures of memory processes that can be targeted for enhancement.

A key part of this foundation is the realization that memory is intrinsically dynamic—the product of several processes interacting on different timescales. When we have an experience, we immediately *encode* it into a memory that persists after the experience ends, then *consolidate* this memory into a more durable state alongside other existing memories, and all the while we can *retrieve* and update the memory based on subsequent experience (Fig. 1A). In this chapter, we review evidence for how these three stages of memory are supported by distributed networks in the human brain. Building on this rich literature, we will consider interventional methods that complement more correlational approaches (e.g., conventional fMRI and EEG) and open up new avenues for developing treatments to enhance or suppress memories. Informed by these existing approaches, in a final section we discuss the unique opportunities that rtfMRI presents for causal experimental investigations of episodic memory, through monitoring, perturbing, and instantiating brain states.

2 Encoding

We are confronted with a barrage of sensory input as we navigate the world. This input is filtered through our perceptual pathways and then must then be recorded in some way so as to inform later behavior when a similar situation or context is encountered. Encoding refers to the process, whereby these perceived events are converted into an enduring memory trace that can be recalled at a later time (Tulving, 1983). This process is not infallible—many factors can degrade the quality of encoding, including the state of the brain at the time of exposure to new information (Daselaar et al., 2009). Understanding the dynamic nature of the brain states that underlie both effective and ineffective encoding could drive the development of neurofeedback-based interventions designed to induce desirable brain states, establishing a causal link between these states and encoding.

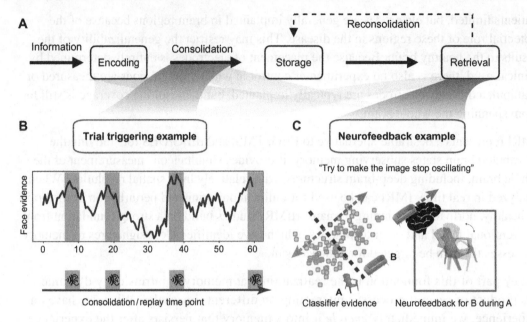

Fig. 1

Stages of memory and types of rtfMRI. (A) As we experience the world, this information is internalized through *encoding*. Over time, encoded information is stabilized through *consolidation* to allow for more permanent storage in memory. These stored memories can later come to mind spontaneously or through cues from the environment, resulting in *retrieval*. Every time we retrieve information, it goes through a process of destabilization and restabilization called reconsolidation. Each of these stages can be investigated with rtfMRI, generally in one of two designs: triggering and neurofeedback. (B) For example, triggering rtfMRI designs can be used to study consolidation. During periods of rest or sleep, classifier evidence can be used to detect *replay* of encoded stimuli. When these states are detected, a sound can be played to disrupt replay and thus impair memory (Schreiner et al., 2015). Varying the timing of the disruption and the brain region used for classification could clarify the nature of this stabilization process. (C) As another example, neurofeedback rtfMRI designs can be used to study retrieval. Consider a pair of objects (e.g., chair and couch). When retrieving one member of the pair cued on the screen (i.e., chair), the visual display can be driven by classifier evidence for the other member (i.e., couch). In the depicted example, the chair is wobbling, but this slows as classifier evidence for the couch increases. As a result, the representations of chair and couch are concurrently active, which may lead to their integration in memory (Ritvo et al., 2019; Schlichting and Preston, 2015).

2.1 Neural basis and measures of encoding

One of the most prominent tasks for studying the dynamic neural states that drive memory encoding is the *subsequent memory paradigm* (Brewer et al., 1998; Wagner et al., 1998). During an initial encoding phase, participants are presented with a series of stimuli (e.g., words or pictures), while their brains are scanned using fMRI. This is followed by a retrieval test, in which participants are asked to judge whether stimuli are "old" or "new." Stimuli from the encoding phase correctly identified as old are labeled as remembered and those incorrectly reported as new are labeled as forgotten. These labels are used to sort the fMRI trials from the encoding phase. Brain activity can be compared between trials with stimuli that were later remembered and trials with stimuli that were later forgotten. This paradigm has yielded a plethora of important discoveries about brain states that are predictive of successful encoding (as indicated by later retrieval).

Many of these results came from univariate analyses in which activity is collapsed across an entire region of interest (ROI) in the brain. This kind of analysis can determine whether an ROI is more active in a particular task or condition. In subsequent memory studies, frontoparietal cortex, medial temporal lobe (MTL) cortex, and the hippocampus consistently show greater activity for remembered relative to forgotten encoding trials, regardless of the type of materials encoded (Uncapher and Wagner, 2009; Kim, 2011). In fact, even before the presentation of a stimulus to be encoded, brain states in MTL cortex and the hippocampus reliably predict subsequent memory (Guderian et al., 2009; Park and Rugg, 2010; Turk-Browne et al., 2006). These encoding states can be considered to be stimulus agnostic, as the stimulus is not yet known to the brain. Other regions are more sensitive to specific types of input. For example, activity in left inferior frontal cortex predicts memory for words, while activity in bilateral fusiform cortices predicts memory for pictures (Uncapher and Wagner, 2009; Kim, 2011). Together, these findings highlight that the most effective encoding state is likely to recruit content-general regions in concert with distributed regions that are more finely tuned to the specific nature of the incoming content.

Memory research has also benefited from the use of multivariate pattern analysis (MVPA; Lewis-Peacock and Norman, 2014). In contrast to the univariate approach of averaging activation across voxels in a region, MVPA exploits the spatial pattern of activity within a region to determine the content or information being represented there. MVPA has been applied in tasks where to-be-remembered information is presented repeatedly during an encoding phase. Researchers measured the neural patterns at each repetition of the same stimulus, then quantified how stable these patterns were across presentations. During encoding, higher pattern similarity across repetitions of the same event was positively associated with performance in later memory tests (Xue et al., 2010; Ward et al., 2013). This effect is most prominent in frontoparietal cortex, visual cortex, and posterior cingulate cortex.

Univariate and multivariate fMRI analyses reveal the role of individual regions in encoding, but how do these regions interact to support this process? Functional connectivity analyses, which measure the correlation of fMRI activity between pairs of brain regions, provide a window into these network dynamics. Successful encoding is generally associated with increased connectivity between frontoparietal cortex, MTL cortex, and the hippocampus (Ranganath et al., 2005; Summerfield et al., 2006). Connectivity among these regions predicts variance in subsequent memory within and across individuals. These analyses also allow the identification of distinct brain networks supporting different aspects or types of memory. For example, resting-state fMRI (i.e., no cognitive task) has been used to identify brain networks with distinct patterns of MTL connectivity (Libby et al., 2012; Kahn et al., 2008): the posterior medial network, composed of regions interconnected with posterior hippocampus (including parahippocampal cortex, retrosplenial cortex, posterior cingulate cortex, and precuneus), and the anterior temporal network, composed of regions interconnected with anterior hippocampus (including perirhinal cortex, anterior temporal cortex, amygdala, and orbitofrontal cortex). These networks have distinct roles, with the anterior temporal network processing items and the posterior medial network processing context (see Ranganath and Ritchey, 2012).

Successful encoding, therefore, relies on the dynamic interaction of spatial patterns of neural activity across distinct networks of brain regions. The most prominent regions identified for encoding processes are the hippocampus, MTL cortex, and frontal cortex, but regions more specific to the type of information encoded are also engaged (e.g., premotor cortex, fusiform gyrus, and posterior parietal cortex). By measuring whole-brain fMRI during encoding and linking these neural measures to later behavioral memory judgments, it is possible to identify which brain states are conducive to memory. Such findings lay the foundation for interventional studies designed to perturb these states to promote or sabotage encoding.

2.2 Methodological approaches for perturbing encoding

Interventions have been used to influence activity in the brain regions and networks underlying memory encoding, often with the intention of nudging brain states either toward or away from optimal encoding states during a memory task. For example, a TMS study (Tambini et al., 2018) indirectly targeted the hippocampus by stimulating posterior inferior parietal cortex (pIPC), a region robustly connected with the hippocampus, during the encoding of object-location associations. This led to a selective enhancement in associative memory (see also Wang et al., 2014), which is primarily supported by the hippocampus, but not item memory, which can be supported by cortical regions outside of the hippocampus. Although TMS cannot directly target deeper brain structures, this study elegantly circumvented this constraint, establishing that pIPC stimulation likely impacted hippocampal activity. Resonating with that work, a later concurrent fMRI-TMS study convincingly demonstrated that delivering TMS to the parietal cortex during encoding led to an immediate impact on hippocampal activity and improved memory formation (Hermiller et al., 2020). Other TMS studies targeted left dorsolateral prefrontal cortex (PFC) during encoding of verbal and nonverbal material and observed downstream effects on memory (Gagnon et al., 2010, 2011).

Unlike TMS, DES can directly perturb the hippocampus and other deep-brain structures. Due to its invasive nature, however, DES is only conducted in patients when it is medically necessary. In epilepsy, electrodes are implanted in the brain for 1–2 weeks to monitor seizures and identify their source location prior to neurosurgery. During this time, electrical potentials are recorded and can be linked to experimental tasks; this method is often referred to as iEEG. Near the end of a monitoring period, current is applied to the same electrodes to stimulate the neural tissue where they terminate. Because electrodes are often implanted in the MTL cortex and hippocampus (common sites of seizures and sclerosis in epilepsy), these patients provide a rare opportunity to probe for causal effects in memory.

DES applied in the MTL cortex and hippocampal formation leads to variable effects (see Suthana and Fried, 2014). This highlights the complexity of these regions and the distributed nature of the representations they encode. For instance, stimulating entorhinal cortex (a subregion of MTL cortex) during encoding has been shown to enhance spatial memory, while stimulating the hippocampus proper had no measurable impact (Suthana et al., 2012). A later study reported that stimulation of either entorhinal cortex or hippocampus during encoding impaired both verbal free recall and spatial memory performance (Jacobs et al., 2016). In the spatial memory task, participants were placed randomly in an open arena with distant landmarks and automatically moved toward a target that was not visible until they started moving. That is, there was no consistent relationship between the person's initial position and the invisible target, preventing an egocentric map and biasing participants toward an allocentric perspective (i.e., based on spatial relationships between targets and external boundaries). Stimulation only impaired spatial memory for locations farther away from boundaries and memory for the temporal ordering of words, both of which require keeping track of relations, the specialty of the hippocampus (Goyal et al., 2018).

Expanding on these results and mirroring the fMRI studies discussed earlier, a recent study showed that subsequent memory can be predicted from hippocampal iEEG recordings acquired during encoding (Ezzyat et al., 2017). This provided a target for perturbing encoding, which was pursued with DES in a later session with the same patients. Specifically, during the encoding of a word list, DES was applied to the hippocampus and MTL cortex when possible. This stimulation caused neither an overall increase nor decrease in memory performance. Rather, an interaction was observed, helping to clarify the earlier inconsistent results: when the brain was already in a good encoding state (based on iEEG signal decoding), stimulation disrupted this state and impaired memory; however, when the brain was in a bad encoding state, stimulation nudged the brain toward a better encoding state, which in turn improved free-recall performance (Ezzyat et al., 2017). This confirms the existence and causal role of encoding states as an explanation for variability in memory within a person over time. There is now also evidence for variability in the impact of stimulation on memory across individuals (Kucewicz et al., 2018).

Temporal dynamics in encoding states can be leveraged for closed-loop memory improvement using DES (Ezzyat et al., 2018). In this work, pattern classifiers were trained on iEEG recording data from a patient to distinguish encoding states likely to yield later retrieval or forgetting. The patient then underwent an additional memory task with stimulation applied during encoding. However, rather than randomly assigning trials or time periods for stimulation, the pretrained classifiers were used to parse incoming data and detect bad encoding states (i.e., those associated with forgetting). When detected, these states were perturbed using stimulation to the lateral temporal cortex. Stimulation disrupted the negative encoding states, yielding improved memory not only for items present during stimulation, but also for items presented nearby in time to the stimulation.

Together, these results indicate that manipulations of a wide range of regions can affect encoding, and that the impact of stimulation depends on the currently unfolding brain state of the individual. In other words, to be confident about when and how to perturb brain states, it is necessary to monitor brain states in real time. Applying rtfRMI to influence memory performance is a new frontier, but one early study demonstrated the promise of this approach (Yoo et al., 2012). Participants were tasked with encoding a set of scenes. In an initial study (not conducted in real-time), the researchers established that low prestimulus activation in the parahippocampal place area (PPA) was associated with improved subsequent memory. In the next study, PPA activity during encoding was measured in real time. When low PPA activation was detected, presentation of a new scene was triggered. In other words, researchers identified a state that was conducive to encoding in real time and supplied new information for the participant to learn during that time. As a control, other trials were triggered when high PPA activation was detected. Indeed, scenes triggered by low but not high PPA activity were later better remembered. Although this study did not use neurofeedback to change the participant's brain state, it identified optimal or suboptimal encoding states, and determined the timing of encoding opportunities accordingly.

3 Consolidation

Once new information has been encoded into memory, it must be accommodated alongside existing memories and maintained in a durable state for later retrieval. Consolidation is the time-dependent process, whereby newly encoded information is stabilized and stored more permanently in long-term memory. This process can be discussed at two different levels of description, the cellular/synaptic level and the systems level (Dudai, 2012), which unfold along different timescales. Synaptic consolidation occurs in the local neural circuit that is engaged in encoding the memory, and refers to the time-dependent stabilization of changes in synaptic efficacy in this circuit that often occurs within seconds after encoding. In contrast, systems consolidation occurs in a more distributed set of regions across the brain, and refers to the reorganization of neural circuits to allow the more permanent storage of the new information. Here, we focus exclusively on the latter process of systems consolidation, which can be studied with fMRI.

3.1 Neural basis and measures of consolidation

Theories about systems consolidation primarily focus on the interaction between the hippocampus and neocortex. According to the *standard consolidation theory* (Marr et al., 1991), newly formed memories are initially dependent on a network of brain regions comparable to those implicated during encoding, including the hippocampus, MTL cortex, and neocortical areas involved in the experience. The hippocampus serves as a fast learner, rapidly binding the features of an experience. In contrast, the neocortex is a slow learner, building longer lasting but less detailed representations while avoiding interference with existing memories. Specifically, following encoding, the hippocampal state associated with the memory is repeatedly reinstated during sleep or rest, and this repetition through replay leads to gradual changes in neocortical circuits. Once completed, the memories no longer depend upon the hippocampus. Standard consolidation theory was initially supported by findings from amnesic patients who had hippocampal lesions but mostly intact neocortex (Corkin, 2013). This pattern of pathology is associated with a preserved ability to recall semantic knowledge and older memories that have undergone consolidation, but sweeping impairments in the acquisition of new episodic memories.

Later studies found evidence that hippocampal lesions can also lead to deficits for older episodic memories, indicating that remote memory does not always become independent from the hippocampus (see Frankland and Bontempi, 2005). This can be accounted for by *multiple trace theory* (Nadel and Moscovitch, 1997), in which hippocampal replay leads to multiple memory traces for the same information. That is, the hippocampus stores a "pointer" or "index" to a specific distributed pattern of cortical activity. Because similar traces reference highly overlapping neocortical networks, their accumulation produces abstract, gist-like long-term representations. However, these memories remain anchored in the hippocampus such that the loss of this index after hippocampal lesion renders the neocortical traces inaccessible. The *complementary learning systems* (CLS) theory (McClelland et al., 1995) can also account for these results. According to CLS, the hippocampal replay trains cortex to represent abstractions across multiple replayed episodes, rather than simply transferring individual episodic memories to cortex; as such, memory for individual episodes will continue to depend on hippocampus, unless they are replayed very extensively.

The traditional view of consolidation posits that it occurs once, after which the consolidated memory is considered fixed (McGaugh, 1966). However, if a consolidated memory is cued for retrieval, it can become labile again and subject to change, prior to a period of *reconsolidation* (Misanin et al., 1968; Nader et al., 2000). Although many studies of reconsolidation focus on fear conditioning (Nader et al., 2000; Schiller et al., 2010), reconsolidation has since been reported in several memory protocols (see Nader and Hardt, 2009; Dudai, 2012). These and other studies of consolidation highlight the dynamic nature of memory traces: they are formed, replayed, stored, reactivated, and modified repeatedly over time. With this in mind, targeted manipulations that reinstate brain states productive for memory may benefit consolidation and strengthen memories.

3.2 Methodological approaches for perturbing consolidation

Although manipulating the consolidation process directly is less common than manipulating encoding and retrieval, there have been a few attempts using DES. For example, researchers have stimulated memory-relevant brain structures during the consolidation period of a verbal free-recall task (Merkow et al., 2017). DES to MTL cortex during the retention period between encoding and test of a word list impaired later retrieval. Although DES also impaired memory when applied during encoding and retrieval itself, the disruption was greatest during consolidation. This was interpreted as DES interfering with the successful formation of an enduring memory trace, perhaps by preventing replay or rehearsal. Stimulating the amygdala immediately following learning of neutral images can also impact later memory in a positive direction (Inman et al., 2018). Specifically, amygdala stimulation during consolidation increased coherence between the hippocampus and perirhinal cortex during retrieval the following day and improved recognition memory performance.

EEG can also be used to monitor states that are conducive to memory consolidation. In studies using *targeted memory reactivation* (TMR), sleeping participants are reminded of specific episodes of learning from when they were awake, via presentation of sensory cues associated with those episodes (see Paller et al., 2020). These reminders impact hippocampal activity and subsequent memory more during slow wave sleep (SWS) than during rapid eye movement (REM) sleep or wake (e.g., Rasch et al., 2007). SWS can be distinguished from REM using EEG; thus, by monitoring for SWS and presenting cues when this sleep stage is detected, one can optimize the impact on consolidation.

TMR has also been used to show that sleep reminders are more effective at promoting consolidation when they elicit sleep spindle oscillations (Antony et al., 2018; Wang et al., 2019; Schreiner et al., 2015). This association between sleep spindles and memory consolidation presents an excellent target for intervention, made possible by the ability to detect sleep spindles in real time during sleep (Antony et al., 2018). Following a sleep spindle, there is a refractory period during which no new spindles occur. Reasoning that a lack of spindles would decrease the likelihood of reactivation and therefore consolidation, a real-time algorithm was used to present sound cues either immediately following spindles (in the refractory period) or after some time had passed (when spindles could occur again). Spatial memory was better for items cued outside the refractory period, further confirming the role of sleep spindles in effective memory consolidation (Antony et al., 2018).

4 Retrieval

Once new information has been encoded into memory and consolidated, the resultant memory trace can be brought back to mind, either spontaneously as a result of a relevant cue in the environment or intentionally as a result of effortful search. This process of remembering information that has been stored in long-term memory is called retrieval. Successful retrieval involves recapitulating the brain states that were present at encoding. Not surprisingly, and much like encoding and consolidation, memory retrieval is driven by multiple brain circuits distributed across brain regions.

4.1 Neural basis and measures of retrieval

When reviewing encoding, we highlighted brain regions that are more active for information that is subsequently remembered versus forgotten in a later memory test. The neural basis of retrieval has also been studied by sorting brain activity in the memory test itself according to whether each old item is successfully remembered versus forgotten (e.g., Buckner et al., 1998). The regions identified by this retrieval success contrast overlap with the regions involved in encoding (see Spaniol et al., 2009; Rugg and Vilberg, 2013). However, the relative activation in these regions differs: left ventrolateral PFC and MTL regions are more strongly involved in encoding, whereas left superior parietal and dorsolateral and anterior PFC regions are more strongly involved in retrieval. The proposed role of the PFC in retrieval is top-down selection of information, updating of episodic features, and guiding behavioral responses to the task at hand (Eichenbaum, 2000; Rugg et al., 2002). The proposed role of the parietal cortex (in particular, the angular gyrus) is guiding search or attention processes (Cabeza et al., 2012) and binding episodic details (Rugg et al., 2002). In addition to greater activity, the functional connectivity between these regions is higher during successful retrieval and the extent of increased connectivity in this network correlates with individual differences in recollection (King et al., 2015).

Successful retrieval is also associated with the reinstatement of brain states from encoding (see Rissman and Wagner, 2012; Frankland et al., 2019). MVPA studies have revealed that fine-grained spatial patterns of activity corresponding to the encoded content are recapitulated during retrieval (Polyn et al., 2005; Johnson et al., 2009; Kuhl et al., 2011). In one study (Polyn et al., 2005), participants encoded three lists consisting of either faces, places, or objects. During retrieval, participants were asked to freely recall items in any order and regardless of category. Nevertheless, the category of recalled items could be predicted in advance based on whole-brain patterns of activity. That is, returning the brain to a category-specific brain state from encoding facilitated retrieval of items from that category.

The degree to which an encoding brain state is reinstated correlates with memory performance. In one study (Kuhl et al., 2011), participants encoded two lists of word-image pairs. Some words were paired with just one image, whereas others were paired with a face in one list and a scene in the other list. During retrieval, participants were cued with a word and instructed to recall the image that was most recently paired with that word. A classifier was trained to distinguish faces and scenes based on activity patterns in the ventral occipitotemporal cortex. Performance was better when participants were able to recall the specific image compared to when they were only able to recall the category. This suggests a relationship between the fidelity of neural reinstatement and the success and specificity of retrieval. This relationship has since been reported in other modality-specific regions, as well as in frontal and parietal cortices, and is modulated by the hippocampus (Ritchey et al., 2013; Danker et al., 2017; Bosch et al., 2014).

In addition to retrieval success, an "all-or-none" memory measure, several studies have shown that neural reinstatement predicts rich aspects of memory performance during retrieval, such as the level of detail (Wing et al., 2015), vividness (Johnson et al., 2015; St-Laurent et al., 2015; Bone et al., 2020), and confidence (Thakral et al., 2015). These different aspects of memory retrieval seem to be supported by distinct neural mechanisms (Richter et al., 2016), revealing potential targets for memory enhancement through neurofeedback.

Complementing these findings from the fMRI literature, studies using iEEG have tracked the temporal dynamics associated with retrieval at millisecond resolution. Successful retrieval is associated with greater connectivity among various regions including the MTL, PFC, and parietal cortex (Watrous et al., 2013). In a more recent study (Vaz et al., 2020), single-unit spikes and local field potentials were recorded while participants performed a memory task. Ripple oscillations in the temporal cortex were found to reflect bursts of single-unit spiking activity organized into memory-specific sequences. These sequences occurred repeatedly during memory formation. Most intriguingly, these sequences were also replayed during successful retrieval and the extent of this replay in temporal cortex was associated with ripples in MTL. These results demonstrate that memory retrieval is supported by a reinstatement of a temporally stereotyped pattern of neural activity that was present during encoding.

Together, these findings suggest that successful memory retrieval is accompanied by coordinated activity between memory systems and the frontoparietal cortex, often recapitulating spatiotemporal patterns of activity that were present during initial encoding. However, due to the correlational nature of the methods used in these studies, they cannot pinpoint the causal roles of the different brain regions or rule out the possibility that some of the correlations observed between brain states and retrieval (e.g., reinstatement) may be epiphenomenal. Using rtfMRI, participants could be trained to target or elicit activity patterns in retrieval-related brain regions. By observing the effects on performance, the relative roles of these regions and the directionality of their interactions could be inferred. To a more practical end, neurofeedback could be used to impose beneficial retrieval states.

4.2 Methodological approaches for perturbing retrieval

The idea that perturbation of the brain can prompt memory retrieval has a long history, going back to pioneering studies in which brain stimulation caused deja vu, a memory phenomenon akin to familiarity (Penfield and Perot, 1963). This direct link between induced brain activity and memory retrieval has been replicated more systematically (Jacobs et al., 2012). Stimulation at sites throughout the temporal lobe is associated with phenomena resembling memory retrieval (see Selimbeyoglu and Parvizi, 2010). In right dorsolateral PFC, excitatory TMS during retrieval leads to faster memory response times, suggestive of increased retrieval efficiency, whereas inhibitory TMS reduces memory accuracy (Gagnon et al., 2011). In precuneus, TMS selectively improves source memory (Bonnì et al., 2015). In addition to the memory benefit observed in healthy young adult population, repetitive TMS applied to the precuneus has been shown to improve retrieval-related symptoms of Alzheimer's disease (Koch et al., 2018).

Rather than focusing on a single site, one recent study targeted multiple brain regions simultaneously (Kim et al., 2018). Patients navigated a virtual city to visit five stores. Later, they had to identify where the stores were located (i.e., spatial memory) and the order in which they visited them (i.e., temporal memory). The functional connectivity between left inferior temporal sulcus and left middle frontal gyrus was selectively associated with spatial memory but not with temporal memory. In a clear demonstration of functional specificity, stimulating these network hubs just prior to retrieval impaired spatial but not temporal memory.

We have thus far discussed memory retrieval as it is studied in the laboratory. Participants are presented with a set of items and are later tested to see which ones are remembered. Another form of memory retrieval involves recapitulating one's own autobiographical experiences when prompted (e.g., Benoit and Schacter, 2015). This process too can be influenced by direct manipulation of brain states. In a recent study, researchers applied TMS to angular gyrus during an autobiographical recall task. When participants were asked to recall an event from the last 5 years of their life, memories recounted during TMS had fewer episodic details (Thakral et al., 2017). This provides evidence for the necessity of the angular gyrus in retrieving specific contextual details from memory.

Leveraging the idea that reinstatement of relevant brain states drives successful retrieval, a recent study used closed-loop rtfMRI to directly test whether context reinstatement leads to better memory retrieval (deBettencourt et al., 2019). In this study (Fig. 2A), two contexts were created by interspersing images of either scenes or faces between words from two different lists during encoding. Prior to recall, the participants were instructed to reinstate the context from one of the lists. They were provided with a visual neurofeedback display, which was a weighted blend of a face and a scene. Using a classifier trained to distinguish brain activity

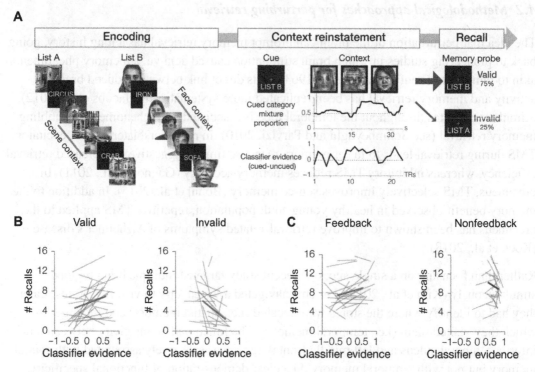

Fig. 2

Neurofeedback helps to reveal a relationship between context reinstatement and memory retrieval (deBettencourt et al., 2019). (A) Participants first encoded two lists of words paired with a visual context of scenes or faces. They were then cued to reinstate one of the two contexts during neurofeedback with the aid of composite face/scene images. The mixture proportion of the two categories in the composite image was determined by the classifier evidence for the cued relative to uncued category context, based on real-time decoding of incoming brain images. Finally, participants were cued to recall words from one of the two lists, which could either be valid (matching the context cued for reinstatement during neurofeedback) or invalid (mismatching the reinstated context). (B) Context reinstatement as measured by classifier evidence benefited the recall of words when valid (*left*) but hurt recall when invalid (*right*). (C) The relationship between neural context reinstatement and memory recall performance was only detectable with neurofeedback (*left*). When the image was set to always be fully coherent (i.e., containing only the cued category), and thus decoupled from neural reinstatement, there was no relationship between neural reinstatement and memory performance (*right*). *Adapted with permission from deBettencourt, M.T., Turk-Browne, N.B., Norman, K.A., 2019. Neurofeedback helps to reveal a relationship between context reinstatement and memory retrieval. NeuroImage 200, 292–301.*

patterns for faces versus scenes, the visibility of the cued context in the display tracked the degree of classifier evidence for the cued context in the brain. For example, if cued to reinstate the context of the list interspersed with scenes, the more the participant's brain contained information about scenes, the more strongly the scene appeared in the face/scene blend. This created a positive feedback loop that amplified subtle inflections in brain states. Importantly, the cued context was not always a valid indicator of which list would ultimately be tested. For example, sometimes participants were cued to reinstate a scene context, but then told to recall the words from the list with the face context. Higher levels of neural context reinstatement (operationalized in terms of classifier evidence for the cued context) were associated with better recall if the test list matched the reinstated context and worse recall if the participants were asked to reinstate the wrong context (Fig. 2B). Critically, this relationship between neural context reinstatement and free recall was only detectable with neurofeedback; it was eliminated in a control group who were presented with fully coherent images of a category as contextual retrieval cues irrespective of brain states (Fig. 2C).

5 Studying memory using real-time fMRI

fMRI has proven useful for understanding memory because it provides whole-brain coverage, can be used noninvasively in the healthy brain, and allows neural data to be collected concurrently with all three stages of memory reviewed earlier. rtfMRI confers additional advantages for memory research, complementing conventional fMRI by establishing and manipulating brain-behavior relationships and testing causal hypotheses about memory processes. Given that memory is supported by interactions across widely distributed brain regions, especially deep-brain structures such as the hippocampus and MTL cortex, rtfMRI provides advantages relative to other tools (e.g., TMS or DES) that do not provide access to the whole brain. With the recent developments in MRI technology and computational tools for fMRI data analysis (Cohen et al., 2017), rtfMRI provides alluring new opportunities to study the spatial and temporal dynamics of the neural mechanisms underlying memory.

The most defining characteristic of rtfMRI is that the incoming volumes of whole-brain data are analyzed on the fly (often in under a few seconds) and the results are used to modify the ongoing experiment. Paradigms using these methods typically fall into two broad categories: triggering and neurofeedback. In a triggering design (Fig. 1B), the goal is to determine the timing and content of stimulus presentations based on the ongoing brain states of participants. Volumes are analyzed as they are collected and compared to some researcher-defined benchmark. Then, researchers simply wait for the desired state, and when it is detected, trigger a particular type of trial, such as a new item to encode (Yoo et al., 2012).

In a neurofeedback design (Fig. 1C), the primary goal is to induce a target brain state (e.g., activation in a certain brain region or a particular spatial pattern) in the participants. As each incoming volume is collected and analyzed, feedback is given based on some measure of the similarity of the current brain state to the desired brain state. The most common way of providing feedback is via a visual signal that scales with the similarity to the target brain state (e.g., a looming circle; Shibata et al., 2011). In this case, the underlying mechanism can be seen as a version of operant conditioning where participants learn to self-regulate brain activity instead of behavior, via repeated trial and error, to maximize the feedback signal. More recently, some neurofeedback studies have provided feedback signals that are more integrated into the experiment, often referred to as closed loop (deBettencourt et al., 2015, 2019; Mennen et al., 2021). For example, similarity to the target brain state may be used to control task difficulty (deBettencourt et al., 2019), such that successful regulation of brain activity is rewarded with an easier task. Both triggering and neurofeedback paradigms can be based on the univariate activation in one region, the functional connectivity between regions, a multivariate pattern of activity across voxels, or even a combination of these measures. As a result of the flexibility of this method, there are many opportunities for using rtfMRI to study the mechanics underlying memory. Below, we highlight just a few.

5.1 Enhancing encoding or retrieval with real-time fMRI

Successful memory depends not just on the activation of one single region but rather, on the interaction and coordination of distributed brain networks. Recently, neurofeedback has been applied to enhance functional networks relevant for behavior and yielded some promising results (e.g., Megumi et al., 2015; Ramot et al., 2017; Yamashita et al., 2017; Scheinost et al., 2020). A potential application of rtfMRI is to use neurofeedback to train participants to induce optimal encoding or retrieval states by targeting the functional networks identified in the previous studies as being critical to these processes. In this way, participants can be taught how to attain the optimal encoding or retrieval brain states, so that they can learn to regulate their own functional networks to improve performance going forward.

In addition to being a potential novel tool for memory enhancement, using neurofeedback to target encoding versus retrieval networks could also answer important theoretical questions that are not easily addressed with conventional neuroimaging methods. Encoding and retrieval involve overlapping brain regions in the MTL cortex, hippocampus, PFC, and parietal cortex (see Spaniol et al., 2009; Rugg and Vilberg, 2013). Using neurofeedback to target these regions during encoding and retrieval may shed light on the different roles they play in these processes. For instance, we know which regions are implicated in encoding, and have identified sets of regions whose connectivity is associated with better subsequent memory. However, using traditional methods, it is difficult to pinpoint which regions are the most pivotal in driving encoding processes, or the directionality of these regional interactions. Recent advances in computational modeling of network dynamics suggest that some brain regions will have a much broader influence over global brain states than others (Bassett and Khambhati, 2017; Muldoon et al., 2016). Assuming that this principle extends to the networks that drive encoding as well, rtfMRI could be used to identify and subsequently target the regions most likely to propagate changes in connectivity across the entire network. Specifically, individual nodes in the encoding network could be systematically upregulated using neurofeedback to determine which regions most effectively propagate changes in the activity or connectivity of the entire network. The insights gained from this approach could lead to the development of more targeted intervention procedures for memory enhancement.

5.2 Inducing or disrupting item or category-specific representations

Hippocampal replay during consolidation of learned information improves later memory (see Foster, 2017; Tambini and Davachi, 2019). As discussed earlier, EEG can be used to detect sleep stages and spindles in real time, and both types of information can be used to optimize the timing of TMR cues. rtfMRI has complementary strengths and weaknesses from EEG with regard to studying and promoting consolidation. Due to its lower temporal resolution, fMRI is less useful than EEG for sleep staging and spindle tracking. On the positive side, the superior spatial resolution of fMRI can potentially provide a more specific way of monitoring or instantiating replay in one or several regions. The spatial resolution of fMRI is also advantageous when it comes to tracking the specific content of the replayed information. Although there have been some basic successes in decoding the content of replayed memories during sleep with EEG (faces vs. scenes: Cairney et al., 2018; Schönauer et al., 2017; left- vs. right-side movements: Wang et al., 2019), the spatial blurring of EEG places an upper bound on the resolution of decoding. By contrast, fMRI has been used to decode the replay of more fine-grained content (e.g., specific images of satellites within categories: Schapiro et al., 2018).

Using rtfMRI, researchers could apply both triggering and neurofeedback approaches to study memory consolidation. Scans during an initial encoding phase could be used to quantify the spatial patterns of brain activity associated with exposure to a particular item, category of items, or context. Next, while participants are awake but at rest in a subsequent phase, researchers could extract information about the participant's internal representations by analyzing multivoxel patterns from each incoming volume. By monitoring the moment-to-moment fluctuations in internal states, activity consistent with the prescribed stimulus or category could be detected and used to precisely time an experimental intervention (Fig. 1B). For example, if trying to prevent replay of a particular face, activation of that face representation, detected in real time, could be met with distracting sounds, which have been shown to disrupt replay (Schreiner et al., 2015). Further, the target brain region and timing of interference could be manipulated to establish the causal roles of brain regions in replay during consolidation.

Although triggering approaches could help reveal mechanisms of consolidation by disrupting replay, neurofeedback approaches might have more potential for real-world application. Namely, participants could be trained to become better at replaying or to learn mental strategies that promote replay. That is, during a postencoding period, researchers could display a continuously changing feedback signal to a participant, reflecting classifier evidence in favor of a target item or category whose memory they are trying to enhance. By selectively targeting the hippocampus or different neocortical regions, this approach could help disentangle the relative contributions of hippocampal versus cortical replay to later memory, and establish the direction of information flow between the hippocampus and cortex (see Rothschild et al., 2017).

5.3 Testing theories of learning-related change

As we learn, representations in memory are constantly reorganized. Memories are weakened and strengthened, but can also become more or less similar to one another. One theory of neuroplasticity, the *nonmonotonic plasticity hypothesis* (NMPH; Ritvo et al., 2019) proposes that these changes, both in individual memories and in the relationships between them, are driven by varying degrees of concurrent activation across memories (Detre et al., 2013; Hulbert and Norman, 2015; Newman and Norman, 2010). According to the NMPH, the degree of shared activation among two memory representations will determine whether they integrate or differentiate: while strong coactivation will lead to integration of two memories, moderate coactivation will lead to their differentiation, and lower levels of coactivation will lead to no change in the similarity structure of the memories.

It is challenging to test this hypothesis using traditional fMRI methods, because there is no way of knowing a priori where a particular experimental condition will fall on the continuum from low coactivation to moderate coactivation (leading to differentiation) to strong coactivation (leading to integration). This is further complicated by the fact that coactivation levels can vary across individuals and across trials within a particular experimental condition. One approach to this problem is to include a variety of conditions meant to evoke different levels of activity, measure those levels of activity post hoc using MVPA, and then relate measured activity to representational change, all the while hoping that enough observations are collected at each level of coactivity to test the predictions of the NMPH. rtfMRI could provide a more efficient way of testing these predictions: specifically, one could estimate the neural representations of a pair of items (A and B) within each individual. Then, during presentation of the B item, neurofeedback could be used to reward participants for activating the A item to a particular "target" level, without actually displaying A to the participant. For example, if participants were rewarded for strong A activation during the presentation of B, this should induce strong coactivation of A and B, leading to integration of the two memories (Fig. 1C). More generally, this approach provides an exciting opportunity to establish a causal relationship between particular levels of coactivation of memories, representational changes in the brain, and behavioral effects of these changes.

5.4 Leveraging expert brain states to enhance learning

Memory in the real world often deals with complex, abstract concepts that are learned gradually and intermixed with other information. Moreover, there are dramatic differences in how well people learn or remember when presented with the same content (Jonassen and Grabowski, 2012). What underlying neural mechanisms could explain such individual differences? Furthermore, could we train individuals to become better at learning a certain topic by teaching them how to modulate their own brain activity?

Previous studies have found that comprehension and memory of narratives can be predicted from the similarity between the neural patterns in listeners and that of the speaker (Hasson et al., 2012; Nguyen et al., 2019; Stephens et al., 2010). The efficacy of learning could thus be predicted by the neural similarity between a teacher/expert and students (Meshulam et al., 2021). This could be leveraged by rtfMRI studies that directly reward similarity to a teacher's neural patterns and measure the effect on later comprehension and learning of the presented content. Specifically, one could measure the dynamic brain states present in a set of teachers or experts, while they are outlining a particularly difficult concept. As a student is learning, their dynamic brain states could be analyzed in real time, and feedback given to nudge their brains toward (or away from) states that more closely resemble those observed in the experts. Researchers could then probe for differences in performance as a result of this neurofeedback manipulation. In addition to attempting to induce appropriate brain states for learning, the similarity of brain states could be used to provide a sensitive measure of learning in real time, especially in cases where the strategy for improvement might not be easily verbalized. Techniques like these have value for basic science by establishing causal links between changes in brain states and the efficacy of learning, but could also eventually find application in pedagogical settings (perhaps with different and more cost-efficient neural technologies) for brain-based education and evaluation.

6 Conclusion

Memory is fundamental to every aspect of the mind and brain, and ultimately may underlie all rtfMRI training effects described in this book. Our focus in this chapter, however, was on what could be learned in the other direction, using rtfMRI to understand memory itself. Memory processes are underpinned by dynamic processes in the hippocampus and MTL cortex, and more broadly throughout cortex. The enterprise of using rtfMRI to study these processes is still in its infancy, relative to other clinical and basic cognitive approaches. Several other methods (e.g., DES, TMS, EEG) have been used to monitor or manipulate these neural circuits and shed light on how they support memory, albeit with mixed results. We propose that rtfMRI, through broad sampling of the whole brain with relatively high spatial sensitivity (especially to deep-brain memory structures), will allow for more flexible control over the neural processes driving encoding, consolidation, and retrieval. Complementing other methods, rtfMRI provides unprecedented opportunities to monitor, perturb, and instantiate brain states, in order to draw causal inferences about how brain dynamics support optimal memory performance and guide the development of memory enhancement strategies.

References

Antony, J.W., Piloto, L., Wang, M., Pacheco, P., Norman, K.A., Paller, K.A., 2018. Sleep spindle refractoriness segregates periods of memory reactivation. Curr. Biol. 28 (11), 1736–1743.
Bassett, D.S., Khambhati, A.N., 2017. A network engineering perspective on probing and perturbing cognition with neurofeedback. Ann. N. Y. Acad. Sci. 1396 (1), 126–143.

Benoit, R.G., Schacter, D.L., 2015. Specifying the core network supporting episodic simulation and episodic memory by activation likelihood estimation. Neuropsychologia 75 (1), 450–457.

Bone, M.B., Ahmad, F., Buchsbaum, B.R., 2020. Feature-specific neural reactivation during episodic memory. Nat. Commun. 11 (1), 1–13.

Bonnì, S., Veniero, D., Mastropasqua, C., Ponzo, V., Caltagirone, C., Bozzali, M., Koch, G., 2015. TMS evidence for a selective role of the precuneus in source memory retrieval. Behav. Brain Res. 282, 70–75.

Bosch, S.E., Jehee, J.F.M., Fernández, G., Doeller, C.F., 2014. Reinstatement of associative memories in early visual cortex is signaled by the hippocampus. J. Neurosci. 34 (22), 7493–7500.

Brewer, J.B., Zhao, Z., Desmond, J.E., Glover, G.H., Gabrieli, J.D.E., 1998. Making memories: brain activity that predicts how well visual experience will be remembered. Science 281 (5380), 1185–1187.

Buckner, R.L., Koutstaal, W., Schacter, D.L., Dale, A.M., Rotte, M., Rosen, B.R., 1998. Functional-anatomic study of episodic retrieval: II. Selective averaging of event-related fMRI trials to test the retrieval success hypothesis. NeuroImage 7 (3), 163–175.

Cabeza, R., Ciaramelli, E., Moscovitch, M., 2012. Cognitive contributions of the ventral parietal cortex: an integrative theoretical account. Trends Cogn. Sci. 16 (6), 338–352.

Cairney, S.A., El Marj, N., Staresina, B.P., et al., 2018. Memory consolidation is linked to spindle-mediated information processing during sleep. Curr. Biol. 28 (6), 948–954.

Cohen, J.D., Daw, N., Engelhardt, B., Hasson, U., Li, K., Niv, Y., Norman, K.A., Pillow, J., Ramadge, P.J., Turk-Browne, N.B., et al., 2017. Computational approaches to fMRI analysis. Nat. Neurosci. 20 (3), 304–313.

Corkin, S., 2013. Permanent Present Tense: The Unforgettable Life of the Amnesic Patient, HM. Basic Books (AZ), New York, NY.

Danker, J.F., Tompary, A., Davachi, L., 2017. Trial-by-trial hippocampal encoding activation predicts the fidelity of cortical reinstatement during subsequent retrieval. Cereb. Cortex 27 (7), 3515–3524.

Daselaar, S.M., Prince, S.E., Dennis, N.A., Hayes, S.M., Kim, H., Cabeza, R., 2009. Posterior midline and ventral parietal activity is associated with retrieval success and encoding failure. Front. Hum. Neurosci. 3, 13.

deBettencourt, M.T., Cohen, J.D., Lee, R.F., Norman, K.A., Turk-Browne, N.B., 2015. Closed-loop training of attention with real-time brain imaging. Nat. Neurosci. 18 (3), 470–475.

deBettencourt, M.T., Turk-Browne, N.B., Norman, K.A., 2019. Neurofeedback helps to reveal a relationship between context reinstatement and memory retrieval. NeuroImage 200, 292–301.

Detre, G.J., Natarajan, A., Gershman, S.J., Norman, K.A., 2013. Moderate levels of activation lead to forgetting in the think/no-think paradigm. Neuropsychologia 51 (12), 2371–2388.

Dudai, Y., 2012. The restless engram: consolidations never end. Annu. Rev. Neurosci. 35, 227–247.

Eichenbaum, H., 2000. A cortical-hippocampal system for declarative memory. Nat. Rev. Neurosci. 1 (1), 41–50.

Ezzyat, Y., Kragel, J.E., Burke, J.F., Levy, D.F., Lyalenko, A., Wanda, P., O'Sullivan, L., Hurley, K.B., Busygin, S., Pedisich, I., et al., 2017. Direct brain stimulation modulates encoding states and memory performance in humans. Curr. Biol. 27 (9), 1251–1258.

Ezzyat, Y., Wanda, P.A., Levy, D.F., Kadel, A., Aka, A., Pedisich, I., Sperling, M.R., Sharan, A.D., Lega, B.C., Burks, A., et al., 2018. Closed-loop stimulation of temporal cortex rescues functional networks and improves memory. Nat. Commun. 9 (1), 1–8.

Foster, D.J., 2017. Replay comes of age. Annu. Rev. Neurosci. 40, 581–602.

Frankland, P.W., Bontempi, B., 2005. The organization of recent and remote memories. Nat. Rev. Neurosci. 6 (2), 119–130.

Frankland, P.W., Josselyn, S.A., Köhler, S., 2019. The neurobiological foundation of memory retrieval. Nat. Neurosci. 22 (10), 1576–1585.

Gagnon, G., Blanchet, S., Grondin, S., Schneider, C., 2010. Paired-pulse transcranial magnetic stimulation over the dorsolateral prefrontal cortex interferes with episodic encoding and retrieval for both verbal and non-verbal materials. Brain Res. 1344, 148–158.

Gagnon, G., Schneider, C., Grondin, S., Blanchet, S., 2011. Enhancement of episodic memory in young and healthy adults: a paired-pulse TMS study on encoding and retrieval performance. Neurosci. Lett. 488 (2), 138–142.

Goyal, A., Miller, J., Watrous, A.J., Lee, S.A., Coffey, T., Sperling, M.R., Sharan, A., Worrell, G., Berry, B., Lega, B., et al., 2018. Electrical stimulation in hippocampus and entorhinal cortex impairs spatial and temporal memory. J. Neurosci. 38 (19), 4471–4481.

Guderian, S., Schott, B.H., Richardson-Klavehn, A., Düzel, E., 2009. Medial temporal theta state before an event predicts episodic encoding success in humans. Proc. Natl. Acad. Sci. 106 (13), 5365–5370.

Hanlon, C., 2017. Blunt or precise? A note about the relative precision of figure-of-eight rTMS coils. Brain Stimul. 10 (2), 338–339.

Hasson, U., Ghazanfar, A.A., Galantucci, B., Garrod, S., Keysers, C., 2012. Brain-to-brain coupling: a mechanism for creating and sharing a social world. Trends Cogn. Sci. 16 (2), 114–121.

Hermiller, M.S., Chen, Y.F., Parrish, T.B., Voss, J.L., 2020. Evidence for immediate enhancement of hippocampal memory encoding by network-targeted theta-burst stimulation during concurrent fMRI. J. Neurosci. 40 (37), 7155–7168.

Hulbert, J.C., Norman, K.A., 2015. Neural differentiation tracks improved recall of competing memories following interleaved study and retrieval practice. Cereb. Cortex 25 (10), 3994–4008.

Inman, C.S., Manns, J.R., Bijanki, K.R., Bass, D.I., Hamann, S., Drane, D.L., Fasano, R.E., Kovach, C.K., Gross, R.E., Willie, J.T., 2018. Direct electrical stimulation of the amygdala enhances declarative memory in humans. Proc. Natl. Acad. Sci. 115 (1), 98–103.

Jacobs, J., Lega, B., Anderson, C., 2012. Explaining how brain stimulation can evoke memories. J. Cogn. Neurosci. 24 (3), 553–563.

Jacobs, J., Miller, J., Lee, S.A., Coffey, T., Watrous, A.J., Sperling, M.R., Sharan, A., Worrell, G., Berry, B., Lega, B., et al., 2016. Direct electrical stimulation of the human entorhinal region and hippocampus impairs memory. Neuron 92 (5), 983–990.

Johnson, J.D., McDuff, S.G.R., Rugg, M.D., Norman, K.A., 2009. Recollection, familiarity, and cortical reinstatement: a multivoxel pattern analysis. Neuron 63 (5), 697–708.

Johnson, M.K., Kuhl, B.A., Mitchell, K.J., Ankudowich, E., Durbin, K.A., 2015. Age-related differences in the neural basis of the subjective vividness of memories: evidence from multivoxel pattern classification. Cogn. Affect. Behav. Neurosci. 15 (3), 644–661.

Jonassen, D.H., Grabowski, B.L., 2012. Handbook of Individual Differences, Learning, and Instruction. Routledge, New York, NY.

Kahn, I., Andrews-Hanna, J.R., Vincent, J.L., Snyder, A.Z., Buckner, R.L., 2008. Distinct cortical anatomy linked to subregions of the medial temporal lobe revealed by intrinsic functional connectivity. J. Neurophysiol. 100 (1), 129–139.

Kim, H., 2011. Neural activity that predicts subsequent memory and forgetting: a meta-analysis of 74 fMRI studies. NeuroImage 54 (3), 2446–2461.

Kim, K., Schedlbauer, A., Rollo, M., Karunakaran, S., Ekstrom, A.D., Tandon, N., 2018. Network-based brain stimulation selectively impairs spatial retrieval. Brain Stimul. 11 (1), 213–221.

King, D.R., de Chastelaine, M., Elward, R.L., Wang, T.H., Rugg, M.D., 2015. Recollection-related increases in functional connectivity predict individual differences in memory accuracy. J. Neurosci. 35 (4), 1763–1772.

Koch, G., Bonnì, S., Pellicciari, M.C., Casula, E.P., Mancini, M., Esposito, R., Ponzo, V., Picazio, S., Di Lorenzo, F., Serra, L., et al., 2018. Transcranial magnetic stimulation of the precuneus enhances memory and neural activity in prodromal Alzheimer's disease. NeuroImage 169, 302–311.

Kucewicz, M.T., Berry, B.M., Miller, L.R., Khadjevand, F., Ezzyat, Y., Stein, J.M., Kremen, V., Brinkmann, B.H., Wanda, P., Sperling, M.R., et al., 2018. Evidence for verbal memory enhancement with electrical brain stimulation in the lateral temporal cortex. Brain 141 (4), 971–978.

Kuhl, B.A., Rissman, J., Chun, M.M., Wagner, A.D., 2011. Fidelity of neural reactivation reveals competition between memories. Proc. Natl. Acad. Sci. 108 (14), 5903–5908.

Kuhl, B.A., Rissman, J., Wagner, A.D., 2012. Multi-voxel patterns of visual category representation during episodic encoding are predictive of subsequent memory. Neuropsychologia 50 (4), 458–469.

Lewis-Peacock, J.A., Norman, K.A., 2014. Multi-voxel pattern analysis of fMRI data. Cogn. Neurosci. 512, 911–920.

Libby, L.A., Ekstrom, A.D., Ragland, J.D., Ranganath, C., 2012. Differential connectivity of perirhinal and parahippocampal cortices within human hippocampal subregions revealed by high-resolution functional imaging. J. Neurosci. 32 (19), 6550–6560.

Marr, D., Willshaw, D., McNaughton, B., 1991. Simple memory: a theory for archicortex. In: From the Retina to the Neocortex, Springer, pp. 59–128.

McClelland, J.L., McNaughton, B.L., O'Reilly, R.C., 1995. Why there are complementary learning systems in the hippocampus and neocortex: insights from the successes and failures of connectionist models of learning and memory. Psychol. Rev. 102 (3), 419–457.

McGaugh, J.L., 1966. Time-dependent processes in memory storage. Science 153 (3742), 1351–1358.

Megumi, F., Yamashita, A., Kawato, M., Imamizu, H., 2015. Functional MRI neurofeedback training on connectivity between two regions induces long-lasting changes in intrinsic functional network. Front. Hum. Neurosci. 9, 160.

Mennen, A.C., Turk-Browne, N.B., Wallace, G., Seok, D., Jaganjac, A., Stock, J., deBettencourt, M.T., Cohen, J.D., Norman, K.A., Sheline, Y.I., 2021. Cloud-based fMRI neurofeedback to reduce the negative attentional bias in depression: a proof-of-concept study. Biol. Psychiatry Cogn. Neurosci. Neuroimaging 6 (4), 490–497.

Merkow, M.B., Burke, J.F., Ramayya, A.G., Sharan, A.D., Sperling, M.R., Kahana, M.J., 2017. Stimulation of the human medial temporal lobe between learning and recall selectively enhances forgetting. Brain Stimul. 10 (3), 645–650.

Meshulam, M., Hasenfratz, L., Hillman, H., Liu, Y.-F., Nguyen, M., Norman, K.A., Hasson, U., 2021. Neural alignment predicts learning outcomes in students taking an introduction to computer science course. Nat. Commun. 12 (1), 1–14.

Misanin, J.R., Miller, R.R., Lewis, D.J., 1968. Retrograde amnesia produced by electroconvulsive shock after reactivation of a consolidated memory trace. Science 160 (3827), 554–555.

Muldoon, S.F., Pasqualetti, F., Gu, S., Cieslak, M., Grafton, S.T., Vettel, J.M., Bassett, D.S., 2016. Stimulation-based control of dynamic brain networks. PLoS Comput. Biol. 12 (9), e1005076.

Nadel, L., Moscovitch, M., 1997. Memory consolidation, retrograde amnesia and the hippocampal complex. Curr. Opin. Neurobiol. 7 (2), 217–227.

Nader, K., Hardt, O., 2009. A single standard for memory: the case for reconsolidation. Nat. Rev. Neurosci. 10 (3), 224–234.

Nader, K., Schafe, G.E., Le Doux, J.E., 2000. Fear memories require protein synthesis in the amygdala for reconsolidation after retrieval. Nature 406 (6797), 722–726.

Newman, E.L., Norman, K.A., 2010. Moderate excitation leads to weakening of perceptual representations. Cereb. Cortex 20 (11), 2760–2770.

Nguyen, M., Vanderwal, T., Hasson, U., 2019. Shared understanding of narratives is correlated with shared neural responses. NeuroImage 184, 161–170.

Paller, K.A., Mayes, A.R., Antony, J.W., Norman, K.A., 2020. Replay-based consolidation governs enduring memory storage. In: Poeppel, D., Mangun, G.R., Gazzaniga, M.S. (Eds.), The Cognitive Neurosciences. MIT Press, Cambridge, MA, pp. 265–276.

Park, H., Rugg, M.D., 2010. Prestimulus hippocampal activity predicts later recollection. Hippocampus 20 (1), 24–28.

Penfield, W., Perot, P., 1963. The brain's record of auditory and visual experience: a final summary and discussion. Brain 86 (4), 595–696.

Polyn, S.M., Natu, V.S., Cohen, J.D., Norman, K.A., 2005. Category-specific cortical activity precedes retrieval during memory search. Science 310 (5756), 1963–1966.

Ramot, M., Kimmich, S., Gonzalez-Castillo, J., Roopchansingh, V., Popal, H., White, E., Gotts, S.J., Martin, A., 2017. Direct modulation of aberrant brain network connectivity through real-time neurofeedback. Elife 6, e28974.

Ranganath, C., Ritchey, M., 2012. Two cortical systems for memory-guided behaviour. Nat. Rev. Neurosci. 13 (10), 713–726.

Ranganath, C., Heller, A., Cohen, M.X., Brozinsky, C.J., Rissman, J., 2005. Functional connectivity with the hippocampus during successful memory formation. Hippocampus 15 (8), 997–1005.

Rasch, B., Büchel, C., Gais, S., Born, J., 2007. Odor cues during slow-wave sleep prompt declarative memory consolidation. Science 315 (5817), 1426–1429.

Richter, F.R., Cooper, R.A., Bays, P.M., Simons, J.S., 2016. Distinct neural mechanisms underlie the success, precision, and vividness of episodic memory. Elife 5, e18260.

Rissman, J., Wagner, A.D., 2012. Distributed representations in memory: insights from functional brain imaging. Annu. Rev. Psychol. 63, 101–128.

Ritchey, M., Wing, E.A., LaBar, K.S., Cabeza, R., 2013. Neural similarity between encoding and retrieval is related to memory via hippocampal interactions. Cereb. Cortex 23 (12), 2818–2828.

Ritvo, V.J.H., Turk-Browne, N.B., Norman, K.A., 2019. Nonmonotonic plasticity: how memory retrieval drives learning. Trends Cogn. Sci. 23 (9), 726–742.

Rothschild, G., Eban, E., Frank, L.M., 2017. A cortical-hippocampal-cortical loop of information processing during memory consolidation. Nat. Neurosci. 20 (2), 251–259.

Rugg, M.D., Vilberg, K.L., 2013. Brain networks underlying episodic memory retrieval. Curr. Opin. Neurobiol. 23 (2), 255–260.

Rugg, M.D., Otten, L.J., Henson, R.N.A., 2002. The neural basis of episodic memory: evidence from functional neuroimaging. Philos. Trans. R. Soc. Lond. B Biol. Sci. 357 (1424), 1097–1110.

Schapiro, A.C., McDevitt, E.A., Rogers, T.T., Mednick, S.C., Norman, K.A., 2018. Human hippocampal replay during rest prioritizes weakly learned information and predicts memory performance. Nat. Commun. 9 (1), 1–11.

Scheinost, D., Hsu, T.W., Avery, E.W., Hampson, M., Constable, R.T., Chun, M.M., Rosenberg, M.D., 2020. Connectome-based neurofeedback: a pilot study to improve sustained attention. NeuroImage 12, 116684.

Schiller, D., Monfils, M.-H., Raio, C.M., Johnson, D.C., LeDoux, J.E., Phelps, E.A., 2010. Preventing the return of fear in humans using reconsolidation update mechanisms. Nature 463 (7277), 49–53.

Schlichting, M.L., Preston, A.R., 2015. Memory integration: neural mechanisms and implications for behavior. Curr. Opin. Behav. Sci. 1, 1–8.

Schönauer, M., Alizadeh, S., Jamalabadi, H., Abraham, A., Pawlizki, A., Gais, S., 2017. Decoding material-specific memory reprocessing during sleep in humans. Nat. Commun. 8 (1), 1–9.

Schreiner, T., Lehmann, M., Rasch, B., 2015. Auditory feedback blocks memory benefits of cueing during sleep. Nat. Commun. 6 (1), 1–11.

Selimbeyoglu, A., Parvizi, J., 2010. Electrical stimulation of the human brain: perceptual and behavioral phenomena reported in the old and new literature. Front. Hum. Neurosci. 4, 46.

Shibata, K., Watanabe, T., Sasaki, Y., Kawato, M., 2011. Perceptual learning incepted by decoded fMRI neurofeedback without stimulus presentation. Science 334 (6061), 1413–1415.

Spaniol, J., Davidson, P.S.R., Kim, A.S.N., Han, H., Moscovitch, M., Grady, C.L., 2009. Event-related fMRI studies of episodic encoding and retrieval: meta-analyses using activation likelihood estimation. Neuropsychologia 47 (8–9), 1765–1779.

St-Laurent, M., Abdi, H., Buchsbaum, B.R., 2015. Distributed patterns of reactivation predict vividness of recollection. Cogn. Neurosci. 27 (10), 2000–2018.

Stephens, G.J., Silbert, L.J., Hasson, U., 2010. Speaker-listener neural coupling underlies successful communication. Proc. Natl. Acad. Sci. 107 (32), 14425–14430.

Summerfield, C., Greene, M., Wager, T., Egner, T., Hirsch, J., Mangels, J., 2006. Neocortical connectivity during episodic memory formation. PLoS Biol. 4 (5), 855–864.

Suthana, N., Fried, I., 2014. Deep brain stimulation for enhancement of learning and memory. NeuroImage 85, 996–1002.

Suthana, N., Haneef, Z., Stern, J., Mukamel, R., Behnke, E., Knowlton, B., Fried, I., 2012. Memory enhancement and deep-brain stimulation of the entorhinal area. N. Engl. J. Med. 366 (6), 502–510.

Tambini, A., Davachi, L., 2019. Awake reactivation of prior experiences consolidates memories and biases cognition. Trends Cogn. Sci. 23 (10), 876–890.

Tambini, A., Nee, D.E., D'Esposito, M., 2018. Hippocampal-targeted theta-burst stimulation enhances associative memory formation. J. Cogn. Neurosci. 30 (10), 1452–1472.

Thakral, P.P., Wang, T.H., Rugg, M.D., 2015. Cortical reinstatement and the confidence and accuracy of source memory. NeuroImage 109, 118–129.

Thakral, P.P., Madore, K.P., Schacter, D.L., 2017. A role for the left angular gyrus in episodic simulation and memory. J. Neurosci. 37 (34), 8142–8149.

Tulving, E., 1983. Elements of Episodic Memory. Oxford University Press, Oxford.

Turk-Browne, N.B., Yi, D.-J., Chun, M.M., 2006. Linking implicit and explicit memory: common encoding factors and shared representations. Neuron 49 (6), 917–927.

Uncapher, M.R., Wagner, A.D., 2009. Posterior parietal cortex and episodic encoding: insights from fMRI subsequent memory effects and dual-attention theory. Neurobiol. Learn. Memory 91 (2), 139–154.

Vaz, A.P., Wittig, J.H., Inati, S.K., Zaghloul, K.A., 2020. Replay of cortical spiking sequences during human memory retrieval. Science 367 (6482), 1131–1134.

Wagner, A.D., Schacter, D.L., Rotte, M., Koutstaal, W., Maril, A., Dale, A.M., Rosen, B.R., Buckner, R.L., 1998. Building memories: remembering and forgetting of verbal experiences as predicted by brain activity. Science 281 (5380), 1188–1191.

Wang, J.X., Rogers, L.M., Gross, E.Z., Ryals, A.J., Dokucu, M.E., Brandstatt, K.L., Hermiller, M.S., Voss, J.L., 2014. Targeted enhancement of cortical-hippocampal brain networks and associative memory. Science 345 (6200), 1054–1057.

Wang, B., Antony, J.W., Lurie, S., Brooks, P.P., Paller, K.A., Norman, K.A., 2019. Targeted memory reactivation during sleep elicits neural signals related to learning content. J. Neurosci. 39 (34), 6728–6736.

Ward, E.J., Chun, M.M., Kuhl, B.A., 2013. Repetition suppression and multi-voxel pattern similarity differentially track implicit and explicit visual memory. J. Neurosci. 33 (37), 14749–14757.

Watrous, A.J., Tandon, N., Conner, C.R., Pieters, T., Ekstrom, A.D., 2013. Frequency-specific network connectivity increases underlie accurate spatiotemporal memory retrieval. Nat. Neurosci. 16 (3), 349–356.

Wing, E.A., Ritchey, M., Cabeza, R., 2015. Reinstatement of individual past events revealed by the similarity of distributed activation patterns during encoding and retrieval. J. Cogn. Neurosci. 27 (4), 679–691.

Xue, G., Dong, Q., Chen, C., Lu, Z., Mumford, J.A., Poldrack, R.A., 2010. Greater neural pattern similarity across repetitions is associated with better memory. Science 330 (6000), 97–101.

Yamashita, A., Hayasaka, S., Kawato, M., Imamizu, H., 2017. Connectivity neurofeedback training can differentially change functional connectivity and cognitive performance. Cereb. Cortex 27 (10), 4960–4970.

Yoo, J.J., Hinds, O., Ofen, N., Thompson, T.W., Whitfield-Gabrieli, S., Triantafyllou, C., Gabrieli, J.D.E., 2012. When the brain is prepared to learn: enhancing human learning using real-time fMRI. NeuroImage 59 (1), 846–852.

CHAPTER 6

Using fMRI neurofeedback to interrogate emotion, motivation, and social neurocognition

Kathryn C. Dickerson[a] **and R. Alison Adcock**[a,b,c]

[a]*Department of Psychiatry & Behavioral Sciences, Center for Cognitive Neuroscience, Duke University, Durham, NC, United States,* [b]*Department of Psychology & Neuroscience, Center for Cognitive Neuroscience, Duke University, Durham, NC, United States,* [c]*Department of Neurobiology, Center for Cognitive Neuroscience, Duke University, Durham, NC, United States*

1 Introduction

Among the most exciting aspects of real-time functional magnetic resonance imaging (rtfMRI) neurofeedback is that it allows access to aspects of the human experience that are highly individual and have traditionally been defined in terms of subjective experience. Emotion, motivation, and social cognition are among the most mysterious and complex aspects of human behavior. These functions have previously been interrogated mainly using an experimenter's informed but imperfect guess at effective external triggers (e.g., food, money) and validated with participant introspection or retrospection. Dynamic access to neural events that coincide with affective experience offers a tremendous new advantage for the basic neuroscience of affective and social brain function.

In this chapter, we examine the subfield of rtfMRI neurofeedback studies that explore questions related to social and affective neuroscience. The use of fMRI neurofeedback permits scientists to tackle compelling questions such as: Can people regulate brain areas involved in emotion, motivation, or reward processing, which have often traditionally been viewed as ancient, primitive, and beyond volitional control? Can they learn to incorporate these skills into daily life? Can they modulate brain activity during pain processing? How do networks in the brain change when a single brain region is regulated? A primary and foundational research question in this field centers on understanding whether individuals can regulate brain activity within a certain region of interest or circuit and its associated brain networks. A secondary, equally important question, is whether this leads to behavioral changes. We will explore both of these questions throughout this chapter as we examine how scientists use rtfMRI neurofeedback within the domain of social and affective neuroscience.

fMRI Neurofeedback. https://doi.org/10.1016/B978-0-12-822421-2.00001-6

We begin by giving a brief overview of the neural systems engaged in social and affective processes and the regions of interest targeted in prior neurofeedback studies. We then examine common research questions, and discuss representative empirical studies using rtfMRI neurofeedback within the domain of social and affective neuroscience. We conclude by discussing exciting open questions and future directions.

2 Social and affective neuroscience

Emotions, motivations, and the intersubjectivity arising from interactions with others are some of the most mysterious and complex aspects of human behavior. The field of affective neuroscience examines the generation, expression, and regulation of emotions and motivational states, and explores behavioral, physiological, and neural markers of these states. Brain regions implicated in emotional experiences include limbic regions such as the amygdala and hippocampus; subcortical areas including the basal ganglia, cingulate cortex, insula, and midbrain nuclei; and cortical areas including the prefrontal cortex (Cromwell et al., 2020).

Importantly, although emotion is frequently conceptualized (and studied) as a reaction to events in the world, affective states are often *anticipatory* of predicted outcomes: worry and excitement are common examples. These and other predictive affective states are important determinants of our experience of the world, and regulate its representation in memory (Murty and Alison Adcock, 2017; Dickerson and Adcock, 2018) which, in turn, guides future behavior. The impact of predictive affect on experience and behavior makes clear that affect regulation should continue to be a priority target for therapeutic interventions in mental health. The human ability to generate internal representations (ideas and images) also makes these target processes for neurofeedback directed at regulating affect. The extended time course of affective changes and their impact on cognition is especially appropriate for neurofeedback interventions using fMRI, because these are well matched to the temporal resolution dictated by the hemodynamic lag for continuous-feedback studies.

These are some of the reasons our research group has studied and aimed to characterize anticipatory affect. We have focused on anticipatory affect in the context of *motivation* because motivation manifests in both behavioral and cognitive outcomes and subjective states attached to the predicted events. This approach has allowed us to characterize several distinct motivational states at the behavioral, cognitive, and neural levels. Many readers will be familiar with distinctions like approach versus avoidance that make reference to incentives and goals, or intrinsic versus extrinsic, which likewise localize the goals, but remain agnostic to their implications for subjective experience of these anticipatory affects.

As might be predicted from a perspective that predictive affect filters experience, we have found that it is how the brain *responds* to an incentive that determines its impact on learning and memory—not its objective value or valence. Our work suggests additional distinctions related to the quality of evidence for a course of action and to neurotransmitter distribution systems, although we use incentive valence to elicit these motivations: Interrogative states, which are more common during reward anticipation, can be contrasted with imperative states, which are more commonly elicited by threats (Murty and Alison Adcock, 2017; Dickerson and Adcock, 2018). We have previously demonstrated that these motivational states produce distinct configurations of neuromodulatory networks. Interrogative motivated states engage the ventral tegmental area (VTA) which supports hippocampal-dependent encoding. Imperative motivated states engage a different neural network, namely the amygdala and cortical medial temporal lobe. These anticipatory states bias ongoing perceptual and cognitive processing and influence the physiology of memory systems both at the time of encoding (Murty et al., 2016) and during consolidation (Murty et al., 2017) to yield distinct forms of memory—either relational (VTA-hippocampus) or sparse representation of behaviorally relevant features (amygdala-medial temporal lobe). Importantly, imperative states can emerge in the presence of reward incentives, and not only when those incentives present objectively "high" stakes. Why an individual may construe an opportunity as a threat and whether we can correct this bias is a focus of our ongoing research.

Social neuroscience is a relatively new, interdisciplinary field focused on examining how humans interact and the neural substrates that support social behavior. Neural regions involved in these processes include the amygdala, temporal parietal junction, superior temporal sulcus, and medial prefrontal cortex (Gilam and Hendler, 2016). Relative to affective neuroscience, significantly less research has used rtfMRI neurofeedback to address research questions in the domain of social neuroscience. Work discussed in this chapter includes examining the efficacy of using social stimuli (e.g., a smiling face) for neurofeedback rather than typical informational neurofeedback stimuli (e.g., a thermometer). We expect rtfMRI neurofeedback studies in social neuroscience to be a growing area, especially as technological advances push the boundaries of what is achievable within this domain, extending studies of neural coordination during social interactions (e.g., neural synchrony) currently shown using other physiological modalities (Quiñones-Camacho et al., 2019; Cheong et al., 2020). For example, the recent development of hyperscanning may allow researchers to conduct a rtfMRI study collecting data from more than one person simultaneously. This opens the opportunity for brain-to-brain communication, which can be particularly interesting for social neuroscience questions (e.g., exploring a complex topic such as trust between friends).

Given the profound role of emotions in the human experience, and the observation that emotion dysregulation is implicated in many psychological disorders, it is not surprising that both translational and basic science researchers want to understand whether and how humans can regulate regions involved in the generation, expression, or regulation of affect. Understanding if humans can volitionally control activation within affective brain regions promises to not only deepen our understanding of the mechanisms of these neural systems, but also holds promise for novel clinical treatments. For example, if people can volitionally increase activation of neural substrates of motivation, as discussed in this chapter, this ability could be harnessed to improve learning and memory and may also prove to be a powerful tool for individuals with disorders where motivation is characteristically low, such as depression or attention deficit hyperactivity disorder (ADHD).

3 Learning from neurofeedback: Assessments, evidence, and mechanisms

Neurofeedback is a dynamic method of perturbing brain systems, and its impacts manifest over multiple timescales, via multiple mechanisms, implying multiple forms of plasticity and learning. Thus, in addition to considering psychological and computational functions and the neural systems involved in these functions, we must also consider possible plastic mechanisms in evaluating the implications of neurofeedback research findings. These aspects of interpretation are especially relevant in the domains of affect and social function because many different mechanisms of learning contribute to adaptive functioning in these domains. However, these mechanistic considerations are also relevant to other studies of higher order cognition.

A first fundamental question to be addressed in such studies is: Does the introduction of neurofeedback impact regulation of a neural system at all? Establishing this impact is often approached by comparing attempted regulation using veridical neurofeedback from a region of interest during a specific goal (the experimental condition: e.g., upregulate the amygdala) to baseline trials (e.g., rest or backward counting) and/or regulation using altered feedback or feedback from a control brain region (see Fig. 1 for an example task design). The demonstration that a region's dynamic range of activation changes selectively when veridical feedback is provided supports a conclusion that the neurofeedback enhances regulation

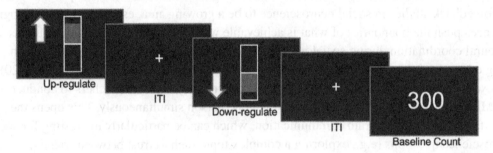

Fig. 1

Example real-time fMRI neurofeedback task design. Many rtMRI experiments examining emotion and motivational processes involve up- and/or downregulation of a specified region of interest (ROI). This example task shows three conditions commonly used in rtfMRI neurofeedback paradigms. Indicated by the *up-arrow*, subjects are asked to increase the height of the feedback bar by performing some cognitive task (e.g., recalling a positive autobiographical memory). In contrast, indicated by the *down-arrow*, subjects are asked to decrease the height of the feedback bar (e.g., using an emotion regulation strategy). As a control condition, subjects are asked to count backward by a given increment (e.g., 4), beginning at a specified value (e.g., 300). Passive rest is another common baseline condition. By comparing activation in up- and/or downregulation trials to baseline, scientists examine whether individuals can volitionally regulate the neural region of interest.

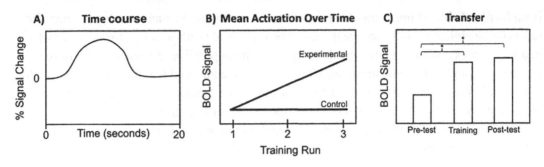

Fig. 2

Example post hoc analyses of hypothetical rtfMRI neurofeedback data. Many rtfMRI neurofeedback experiments involve up- and/or downregulation of a region of interest (ROI), depending on the constructs being studied. Above are example analyses scientists may use to examine upregulation of a region of interest (ROI) in rtfMRI paradigms. (A) Trial level: time course data examines the percent BOLD signal change of a particular ROI within a given time period (e.g., upregulation trials). This is typically examined at the trial level within one or multiple subjects. (B) Group run level: scientists also commonly examine how mean activation changes over the course of NF training (e.g., runs). Here we can see that the experimental group increases BOLD activation throughout training, while the control group does not. (C) Group mean data across runs: many paradigms examine whether individuals can reproduce regulation of a given ROI after NF training (referred to as transfer). This is commonly done by including a pre- and posttest that are similar in design to the training runs, but do not contain NF. Here we see individuals upregulate the ROI both during and after training. Furthermore, posttest activation is significantly higher than the pretest activation, indicating learning.

of the target (see Fig. 2 for example common post hoc analyses of hypothetical rtfMRI data and Chapter 3 for further discussion of the various methods for assessing impacts of neurofeedback on brain regulation).

The demonstration that neurofeedback enhances regulation is one important contribution to our body of knowledge. A separate contribution, however, is to demonstrate **learning** to regulate brain systems. Claims about learning from neurofeedback require not only a demonstration that neurofeedback changes brain activation while it is being delivered, but also a change in activation over time (that is specific to veridical feedback). This can be established in several ways: for example an increase over time—a learning curve— in dynamic range of activation or pattern similarity during neurofeedback training (as illustrated in Fig. 2B). Another sort of evidence for learning involves the **transfer** of the ability to regulate, that is reproducing the regulation in new experimental contexts without feedback (shown in Fig. 2C) or—the ultimate goal for many clinical applications—in daily life.

The term "transfer" to describe the ability to regulate a target region in untrained contexts (and in a posttest relative to a pretest without feedback) reflects the influence of conventions from **feedback-based instrumental reinforcement learning**. In such paradigms, 'transfer' refers to the ability of skills once acquired to be replicated (with some performance cost) in a new context. While this may be the only mechanism possible in some paradigms (e.g., implicit training), other paradigms are likely to involve additional learning mechanisms which may contribute to the long-term impact of neurofeedback training. An important elaboration of our current dominant paradigms is to consider the contributions of other learning mechanisms besides feedback-based instrumental reinforcement to the changes seen after neurofeedback training.

These additional possible mechanisms include (among others) **metacognition**, in which participants explore multiple regulation strategies and evaluate their efficacy comparatively, and explicit **episodic memory** for the overall neurofeedback training session (for examples see MacInnes et al., 2016; MacDuffie et al., 2018). These mechanisms have qualitatively different temporal dynamics from reinforcement learning, including nonlinear learning curves, and may also impact future behavior. For example, metacognitive strategy evaluation during feedback learning may result in transfer that shows no decrement but rather a counterintuitive performance gain after removing the feedback signal in a posttest. We previously hypothesized that episodic memory for the novel and salient demonstration of brain-behavior relationships during a neurofeedback training session may change future behavior via increased motivation, arising from amplifying the perceived utility of regulation (MacDuffie et al., 2018). Learning to regulate affective brain systems, like many complex learning problems, involves multiple memory systems.

4 Using fMRI neurofeedback to study social and affective neuroscience questions

Scientists are actively examining several interesting research questions within brain regions involved in the generation and expression of affect. Core themes include reward processing, generation of motivational states, emotion regulation, empathy, and pain processing. In the following sections we explore each of these topics in depth, examining what scientists have discovered thus far and identifying areas for future discovery. See Fig. 3 for an overview.

The majority of studies discussed in this chapter have focused on giving research participants neurofeedback from an individual neural region within the affective brain (e.g., amygdala). Of course no single brain area operates in isolation and thus scientists also often examine neural networks engaged during neurofeedback or changes in connectivity among brain regions following neurofeedback training. Less work has been devoted to examining neurofeedback based on connectivity between multiple regions and this remains an area for future research.

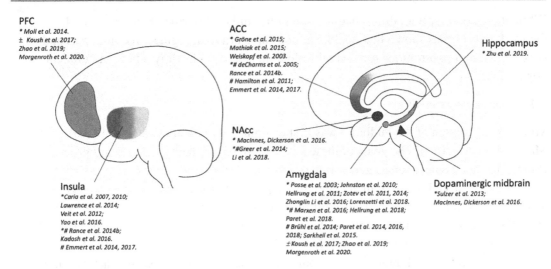

PFC
* Moll et al. 2014.
± Koush et al. 2017;
Zhao et al. 2019;
Morgenroth et al. 2020.

ACC
* Gröne et al. 2015;
Mathiak et al. 2015;
Weiskopf et al. 2003.
*# deCharms et al. 2005;
Rance et al. 2014b.
Hamilton et al. 2011;
Emmert et al. 2014, 2017.

Hippocampus
* Zhu et al. 2019.

NAcc
* MacInnes, Dickerson et al. 2016.
*#Greer et al. 2014;
Li et al. 2018.

Insula
*Caria et al. 2007, 2010;
Lawrence et al. 2014;
Veit et al. 2012;
Yao et al. 2016.
*# Rance et al. 2014b;
Kadosh et al. 2016.
Emmert et al. 2014, 2017.

Amygdala
* Posse et al. 2003; Johnston et al. 2010;
Hellrung et al. 2011; Zotev et al. 2011, 2014;
Zhonglin Li et al. 2016; Lorenzetti et al. 2018.
*# Marxen et al. 2016; Hellrung et al. 2018;
Paret et al. 2018.
Brühl et al. 2014; Paret et al. 2014, 2016,
2018; Sarkheil et al. 2015.
± Koush et al. 2017; Zhao et al. 2019;
Morgenroth et al. 2020.

Dopaminergic midbrain
*Sulzer et al. 2013;
MacInnes, Dickerson et al. 2016.

Fig. 3

Neuroanatomical regions commonly studied in affective real-time fMRI neurofeedback studies. Color shading indicates the following affective domains: black = reward and motivational processing, light gray = empathy, medium gray = emotion regulation, and dark gray = pain processing. *PFC*, prefrontal cortex; *ACC*, anterior cingulate cortex; *NAcc*, nucleus accumbens. * denotes studies referenced in this chapter examining volitional upregulation of the ROI; # denotes studies referenced in this chapter examining downregulation of the ROI. ± denotes connectivity-based studies referenced in this chapter.

4.1 Reward processing and generation of motivated states

Research investigating regulation of reward and motivation processes within healthy adults using rtfMRI neurofeedback (NF) is only just beginning. To date, only four studies have examined individuals' ability to regulate brain regions involved in generating reward or motivated states, namely the dopamine system. The ability to volitionally control these processes is exciting from both a basic science as well as a clinical applications perspective. The dopamine system is involved in numerous processes critical to adaptive behavior, including motivation (Salamone and Correa, 2012), action initiation (Roitman et al., 2004), action contingency (Tricomi et al., 2004), agency (Leotti and Delgado, 2011), effort allocation (Botvinick et al., 2009), cognitive control (Braver and Barch, 2002), and valuation (Wimmer et al., 2012). Furthermore, disruptions in these systems underlie several neurological and psychological disorders, including depression, Parkinson's disease, ADHD, and substance use disorders (Maia and Frank, 2011).

As described later, two studies to date focused on regulation of the dopaminergic midbrain (Sulzer et al., 2013b; MacInnes et al., 2016) and three studies used the nucleus accumbens (NAcc) (Greer et al., 2014; Li et al., 2018; MacInnes et al., 2016) as their region of interest (part of the basal ganglia that receives substantial input from midbrain dopamine neurons).

While there are important differences between the studies described here, in general, the work thus far has shown that healthy adults can learn to upregulate the midbrain and NAcc, opening opportunities for several follow-up studies in healthy adults and clinical populations.

4.1.1 Dopaminergic midbrain

Volitional regulation of the midbrain was first examined by Sulzer et al. (2013b) and MacInnes et al. (2016). The goals of these studies differed in their focus: reward processing (Sulzer and colleagues) versus generation of motivated states (MacInnes et al., 2016). Sulzer and colleagues asked if young men could utilize pleasant or romantic imagery to increase activation within the midbrain. Their ROI included the ventral tegmental area (VTA) and substantia nigra (SN): midbrain nuclei that contain the majority of dopamine neurons in the brain. Individuals were assigned to receive either valid (often termed veridical) NF from the midbrain or inverted midbrain NF (as a control comparison). They measured activation before (pretest), during (training), and after (posttest) neurofeedback training. Interestingly, both groups were able to increase midbrain activation prior to NF training (pretest). However, only those in the veridical NF group were able to further increase activation during NF training runs relative to the pretest. The authors next examined whether there was an effect of transfer, typically measured as the ability to increase brain activation following removal of the NF training stimulus. As discussed before, this is an important metric of learning in NF studies as it indicates that individuals are able to recreate engagement of a ROI in a novel context. This metric is important for potential extrapolation to real-world contexts outside of the research MRI environment.

In this study, Sulzer et al. (2013b) observed no evidence of transfer: participants were unable to recreate increased activation of the midbrain observed during training in the posttest. This finding is characteristic of many neurofeedback studies: participants succeed at increasing brain activation while interacting with the NF stimulus directly, but they are unable to recreate that activation once the NF stimulus is removed. Sulzer and colleagues also reported activation in several other areas of the brain including the hippocampus, striatum, and cingulate (among others) during neurofeedback trials compared to rest. The authors concluded that individuals can regulate midbrain activation and that receiving NF boosts their ability to do so. Limitations of this study include the choice of control group, examining the question in men only (pilot work by the group determined using romantic imagery in men produced reliable midbrain activation), and not exploring potential downstream behavioral impacts of midbrain self-regulation. Choosing a control group is one of the greatest challenges of rtfMRI studies currently. One limitation of using an inverted signal for the control group is that it makes it difficult to understand what is driving the different pattern of activation observed across groups. For example, group differences in regulation could be caused by the veridical signal increasing, which could be a true increase or due to practice effects. The inverted signal could cause confusion among participants, thus not providing a tight control for regulation ability. Including an additional comparison group that does not receive inverted/false feedback would be an important addition to this work.

Work from MacInnes et al. (2016) examined regulation of the dopaminergic midbrain using an approach that focused on the generation of motivated states, rather than reward. They asked men and women to generate personalized motivated states with the goal of increasing activation within the VTA (note, this ROI did not include the SN given its involvement in motor rather than affective processes). Healthy adults were assigned to one of four groups: veridical VTA NF, veridical NAcc NF, sham NF (noise that was portrayed as real NF), or visual control (here a predictable moving stimulus that participants knew did not reflect brain activation but was a cue to focus on during the regulation task). In this study, individuals in the VTA NF group were initially unable to increase activation within the VTA during the pretest (prior to NF training). As predicted, the veridical VTA group showed increased activation during NF training. Importantly, the veridical VTA group also generalized this skill. The veridical VTA group reproduced VTA activation when NF was removed following training, in the posttest. This transfer was the first evidence of such learning from neurofeedback for brain reward systems. Excitingly, VTA activation was also sustained over a relatively long period of time (20 s) in the posttest. This pattern is important because dopaminergic neurons fire to unexpected stimuli with a rapid burst of firing, corresponding to a short peak in the blood oxygenation level-dependent (BOLD) response measured via fMRI (4–6 s) (Knutson et al., 2001; Delgado et al., 2000). Thus the enhanced, sustained activation observed here supports the hypothesis of engagement of motivational states, beyond mere reward responses, and was an important novel contribution to the field.

Neither the sham or visual control groups demonstrated enhanced VTA responses during the pretest, training phase, or posttest. (See the Section 4.1.2 later for results from the veridical NAcc group.) Thus receipt of valid VTA NF was critical for participants to learn to self-activate the VTA. The authors also examined changes in functional connectivity among reward regions, including the VTA, NAcc, hippocampus, and caudate nucleus. Increased connectivity was observed between the VTA and hippocampus and the NAcc and hippocampus in the posttest relative to the pretest, suggesting plasticity within this network. A main limitation of this study was not examining downstream behavioral impacts of VTA regulation.

Taken together these studies suggest that individuals can volitionally modulate midbrain activity in the presence of reward cues (Sulzer et al., 2013b) and can also learn to do so even without external rewards or cues (MacInnes et al., 2016). Interestingly, although both of these studies focused on upregulation of the midbrain dopamine system using rtfMRI NF, the research question, approach, and conclusions one can draw differ. Differences in study design include selection of participants (men only versus men and women),

ROI (VTA/SN versus VTA only), suggested regulation strategy (romantic imagery vs. motivated states and metacognitive evaluation of strategies), stimuli (smiling face vs. nonvalenced cue), and choice of methodological parameters (2 s versus 1 s TR). These are noted here to bring awareness that there are many approaches to designing and analyzing rtfMRI studies. Furthermore, depending on the research question and approach, these choices can directly impact the observed results.

4.1.2 Nucleus accumbens

Greer and colleagues were the first to examine volitional regulation of the NAcc using rtfMRI neurofeedback (Greer et al., 2014). The NAcc is part of the ventral striatum in the basal ganglia and receives significant input from the dopaminergic midbrain. Often conceptualized as merely a reward region, the NAcc's role in behavior is more nuanced: its function is central to many processes including action selection, approaching motivationally relevant information, improving action efficiency, and goal-directed behavior (Floresco, 2015).

In this first study examining regulation of the NAcc, Greer and colleagues asked if healthy adults could volitionally up- and downregulate this region by thinking about exciting or boring events, respectively. Participants successfully increased NAcc activation in the pretest, training runs, and posttest. However, activation in the posttest was not significantly greater than training or pretest activation. Although participants were able to increase NAcc, they were unable to significantly decrease activation in the NAcc. One explanation the authors offer for this dichotomy is that dopamine signals convey information about goal achievement (among other things); therefore successful downregulation of the NAcc could cause an increase in dopamine responses, paradoxically canceling out any decreased activation. Greer and colleagues concluded that individuals can increase, but not decrease, activation of the NAcc. While an important first study, this work did not include a control group and did not examine changes in behavior based on NAcc activation. Future studies examining upregulation of the NAcc could explore the behavioral impacts of NAcc regulation, including modification of motivational, learning, or decision-making processes.

As part of the examination of regulation of the VTA, MacInnes and Dickerson et al. also examined healthy adults' ability to increase activation within the NAcc using motivational strategies (MacInnes et al., 2016). Unlike the adults who received NF from the VTA, those who received NF from the NAcc were unable to significantly increase activation above baseline prior to, during, or following NAcc NF. What can account for the differences observed between the findings of MacInnes and Dickerson et al., and those of Greer and colleagues? MacInnes and Dickerson et al. were interested in exploring the temporal dynamics of both the VTA and NAcc signal. They were interested in examining sustained activation of these regions, which may signal motivational processes, rather than a rapid reward response. Thus MacInnes and Dickerson et al. examined the mean activation over a relatively long period of time (20 s). Greer and colleagues, on the other hand, were not explicitly examining motivation at this longer timescale. Rather, they focused on immediate activation (which tended to be the strongest activation) using positive, exciting, and or arousing mental imagery. In order to more directly compare these findings, MacInnes and colleagues performed the same analysis as Greer et al., and replicated their findings: significant NAcc activation in the pretest, training, and posttest phases. This example again highlights the fact that analysis choices scientists make can have a significant impact on the observed findings.

The most recent study to examine regulation of the NAcc in healthy adults was performed by Li et al. (2018). They asked female participants to both increase (regulation blocks) and decrease (baseline blocks) NAcc activity by anticipating exciting events or doing mental math (respectively) during two rtfMRI training sessions. A key focus of this paper was examining individual differences in the ability to regulate NAcc as well as personality measures that may track NAcc regulation. Based on NAcc activation, the authors divided participants into learners and nonlearners. To characterize these groups they subtracted the NAcc activation in each baseline block from the subsequent regulation block. They then examined if this difference score changed over time. If the NAcc activation in regulation vs. baseline blocks increased over time in one or both sessions, they labeled the participant as a learner, otherwise they characterized her as a nonlearner.

One of the most interesting parts of this study is the characterization of individual differences in NAcc response and its relationship with personality measures and motivational tasks. The authors examined how self-regulation of the NAcc impacts behavior. Participants in the study completed the Temporal Experience Pleasure Scale (TEPS) (Gard et al., 2006) and Behavioral Inhibition System/Behavioral Activation System scale (BIS/BAS) (Carver and White, 1994) questionnaires as well as the Effort Expenditure for Rewards Task (EEfRT) (Treadway et al., 2009) and the Anticipatory and Consummatory Pleasure Task (ACP) (Heerey and Gold, 2007) prior to and following rtfMRI training. In addition, they completed the Monetary Incentive Delay task (MID) (Knutson et al., 2001) pre- and post-rtfMRI training while inside the MRI scanner.

The authors found that about 70% of women in the experimental group were able to regulate the NAcc in at least one session. Compared to the nonlearning group, the learning group had several markers of enhanced motivation as indicated by both the questionnaire findings and performance on the tasks. For example, the learning group had a higher BAS-Drive score than the nonlearning group at baseline. This could indicate differences in trait motivation across individuals who learn versus those who do not learn NAcc regulation. Future studies could test the reliability of this observation by using this measure at baseline to try to predict which individuals learn to regulate reward regions.

The authors also observed that after rtfMRI NF training, the learning group demonstrated an increased press rate during the anticipation phase of the ACP task (anticipation of viewing positive and avoiding negative pictures) and faster reaction time during anticipation of monetary gains and losses following NF training. (Note the nonlearning group also showed increased reaction time to monetary gain trials following NF training).

Though the authors had a control group who received NF from the posterior parahippocampal gyrus, the group was small ($N = 5$). In addition, a main limitation of this work is that there was no pre- or posttest; the rt-fMRI sessions all included a neurofeedback stimulus. Thus it is not possible to test transfer of NAcc regulation outside of the NF context. Li and colleagues concluded that individuals can regulate the NAcc and that this may improve motivated behavior (as measured by press rate and reaction time) on certain tasks.

4.1.3 Interim summary

Taken as a whole, the studies discussed in this section suggest that individuals can regulate the dopaminergic midbrain and the NAcc and that increased NAcc activation may affect motivated behavior. These results have important basic science and clinical implications (see, e.g., Chapter 9 for clinical applications to addiction). The dopamine system is involved in numerous processes critical to adaptive behavior, including motivation (Salamone and Correa, 2012), action initiation (Roitman et al., 2004), action contingency (Tricomi et al., 2004), agency (Leotti and Delgado, 2011), effort allocation (Botvinick et al., 2009), cognitive control (Braver and Barch, 2002), and valuation (Wimmer et al., 2012). As such, learning to engage this system on demand has many exciting applications. For example, upregulation of dopamine regions could improve effort allocation or cognitive control, ultimately enhancing adaptive behavior. There are also numerous clinical applications given that the dopamine system is disrupted in several disorders, including schizophrenia, ADHD, substance abuse disorders, and depression (Maia and Frank, 2011).

Yet, even in the four studies discussed here there is great variability in the results observed and the conclusions one can draw. This serves as a reminder that real-time fMRI is a relatively novel field. As such, there is great heterogeneity in how scientists design, execute, and analyze rt-fMRI studies. For example, there are many software packages scientists can use during the data collection phase, with many groups using custom in-house software. There are several approaches used when collecting the data (single ROI, functional connectivity, MVPA, etc.) and analyzing the results (peak time-point, time series, regressing out physiological noise). One of the greatest challenges lies with deciding on control conditions and groups [yoked sham NF vs. veridical NF from a control ROI vs. random noise; for a discussion on this topic see (Sorger et al., 2019)]. All this variability makes it difficult to make firm conclusions when extrapolating across studies. As more research is conducted with rt-fMRI neurofeedback, we expect to have more definitive answers to the many pressing questions remaining in this field.

4.2 Emotion regulation

The ability to regulate one's emotions is critical to adaptive behavior (Hartley and Phelps, 2010). It is no surprise therefore that a substantial amount of rtfMRI NF studies to date have examined this important research question (for review, see Linhartová et al., 2019). In the relatively nascent field of rtfMRI neurofeedback, perhaps the most highly studied brain region to date has been the amygdala (for review, see Barreiros et al., 2019). Here we will discuss representative empirical findings examining regulation of the amygdala in social and affective neuroscience (see Chapter 8 for clinical studies examining this question). While the amygdala has dominated the field of emotion regulation rtfMRI NF research, there has also been interesting work focusing on other parts of the emotion network, including the hippocampus, insula, and anterior cingulate cortex (ACC), which we will also discuss here. Readers who are excited to learn more about this work are referred to (Linhartová et al., 2019) for a recent systematic literature review.

4.2.1 Amygdala

There have been nearly twenty rt-fMRI studies to date focusing on emotion regulation using rtfMRI neurofeedback from the amygdala (for review, see Barreiros et al., 2019). In the present chapter we will highlight a few papers to illustrate the types of questions scientists are exploring in healthy adults. The vast majority of work examining amygdala regulation has focused on upregulation (Johnston et al., 2010; Li et al., 2016; Lorenzetti et al., 2018; Posse et al., 2003; Zotev et al., 2011, 2014), though some studies have examined downregulation (Brühl et al., 2014; Paret et al., 2014; Sarkheil et al., 2015), or up- and downregulation (Hellrung et al., 2018; Marxen et al., 2016; Paret et al., 2018).

One of the first studies to take advantage of rt-fMRI technology and examine emotion regulation in the amygdala was conducted by Posse and colleagues (Posse et al., 2003). In this proof-of-concept study, healthy adults viewed sad or neutral faces as part of an emotion induction paradigm and reported their level of sadness following each face. Unlike the majority of neurofeedback studies that use visual feedback, here the authors provided feedback to participants by verbally telling them the degree of activation within their amygdala. As hypothesized, self-reported sadness and amygdala activation were correlated during the majority of sad trials (78%) and the minority of neutral trials (14%). This early study did not use a control group, did not have a pre- or posttest, and the sample size was quite small (six participants total). However, the authors examined their effect across hundreds of trials and scanned some participants more than once to examine reproducibility of their findings. The authors concluded that amygdala activation in response to sad mood could be observed at the single trial level using rt-fMRI. The findings from this proof-of-concept study are consistent with the wide body of research implicating the amygdala with negative mood (for example, see Schaefer et al., 2002).

An interesting line of more recent research has examined regulation of the amygdala by utilizing positive autobiographical memory recall (Zotev et al., 2011, 2013). We will discuss the initial study that used this paradigm in healthy adult volunteers here; please see Chapter 8 for discussion of a line of research using this paradigm in individuals with major depressive disorder. In the initial study (Zotev et al., 2011), healthy adults were assigned to either the experimental or control group. Participants aimed to increase activation in the amygdala (experimental group) or a brain region not engaged in emotional processing, the horizontal segment of the intraparietal sulcus (HIPS; control group), by recalling positive autobiographical memories. Individuals in the experimental group increased activation in the amygdala during training and a posttest (transfer) run. Those in the control group were unable to regulate amygdala activation and neither group activated the HIPS. The authors concluded that healthy adults could learn to control amygdala activation by thinking about positive autobiographical memories when provided with amygdala neurofeedback, an important finding they have pursued in clinical populations.

Hellrung and colleagues recently used the same paradigm as developed by Zotev et al. (2011) to examine an important methodological question: whether intermittent or continuous NF is more effective for learning (Hellrung et al., 2018). The majority of studies to date use continuous NF (e.g., a moving thermometer updates each NF value as soon as it is acquired). However, NF paradigms are cognitively demanding and subjectively, participants often report fatigue at the end of the rtfMRI session. In the present paper, the authors investigated if providing intermittent NF (here conceptualized as one summary value at the end of each trial) would be more effective than continuous NF. They assigned individuals to one of three groups: no NF, continuous NF, or intermittent NF. Individuals who did not receive NF failed to learn to regulate the amygdala. Interestingly, those who received intermittent NF performed better during training compared to the continuous NF group in terms of improvement across training runs, although this difference was not significant. In addition, the authors found increased activation in regions involved in cognitive load, including the insula and inferior frontal gyrus, in the continuous NF group relative to the intermittent NF group (in the last training run). Interestingly, there was no difference in amygdala regulation across the intermittent and continuous NF groups in the transfer run (both significantly increased amygdala activation), suggesting both NF methods lead to the ability to self-regulate the amygdala. Thus while this paper suggests some (nonsignificant) differences during training between the continuous and intermittent NF group, more research should examine this important question. Indeed, many open questions remain regarding how individuals learn from neurofeedback (for discussion of these ideas, see Emmert et al., 2016; Oblak et al., 2017; Sitaram et al., 2017).

While the majority of studies have focused on increasing amygdala activation (Johnston et al., 2010; Li et al., 2016; Lorenzetti et al., 2018; Posse et al., 2003; Zotev et al., 2011, 2014), some studies have examined both up- and downregulation of the amygdala

(Hellrung et al., 2018; Marxen et al., 2016; Paret et al., 2018) or focused solely on downregulation (Brühl et al., 2014; Paret et al., 2014; Sarkheil et al., 2015; see Linhartová et al., 2019 for review). Paret and colleagues have been interested in examining whether healthy adults can learn to downregulate amygdala activity (Paret et al., 2014, 2016, 2018) given hyperactivity of this region is implicated in psychological disorders including borderline personality disorder. In their initial study with healthy adults, women were randomly assigned to receive NF from either the amygdala or the basal ganglia (served as a control ROI). During training, participants viewed either aversive images or control scrambled images. On each trial they were instructed to regulate their emotions while viewing an aversive image or simply to view it (with no emotion regulation). Individuals in both groups were able to decrease activation in the amygdala during regulate trials compared with view trials; however, these differences were not significant after correcting for multiple comparisons. Similarly, the experimental group decreased activation in the right amygdala during the transfer run (though again this effect did not remain after correcting for multiple comparisons). While the results are in the expected direction in this initial study, further work is required to determine if individuals can significantly downregulate the amygdala. Further, this initial study did not include a pretest, making it impossible to compare activation in the posttest to a similar condition prior to training.

In sum, a growing body of research indicates that healthy adults can volitionally upregulate activation in the amygdala using a variety of emotion regulation strategies (see Barreiros et al., 2019 for a systematic review of these findings). While initial results show promise, more work is needed to determine whether adults can downregulate amygdala activation. Given the critical role of the amygdala in emotional processing, perception, attention, learning, and memory modification (for review, see Phelps and LeDoux, 2005), understanding the ability to modify it on demand has important basic science and clinical applications.

4.2.2 Hippocampus

Relatively less research has been devoted to investigating affective questions using the hippocampus as an ROI in healthy individuals. This may be because NF studies examining the hippocampus focus on memory, rather than affect per se (see Chapter 5 for NF studies of memory). Recently, Zhu and colleagues recruited healthy adults to randomly receive neurofeedback from either the hippocampus (experimental group) or the intraparietal sulcus (control group) (Zhu et al., 2019). All participants completed two fMRI sessions, each containing one rest run and two training runs. During the NF regulate trials, participants were instructed to increase activation within their assigned ROI by thinking about positive autobiographical memories. Interestingly, in this study, NF was delivered as a numerical value (e.g., + 1.45); no graphical display was used. During view trials, participants viewed positive images and tried to imagine experiencing the depicted situation (e.g., birthday party). Count trials served as a baseline (participants counted backward). Participants in the experimental group observed increased activation in the hippocampus for the comparison of regulate > baseline over training runs (run 4 > run 1). This pattern was not observed for the comparison of view > baseline and was also not observed in the control group. However, one limitation of this work is the way the data are analyzed. The authors report only *t*-tests, which are modest; they did not report ANOVA results. Furthermore, this study did not include a pre- and posttest, making the comparison across test runs impossible. Thus, while this line of work holds promise, these results should be interpreted with caution and replicated.

4.2.3 Insula

Given the insula's role in emotion and affective processing (Simmons et al., 2013), scientists have examined healthy adults' ability to voluntarily regulate the insula using emotion regulation techniques (see Linhartová et al., 2019 for review). Caria and colleagues have examined this question across a series of experiments beginning by asking whether individuals can upregulate insula activation by recalling personal emotional memories. Participants were assigned to either the experimental group or one of two control groups (Caria et al., 2007). Those in the experimental group received neurofeedback from the right anterior insula (RAI). To account for global signal fluctuations, signal in a control ROI (whole brain slice) was subtracted from the RAI. During regulation trials participants were instructed to try to increase activation in the RAI by recalling personal emotional memories (either positive or negative). Individuals were allowed to explore to identify strategies that were effective for them. During baseline trials participants counted backward and tried to decrease activation in the RAI. Three subjects each participated in two control conditions: sham neurofeedback (from a background ROI) or no neurofeedback. Individuals in the experimental group successfully increased activation in the RAI during training and posttest (transfer). Similar, though weaker, activation was observed in the left anterior insula. During training, a linear increase in activation across the four training runs was observed. Neither control group successfully increased RAI activation. Furthermore, analysis from control brain regions did not exhibit the same pattern of activation as observed in the RAI, indicating specificity of the effect. This was the first study to demonstrate volitional activation of the insula using rtfMRI neurofeedback. Limitations of this study include a small sample size and lack of a pretest in the experimental design. Not all NF studies include a pretest, in fact many do not, and there is no standard to date for the structure of NF studies. However, including a pretest is an important way to measure an individual's baseline ability to up- or downregulate an ROI prior to training with NF.

Caria and colleagues built upon their initial study and next asked if insula self-regulation would impact behavioral responses (arousal and valence ratings) to emotional stimuli viewed after regulation (Caria et al., 2010). The authors hypothesized that individuals who learned to increase activation in the insula would have a greater response to aversive images. Participants were assigned to one of three groups, using the same experimental design and task as described in (Caria et al., 2007): veridical insula neurofeedback (experimental), sham neurofeedback from a large control ROI, or no feedback (imagery only). In this study, after both regulation and rest trials participants viewed one emotionally neutral or negative image from the International Affective Picture System (IAPS) and rated their arousal and valence levels using the Self-Assessment Manikin (SAM). Only individuals in the experimental group increased activation in the left insula. As predicted, those in the experimental group who learned to increase activation in the left insula reported a greater negative response to aversive IAPS images. Neither control group demonstrated regulation of the insula or a relationship between insula activation and emotional ratings of images. An important caveat of this work is that the study did not include a pre- or posttest in the experimental design, making it not possible to assess transfer of regulation of activation in this region. The sample sizes were also relatively low.

Veit and colleagues extended this line of work by examining connectivity with the insula during self-regulation while viewing threat-related imagery (Veit et al., 2012). Participants viewed threat-related or neutral images and were instructed to increase insula activation (upregulate), decrease insula activation (downregulate), or merely view the images (no regulation). Consistent with the prior work, participants learned to upregulate insula activation. Insula downregulation had not yet been examined, and here individuals were unable to do so. The authors also examined whole brain activation and connectivity with the insula using a psychophysical interaction (PPI) analysis. In addition to the insula, the ventrolateral PFC (VLPFC), cingulate cortex, and frontal operculum were engaged during upregulation. During downregulation, the medial frontal cortex, ACC, VLPFC, and frontal inferior operculum were recruited. Similar to the studies before, this experiment did not have a pre- or posttest to examine transfer. It also had a small sample (11 participants) and did not include a control group.

In summary, an increasing number of related studies have shown that adults can learn to upregulate insula activation using fMRI neurofeedback during training (see Kadosh et al., 2016 for work in children and adolescents), with one study demonstrating upregulation during transfer (Caria et al., 2007). There have been mixed results regarding the impact of successful insula upregulation on individuals' mood (see Caria et al., 2010; Lawrence et al., 2014) and no evidence of a relationship between insula upregulation and arousal (as measured by skin conductance responses in Lawrence et al., 2014). Thus, while individuals are able to increase insula activity, there is no evidence to date of the ability to downregulate insula activity.

4.2.4 Anterior cingulate cortex

The anterior cingulate cortex (ACC) is a region involved in many complex cognitive processes, including emotional processing, generation of affective states, and error detection among others (for review see Critchley, 2005). The ACC is believed to play a role in several different psychopathologies, including unipolar depression, bipolar depression, and obsessive compulsive disorder. As such, it has been the focus for multiple rtfMRI NF studies as a means to study social and affective processes both to understand basic functioning of the region as well as to lay the groundwork for studies with patient populations (see Linhartová et al., 2019 for review).

Hamilton and colleagues were one of the first to examine regulation of the ACC in healthy adults (Hamilton et al., 2011; see Weiskopf et al., 2003 for example data in one participant showing ACC regulation). The specific area within the ACC they examined was the subgenual ACC (sACC)—a region involved in affective processing and implicated in depression (Drevets et al., 2008). In this study, healthy adults were recruited to learn to downregulate sACC activation. Individuals were assigned to the experimental (real NF) or control group (yoked, sham NF). All participants completed a pretest, two NF runs, and a posttest. Participants were instructed to use strategies to increase positive mood as a means of decreasing sACC activation. Individuals in the experimental group were able to significantly decrease sACC activation during the training runs, but not the pre- or posttest. Those in the control group were unable to decrease sACC activation in any run (test or training). Furthermore, the experimental group showed decreased correlation between the sACC and posterior cingulate cortex during NF runs relative to the test runs, while the control group showed the opposite pattern of results. This study demonstrated that individuals could learn to downregulate sACC activation during training, if given valid NF. This set the stage for future studies in healthy and adult populations, including work by Gröne and colleagues who compared ACC regulation using rt-fMRI NF in a 3T versus 7T scanner and found it effective at both field strengths, but no evidence for improvement at 7T (Gröne et al., 2015).

Recently Mathiak and colleagues began investigating whether individuals could learn to regulate the ACC using social reward as neurofeedback. An initial pilot study in one subject provided the proof of concept for this work (Mathiak et al., 2010). The authors then followed up by examining this question in a larger group of healthy adults where they compared receipt of social NF (smiling face) to standard NF (moving bar display) (Mathiak et al., 2015). Participants were assigned to the social or standard NF condition and were instructed to try to upregulate activation within the ACC during NF trials and to count backward during baseline trials. To increase ACC activity, they were encouraged to focus on thinking about a body perception, performing a hobby, or recalling positive autobiographical memories. Participants completed three NF sessions within one week. Each session consisted of a pretest, three training runs, and a posttest. The authors hypothesized both groups would learn to regulate the ACC, but the social NF group would demonstrate higher ACC activation, greater recruitment of other reward regions, greater ACC activation during the posttest (transfer), and better generalization to a cognitive task that engages the ACC. Consistent with their hypotheses, both groups increased activation in the ACC, with the social group showing greater activation during training. There was also stronger activation in reward-related regions during training in the social group. While there was no difference between groups during the posttest (transfer), there was an effect in the expected direction during generalization to a cognitive interference task (though no behavioral differences in task performance were observed across groups).

Limitations of this study include a relatively small sample size and nonrandom group assignment (participants were assigned sequentially). It is also an open question regarding how to effectively deliver social NF. In this paper, the authors used a smiling face as positive feedback and a neutral face as a baseline stimulus. However, neutral faces are often interpreted as ambiguous and thus many people find them affectively negative (Lee et al., 2008). Relatedly, in the posttest (no NF) the authors used a slightly smiling face as the stimulus, which is (by design) somewhere in between a neutral face and a smiling face. It is an open question about what the appropriate stimulus should be for the test phase in such a study. Thus this experiment is an interesting start to the examination of using social NF as a means to study engagement of affective regions. We predict more research will be directed at this interesting question.

In summary, several studies have examined healthy adults' ability to regulate the ACC. Evidence to date suggests that individuals can up- and downregulate the ACC which has interesting implications for basic science applications such as improving affective processing, error detection, and cognitive control, all which remain to be further explored.

4.2.5 Multiple ROIs and functional connectivity-based neurofeedback

Most of the work using rt-fMRI NF has focused on delivering NF from a single ROI. Recently, however, studies are beginning to examine delivery of NF from multiple ROIs (see Ruiz et al., 2014; Linhartová et al., 2019 for reviews). One approach for doing this is to first identify brain regions engaged in a cognitive process and then create a mask from the entire network. One example of this in the domain of social and affective neuroscience is work done by Moll and colleagues (Moll et al., 2014). In their study, the authors examined activation of brain regions engaged during generation of affiliative emotions, such as affection or tenderness. Participants received either valid NF (experimental group) or random NF (control group). All individuals were instructed to recall positive autobiographical memories related to: tenderness/affection (e.g., visiting a loved one), pride (e.g., recognition of one's achievements), or neutral (e.g., shopping). The ROI used for NF was a mask of many brain regions defined by data from an independent study examining affiliative emotions. The mask included parts of the prefrontal cortex, temporal lobe, parietal cortex, cingulate cortex, and other subcortical areas involved in social emotions. The authors trained a support vector machine (SVM) classifier to discriminate between brain activity patterns associated with tenderness/affection and pride (see Chapter 2 for more details about training brain patterns using NF). In support of their hypothesis, participants in the experimental, but not control group, were able to use the NF to increase brain responses to tenderness/affection. The authors were excited that they were able to demonstrate regulation of the neural signatures of a complex emotion like tenderness/affection as it has implications for improving wellbeing in both healthy adults and clinical populations.

Another approach is using connectivity-based neurofeedback (see Yamada et al., 2017 for review). In one of the first demonstrations of this type of study, Koush and colleagues used their novel real-time dynamic causal modeling method (Koush et al., 2013), which allows for model comparison of different effective connectivity patterns within the brain in real time. In a subsequent study, the authors examined whether participants could learn to selectively control connectivity from the dorsomedial prefrontal cortex (dmPFC) to the amygdala, but not the other way around (amygdala to dmPFC; Koush et al., 2017). The authors demonstrated, for the first time, that individuals can learn to increase top-down connectivity of the dmPFC to the amygdala. Furthermore, the degree of learning (here defined as slope) was associated with valence ratings of emotional stimuli. Importantly, only the experimental group, but not a control group that received sham feedback, showed learned control of this network. This is a very promising finding, tempered only by a small sample size and somewhat small statistical effects.

Functional connectivity-based neurofeedback is beginning to be used to address clinically oriented questions in healthy adults. Two recent studies used this method to examine changes in connectivity in healthy individuals with high trait anxiety. The first study, by Zhao et al. (2019), used rtfMRI to try to enhance connectivity between the ventrolateral PFC (vlPFC) and amygdala while participants viewed threatening stimuli. Excitingly, only the vlPFC-amygdala pathway (and not the control pathway, focused on motor regions) increased connectivity following training. Furthermore, strong connectivity was associated with greater reduction in anxiety. Lastly, the increased connectivity was observed at a follow-up session 3-days posttraining (transfer test, no NF). The results from this proof-of-concept study are very compelling. Note, this study only recruited male participants, thus future work should examine this important question in female participants as well.

A recent study examined a related topic, attention and resting state networks in men and women with high trait anxiety, but focused on changes in connectivity between a different set of regions: the DLPFC and ACC (Morgenroth et al., 2020). Similar to Zhao and colleagues, Morgenroth and colleagues' effects were specific to the manipulation. Here, functional connectivity increased between the DLPFC-ACC following veridical, but not control NF (yoked sham NF). In this study, the experimental group showed increased DLPFC-ACC connectivity, decreased anxiety levels, and importantly a relationship between the two. Interestingly, in a more inferior part of the ACC, the authors observed decreased connectivity between the DLPFC-ACC, which was also associated with decreased anxiety. The authors conclude that individuals in the experimental group were able to regulate connectivity between the DLPFC-ACC and this was associated with decreased anxiety. Note, there was also no change in performance on an attention task following NF training.

Taken together, these studies (Koush et al., 2017; Zhao et al., 2019; Morgenroth et al., 2020) provide a very promising initial body of work examining changes in functional connectivity, self-report measures, and behavior using connectivity-based NF. Future research will likely continue to use the approach of providing NF from a network of regions, rather than a single ROI, especially as researchers continue to ask increasingly complex questions where one-to-one mapping of a cognitive process and a single brain region does not exist. This approach also allows for greater flexibility across individuals in terms of the brain areas recruited in a cognitive process (e.g., ACC, insula) and the degree to which they are engaged (e.g., high ACC activation and low insula for subject 1; low ACC and high insula for subject 2). However, it is important to note that research using functional connectivity-based rtfMRI must take care as recent work points to strong correlations between physiological artifacts and functional connectivity estimates (Weiss et al., 2020). Further investigation into this relationship and how to correct for it is certainly warranted.

4.2.6 Interim summary

Taken as a whole, the studies discussed in this section suggest that individuals can regulate multiple individual neural regions engaged in emotion regulation, including the amygdala, hippocampus, insula, and ACC (for review see Linhartová et al., 2019). The degree of success in regulating these regions is variable. Furthermore, continued research on the many potential behavioral implications of learned regulation of these regions, including improved attention, memory, cognitive control, and emotion regulation, is anticipated with great excitement in the field.

4.3 Empathy

4.3.1 Insula

The insula is involved in several facets of emotional processing (Simmons et al., 2013). In addition to the work that has been done on general emotional regulation, scientists have also examined the role of the insula in empathy using real-time fMRI NF (Yao et al., 2016; Kanel et al., 2019). In one example study, Yao and colleagues asked whether healthy adults could learn to regulate the insula and what effect this would have on empathy for pain processing (Yao et al., 2016). The authors adapted the task from (Caria et al., 2010). During regulation trials, participants in the experimental group were instructed to increase activation displayed on a thermometer stimulus by recalling or imagining negative emotional or autobiographical events. Both regulation and baseline trials were followed by an image of a painful scene and then participants provided empathy and arousal ratings. Two days following the NF training session, participants returned for a follow-up assessment that was similar to the training session, but contained no NF (a posttest). Participants were asked to increase insula activation based on what they learned during training. Individuals in the control group completed the same protocol except they received NF from a large control ROI. The authors reported that individuals in the experimental, but not control, group increased activation within the insula during session one. This effect was maintained two days later during follow-up. Furthermore, the experimental group had increased empathy to painful pictures relative to the control group and there was a relationship between empathy ratings and insula activation in the experimental group only. Lastly the authors observed increased connectivity between the insula and regions of the prefrontal cortex across training.

These findings are exciting as they demonstrate learned regulation of the insula, an effect that is maintained two days later at follow-up in the absence of NF. Furthermore, this volitional regulation was related to empathy ratings while viewing painful images. These findings have important clinical potential for individuals who have abnormal emotional processing, particularly those who struggle with empathy.

4.4 Pain processing

4.4.1 Anterior cingulate cortex and insula cortex

One of the first seminal empirical papers using rt-fMRI NF to examine regulation of an individual neural region was conducted with healthy adult volunteers (and those with chronic pain) on the topic of pain perception. deCharms and colleagues asked whether individuals could learn to control the rostral ACC (rACC) and if so, if that would impact pain perception (de Charms et al., 2005). During training runs, the task consisted of rest (baseline), increase, and decrease trials. During the first half of the increase and decrease trials, healthy participants received a nociceptive thermal stimulus on the hand. They were provided with several strategies to try to increase or decrease their pain perception. In addition, they received NF regarding their degree of success in regulating rACC activation. Subjects completed a localizer run, three training runs, and a posttest (no NF). Several control groups were included in this study, including no NF groups, NF from a control ROI, and yoked sham control (participants in this group received NF from someone in the experimental group). The authors defined learning as a greater difference between increase and decrease trials in the last run of training relative to the first run, which they observed. The effect was also present in the posttest (relative to training run 1). Excitingly, pain perception also changed throughout training, such that participants rated painful stimuli as more painful when they were increasing rACC activity than decreasing it (upregulation > downregulation). Furthermore, there was a positive, linear relationship between changes in pain perception and rACC activation. These effects were significantly larger in the experimental group than any of the control groups. The authors found similar effects in the patient group (see Chapter 11 for more about pain research using rt-fMRI NF in patient populations). In sum, the authors found that individuals can learn to control the rACC and that this impacts their pain perception. This was a seminal paper at the time and helped garner enthusiasm for research in the field of rtfMRI NF.

Recently, Rance and colleagues followed up on the initial work by deCharms and examined the ability of healthy adults to up- and downregulate two regions strongly engaged in pain processing: the rACC and insula (Rance et al., 2014b; see also Emmert et al., 2014, 2017 for additional work examining rt-fMRI NF from the ACC and insula related to pain processing). The authors were interested in examining the specificity and relative impact the rACC and insula have on pain intensity and emotional responses. Healthy adults participated in four consecutive scanning days that included a baseline run and 24 training trials. On each day participants attempted to up- or downregulate the rACC or insula (each person completed training with all four conditions: rACC upregulation, rACC downregulation, etc.). Training trials consisted of six regulation phases and six nonregulation phases (where participants performed mental math). During regulation phases individuals received painful electrical stimulation to the hand and received NF regarding ROI activation in either the rACC or insula.

Unlike de Charms et al. (2005), participants here were instructed to try to regulate the NF, but were not informed that it may be related to pain processing. They were allowed to use any strategy they liked, aside from body movement. Participants learned to up- and downregulate the insula, but were only able to significantly downregulate the rACC. Interestingly, modulation of these two ROIs (rACC and insula) was not correlated. The authors also did not observe an impact on either of the individual ROI's activation with pain intensity or unpleasantness ratings. The lack of relationship with pain intensity differs from what deCharms and colleagues observed. A major difference between these two studies is how individuals were instructed to regulate the brain regions: de Charms et al. (2005) told subjects to use strategies related to pain regulation, while Rance and colleagues did not instruct them to use pain-related strategies. In addition, participants in the deCharms study significantly upregulated ACC activation, whereas those in this study did not. Either or both of these differences could have had a significant impact on subjective pain perception. Despite the fact that Rance and colleagues did not observe a relationship between pain ratings and either individual ROI's activation, they did observe lower unpleasantness ratings correlated with increased insula activation when it was disengaged from the rACC. This suggests that interactions between these regions may impact subjective pain responses, an idea the authors further explore in a second study (Rance et al., 2014a). Note, there was no relationship between brain activation and subjective measures of pain (intensity or unpleasantness) in this second study as well.

4.4.2 Interim summary

In sum, there is evidence that healthy adults can regulate both the ACC and the insula while experiencing a painful stimulus. The impact this neural regulation has on perceptions of pain is mixed, with only one study showing a relationship between ACC activation and self-assessed pain ratings (de Charms et al., 2005). Given the difficulty treating pain, particularly chronic pain, understanding if and how rtfMRI NF can provide novel therapies for patients is an important area for future research.

5 Conclusions and future directions

The goal of this chapter is to examine the burgeoning field of rtfMRI NF studies on social and affective neuroscience. Many exciting findings have been reported to date, including volitional control of areas involved in the generation, expression, and regulation of emotions; reward processing and motivated states; as well as pain processing (including empathy for pain). Specifically evidence to date suggests that individuals can upregulate the amygdala (for review, see Barreiros et al., 2019), hippocampus (Zhu et al., 2019), insula and anterior cingulate cortex (for review, see Linhartová et al., 2019). Evidence for successful downregulation is less strong: data on downregulation of the amygdala looks promising (Paret et al., 2014), but more work needs to be done to further examine this question in multiple ROIs.

Regarding reward processing and generation of motivated states, there is evidence that healthy adults can upregulate both the dopaminergic midbrain (VTA/SN) (Sulzer et al., 2013b; MacInnes et al., 2016) and NAcc (Greer et al., 2014; MacInnes et al., 2016; Li et al., 2018). However, there is no evidence to date that individuals can downregulate the midbrain or the NAcc; though only the NAcc has been tested. Greer and colleagues suggested it may be difficult to achieve successful downregulation of regions like the midbrain and NAcc that are strongly engaged in reward processing when participants receive an ongoing feedback signal (Greer et al., 2014). Dopamine neurons signal goal achievement (Howe et al., 2013), among other things. Thus if an individual succeeds at downregulating a dopamine-rich area, and dopamine neurons then burst indicating goal achievement, this may cancel out any potential successful downregulation. For protocols aiming to downregulate reward circuitry, intermittent feedback may be preferable to continuous feedback for these reasons.

More limited work has been conducted in the domain of pain processing in healthy adults. Evidence suggests individuals can volitionally regulate the ACC (Rance et al., 2014b; de Charms et al., 2005) and have shown bidirectional control of the insula (up- and downregulation; Rance et al., 2014b). In addition, volitional upregulation of the insula has also been observed during empathy for pain processing (Yao et al., 2016). Decidedly less work has explicitly examined social neuroscience research questions (for example, see Mathiak et al., 2015), leaving this area open for future research.

Most studies on affective and social neuroscience using rtfMRI NF have been proof of concept in nature, aiming to demonstrate whether an area of interest can be up- and/or downregulated via neurofeedback. As such, not all studies have included important experimental design parameters such as control groups or pre- and posttests to examine generalization to nonfeedback contexts. Including a posttest to evaluate regulation in the absence of feedback is critical for demonstrating the utility of brain regulation in the real world; modifying brain activity only within the MRI environment is much less relevant for daily life. The field of rtfMRI neurofeedback is relatively novel, and firm guidelines have yet to be established standardizing rtfMRI NF study design. However, as the field grows, scientists are actively thinking about the important aspects of experimental design in order to more deeply examine the many open questions remaining in this field (for examples, see Sorger et al., 2019; Paret et al., 2019; Rance et al., 2018; Oblak et al., 2017; Emmert et al., 2016; Sulzer et al., 2013a; Caria et al., 2012; Sitaram et al., 2017; MacInnes and Dickerson, 2018).

Many important research questions remain unanswered in the domain of social and affective neuroscience that can be addressed using rtfMRI NF. A primary one is how volitional up- and downregulation of a neural region changes behavior and neural networks. Many of the initial proof-of-concept papers described here examined whether control of a region could be achieved. The logical next step is to examine the impact of regulation of various brain regions on both behavioral outcomes and brain plasticity. A great example of this in the work described here is the study by Yao and colleagues (Yao et al., 2016) who examined volitional regulation of the insula and the effect of that regulation on brain networks and behavior. The authors used a pretest, training, posttest design that included a two-day follow-up. In addition to the experimental group that received valid insula NF, they included a control group that received valid NF from a control brain region. Individuals in the experimental, but not control, group increased activation within the insula during session one. This effect was maintained two days later at follow-up. Furthermore, the experimental group had increased empathy to painful pictures relative to the control group and there was a correlation between empathy ratings and insula activation in the experimental group only. Lastly the authors observed increased connectivity between the insula and regions of the prefrontal cortex across training. The contributions of this study go far beyond understanding volitional regulation of the insula; they contribute to a deeper understanding of the role of this region in empathy. As the rtfMRI NF community grows we expect many more studies to examine not only whether a given region can be up- or downregulated, but what the impacts of such volitional regulation are on the rest of the brain and behavior.

Real-time fMRI NF has the potential to contribute to science in unique ways as it allows individuals to harness the power of their own brain and dynamically adapt it as needed. As such there are many exciting questions that can be answered that have the potential to both deepen our understanding of the affective and social brain, as well as to improve human health and wellbeing.

References

Barreiros, A.R., Almeida, I., Correia, B.R., Castelo-Branco, M., 2019. Amygdala modulation during emotion regulation training with fMRI-based neurofeedback: a systematic review. Front. Hum. Neurosci. 13, 89.

Botvinick, M.M., Huffstetler, S., McGuire, J.T., 2009. Effort discounting in human nucleus accumbens. Cogn. Affect. Behav. Neurosci. 9 (1), 16–27.

Braver, T.S., Barch, D.M., 2002. A theory of cognitive control, aging cognition, and neuromodulation. Neurosci. Biobehav. Rev. 26 (7), 809–817.

Brühl, A.B., Scherpiet, S., Sulzer, J., Stämpfli, P., Seifritz, E., Herwig, U., 2014. Real-time neurofeedback using functional MRI could improve down-regulation of amygdala activity during emotional stimulation: a proof-of-concept study. Brain Topogr. 27 (1), 138–148.

Caria, A., Veit, R., Sitaram, R., Lotze, M., Weiskopf, N., Grodd, W., Birbaumer, N., 2007. Regulation of anterior insular cortex activity using real-time fMRI. NeuroImage 35 (3), 1238–1246.

Caria, A., Sitaram, R., Veit, R., Begliomini, C., Birbaumer, N., 2010. Volitional control of anterior insula activity modulates the response to aversive stimuli. A real-time functional magnetic resonance imaging study. Biol. Psychiatry 68 (5), 425–432.

Caria, A., Sitaram, R., Birbaumer, N., 2012. Real-time fMRI: a tool for local brain regulation. Neuroscientist 18 (5), 487–501.

Carver, C.S., White, T.L., 1994. Behavioral inhibition, behavioral activation, and affective responses to impending reward and punishment: the BIS/BAS scales. J. Pers. Soc. Psychol. 67 (2), 319.

Cheong, J.H., Molani, Z., Sadhukha, S., Chang, L.J., 2020. Synchronized affect in shared experiences strengthens social connection., https://doi.org/10.31234/osf.io/bd9wn.

Critchley, H.D., 2005. Neural mechanisms of autonomic, affective, and cognitive integration. J. Comp. Neurol. 493 (1), 154–166.

Cromwell, H.C., Abe, N., Barrett, K.C., Caldwell-Harris, C., Gendolla, G.H.E., Koncz, R., Sachdev, P.S., 2020. Mapping the interconnected neural systems underlying motivation and emotion: a key step toward understanding the human affectome. Neurosci. Biobehav. Rev. 113 (February), 204–226.

de Charms, R.C., Maeda, F., Glover, G.H., Ludlow, D., Pauly, J.M., Soneji, D., Gabrieli, J.D.E., Mackey, S.C., 2005. Control over brain activation and pain learned by using real-time functional MRI. Proc. Natl. Acad. Sci. U. S. A. 102 (51), 18626–18631.

Delgado, M.R., Nystrom, L.E., Fissell, C., Noll, D.C., Fiez, J.A., 2000. Tracking the hemodynamic responses to reward and punishment in the striatum. J. Neurophysiol. 84 (6), 3072–3077.

Dickerson, K.C., Adcock, R.A., 2018. Motivation and memory. In: Wixted, J.T. (Ed.), Stevens' Handbook of Experimental Psychology and Cognitive Neuroscience. 50. John Wiley & Sons, Inc., Hoboken, NJ, USA, pp. 1–36.

Drevets, W.C., Savitz, J., Trimble, M., 2008. The Subgenual anterior cingulate cortex in mood disorders. CNS Spectrums 13 (8), 663–681.

Emmert, K., Breimhorst, M., Bauermann, T., Birklein, F., Van De Ville, D., Haller, S., 2014. Comparison of anterior cingulate vs. insular cortex as targets for real-time fMRI regulation during pain stimulation. Front. Behav. Neurosci. 8 (October), 350.

Emmert, K., Kopel, R., Sulzer, J., Brühl, A.B., Berman, B.D., Linden, D.E.J., Horovitz, S.G., et al., 2016. Meta-analysis of real-time fMRI neurofeedback studies using individual participant data: how is brain regulation mediated? NeuroImage 124 (Pt A), 806–812.

Emmert, K., Breimhorst, M., Bauermann, T., Birklein, F., Rebhorn, C., Van De Ville, D., Haller, S., 2017. Active pain coping is associated with the response in real-time fMRI neurofeedback during pain. Brain Imaging Behav. 11 (3), 712–721.

Floresco, S.B., 2015. The nucleus accumbens: an interface between cognition, emotion, and action. Annu. Rev. Psychol. 66 (January), 25–52.

Gard, D.E., Gard, M.G., Kring, A.M., John, O.P., 2006. Anticipatory and consummatory components of the experience of pleasure: a scale development study. J. Res. Pers. 40 (6), 1086–1102.

Gilam, G., Hendler, T., 2016. With love, from me to you: embedding social interactions in affective neuroscience. Neurosci. Biobehav. Rev. 68 (September), 590–601.

Greer, S.M., Trujillo, A.J., Glover, G.H., Knutson, B., 2014. Control of nucleus accumbens activity with neurofeedback. NeuroImage 96 (August), 237–244.

Gröne, M., Dyck, M., Koush, Y., Bergert, S., Mathiak, K.A., Alawi, E.M., Elliott, M., Mathiak, K., 2015. Upregulation of the rostral anterior cingulate cortex can alter the perception of emotions: fMRI-based neurofeedback at 3 and 7 T. Brain Topogr. 28 (2), 197–207.

Hamilton, J.P., Glover, G.H., Hsu, J.-J., Johnson, R.F., Gotlib, I.H., 2011. Modulation of Subgenual anterior cingulate cortex activity with real-time neurofeedback. Hum. Brain Mapp. 32 (1), 22–31.

Hartley, C.A., Phelps, E.A., 2010. Changing fear: the neurocircuitry of emotion regulation. Neuropsychopharmacology 35 (1), 136–146.

Heerey, E.A., Gold, J.M., 2007. Patients with schizophrenia demonstrate dissociation between affective experience and motivated behavior. J. Abnorm. Psychol. 116 (2), 268–278.

Hellrung, L., Dietrich, A., Hollmann, M., Pleger, B., Kalberlah, C., Roggenhofer, E., Villringer, A., Horstmann, A., 2018. Intermittent compared to continuous real-time fMRI neurofeedback boosts control over amygdala activation. NeuroImage 166 (February), 198–208.

Howe, M.W., Tierney, P.L., Sandberg, S.G., Phillips, P.E.M., Graybiel, A.M., 2013. Prolonged dopamine signalling in striatum signals proximity and value of distant rewards. Nature 500 (7464), 575–579.

Johnston, S.J., Boehm, S.G., Healy, D., Goebel, R., Linden, D.E.J., 2010. Neurofeedback: a promising tool for the self-regulation of emotion networks. NeuroImage 49 (1), 1066–1072.

Kadosh, K., Luo, Q., de Burca, C., Sokunbi, M.O., Feng, J., Linden, D.E.J., Lau, J.Y.F., 2016. Using real-time fMRI to influence effective connectivity in the developing emotion regulation network. NeuroImage 125 (January), 616–626.

Kanel, D., Al-Wasity, S., Stefanov, K., Pollick, F.E., 2019. Empathy to emotional voices and the use of real-time fMRI to enhance activation of the anterior insula. NeuroImage 198 (September), 53–62.

Knutson, B., Fong, G.W., Adams, C.M., Varner, J.L., Hommer, D., 2001. Dissociation of reward anticipation and outcome with event-related fMRI. Neuroreport 12 (17), 3683–3687. https://doi.org/10.1097/00001756-200112040-00016.

Koush, Y., Rosa, M.J., Robineau, F., Heinen, K., Rieger, S.W., Weiskopf, N., Vuilleumier, P., Van De Ville, D., Scharnowski, F., 2013. Connectivity-based neurofeedback: dynamic causal modeling for real- time fMRI. NeuroImage 81 (November), 422–430.

Koush, Y., Meskaldji, D.-E., Pichon, S., Rey, G., Rieger, S.W., Linden, D.E.J., Van De Ville, D., Vuilleumier, P., Scharnowski, F., 2017. Learning control over emotion networks through connectivity-based neurofeedback. Cereb. Cortex 27 (February), 1193–1202.

Lawrence, E.J., Li, S., Barker, G.J., Medford, N., Dalton, J., Steve C. R. Williams, Niels Birbaumer, et al., 2014. Self-regulation of the anterior insula: reinforcement learning using real-time fMRI neurofeedback. NeuroImage 88 (March), 113–124.

Lee, E., In Kang, J., Park, I.H., Kim, J.-J., An, S.K., 2008. Is a neutral face really evaluated as being emotionally neutral? Psychiatry Res. 157 (1–3), 77–85.

Leotti, L.A., Delgado, M.R., 2011. The inherent reward of choice. Psychol. Sci. 22 (10), 1310–1318.

Li, Z., Tong, L., Wang, L., Li, Y., He, W., Guan, M., Yan, B., 2016. Self-regulating positive emotion networks by feedback of multiple emotional brain states using real-time fMRI. Exp. Brain Res. 234 (12), 3575–3586.

Li, Z., Zhang, C.-Y., Huang, J., Wang, Y., Yan, C., Li, K., Zeng, Y.-W., et al., 2018. Improving motivation through real-time fMRI-based self-regulation of the nucleus Accumbens. Neuropsychology 32 (6), 764–776.

Linhartová, P., Látalová, A., Kóša, B., Kašpárek, T., Schmahl, C., Paret, C., 2019. fMRI neurofeedback in emotion regulation: a literature review. NeuroImage 193 (June), 75–92.

Lorenzetti, V., Melo, B., Basílio, R., Suo, C., Yücel, M., Tierra-Criollo, C.J., Moll, J., 2018. Emotion regulation using virtual environments and real-time fMRI neurofeedback. Front. Neurol. 9 (July), 390.

MacDuffie, K.E., MacInnes, J., Dickerson, K.C., Eddington, K.M., Strauman, T.J., Alison Adcock, R., 2018. Single session real-time fMRI neurofeedback has a lasting impact on cognitive behavioral therapy strategies. NeuroImage Clin. 19 (June), 868–875.

MacInnes, J.J., Dickerson, K.C., 2018. Real-time functional magnetic resonance imaging. In: eLS. John Wiley & Sons, Ltd.

MacInnes, J.J., Dickerson, K.C., Chen, N.-K., Alison Adcock, R., 2016. Cognitive neurostimulation: learning to volitionally sustain ventral tegmental area activation. Neuron 89 (6), 1331–1342.

Maia, T.V., Frank, M.J., 2011. From reinforcement learning models to psychiatric and neurological disorders. Nat. Neurosci. 14 (2), 154–162.

Marxen, M., Jacob, M.J., Müller, D.K., Posse, S., Ackley, E., Hellrung, L., Riedel, P., Bender, S., Epple, R., Smolka, M.N., 2016. Amygdala regulation following fMRI-neurofeedback without instructed strategies. Front. Hum. Neurosci. 10, 183. https://doi.org/10.3389/fnhum.2016.00183.

Mathiak, K.A., Koush, Y., Dyck, M., Gaber, T.J., Alawi, E., Zepf, F.D., Zvyagintsev, M., Mathiak, K., 2010. Social reinforcement can regulate localized brain activity. Eur. Arch. Psychiatry Clin. Neurosci. 260 (Suppl 2), S132–S136.

Mathiak, K.A., Alawi, E.M., Koush, Y., Dyck, M., Cordes, J.S., Gaber, T.J., Florian D. Zepf, et al., 2015. Social reward improves the voluntary control over localized brain activity in fMRI-based neurofeedback training. Front. Behav. Neurosci. 9 (June), 136.

Moll, J., Weingartner, J.H., Bado, P., Basilio, R., Sato, J.R., Melo, B.R., Bramati, I.E., de Oliveira-Souza, R., Zahn, R., 2014. Voluntary enhancement of neural signatures of affiliative emotion using FMRI neurofeedback. PLoS One 9 (5), e97343.

Morgenroth, E., Saviola, F., Gillen, J., Allen, B., Lührs, M., Eysenck, M.W., Allen, P., 2020. Using connectivity-based real-time fMRI neurofeedback to modulate attentional and rest state networks in people with high trait anxiety. Neuroimage Clin. 25, 102191.

Murty, V.P., Alison Adcock, R., 2017. Distinct medial temporal lobe network states as neural contexts for motivated memory formation. In: Hannula, D.E., Duff, M.C. (Eds.), The Hippocampus from Cells to Systems: Structure, Connectivity, and Functional Contributions to Memory and Flexible Cognition. Springer International Publishing, New York, USA, pp. 467–501.

Murty, V.P., LaBar, K.S., Adcock, R.A., 2016. Distinct medial temporal networks encode surprise during motivation by reward versus punishment. Neurobiol. Learn. Mem. 134 (Pt A), 55–64.

Murty, V.P., Alexa, T., Alison Adcock, R., Davachi, L., 2017. Selectivity in postencoding connectivity with high-level visual cortex is associated with reward-motivated memory. J. Neurosci. Off. J. Soc. Neurosci. 37 (3), 537–545.

Oblak, E.F., Lewis-Peacock, J.A., Sulzer, J.S., 2017. Self-regulation strategy, feedback timing and hemodynamic properties modulate learning in a simulated fMRI neurofeedback environment. PLoS Comput. Biol. 13 (7), e1005681.

Paret, C., Kluetsch, R., Ruf, M., Demirakca, T., Hoesterey, S., Ende, G., Schmahl, C., 2014. Down-regulation of amygdala activation with real-time fMRI neurofeedback in a healthy female sample. Front. Behav. Neurosci. 8 (September), 299.

Paret, C., Ruf, M., Gerchen, M.F., Kluetsch, R., Demirakca, T., Jungkunz, M., Bertsch, K., Schmahl, C., Ende, G., 2016. fMRI neurofeedback of amygdala response to aversive stimuli enhances prefrontal–limbic brain connectivity. NeuroImage 125 (January), 182–188.

Paret, C., Zähringer, J., Ruf, M., Gerchen, M.F., Mall, S., Hendler, T., Schmahl, C., Ende, G., 2018. Monitoring and control of amygdala neurofeedback involves distributed information processing in the human brain. Hum. Brain Mapp. 39 (7), 3018–3031. https://doi.org/10.1002/hbm.24057.

Paret, C., Goldway, N., Zich, C., Keynan, J.N., Hendler, T., Linden, D., Kadosh, K.C., 2019. Current progress in real-time functional magnetic resonance-based neurofeedback: methodological challenges and achievements. NeuroImage 202 (November), 116107.

Phelps, E.A., LeDoux, J.E., 2005. Contributions of the amygdala to emotion processing: from animal models to human behavior. Neuron 48 (2), 175–187.

Posse, S., Fitzgerald, D., Gao, K., Habel, U., Rosenberg, D., Moore, G.J., Schneider, F., 2003. Real-time fMRI of temporolimbic regions detects amygdala activation during single-trial self-induced sadness. NeuroImage 18 (3), 760–768.

Quiñones-Camacho, L.E., Fishburn, F.A., Catalina Camacho, M., Hlutkowsky, C.O., Huppert, T.J., Wakschlag, L.S., Perlman, S.B., 2019. Parent-child neural synchrony: a novel approach to elucidating dyadic correlates of preschool irritability. J. Child Psychol. Psychiatry 61 (11), 1213–1223. https://doi.org/10.1111/jcpp.13165.

Rance, M., Ruttorf, M., Nees, F., Schad, L.R., Flor, H., 2014a. Neurofeedback of the difference in activation of the anterior cingulate cortex and posterior insular cortex: two functionally connected areas in the processing of pain. Front. Behav. Neurosci. 8, 357. https://doi.org/10.3389/fnbeh.2014.00357.

Rance, M., Ruttorf, M., Nees, F., Schad, L.R., Flor, H., 2014b. Real time fMRI feedback of the anterior cingulate and posterior insular cortex in the processing of pain. Hum. Brain Mapp. 35 (12), 5784–5798.

Rance, M., Walsh, C., Sukhodolsky, D.G., Pittman, B., Qiu, M., Kichuk, S.A., Wasylink, S., et al., 2018. Time course of clinical change following neurofeedback. NeuroImage 181 (November), 807–813.

Roitman, M.F., Stuber, G.D., Phillips, P.E.M., Wightman, R.M., Carelli, R.M., 2004. Dopamine operates as a subsecond modulator of food seeking. J. Neurosci. Off. J. Soc. Neurosci. 24 (6), 1265–1271.

Ruiz, S., Buyukturkoglu, K., Rana, M., Birbaumer, N., Sitaram, R., 2014. Real-time fMRI brain computer interfaces: self-regulation of single brain regions to networks. Biol. Psychol. 95 (January), 4–20.

Salamone, J.D., Correa, M., 2012. The mysterious motivational functions of mesolimbic dopamine. Neuron 76 (3), 470–485.

Sarkheil, P., Zilverstand, A., Kilian-Hütten, N., Schneider, F., Goebel, R., Mathiak, K., 2015. fMRI feedback enhances emotion regulation as evidenced by a reduced amygdala response. Behav. Brain Res. 281 (March), 326–332.

Schaefer, S.M., Jackson, D.C., Davidson, R.J., Aguirre, G.K., Kimberg, D.Y., Thompson-Schill, S.L., 2002. Modulation of amygdalar activity by the conscious regulation of negative emotion. J. Cogn. Neurosci. 14 (6), 913–921.

Simmons, W.K., Avery, J.A., Barcalow, J.C., Bodurka, J., Drevets, W.C., Bellgowan, P., 2013. Keeping the body in mind: insula functional organization and functional connectivity integrate interoceptive, exteroceptive, and emotional awareness. Hum. Brain Mapp. 34 (11), 2944–2958.

Sitaram, R., Ros, T., Stoeckel, L., Haller, S., Scharnowski, F., Lewis-Peacock, J., Weiskopf, N., et al., 2017. Closed-loop brain training: the science of neurofeedback. Nat. Rev. Neurosci. 18 (2), 86–100.

Sorger, B., Scharnowski, F., Linden, D.E.J., Hampson, M., Young, K.D., 2019. Control freaks: towards optimal selection of control conditions for fMRI neurofeedback studies. NeuroImage 186 (February), 256–265.

Sulzer, J., Haller, S., Scharnowski, F., Weiskopf, N., Birbaumer, N., Blefari, M.L., Bruehl, A.B., et al., 2013a. Real-time fMRI neurofeedback: progress and challenges. NeuroImage 76 (August), 386–399.

Sulzer, J., Sitaram, R., Blefari, M.L., Kollias, S., Birbaumer, N., Stephan, K.E., Luft, A., Gassert, R., 2013b. Neurofeedback-mediated self-regulation of the dopaminergic midbrain. NeuroImage 83 (December), 817–825.

Treadway, M.T., Buckholtz, J.W., Schwartzman, A.N., Lambert, W.E., Zald, D.H., 2009. Worth the 'EEfRT'? The effort expenditure for rewards task as an objective measure of motivation and anhedonia. PLoS One 4 (8), e6598.

Tricomi, E.M., Delgado, M.R., Fiez, J.A., 2004. Modulation of caudate activity by action contingency. Neuron 41 (2), 281–292.

Veit, R., Singh, V., Sitaram, R., Caria, A., Rauss, K., Birbaumer, N., 2012. Using real-time fMRI to learn voluntary regulation of the anterior insula in the presence of threat-related stimuli. Soc. Cogn. Affect. Neurosci. 7 (6), 623–634.

Weiskopf, N., Veit, R., Erb, M., Mathiak, K., Grodd, W., Goebel, R., Birbaumer, N., 2003. Physiological self-regulation of regional brain activity using real-time functional magnetic resonance imaging (fMRI): methodology and exemplary data. NeuroImage 19 (3), 577–586.

Weiss, F., Zamoscik, V., Schmidt, S.N.L., Halli, P., Kirsch, P., Gerchen, M.F., 2020. Just a very expensive breathing training? Risk of respiratory artefacts in functional connectivity-based real-time fMRI neurofeedback. NeuroImage 210 (April), 116580.

Wimmer, G.E., Daw, N.D., Shohamy, D., 2012. Generalization of value in reinforcement learning by humans. Eur. J. Neurosci. 35 (7), 1092–1104.

Yamada, T., Hashimoto, R.-i., Yahata, N., Ichikawa, N., Yoshihara, Y., Okamoto, Y., Kato, N., Takahashi, H., Kawato, M., 2017. Resting-state functional connectivity-based biomarkers and functional MRI-based neurofeedback for psychiatric disorders: a challenge for developing theranostic biomarkers. Int. J. Neuropsychopharmacol. 20 (10), 769–781.

Yao, S., Becker, B., Geng, Y., Zhao, Z., Xu, X., Zhao, W., Ren, P., Kendrick, K.M., 2016. Voluntary control of anterior insula and its functional connections is feedback-independent and increases pain empathy. NeuroImage 130 (April), 230–240.

Zhao, Z., Yao, S., Li, K., Sindermann, C., Zhou, F., Zhao, W., Li, J., Lührs, M., Goebel, R., Kendrick, K.M., Becker, B., 2019. Real-time functional connectivity-informed neurofeedback of amygdala-frontal pathways reduces anxiety. Psychother. Psychosom. 88, 5–15.

Zhu, Y., Gao, H., Tong, L., Li, Z., Wang, L., Zhang, C., Yang, Q., Yan, B., 2019. Emotion regulation of hippocampus using real-time fMRI neurofeedback in healthy human. Front. Hum. Neurosci. 13 (July), 242.

Zotev, V., Krueger, F., Phillips, R., Alvarez, R.P., Kyle Simmons, W., Bellgowan, P., Drevets, W.C., Bodurka, J., 2011. Self-regulation of amygdala activation using real-time FMRI neurofeedback. PLoS One 6 (9), e24522.

Zotev, V., Phillips, R., Young, K.D., Drevets, W.C., Bodurka, J., 2013. Prefrontal control of the amygdala during real-time fMRI neurofeedback training of emotion regulation. PLoS One 8 (11), e79184.

Zotev, V., Phillips, R., Yuan, H., Misaki, M., Bodurka, J., 2014. Self-regulation of human brain activity using simultaneous real-time fMRI and EEG neurofeedback. NeuroImage 85 (Pt 3), 985–995.

Introduction to clinical section

David Linden

School for Mental Health and Neuroscience, Faculty of Health, Medicine and Life Sciences, Maastricht University, Maastricht, Netherlands

Brain diseases pose an increasing challenge to health systems worldwide. The aging of our populations entails increasing prevalence of neurodegenerative diseases, which generally have no established cure. Psychological disorders with onset in adolescence and early adulthood such as addiction are also on the rise. As a side note, I have to mention that I include mental or psychological disorders under the label "brain diseases" because they manifest through changes in brain function, even if their causes are multifaceted and involve multiple bio-psycho-social factors. It has been argued that we are even in the midst of an international mental health crisis, with a quarter or more of the population being affected by a mental disorder at some point in their lives, and depression being the single most prominent cause of disability. At the same time we are seeing stagnation in therapeutic innovation, with many pharmaceutical companies abandoning their neuroscience programs because of high costs and low success rates of new drugs. It is thus understandable that there is considerable interest in new neuromodulation treatments that utilize the successes of the last three decades of human neuroscience and provide new therapeutic avenues for diseases that are currently difficult to treat or have high numbers of treatment-refractory patients. Almost all brain diseases fall into one of these categories, for example, neurodegenerative diseases have no causal treatments, and their symptomatic treatments either have very limited effects (as in Alzheimer's disease) or major side effects (as in Parkinson's disease). Some of the mental disorders are very difficult to treat, for example autism, others have established and very effective treatments (e.g., antidepressants for depression) but still considerable numbers of treatment-refractory patients.

Over the last 15 years, research groups have increasingly sought to develop and evaluate clinical neurofeedback paradigms with fMRI, and in this section we will review many of the relevant papers, but also explain the steps that are necessary for the design of your first clinical neurofeedback study. In the first chapter of this section, *Design of clinical studies in neurofeedback*, I introduce the Framework for the Development and Evaluation of Complex Interventions and use it as guiding principle for the further development of clinical neurofeedback protocols. I also discuss some of the challenges of designing clinical neurofeedback trials such as choosing the appropriate control intervention or achieving the right balance between power and use of resources. The most extensive work in clinical fMRI neurofeedback has so far been conducted on emotion regulation disorders such as depression, posttraumatic stress disorder (PTSD), and other anxiety disorders. This literature is reviewed in the chapter by Kymberly Young, Naomi Fine, and Talma Hendler, who also expand on some of the general design questions outlined in my chapter. In their chapter on *The treatment and study of psychiatric disorders with fMRI neurofeedback*, Zhiying Zhao, Emma Romaker, and Michelle Hampson cover the other mental and behavioral disorders for which neurofeedback-based treatment protocols have been piloted. A common theme of many of these studies is the combination of symptom provocation strategies such as contamination imagery in obsessive compulsive disorder (OCD) or presentation of substance-related cues in alcohol use disorder in combination with self-regulation training of the relevant neural circuits. Another theme common to these psychiatric applications (as well as those in emotion regulation disorders) is how to combine neurofeedback with psychological therapies such as cognitive behavioral therapy (CBT). The topic of (virtual) psychotherapy comes up again in the chapter on *Implicit training as a clinical tool* by Ai Koizumi and Mitsuo Kawato. This chapter introduces the clinical potential of Decoded Neurofeedback (DecNef) which aims to automatically detect neural patterns associated with specific mental states or stimuli, which can then be (positively or negatively) reinforced. Koizumi and Kawato explain how this method could be used as implicit exposure therapy, for example for phobias. The theoretical attraction is that it would enable working with the neural representations of the feared scenarios rather than inducing the scenarios explicitly—overcoming some of the distressing aspects of real or imaginary exposure.

Moving from psychiatry to neurology, I discuss the rationale for *Haemodynamic neurofeedback in neurorehabilitation*. Although theoretically attractive because of the substantial knowledge about dysfunctional brain circuits, particularly in Parkinson's disease, this area has not progressed as much (in terms of size of studies and level of evidence) as the psychiatric applications, and I discuss some of the particular challenges in setting up neurofeedback studies in neurodegenerative disorders and stroke. The section closes with an outlook on *Translation to the clinic and other modalities* by Jessica Taylor, Itamar Jalon, Toshinori Chiba, Tomokazu Motegi, Mitsuo Kawato, and Talma Hendler. This chapter considers the technological and methodological gaps and hurdles along the way to reach scaled (accessible and cost effective) and precise (mechanism driven) clinical translation of neurofeedback. It brings up the question how we will define "smart" neural markers for modulation in the future and reviews the properties of the different (univariate and multivariate) neurofeedback techniques. It also explains ways of "scaling up" neurofeedback that make it independent from continuous access to MRI systems, for example through transfer to ambulatory EEG or other mobile devices. One important aspect that relates to all the clinical chapters but is explicitly addressed here is how to personalize neurofeedback. Personalized or "precision" medicine is a topical issue in current clinical neuroscience and mental health research, and neurofeedback seems to be particularly suited to this agenda.

We are aware that readers will also be interested in a summary of the level of clinical evidence available for these different neurofeedback applications, which is why we have added an overview of the main clinical studies and the reported effects on clinical and neural measures in Table 1. We have incorporated work published until June 2020 and would encourage readers regularly to check for updates on scientific citation systems such as pubmed (https://pubmed.ncbi.nlm.nih.gov/) as well as the clinical trials database such as https://clinicaltrials.gov.

Table 1: Summary of patient studies with fMRI neurofeedback.

Disorder		Study[a]	Sample size NF group (based on completed intervention/clinical assessment)	Successful self-regulation (within group)	Significant symptom change in NF group (clinical scales only)	Control group or condition[b]	Participant blinding	Sample size control	Significant gp diff biomarker change	Significant gp diff symptom change
Depression	Clinical population	Zahn et al. (2019)	14	Yes (pre-post training comparison)	N/A	Control NF	Yes	14	Yes	N/A
		Mehler et al. (2018)	16	Yes (baseline comparison)	Yes	Control NF	No	16	No	No
		Young et al. (2017)	19	Yes (baseline comparison)	Yes	Control NF	Yes	17	Yes	Yes
		Hamilton et al. (2016)	10	Not reported	N/A	Yoked NF	Not reported	10	Yes	N/A
		Schnyer et al. (2015)	7	Not reported	N/A	No	N/A	N/A	N/A	N/A
		Young et al. (2014)	14	Yes (baseline comparison)	N/A	Control NF	Yes	7	Yes	N/A
		Linden et al. (2012)	8	Yes (baseline comparison)	Yes	Mental imagery outside MRI	No	8	N/A	Yes
PTSD	Clinical population	Fruchtman et al. (2019)	13	Yes (baseline comparison)	Yes	Control NF + no NF	No	13+14	Yes	Yes
		Chiba et al. (2019)	4	Not reported	Yes	No	N/A	N/A	N/A	N/A
		Zotev et al. (2018)	15	Yes (baseline comparison)	Yes	Control NF	Yes	8	Yes	No
		Zweerings et al. (2018)	9	Yes (increase over sessions)	N/A	Same paradigm, in healthy controls	No	9	N/A	N/A
		Nicholson et al. (2018)	14	Yes (compared to control condition)	N/A	No	N/A	N/A	N/A	N/A

Continued

Table 1: Summary of patient studies with fMRI neurofeedback—cont'd

Disorder		Study[a]	Sample size NF group (based on completed intervention/clinical assessment)	Successful self-regulation (within group)	Significant symptom change in NF group (clinical scales only)	Control group or condition[b]	Participant blinding	Sample size control	Significant gp diff biomarker change	Significant gp diff symptom change
Phobia	Subclinical population	Taschereau-Dumouchel et al. (2018)	17	Yes	Yes - GSR decrease	Target versus control phobia	Yes	17	N/A	N/A
Addiction	Clinical population	Hartwell et al. (2016)	16	No[c]	Yes (within session)	No feedback	No	17	No	Yes (within session)
		Karch et al. (2015)	13	Yes	Trend	Feedback gp from diff area	Yes	2	No	No
		Hanlon et al. (2013)	9	Yes (vACC, within session)	Yes (within session)	No	N/A	N/A	N/A	N/A
		Li et al. (2013)	10	No[c]	No[c]	No	N/A	N/A	N/A	N/A
		Canterberry et al. (2013)	9	No[c]	Yes (within session)	No	N/A	N/A	N/A	N/A
	Subclinical population	Kirschner et al. (2018)	22	Yes	No	Same paradigm in healthy controls	N/A	N/A	N/A	N/A
		Kirsch et al. (2016)	13	Yes	No	Yoked sham and No feedback	13 yoked 12 no fdbk	Yes No	Yes	No
Schizophrenia	Clinical population	Okano et al. (2020)	10	Yes	Yes	Different task and region	No	7 (same subjects)	No	No
		Bauer et al. (2020)	10	Yes	Yes	Different task and region	No	7 (same subjects)	N/A	N/A
		Zweerings et al. (2019)	21	Yes	No	No control, only active groups	N/A	N/A	N/A	N/A
		Orlov et al. (2018)	12	Trend/Yes	No	No	N/A	N/A	N/A	N/A
		Cordes et al. (2015)	11	No	No	Same paradigm in healthy controls	N/A	N/A	N/A	N/A
OCD	Subclinical population	Scheinost et al. (2013)	10	Yes	Yes	Yoked sham	Yes	10	No	Yes

Table 1: Summary of patient studies with fMRI neurofeedback—cont'd

Disorder		Study[a]	Sample size NF group (based on completed intervention/clinical assessment)	Successful self-regulation (within group)	Significant symptom change in NF group (clinical scales only)	Control group or condition[b]	Participant blinding	Sample size control	Significant gp diff biomarker change	Significant gp diff symptom change
Parkinson's disease	Clinical population	Subramanian et al. (2016)	13	Yes (baseline comparison)	Yes	Wii-Fit training	No	13	N/A	No
		Subramanian et al. (2011)	5	Yes (baseline comparison)	Yes	Mental imagery during fMRI without NF	No	5	Yes	Yes
Alzheimer's disease	Prodromal AD	Hohenfeld et al. (2017)	10	No	N/A	Same paradigm in healthy controls	No	4	No	N/A
Tourette syndrome	Clinical population	Sukhodolsky et al. (2020)	21 total 11 in arm 1	No	Yes	Yoked sham	Yes	21 total 10 in arm 1	No/Yes[d]	Yes
ADHD	Clinical population	Zilverstand et al. (2017)	7	Yes	No	No feedback	No	6	No	No
		Alegria et al. (2017)	18	Yes	Yes	Feedback gp from diff area	No	13	Yes	No
ASD	Clinical population	Ramot et al. (2017)	17	Yes	No	Orthogonal fdbk in healthy subs	Yes	10	Yes	No
Aphasia	Clinical population	Sreedharan et al. (2019)	4	Yes (baseline comparison)	N/A	Standard care group	No	4	No	N/A
Huntington's Disease	Clinical population	Papoutsi et al. (2018)	10	Yes (increase over time)	N/A	No	N/A	N/A	No	N/A
Tinnitus	Clinical population	Emmert et al. (2017)	7	Yes (downregulation)	No	Intermittent feedback	No	7	No	No

Continued

Table 1: Summary of patient studies with fMRI neurofeedback—cont'd

Disorder	Study[a]	Sample size NF group (based on completed intervention/clinical assessment)	Successful self-regulation (within group)	Significant symptom change in NF group (clinical scales only)	Control group or condition[b]	Participant blinding	Sample size control	Significant gp diff biomarker change	Significant gp diff symptom change
Pain — Clinical population	Goldway et al. (2019)	25	Yes	Yes (at follow-up)	Feedback from diff. Patients	Yes	9	Yes	Yes (at follow-up)
Clinical and Subclinical population	Guan et al. (2015)	8	Yes	No	Feedback from diff. area	Yes	6	Yes	Yes
	De Charms et al. (2005)	8 patients 8 healthy participants	N/A (patients) Yes (healthy participants)	Yes	Autonomic Biofeedback (patients) Various (healthy participants)	No	4 patients 28 healthy participants	N/A (patients) Yes (healthy participants)	Yes
Borderline Personality Disorder — Clinical population	Zaehringer et al. (2019)	24	Yes	Yes	No	N/A	N/A	N/A	N/A
Clinical population	Paret et al. (2016)	8	Yes	No	No	N/A	N/A	N/A	N/A

[a]Studies only included if (1) they were large enough for group-level statistics and (2) they were specifically measuring symptoms relevant to the disorder either in a patient or subclinical population and examining changes in those symptoms pre- to post-NF.

[b]Control group here specifically refers to a group that receives an intervention designed to control for nonspecific effects of the intervention.

[c]"Significant" "changes" here mean changes over time while the same mental task is performed. Specifically, if subjects are instructed to control symptoms during feedback, changes relative to runs where they are encouraged to experience symptoms are not included.

[d]No for the registered outcome measures, but Yes in an exploratory measure.

References

Alegria, A.A., et al., 2017. Real-time fMRI neurofeedback in adolescents with attention deficit hyperactivity disorder. Hum. Brain Mapp. 38, 3190–3209.

Bauer, C.C.C., et al., 2020. Real-time fMRI neurofeedback reduces auditory hallucinations and modulates resting state connectivity of involved brain regions: part 2: default mode network -preliminary evidence. Psychiatry Res. 284, 112770.

Canterberry, M., et al., 2013. Sustained reduction of nicotine craving with real-time neurofeedback: exploring the role of severity of dependence. Nicotine Tob. Res. 15, 2120–2124.

Chiba, T., et al., 2019. Current status of neurofeedback for post-traumatic stress disorder: a systematic review and the possibility of decoded neurofeedback. Front. Hum. Neurosci. 13, 233.

Cordes, J.S., et al., 2015. Cognitive and neural strategies during control of the anterior cingulate cortex by fMRI neurofeedback in patients with schizophrenia. Front. Behav. Neurosci. 9, 169.

de Charms, R., et al., 2005. Control over brain activation and pain learned by using real-time functional MRI. Proc. Natl. Acad. Sci. U. S. A. 102, 18626–18631.

Emmert, K., et al., 2017. Continuous vs. intermittent neurofeedback to regulate auditory cortex activity of tinnitus patients using real-time fMRI – a pilot study. Neuroimage Clin. 14, 97–104.

Fruchtman, T., Cohen, A., Jaljuli, I., Keynan, J.N., Drori, G., Routledge, E., Krasnoshtein, M., Hendler, T., 2019. Feasibility and effectiveness of personalized amygdala-related neurofeedback for post-traumatic stress disorder. https://psyarxiv.com/qmsz3/.

Goldway, N., et al., 2019. Volitional limbic neuromodulation exerts a beneficial clinical effect on fibromyalgia. NeuroImage 186, 758–770.

Guan, M., et al., 2015. Self-regulation of brain activity in patients with postherpetic neuralgia: a double-blind randomized study using real-time FMRI neurofeedback. PLoS One 10, e0123675.

Hamilton, J.P., et al., 2016. Effects of salience-network-node neurofeedback training on affective biases in major depressive disorder. Psychiatry Res. Neuroimaging 249, 91–96.

Hanlon, C.A., et al., 2013. Reduction of cue-induced craving through realtime neurofeedback in nicotine users: the role of region of interest selection and multiple visits. Psychiatry Res. 213, 79–81.

Hartwell, K.J., et al., 2016. Individualized real-time fMRI neurofeedback toattenuate craving in nicotine-dependent smokers. J. Psychiatry Neurosci. 41, 48–55.

Hohenfeld, C., et al., 2017. Cognitive improvement and brain changes after real-time functional MRI neurofeedback training in healthy elderly and prodromal Alzheimer's disease. Front. Neurol. 8, 384.

Karch, S., et al., 2015. Modulation of craving related brain responses using real-time fMRI in patients with alcohol use disorder. PLoS One 10, e0133034.

Kirsch, M., Gruber, I., Ruf, M., Kiefer, F., Kirsch, P., 2016. Real-time functional magnetic resonance imaging neurofeedback can reduce striatal cue-reactivity to alcohol stimuli. Addict. Biol. 21, 982–992.

Kirschner, M., et al., 2018. Self-regulation of the dopaminergic reward circuit in cocaine users with mental imagery and neurofeedback. EBioMedicine 37, 489–498.

Li, X., Hartwell, K.J., Borckardt, J., Prisciandaro, J.J., Saladin, M.E., Morgan, P.S., Johnson, K.A., Lematty, T., Brady, K.T., George, M.S., 2013. Volitional reduction of anterior cingulate cortex activity produces decreased cue craving in smoking cessation: a preliminary real-time fMRI study. Addict. Biol. 18(4), 739-748. https://doi.org/10.1111/j.1369-1600.2012.00449.x.

Linden, D.E.J., et al., 2012. Real-time self-regulation of emotion networks in patients with depression. PLoS One 7, e38115.

Mehler, D.M.A., et al., 2018. Targeting the affective brain-a randomized controlled trial of real-time fMRI neurofeedback in patients with depression. Neuropsychopharmacology 43 (13), 2578–2585.

Nicholson, A.A., et al., 2018. Intrinsic connectivity network dynamics in PTSD during amygdala downregulation using real-time fMRI neurofeedback: a preliminary analysis. Hum. Brain Mapp. 39, 4258–4275.

Okano, K., et al., 2020. Real-time fMRI feedback impacts brain activation, results in auditory hallucinations reduction: part 1: superior temporal gyrus – preliminary evidence. Psychiatry Res. 286, 112862.

Orlov, N.D., et al., 2018. Real-time fMRI neurofeedback to down-regulate superior temporal gyrus activity in patients with schizophrenia and auditory hallucinations: a proof-of-concept study. Transl. Psychiatry 8, 46.

Papoutsi, M., et al., 2018. Stimulating neural plasticity with real-time fMRI neurofeedback in Huntington's disease: a proof of concept study. Hum. Brain Mapp. 39, 1339–1353.

Paret, C., et al., 2016. Alterations of amygdala-prefrontal connectivity with real-time fMRI neurofeedback in BPD patients. Soc. Cogn. Affect. Neurosci. 11, 952–960.

Ramot, M., et al., 2017. Direct modulation of aberrant brain network connectivity through real-time NeuroFeedback. elife 6, e28974.

Scheinost, D., et al., 2013. Orbitofrontal cortex neurofeedback produces lasting changes in contamination anxiety and resting-state connectivity. Transl. Psychiatry 3, e250.

Schnyer, D.M., et al., 2015. Neurocognitive therapeutics: from concept to application in the treatment of negative attention bias. Biol. Mood Anxiety Disord. 5, 1.

Sreedharan, S., Arun, K.M., Sylaja, P.N., Kesavadas, C., Sitaram, R., 2019. Functional connectivity of language regions of stroke patients with expressive aphasia during real-time functional magnetic resonance imaging based neurofeedback. Brain Connect 9, 613–626.

Subramanian, L., et al., 2011. Real-time functional magnetic resonance imaging neurofeedback for treatment of Parkinson's disease. J. Neurosci. 31, 16309–16317.

Subramanian, L., et al., 2016. Functional magnetic resonance imaging neurofeedback-guided motor imagery training and motor training for Parkinson's disease: randomized trial. Front. Behav. Neurosci. 10, 111.

Sukhodolsky, D.G., et al., 2020. Randomized, sham-controlled trial of real-time functional magnetic resonance imaging neurofeedback for tics in adolescents with Tourette syndrome. Biol. Psychiatry 87, 1063–1070.

Taschereau-Dumouchel, V., et al., 2018. Towards an unconscious neural reinforcement intervention for common fears. Proc. Natl. Acad. Sci. U. S. A. 115, 3470–3475.

Young, K.D., et al., 2014. Real-time FMRI neurofeedback training of amygdala activity in patients with major depressive disorder. PLoS One 9, e88785.

Young, K.D., et al., 2017. Randomized clinical trial of real-time fMRI amygdala neurofeedback for major depressive disorder: effects on symptoms and autobiographical memory recall. Am. J. Psychiatry 174 (8), 748–755.

Zaehringer, J., et al., 2019. Improved emotion regulation after neurofeedback: a single-arm trial in patients with borderline personality disorder. Neuroimage Clin. 24, 102032.

Zahn, R., et al., 2019. Blame-rebalance fMRI neurofeedback in major depressive disorder: a randomised proof-of-concept trial. Neuroimage Clin. 24, 101992.

Zilverstand, A., et al., 2017. fMRI neurofeedback training for increasing anterior cingulate cortex activation in adult attention deficit hyperactivity disorder. an exploratory randomized, single-blinded study. PLoS One 12, e0170795.

Zotev, V., et al., 2018. Real-time fMRI neurofeedback training of the amygdala activity with simultaneous EEG in veterans with combat-related PTSD. Neuroimage Clin. 19, 106–121.

Zweerings, J., et al., 2018. Impaired voluntary control in PTSD: probing self-regulation of the ACC with real-time fMRI. Front. Psychiatry 9, 219.

Zweerings, J., et al., 2019. Neurofeedback of core language network nodes modulates connectivity with the default-mode network: a double-blind fMRI neurofeedback study on auditory verbal hallucinations. NeuroImage 189, 533–542.

CHAPTER 7

Design of clinical studies in neurofeedback

David Linden

School for Mental Health and Neuroscience, Faculty of Health, Medicine and Life Sciences, Maastricht University, Maastricht, Netherlands

1 General principles of clinical trial design

Clinical trials are mainly conducted in order to evaluate the safety, feasibility, efficacy, and practicality of therapeutic interventions. Other applications include the assessment of the value of a new diagnostic tool or screening procedure. In the context of this book we are mainly concerned with the first group, the *interventional* trials. Trials generally will not be designed to answer all of these questions. For a new intervention, for example, it will be paramount to address safety and feasibility questions before moving on to efficacy and, ultimately, cost-effectiveness. However, it is prudent to keep all these aspects of the evaluation chain in mind—a new intervention that is unlikely ever to be cost effective has little chance of succeeding on the healthcare market even if it is safe and efficacious and liked by patients. Before a new intervention is introduced into clinical practice it is normally evaluated in a series of clinical trials. Early phase trials focus on safety and feasibility. For pharmacological interventions the first trials may be conducted in healthy volunteers in order to determine safety and in neurofeedback, too, it is common to test new protocols in healthy individuals first, mainly to determine their feasibility (that is, whether participants can actually attain the self-regulation goal). At this stage of safety and feasibility evaluation, only preliminary estimates of efficacy are obtained, which will inform the power calculation of larger trials that will pit the new intervention against a control intervention in a randomized design. Once efficacy has been established by demonstrating superiority compared to a standard intervention (or equivalence to an approved therapy in a so-called noninferiority trial) even larger trials may be needed to observe longer-term effects in clinical practice and determine cost-effectiveness. These *pragmatic* trials are generally conducted after an intervention has been introduced into clinical practice (*postmarketing trials*) and may make use of routinely collected clinical data. In addition to issues of cost-effectiveness and other practicalities, this ongoing monitoring of the effects of a new intervention also serves the purpose of obtaining more detailed safety data because the initial trials, albeit powered for efficacy, may not have been large enough to discover some rarer adverse effects.

fMRI Neurofeedback. https://doi.org/10.1016/B978-0-12-822421-2.00009-0

2 Neurofeedback in the context of the framework for the development of complex interventions

The general principles of trial design, including the five phases from phase 0 (pharmacokinetics) to phase 4 (postmarketing surveillance), were originally conceived for drug studies. Although some of the principles can be transferred to other types of interventions it became clear that nonpharmacological interventions, which often are more complex in the sense that they involve several interacting components, need their own framework for clinical evaluation. The MRC framework for Developing and evaluating complex interventions, first published in 2000 by the UK's Medical Research Council (MRC) and continually updated (Craig et al., 2008; Moore et al., 2015; Möhler et al., 2015), responds to this need. It can be usefully considered for the design of neurofeedback trials because neurofeedback clearly fulfills at least four of the five criteria listed for a complex intervention, "Number of interacting components within the experimental and control interventions," "Number and difficulty of behaviours required by those delivering or receiving the intervention," "Number and variability of outcomes," and "Degree of flexibility or tailoring of the intervention permitted" (Craig et al., 2008). Compared to the 2000 version, the 2008 moved from a linear process modeled on the phases of drug development and evaluation to a cyclical/iterative process involving crosstalk between the components of "development," "feasibility and piloting," "evaluation," and "implementation."

It is worth considering this framework from the perspective of the design of fMRI-neurofeedback (fMRI-NF) interventions and trials. In the development process, most work on the evidence base will have to rely on the effects of broadly related interventions, for example EEG-neurofeedback or mental imagery training, because of the scarcity of evidence on clinical application of fMRI-NF. Often the argument for developing the (potentially more expensive and generally more technically demanding) fMRI-based intervention will be based on *lack* of efficacy of these comparator interventions rather than on the efficacy of similar interventions. Because of this lack of positive empirical evidence the second component, "identifying or developing theory" is particularly important. Because of its close association with neuropsychological/neurophysiological disease models, this part of the development cascade is actually a strength of the fMRI-NF field. Researchers in this field generally develop interventions and select targeted brain signals based on explicit models of dysfunction and/or compensation of the disease in question, or at least based on explicit models of the desired neural training effects. The third component, modeling, is harder to achieve because so little is known about the efficacy of fMRI-NF interventions and the characteristics of likely responders. Generally, such modeling is conducted on the implementation side and assesses features of the practicality and target population of the intervention. However, for fMRI-NF we could also think of neurophysiological in silico approaches based on neural models of the disease and the likely neuroplastic effect of an fMRI-based intervention, which might also give us the much needed estimates of required dose/number of sessions. Programs such as the Virtual Brain Project or the modeling efforts of the Human Brain Project may soon provide the required disease models and could be extended to allow for the modeling of the effects of NF and other neuromodulation treatments (Falcon et al., 2016).

Feasibility assessment is an integral part of the development of an fMRI-NF protocol before it is moved to a full clinical trial. This includes securing the stability of the setup/brain-computer interface and the reliability of target identification, whether this is based on anatomical or functional localizers or multivariate pattern identification. It should also include some evidence for feasibility of the self-regulation protocol, that is, whether a reasonable proportion of patients can actually attain the targeted neural activation/pattern change. Generally this would be preceded by demonstration of feasibility in healthy individuals. One example of this type of process would be our development of an fMRI-NF intervention with a functional localizer of emotion areas, which moved from a single-session study in healthy individuals to a multisession pilot study and on to a multisession randomized trial (Johnston et al., 2011; Linden et al., 2012; Mehler et al., 2018). The entire process from the initial protocol development to the publication of the randomized trial took about ten years. In addition to these neurofeedback-specific considerations of "target engagement," it will also be important to assess feasibility of patient recruitment and retention given the considerable demands on patients' time and concentration. Here, information from other neurofeedback studies or similarly effortful interventions can help obtain estimates for specific patient groups. For example, in Parkinson's disease we obtained high rates of recruitment (32/47 assessed for eligibility) and retention (26/32 randomized patients completing the study) for a 12-week intervention combining fMRI-NF with motor training and involving multiple laboratory and homework sessions (Subramanian et al., 2016) whereas our retention rate was much lower (16/25) for the intervention group of a 6-session fMRI-NF trial in alcohol dependence (Subramanian et al., 2021). Such feasibility trials will also yield important information about effect sizes of changes on clinical and neural measures although, as always, care needs to be taken not to overestimate effect sizes based on relatively small initial samples. Flexible sampling schemes using Bayesian frameworks can be helpful in the design of clinical trials especially where it is difficult to obtain reliable estimates of clinical effect sizes (and thus, a range of possible outcomes needs to be taken into consideration) and where individual treatment costs (e.g., for scan hours) are relatively high. We have therefore started developing trial protocols in fMRI-NF based on Bayesian Sampling Frameworks (Mehler et al., 2020).

The framework lists a range of randomized and nonrandomized designs for evaluation studies, and reasons for choosing between them. Based on the nature of the clinical effects generally expected for neurofeedback trials (emerging over time, not immediately transformative, and thus needing statistical assessment) and the clinical setting, an experimental approach with randomized group allocation will generally be appropriate, but it will always be useful to obtain advice from experts in trials methodology in the design phase of the trial. Longer-term follow-up measures, beyond the immediate postintervention time point, are customary in the potential application areas of neurofeedback in neurology and psychiatry, and may be particularly relevant for fMRI-NF where clinical effects may build up over time and continue to improve after conclusion of the intervention (Rance et al., 2018). Process evaluation is another, often neglected, component of the assessment of complex interventions. It is particularly relevant for an intervention such as neurofeedback that depends on standardized capture and analysis of neural signals and conversion into sensory feedback, as well as (semi-)standardized instructions provided by experimenters, possibly including homework and other instructions for exercises outside the scanner. Documenting these processes and assessing implementation fidelity is thus a crucial component of neurofeedback trials. A crucial first step toward such process evaluation is the systematic documentation of the elements of the intervention. Our recent survey of the community using the Template for Intervention Description and Replication (TIDieR) has revealed that protocols of fMRI-NF interventions still vary widely across research groups (Randell et al., 2018). The increasing use of the Consensus on the reporting and experimental design of clinical and cognitive-behavioral neurofeedback studies (CRED-nf checklist) (Ros et al., 2020) will likely further facilitate standardization and harmonization of protocols and outcome measures.

Another specific concern that is often raised in relation to fMRI-NF is whether it can ever become cost effective. The answer to this question will ultimately hinge on its efficacy and numbers needed to treat. If fMRI-NF interventions were to enhance abstinence rates in alcohol dependence substantially, for example, the gain in quality of life and productivity and savings in other healthcare costs could justify the costs of several MRI sessions and the technical personnel needed to implement the intervention. For an intervention with relatively high base costs (need for availability of/investment in an MRI system) and little potential for efficiency gains for scaling up (as one would obtain with group or internet-based interventions, for example) certain minimum effect size and a certain sustainability of clinical effects would be needed for cost-effectiveness. Present trials rarely include evaluation of this component, and at the current state of the field it would be difficult to do such an evaluation in a meaningful way. Nevertheless, several groups are pursuing transfer technologies such as EEG or near-infrared spectroscopy in order to have lower-cost alternatives for scaling up (see also Chapter 12).

Even if fMRI-NF were shown to be cost effective its implementation in clinical practice may not be straightforward. Availability of MRI systems and properly trained operators will be a point of attention. It would therefore be useful to include nonacademic hospitals as trial sites to demonstrate the feasibility of establishing fMRI-NF outside of research settings and including any challenges encountered along this path in the process evaluation. These considerations vindicate the use of the complex interventions framework for the design and interpretation of fMRI-NF trials, so much so that fMRI-NF can be considered a paradigmatic case for the relevance and applicability of this iterative and intertwined evaluation process.

3 General challenges of NF studies

The choice of control condition for randomized trials of neurofeedback poses particular difficulties, and whatever choice the investigators make, there will almost certainly be questions that cannot be answered with any single design. The traditional choice for EEG-neurofeedback studies has been some sort of sham treatment, which entails recording of EEG but a feedback signal from a different patient (yoked feedback, the most common sham condition in EEG-neurofeedback trials) or a different component of the EEG signal that is not the pathophysiological target of the study. Yoked feedback controls for reward experience at group level (the active and control groups will overall receive identical feedback), but entails the risk that patients become aware of the noncontingency of the feedback and thus would not be blinded to group assignment (and might stop putting effort into the training process). If veridical feedback is employed, but from a different (or random) frequency band or another nontargeted EEG parameter, reward matching is difficult to ensure as the control biomarker may be easier or more difficult to learn to control than the target biomarker. If conscious strategies that are effective for controlling the target biomarker and not the control biomarker are employed by all participants it is likely that the experimental group will do better in controlling the feedback signal than the control group. A greater clinical response in the experimental group in this case cannot be confidently attributed to the neurofeedback training, as it could be due to a greater sense of personal efficacy during training, more positive affect experienced in the study, or different levels of motivation induced by the more positive feedback received. In certain circumstances, this form of control also carries the potential risk that the blind will be damaged. For example, when participants are using strategies they know to be effective in regulating the target area, and when the study cycles between regulate and nonregulate blocks, the participants may notice that the feedback does not seem to change as expected when they engage their regulation strategies. Similarly, if provocative stimuli (symptom-related cues) are used, participants may notice that the feedback does not show target engagement during provocation. Finally, this control condition may be too conservative if there is a correlation between the "sham" (e.g., random frequency bands) and "real" (e.g., sensorimotor rhythm) target, and may be even more problematic if they are anticorrelated, as the sham condition could be suppressing patterns that are believed to be therapeutic. However, one interesting and unique aspect of this form of control condition is that it can control for the possibility that learning to control any aspect of brain function is therapeutic—this is an important feature for studies aiming to clarify the specific role of the target biomarker in symptoms, but could be a drawback for studies where the primary aim is to demonstrate therapeutic value of the neurofeedback intervention, regardless of its mechanism of action.

For fMRI-NF similar considerations apply. Ideally, a trial would demonstrate both clinical efficacy and a specific contribution of the neurofeedback procedures. To demonstrate clinical efficacy (and thus the basic utility of the neurofeedback intervention) a design that compares fMRI-NF as add-on to standard care with standard care (or "treatment-as-usual") alone would be sufficient. This may indeed be a useful first step (after demonstrating basic feasibility, which can be done with a nonrandomized design) before further, more conservative comparisons are undertaken. After all, a treatment that does not add anything to standard care (where such care is available and has an acceptable safety profile) is unlikely to be of interest for clinical practice. However, this comparison does not control for nonspecific effects of the intervention, such as involvement in an interesting project, reward experience, additional contact with research and clinical staff, and mental imagery or other cognitive stimulation if applicable. Various feedback protocols, including yoked NF, NF from another brain region, biofeedback or bidirectional NF, have been proposed because they cover one or several of these potential confounds, but none of them can cover all aspects. For example, we employed feedback from an alternative brain area, the parahippocampal place area (PPA), in our depression trial, where the active arm targeted fronto-limbic emotion areas (Mehler et al., 2018). This approach resulted in groups that were well matched for performance level and reward experience but may have been too conservative because reinforcement of spatial mental imagery (the likely mechanism behind PPA training) may also be desirable for patients with depression. This speaks to the general "problem" that brain areas are interconnected, and it will never be possible to find a brain region or network that is completely unrelated to the targeted pathophysiological process. A detailed overview and discussion of control conditions for fMRI-NF has been provided in a recent review paper (Table 1) (Sorger et al., 2019).

One of the main aims of including control conditions/interventions is to rule out "placebo" effects. This imperative has been transferred to the complex interventions field from that of drug evaluation but entails added complexities that make fully "controlled" trial designs difficult. In general the "placebo effect" is comprised of several components. According to a taxonomy championed by Edzard Ernst, we can distinguish between a "true" placebo effect and several other components of the "perceived" placebo effect (see Fig. 1).

This general taxonomy of placebo effects is a useful starting point for consideration of control conditions but may need to be adjusted for the specific scenarios encountered in neurofeedback trials, particularly for psychiatric indications. Clinician-patient interactions are not just a general component of medical therapies but also integral specific part of many psychiatric (particularly psychotherapeutic) interventions, and thus controlling for them may not be possible in a meaningful way. Similarly, moving toward more socially desirable patterns of thought and behavior is a key component of treatments for addiction, for example. There may also be an overlap or interaction between the neurofeedback training and the "true placebo" effect (in the sense of patient's beliefs). Although demonstration of a significant benefit over the most conservative control intervention will address these issues of overlap

Table 1: Main types of control conditions for neurofeedback studies with their advantages and drawbacks.

Factors to be controlled for to establish causality	No control	No-training Control		Bidirectional-Regulation Control	Placebo Control				Mental-Rehearsal Control	
		Treatment as usual+	List of matched participants/Waitlist+		Alternative feedback		Sham feedback		Inside the MRI scanner	Outside the MRI scanner
					Feedback from an Alternative Brain Signal	Feedback based on non-brain signals	'Yoked' feedback	Artificially generated feedback		
Equal Motivation/ Perception of Success	X	X	X	✓	✓ *@	✓ *@	✓ ^	✓ ^	X	X
Demonstrate neurophysiological specificity	X	X	X	✓	✓ *@	X	X	X	X	X
Exclude placebo effects	X	X	X	✓	✓ *@	✓ *@	✓ ^	✓ ^	X	X
Exclude Global (spatially non-specific) effects	X	X	X	✓	✓	✓	✓	✓	✓	X
Exclude Behavioral effects	X	X	X	X	X	X	X	X	✓	✓
Remarks	Extremely economical	Economical; Crucial (and fairest) control group in clinical context	Very economical	Up- and downregulation of the same region might not always be possible; Not always ethically jestifiable+	Regions' signal properties should be matched across groups; Might be too conservative (critical region might be trained via funtrional connectivity); Risk of unblinding participants	Risk of unblinding participants	Risk of unblinding participants	Should be generated considering properties of the hemodynamic response; Risk of unblinding participants	Not always possible (implicit neurofeedback); Control participants should not be aware of the existence of the neurofeedback group	Not always possible (implicit neurofeedback); Can considerably minimize scanning costs; Control participants should not be aware of the existence of the neurofeedback group

* if ability to control is balanced across groups

^ if subjects are not unblinded by signal not matching mental changes

@ if control signal does not have an antagonistic relationship with the behavioral/clinical variable of interest.

+ signifies a situation in a clinical context.

From Sorger, B., Scharnowski, F., Linden, D.E.J., Hampson, M., Young, K.D., 2019. Control freaks: towards optimal selection of control conditions for fMRI neurofeedback studies. NeuroImage 186, 256–265. https://doi.org/10.1016/j.neuroimage.2018.11.004 with kind permission from Elsevier.

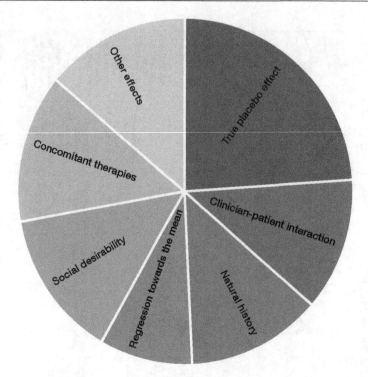

Fig. 1

Factors which can contribute to "perceived" placebo effects in clinical trials. *Adapted with kind permission from Ernst, E., 2007. Placebo: new insights into an old enigma. Drug Discov. Today 12 (9–10), 413–418. https://doi.org/10.1016/j.drudis.2007.03.007. Elsevier. According to the author of the original figure, "effect sizes can vary depending on the exact circumstances of the experiment and are arbitrarily chosen in this graph." The author also explains that factors can overlap, for example "clinician–patient interaction and social desirability could be seen as part of the 'true' placebo effect as they can depend on the belief the patients attributes to them."*

and interaction, it may not be realistic to implement such a control intervention. Firstly, both alternative and sham feedback (see Table 1) incur the possibility that patients actually regulate the target signal (as well). For the alternative feedback this may arise from the functional connectedness between the alternative and target area. For the sham feedback this may arise from partly veridical feedback (e.g., if someone performs well and receives yoked feedback from a good performer, this feedback will still correlate with the trainee's signal and thus provide a partially valid training signal). In addition to these limitations inherent to the neurofeedback design, there is also a practical limitation based on effect sizes. If the active intervention remains better than even the most conservative control interventions, but with loss of so many active components to make the effect size vanishingly small, it may just not be practical to obtain the resources (patient number) to conduct appropriately powered trials (for more thoughts on this, see the following section on depression).

Another challenge that is common to all neurofeedback studies is to define criteria for successful self-regulation performance. For any interpretation of clinical effects it is important to identify the patients who actually achieved a sufficient degree of self-regulation. This aspect has parallels with the determination of target engagement in drug studies or the measurement of individual motor thresholds in transcranial magnetic stimulation trials. However, neurofeedback "target engagement" is much harder to predict on the basis of small pilot studies, and almost impossible to predict for patient groups on the basis of data from healthy individuals. Identification of "regulators" and "non-regulators" is therefore a crucial feature of neurofeedback trials and may warrant additional subgroup analysis that reduces the power of the trial. This effort is further complicated by the lack of standardized criteria for self-regulation "success." The success criteria are generally not preregistered with the rest of the outcome measures although this would be desirable for future clinical trials. Furthermore, they vary greatly across protocols and research groups. The most commonly used criteria are significant difference of activation levels during self-regulation blocks compared to a baseline or mirror condition with similar stimuli but no feedback instructions (Ihssen et al., 2016), activation increase over time (ideally modeled by learning curves) (Thibault et al., 2018), or the improved differentiation between two neural patterns in the case of multivariate or decoded neurofeedback (see Chapter 10). For activation level-based feedback, the use of precision of attaining a specific level rather than upregulating as much as possible might be an attractive, and physiologically meaningful alternative (Mehler et al., 2019). Without predefined self-regulation success criteria it will be very difficult to demonstrate mechanism even in clinical trials that provide evidence for efficacy. At the same time, such success criteria can enable meaningful analyses of single-arm trials, based on the association between neural and clinical responses. Such correlation analyses between (size of the) training effect and clinical improvement are commonly provided in reports on clinical neurofeedback trials but more convincing if they are part of the prespecified analyses, including preregistration of the neural outcome ("success") marker.

4 Considerations for specific disease areas

4.1 Depression

Depression was the first psychiatric indication for which fMRI-NF interventions were developed and is arguably the psychiatric syndrome with the largest evidence base for fMRI-NF (Linden et al., 2012; Mehler et al., 2018; Young et al., 2017). Two recent clinical trials have demonstrated ca. 50% improvement in clinical symptoms after relatively brief (two sessions in the Young et al. study, five sessions in the Mehler et al. study) interventions. However, in one case the improvement was not superior to that observed after the control intervention (Mehler et al., 2018), and in the other case the intervention groups were not matched for success rate/reward (Young et al., 2017). For a relapsing-remitting disorder such as depression, whose established treatments have a high rate of nonspecific effects (Fournier et al., 2010), it is particularly challenging to demonstrate specific effects that exceed the combination of spontaneous remission, improvement on standard care, and placebo effects.

The most conservative designs, by excluding nonspecific effects and their interaction with neurofeedback, run the danger of discarding effective interventions just because they are not statistically superior to a semiactive intervention such as neurofeedback from another disease area (Mehler et al., 2018). After all, there are no completely "passive" control interventions because all interventions will require active collaboration of patients and thus have specific clinical effects in their own right. This difficulty of running trials with interventions that have been artificially created just with the purpose of serving as control conditions is one of the reasons why comparisons between fMRI-NF as add-on to standard care with standard care are so important. Consider the following scenario: A neurofeedback intervention might have an effect size of 0.6 for clinical effects as add-on to standard care, which is a common effect size for add-on antidepressant treatments. A sample size around 60 per group may be sufficient for a properly powered study testing this comparison. However, once all the nonspecific effects of the fMRI-NF procedure have been addressed through a conservative control intervention (see Table 1) the added clinical effect of the fMRI-NF intervention may only have a size of 0.2, resulting in the need for 400 patients or more per group in a standard frequentist design. This study size requires considerable resources, which exceed standard public research funding programs, and patient recruitment across several clinical centers, posing additional challenges for protocol harmonization for multicenter trials. I am not suggesting that the ambition to perform tightly controlled trials for investigation of causal mechanism should be abandoned, but would like to highlight that different designs are appropriate for different questions, and if the aim is to demonstrate basic clinical utility the most conservative design may be neither realistic nor necessary. Although I have addressed these issues in the context of depression trials the highlighted problems apply to all clinical applications of neurofeedback. Another problem with artificial control interventions is that they may create spurious evidence for clinical efficacy for ineffective active interventions if the control intervention has a noxious effect on the patient. For example, sham interventions that unintentionally frustrate or fatigue patients may lead to a worsening of depression symptoms and thus a significant clinical effect for the active intervention that might not be apparent in a comparison with standard care alone.

4.2 Addiction

Clinical trials in substance use disorders can be designed either as relapse prevention trials in currently abstinent patients or to assess symptom/use reduction. Relapse prevention trials address the very important clinical need to stabilize abstinence and prolong abstinence times in patients with alcohol dependence and other dependent use disorder (Cox et al., 2016).

They provide an opportunity to work with highly motivated patients who have been through a detoxification program and are undergoing further addiction treatment. However, they require a very long follow-up time to achieve sufficient power to assess reduction of relapse rates and may be affected by ceiling effects. For example, in our fMRI-NF trial with abstinent patients with alcohol dependence we observed very low relapse rates in the patients who attended follow-up appointments even after one year (Subramanian et al., 2021). Conversely, trials with currently consuming patients with substance use disorders are challenging particularly if the drug use frequently leads to acute intoxication (such as in dependent users of alcohol). Thus many nonabstinent patients with substance dependence may not be able to sustain the concentration and motivation needed to follow through with several sessions of neurofeedback, plus potentially homework assignments, although neurofeedback has been successfully piloted in nicotine-dependent smokers (Hartwell et al., 2016).

Because of the inherent difficulties in designing neurofeedback trials in addiction (particularly alcohol and drug addiction) the field is currently at a crossroads: One strategy would be to integrate neurofeedback into treatments that focus on reduction of consumption and craving rather than promotion of abstinence. Another would be to adapt the design of prevention trials and increase their power through links with routine clinical data that would allow investigators to ascertain outcomes in patients who do not attend follow-ups.

4.3 Neurorehabilitation

Neurofeedback is conceptually attractive for rehabilitation of Parkinson's disease, stroke, and other neurological diseases because of the availability of pathophysiological models that implicate network dysfunction or imbalance that could be rectified by neurofeedback. For example, the hemispheric competition model of stroke could be used to motivate neurofeedback to rebalance ipsi- and contralesional motor cortex, similar to considerations in the development of transcranial brain stimulation interventions (Cunningham et al., 2019). Along similar lines, models of cortico-subcortical interaction in Parkinson's or Huntington's disease can be used to motivate neurofeedback interventions for these neurodegenerative diseases (Papoutsi et al., 2018; Subramanian et al., 2011). These protocols will be discussed in more detail in Chapter 11. Here I will focus on a few issues of feasibility and trial design that pertain to neurological patients. Whereas in our experience feasibility has been a challenge with subacute stroke patients because of patients' multimorbidity and the experience of discomfort while in the scanner, as well as movement artifacts, relatively few concerns of this sort arose in our trials in Parkinson's disease (Subramanian et al., 2016).

How could we then increase the feasibility of neurofeedback protocols for stroke rehabilitation? One option would be to confine the intervention to patients with relatively focal motor impairment and little comorbidity but this would limit the wider clinical utility of the approach. Another would be to target patients in later stages of stroke recovery when some of the acute problems (confusion, somatic comorbidities, psychological consequences of the stroke) have settled but this would risk losing access to the most plastic period of cerebral reorganization after stroke. Another option would be to use more mobile, bedside technologies that are less vulnerable to movement artifacts such as functional near-infrared spectroscopy (fNIRS). FNIRS-NF has indeed been piloted with some success in stroke patients (Mihara and Miyai, 2016) but no evidence from larger RCTs is available as yet.

Another challenge is the choice of target region or network. In neurological disease we are often faced with a pathology that involves irreversible loss of neuronal tissue, such as the core ischemic region in stroke or the loss of dopaminergic neurons in Parkinson's disease. It might still make sense to target these areas of primary damage with neurofeedback, which would be conceptually similar to TMS protocols aiming to activate the lesioned hemisphere after stroke (Hensel et al., 2019), for example in order to prevent spreading of loss of neurons or activate neighboring tissue that might compensate for local losses. Alternatively one might apply neurofeedback in a more general framework of network (re-)balancing, similar to the rationale for deep brain stimulation in PD, and target, for example, the contralesional hemisphere in stroke or the cortical input areas of the subthalamic nucleus in PD (Nachev et al., 2008; Subramanian et al., 2011). Unfortunately it is very difficult to obtain readouts of clinical effects after single sessions or generally over short time courses (days or a few weeks), which means that any of these ideas will probably have to be tested in longer, resource-intensive trials.

A linked problem arises from the low size of clinical effects (at least those so far observed after a few sessions of fMRI-NF). In our studies of PD, we observed improvements on the motor scale of the Unified Parkinson's Disease Rating Scale (UPDRS) around 5 points (Subramanian et al., 2011, 2016) which, albeit exceeding the minimally clinically important difference, is much smaller than the 50% improvements in symptom scores observed after a few sessions of fMRI-NF in depression (Mehler et al., 2018; Young et al., 2017). I would expect effects in neurorehabilitation to scale with the length and intensity of the intervention (at least up to a certain point) and thus longer protocols, involving perhaps 5–10 fMRI sessions and regular homework practice, to provide stronger effects that would also more easily be statistically superior to semiactive interventions (such as the motor training we used in our PD trial; Subramanian et al., 2016). However, at the current level of clinical evidence it may be difficult to persuade funders to invest in trials with even more resource-intensive fMRI-NF protocols, which seems to be one of the reasons for the slow progress of fMRI-NF research in neurorehabilitation. Trials using fMRI-NF (and other complex interventions) may also benefit particularly from novel outcome measures that may be more sensitive than conventional clinical scales, for example ecological momentary assessments of daily functioning and wellbeing and sensor-based assessments of motor function and physiology (Heijmans et al., 2019).

5 Summary

Neurofeedback is a complex intervention. Trials of therapeutic neurofeedback should therefore be conceptualized within the framework of complex interventions, which comprises the interacting phases of "Development," "Feasibility and piloting," "Evaluation," and "Implementation." Because neurofeedback is not only a complex but also an active intervention that relies on the successful collaboration of the patient (as defined by his or her attaining the desired neuroregulation target) careful feasibility testing of new protocols is needed. Another particularly challenging task in the development of neurofeedback protocols and trial design is the choice of control condition. I have argued that no control condition/intervention is perfect and that the choice of control has to be adjusted to the clinical syndrome and evaluation stage. Particular caution needs to be applied when designing artificial interventions that may control for several factors of the neurofeedback process but could be either too conservative (carrying clinical benefits in their own right) or too lenient (if they carry harmful effects) for a sound statistical comparison (and would give rise to ethical concerns, particularly in the latter case). I finally reviewed several challenges for fMRI-NF development in specific clinical areas, mood disorders, addiction, and neurorehabilitation.

References

Cox, W.M., Subramanian, L., Linden, D.E., Lührs, M., McNamara, R., Playle, R., Hood, K., Watson, G., Whittaker, J.R., Sakhuja, R., Ihssen, N., 2016. Neurofeedback training for alcohol dependence versus treatment as usual: study protocol for a randomized controlled trial. Trials 17 (1), 480. https://doi.org/10.1186/s13063-016-1607-7.

Craig, P., Dieppe, P., Macintyre, S., Michie, S., Nazareth, I., Petticrew, M., Guidance, M.R.C., 2008. Developing and evaluating complex interventions: the new Medical Research Council guidance. BMJ 337, a1655.

Cunningham, D.A., Knutson, J.S., Sankarasubramanian, V., Potter-Baker, K.A., Machado, A.G., Plow, E.B., 2019. Bilateral contralaterally controlled functional electrical stimulation reveals new insights into the interhemispheric competition model in chronic stroke. Neurorehabil. Neural Repair 33 (9), 707–717. https://doi.org/10.1177/1545968319863709.

Falcon, M.I., Jirsa, V., Solodkin, A., 2016. A new neuroinformatics approach to personalized medicine in neurology: the virtual brain. Curr. Opin. Neurol. 29 (4), 429–436. https://doi.org/10.1097/WCO.0000000000000344.

Fournier, J.C., DeRubeis, R.J., Hollon, S.D., Dimidjian, S., Amsterdam, J.D., Shelton, R.C., Fawcett, J., 2010. Antidepressant drug effects and depression severity: a patient-level meta-analysis. JAMA 303 (1), 47–53. https://doi.org/10.1001/jama.2009.1943.

Hartwell, K.J., Hanlon, C.A., Li, X., Borckardt, J.J., Canterberry, M., Prisciandaro, J.J., Moran-Santa Maria, M.M., LeMatty, T., George, M.S., Brady, K.T., 2016. Individualized real-time fMRI neurofeedback toattenuate craving in nicotine-dependent smokers. J. Psychiatry Neurosci. 41 (1), 48–55. https://doi.org/10.1503/jpn.140200.

Heijmans, M., Habets, J.G.V., Herff, C., Aarts, J., Stevens, A., Kuijf, M.L., Kubben, P.L., 2019. Monitoring Parkinson's disease symptoms during daily life: a feasibility study. NPJ Parkinsons Dis. 5, 21. https://doi.org/10.1038/s41531-019-0093-5.

Hensel, L., Grefkes, C., Tscherpel, C., Ringmaier, C., Kraus, D., Hamacher, S., Volz, L.J., Fink, G.R., 2019. Intermittent theta burst stimulation applied during early rehabilitation after stroke: study protocol for a randomised controlled trial. BMJ Open 9 (12). https://doi.org/10.1136/bmjopen-2019-034088, e034088.

Ihssen, N., Sokunbi, M.O., Lawrence, A.D., Lawrence, N.S., Linden, D.E., 2016. Neurofeedback of visual food cue reactivity: a potential avenue to alter incentive sensitization and craving. Brain Imaging Behav. 11 (3), 915–924. https://doi.org/10.1007/s11682-016-9558-x.

Johnston, S., Linden, D.E., Healy, D., Goebel, R., Habes, I., Boehm, S.G., 2011. Upregulation of emotion areas through neurofeedback with a focus on positive mood. Cogn. Affect. Behav. Neurosci. 11 (1), 44–51. https://doi.org/10.3758/s13415-010-0010-1.

Linden, D.E., Habes, I., Johnston, S.J., Linden, S., Tatineni, R., Subramanian, L., Sorger, B., Healy, D., Goebel, R., 2012. Real-time self-regulation of emotion networks in patients with depression. PLoS One 7 (6). https://doi.org/10.1371/journal.pone.0038115, e38115.

Mehler, D.M.A., Sokunbi, M.O., Habes, I., Barawi, K., Subramanian, L., Range, M., Evans, J., Hood, K., Lührs, M., Keedwell, P., Goebel, R., Linden, D.E.J., 2018. Targeting the affective brain-a randomized controlled trial of real-time fMRI neurofeedback in patients with depression. Neuropsychopharmacology 43 (13), 2578–2585. https://doi.org/10.1038/s41386-018-0126-5.

Mehler, D.M.A., Williams, A.N., Krause, F., Lührs, M., Wise, R.G., Turner, D.L., Linden, D.E.J., Whittaker, J.R., 2019. The BOLD response in primary motor cortex and supplementary motor area during kinesthetic motor imagery based graded fMRI neurofeedback. NeuroImage 184, 36–44. https://doi.org/10.1016/j.neuroimage.2018.09.007.

Mehler, D.M.A., Williams, A.N., Whittaker, J.R., Krause, F., Lührs, M., Kunas, S., Wise, R.G., Shetty, H.G.M., Turner, D.L., Linden, D.E.J., 2020. Graded fMRI neurofeedback training of motor imagery in middle cerebral artery stroke patients: a preregistered proof-of-concept study. Front. Hum. Neurosci. 14, 226. https://doi.org/10.3389/fnhum.2020.00226.

Mihara, M., Miyai, I., 2016. Review of functional near-infrared spectroscopy in neurorehabilitation. Neurophotonics 3 (3). https://doi.org/10.1117/1.NPh.3.3.031414, 031414.

Möhler, R., Köpke, S., Meyer, G., 2015. Criteria for reporting the development and evaluation of complex interventions in healthcare: revised guideline (CReDECI 2). Trials 16, 204. https://doi.org/10.1186/s13063-015-0709-y.

Moore, G.F., Audrey, S., Barker, M., Bond, L., Bonell, C., Hardeman, W., Moore, L., O'Cathain, A., Tinati, T., Wight, D., Baird, J., 2015. Process evaluation of complex interventions: Medical Research Council guidance. BMJ 350, h1258.

Nachev, P., Kennard, C., Husain, M., 2008. Functional role of the supplementary and pre-supplementary motor areas. Nat. Rev. Neurosci. 9 (11), 856–869.

Papoutsi, M., Weiskopf, N., Langbehn, D., Reilmann, R., Rees, G., Tabrizi, S.J., 2018. Stimulating neural plasticity with real-time fMRI neurofeedback in Huntington's disease: a proof of concept study. Hum. Brain Mapp. 39 (3), 1339–1353. https://doi.org/10.1002/hbm.23921.

Rance, M., Walsh, C., Sukhodolsky, D.G., Pittman, B., Qiu, M., Kichuk, S.A., Wasylink, S., Koller, W.N., Bloch, M., Gruner, P., Scheinost, D., Pittenger, C., Hampson, M., 2018. Time course of clinical change following neurofeedback. NeuroImage 181, 807–813. https://doi.org/10.1016/j.neuroimage.2018.05.001.

Randell, E., McNamara, R., Subramanian, L., Hood, K., Linden, D., 2018. Current practices in clinical neurofeedback with functional MRI-analysis of a survey using the TIDieR checklist. Eur. Psychiatry 50, 28–33. https://doi.org/10.1016/j.eurpsy.2017.10.011.

Ros, T., Enriquez-Geppert, S., Zotev, V., Young, K.D., Wood, G., Whitfield-Gabrieli, S., Wan, F., Vuilleumier, P., Vialatte, F., Van De Ville, D., Todder, D., Surmeli, T., Sulzer, J.S., Strehl, U., Sterman, M.B., Steiner, N.J., Sorger, B., Soekadar, S.R., Sitaram, R., Sherlin, L.H., Schönenberg, M., Scharnowski, F., Schabus, M., Rubia, K., Rosa, A., Reiner, M., Pineda, J.A., Paret, C., Ossadtchi, A., Nicholson, A.A., Nan, W., Minguez, J., Micoulaud-Franchi, J.A., Mehler, D.M.A., Lührs, M., Lubar, J., Lotte, F., Linden, D.E.J., Lewis-Peacock, J.A., Lebedev, M.A., Lanius, R.A., Kübler, A., Kranczioch, C., Koush, Y., Konicar, L., Kohl, S.H., Kober, S.E., Klados, M.A., Jeunet, C., Janssen, T.W.P., Huster, R.J., Hoedlmoser, K., Hirshberg, L.M., Heunis, S.,

Hendler, T., Hampson, M., Guggisberg, A.G., Guggenberger, R., Gruzelier, J.H., Göbel, R.W., Gninenko, N., Gharabaghi, A., Frewen, P., Fovet, T., Fernández, T., Escolano, C., Ehlis, A.C., Drechsler, R., Christopher de Charms, R., Debener, S., De Ridder, D., Davelaar, E.J., Congedo, M., Cavazza, M., Breteler, M.H.M., Brandeis, D., Bodurka, J., Birbaumer, N., Bazanova, O.M., Barth, B., Bamidis, P.D., Auer, T., Arns, M., Thibault, R.T., 2020. Consensus on the reporting and experimental design of clinical and cognitive-behavioural neurofeedback studies (CRED-nf checklist). Brain 143 (6), 1674–1685. https://doi.org/10.1093/brain/awaa009.

Sorger, B., Scharnowski, F., Linden, D.E.J., Hampson, M., Young, K.D., 2019. Control freaks: towards optimal selection of control conditions for fMRI neurofeedback studies. NeuroImage 186, 256–265. https://doi.org/10.1016/j.neuroimage.2018.11.004.

Subramanian, L., Hindle, J.V., Johnston, S., Roberts, M.V., Husain, M., Goebel, R., Linden, D., 2011. Real-time functional magnetic resonance imaging neurofeedback for treatment of Parkinson's disease. J. Neurosci. 31 (45), 16309–16317. https://doi.org/10.1523/JNEUROSCI.3498-11.2011.

Subramanian, L., Morris, M.B., Brosnan, M., Turner, D.L., Morris, H.R., Linden, D.E., 2016. Functional magnetic resonance imaging neurofeedback-guided motor imagery training and motor training for Parkinson's disease: randomized trial. Front. Behav. Neurosci. 10, 111. https://doi.org/10.3389/fnbeh.2016.00111.

Subramanian, L., Skottnik, L., Cox, W.M., Lührs, M., McNamara, R., Hood, K., Watson, G., Whittaker, J.R., Williams, A.N., Sakhuja, R., Ihssen, N., Goebel, R., Playle, R., Linden, D.E.J., 2021. Neurofeedback training versus treatment-as-usual for alcohol dependence: results of an early-phase randomized controlled trial and neuroimaging correlates. Eur. Addict. Res., 1–14.

Thibault, R.T., MacPherson, A., Lifshitz, M., Roth, R.R., Raz, A., 2018. Neurofeedback with fMRI: a critical systematic review. NeuroImage 172, 786–807. https://doi.org/10.1016/j.neuroimage.2017.12.071.

Young, K.D., Siegle, G.J., Zotev, V., Phillips, R., Misaki, M., Yuan, H., Drevets, W.C., Bodurka, J., 2017. Randomized clinical trial of real-time fMRI amygdala neurofeedback for major depressive disorder: effects on symptoms and autobiographical memory recall. Am. J. Psychiatry 174 (8), 748–755. https://doi.org/10.1176/appi.ajp.2017.16060637.

fMRI neurofeedback for disorders of emotion regulation

Kymberly Young[a], Naomi Fine[b], and Talma Hendler[b,c]
[a]Department of Psychiatry, University of Pittsburgh, Pittsburgh, PA, United States [b]School of Psychological Sciences, Tel Aviv University, Tel Aviv, Israel [c]Tel Aviv University, Tel Aviv, Israel

Decades of neuroimaging research have resulted in the identification of regions and networks that function abnormally in various mental illnesses. Neurofeedback (NF) takes advantage of this research by directly modulating these regions in patients. One such brain-mind association has been described for emotion regulation. Emotion regulation is the ability to exert control over the occurrence, intensity, duration, and expression of emotion (Gross, 2007). It involves cognitive and physiological processes such as rethinking challenging situations to reduce anxiety, reducing visible signs of sadness or fear, or focusing on reasons to feel happy or calm. When emotion regulation is absent, deficient, or poorly matched to situational demands, emotional responses may be excessive, inappropriate, or insufficient, as is seen in the context of various psychiatric disorders such as major depressive disorder (MDD), posttraumatic stress disorder (PTSD), and borderline personality disorder (BPD) (Aldao et al., 2010). Neurofeedback is based on the established finding that healthy individuals can learn to control hemodynamic activity in a variety of brain regions implicated in emotional regulation processing, including the insula, amygdala, and ventrolateral prefrontal cortex (PFC) using negative memories and imagery (Johnston et al., 2010), anterior insula using positive and negative imagery (Caria et al., 2007), anterior cingulate cortex by focusing on or away from painful stimuli (deCharms et al., 2005), and amygdala using negative imagery (Posse et al., 2003) or positive autobiographical memories (AM) (Zotev et al., 2011). See Chapter 6 for details of affective neuroscience studies in healthy controls. Intriguingly, emotion regulation and volitional-brain regulation are based on similar psychological processes that include perceptions of the world (or the feedback signal) that are either positively or negatively valued, leading to implementation (explicit or implicit) of mental actions that alter related activation of the brain (Paret and Hendler, 2020). Since modulation of the signal in regions that regulate emotions, such as the amygdala, is feasible among healthy participants, it raises the question regarding its potential transferability to patient populations, and its translation to meaningful behavioral improvements in the clinical

fMRI Neurofeedback. https://doi.org/10.1016/B978-0-12-822421-2.00014-4

domain. The potential therapeutic impact of fMRI neurofeedback has been examined for the following emotion regulation disorders: MDD (Hamilton et al., 2016; Linden et al., 2012; Mehler et al., 2018; Young et al., 2014, 2017b), PTSD (Fruchtman et al., 2019; Gerin et al., 2016; Nicholson et al., 2017; Zotev et al., 2018; Zweerings et al., 2018), BPD (Paret et al., 2016a; Zaehringer et al., 2019), and anxiety/specific phobia (Zilverstand et al., 2015). Table 1 provides an overview of the applications of neurofeedback for disorders of emotion regulation to date. The current chapter focuses on neurofeedback for MDD, PTSD, BPD, and anxiety disorders. A review of the studies on neurofeedback for other psychiatric disorders that are not classified as disorders of emotion regulation is covered in Chapter 9.

The **success** of neurofeedback in a clinical context is defined here as (1) a significant change in the targeted brain activity over the course of the NF training; (2) the ability to maintain the desired change in activity level during a transfer run during which participants engage in the same task as during training, but without the neurofeedback information presented; and (3) a clinically significant change in symptoms or behavior. Furthermore, a correlation between neurofeedback success and clinical change or related behavior provides strong support that the mechanism targeted during neurofeedback is causally related to the pathology of the disorder studied. Hereby we will review approaches and evidence in clinical applications of NF for disorders of emotion regulation.

We suggest two approaches for selecting a region or set of regions to train for clinical neurofeedback studies (Fig. 1).

(1) *Disturbed process approach*: In this approach researchers attempt to train what is considered abnormal to function more normally, or similar to healthy individuals. This approach can be disorder specific or transdiagnostic but requires knowledge of the pathophysiology of the disorder and key mechanisms underlying change. This approach can use a functional localizer scan, but if the process being targeted is a deficit (a region that is recruited in healthy individuals that is not brought on-line in patients), an anatomical localizer should be used. This is the approach taken by Young et al. (2014, 2017b) in their neurofeedback studies for depression to increase the amygdala hemodynamic response during positive memory recall based on findings of decreased amygdala reactivity to positive stimuli in depressed relative to healthy controls. The disturbed processes approach was also implemented in PTSD research—where the focus was decreasing the known hyperactive amygdala response to negative and trauma related stimuli that is observed in PTSD patients relative to healthy controls (Nicholson et al., 2017; Fruchtman et al., 2019).

(2) *Compensatory process approach*: In this approach researchers train individuals to modify neural pathways in order to adjust, or overcome, impaired functions, which might be relevant in more than one-disorder (transdiagnostic function). This approach often uses a functional localizer scan to identify areas that are active during a specific task that are

Table 1: Neurofeedback studies in patients with disorders of emotion regulation.

Study	Disorder	Brain region	Regulation instructions	Control condition	Outcome
Linden et al. (2012)	MDD	Brain areas active while viewing positive pictures	Increase activity	Mental rehearsal outside of the scanner	Decreased depressive symptoms (HDRS)
Young et al. (2014)	MDD	Amygdala	Increase activity	Alternate region of interest	Decreased state anxiety and increased state happiness ratings
Young et al. (2017a,b)	MDD	Amygdala	Increase activity	Alternate region of interest	Decreased depressive symptoms (MADRS, HDRS, BDI)
Hamilton et al. (2016)	MDD	Salience network	Decrease activity	Yoked sham	Decreased emotional response to negative scenes and self-descriptive adjectives
Mehler et al. (2018)	MDD	Brain areas active while viewing positive pictures	Increase activity	Alternate region of interest	*Decreased depressive symptoms (HDRS) in both groups*
Gerin et al. (2016)	PTSD	Amygdala	Decrease activity	None	Promising feasibility data
Nicholson et al. (2017)	PTSD	Amygdala	Decrease activity	None	*No change in symptoms reported*
Zotev et al. (2018)	PTSD	Amygdala	Increase activity	Alternate region of interest	*Decreased symptoms (CAPS) in both groups*
Zweerings et al. (2018)	PTSD	ACC	Decrease activity	Healthy controls	Decreased intrusion and avoidance scores (IES-R), increased positive affect
Fruchtman et al. (2019)	PTSD	Amygdala EFP	Decrease activity	No neurofeedback/treatment as usual	Decreased symptoms (CAPS and PCL)
Paret et al. (2016a,b)	BPD	Amygdala	Decrease activity	None	Decreased dissociative experiences
Zaehringer et al. (2019)	BPD	Amygdala	Decrease activity	None	Decrease in borderline symptoms, startle to negative pictures, and affective instability
Zilverstand et al. (2017)	Anxiety	DLPFC/insula	Increase DLPFC and Decrease insula activity	Mental rehearsal inside of the scanner	*Decrease in anxiety levels in both groups*

Black text in the Outcome column indicates the data supported the hypothesized clinical effect, *gray text* indicates either that no data on clinical effects were presented, or that the data did not support the hypothesized clinical effect. Abbreviations: *ACC*, anterior cingulate cortex; *BDI*, Beck Depression Inventory; *BPD*, borderline personality disorder; *CAPS*, clinician administered PTSD scale; *DLPFC*, dorsolateral prefrontal cortex; *EFP*, electrical finger print; *HDRS*, Hamilton depression rating scale; *MADRS*, Montgomery Asberg Depression Rating Scale; *MDD*, major depressive disorder; *PCL*, PTSD checklist; *PTSD*, posttraumatic stress disorder; *STG*, superior temporal gyrus; *VLPFC*, ventrolateral prefrontal cortex.

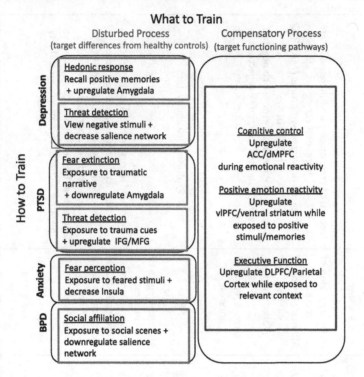

Fig. 1

Approaches for what and how to train in clinical NF. The "What" regards targeted neural region/network. The "How" regards modulated mental process, while considering the relevant disorder.

then selected for training during neurofeedback. This is the approach taken by Linden and colleagues in depression, who focus on training regions such as the ventrolateral prefrontal cortex and insula that function normally in patients with depression while they recall positive memories in order to compensate for the lack of amygdala and salience node network activation (Linden et al., 2012; Mehler et al., 2018).

Both approaches have resulted in clinical improvement in patients, yet it remains an open question as to how to assign patients to each approach. In the following part of the chapter, we will provide an overview of findings derived from these two approaches in studying neurofeedback efficacy in emotion regulation disorders, including MDD, PTSD, BPD, and anxiety/phobia disorders.

1 fMRI neurofeedback for major depressive disorder

Major depressive disorder (MDD) is the leading cause of disability in the United States (World Health Organization, 2004), with the toll on the US society and economy estimated at $210 billion (Greenberg et al., 2015). Up to two-thirds of patients who seek standard pharmacological and/or psychological interventions will not respond, while only one-half of patients who do will achieve sustained remission (Cain, 2007). Therefore there is a need to develop novel therapeutics for MDD and to improve the effectiveness of noninvasive treatments.

Neuroimaging research over decades has identified **neural signatures of depression**. By using what we have learned with respect to how patients' brains react differently than those of healthy individuals, we can identify certain regions that seem to be particularly important in the onset and maintenance of this disorder. By far, the region that has received the most attention is the amygdala (Drevets, 2003). This region plays a critical role in emotional processing and responding/regulation, in neural processing underlying emotional responses to salient environmental stimuli, in generating fight or flight responses to potential threats, and in generating emotional reactions to ambiguous, appetitive, or novel stimuli (Davis and Whalen, 2001; LeDoux, 2003; Phelps and LeDoux, 2005; Sander et al., 2003; Sergerie et al., 2008). Amygdala neurons project to sensory cortical, prefrontal cortical, and other mesiotemporal regions to process environmental information and prompt adaptive behavioral and visceromotor responses (Sah et al., 2003) including emotion regulation (Etkin et al., 2015). While much attention has been focused on the amygdala's role in processing and responding to negative/fearful emotional stimuli (LeDoux, 2003), evidence suggests the amygdala more generally influences the perceived salience of stimuli and events (Davis and Whalen, 2001), and that amygdala BOLD activity increases to both positively and negatively valanced emotional stimuli (Murray, 2007; Namburi et al., 2015; Sergerie et al., 2008; Victor et al., 2010). Abundant evidence suggests amygdala **hemodynamic** response is exaggerated to negative stimuli in MDD (Fu et al., 2004; Siegle et al., 2002). However, extant evidence further suggests MDD-associated abnormalities are "doubly dissociated" from healthy individuals by virtue of their greater amygdala response to negative stimuli and attenuated amygdala response to positive stimuli (Victor et al., 2010).

Evidence also supports a role of the amygdala in recovery from MDD. For example, following successful treatment with selective serotonin reuptake inhibitors (SSRIs), the hyperactivation of the amygdala to negative stimuli decreased while activation of the amygdala to positive stimuli increased (Victor et al., 2010). Increased amygdala activity to the presentation of positive words and decreased activity in response to negative words were also seen following 2 weeks of Cognitive Control Therapy (Siegle et al., 2007). While there is sufficient evidence to suggest decreasing the amygdala response to negative stimuli may be effective at relieving depressive symptoms, neurofeedback studies in depression have focused on the attenuated brain activity seen when processing positive information. This is because of evidence that amygdala responsiveness to positive stimuli is correlated inversely with depression severity (Suslow et al., 2010; Young et al., 2016) and is indistinguishable from controls in patients remitted from MDD (Young et al., 2016), suggesting that decreased activation of the amygdala to positive stimuli is clinically significant and that some antidepressant drugs and cognitive therapies exert their therapeutic effect by normalizing the emotional processing bias. The evidence supporting a role of the amygdala in onset and recovery from MDD, taken together with evidence that the amygdala links the domains of affective experience/response and emotional memory recall, supports using neurofeedback to train patients to regulate their amygdala response to emotional (particularly positive) stimuli. Indeed, the first randomized clinical trial of neurofeedback for MDD focused on increasing the amygdala response to positive autobiographical memories (AMs) (Young et al., 2017b).

1.1 Disturbed process as NF target in MDD

Young and colleagues conducted several studies on the ability of patients with MDD to upregulate their amygdala response to positive autobiographical memories and examined changes in mood, symptoms, and processing biases. In an initial study, depressed patients were indeed able to significantly increase their amygdala BOLD activity over the course of the experiment and maintain it during a transfer run. Following a single session, improvements in mood were observed—specifically, participants who received amygdala neurofeedback were more happy and less depressed, anxious, and irritable after neurofeedback relative to before neurofeedback and to a control group that received neurofeedback from a parietal region putatively not implicated in emotion regulation or depression but which could still be regulated with the strategy of recalling positive memories (Young et al., 2014).

Young et al. (2017b) then went on to conduct a double-blind randomized clinical trial. In this trial participants engaged in two neurofeedback training sessions and completed measures of symptoms and processing biases 1 week before and after the neurofeedback training. Clinical measures included both self-report (Beck Depression Inventory-II) and clinically administered assessments [Montgomery-Åsberg Depression Rating Scale (MADRS), Hamilton Rating Scale for Depression-21 (HDRS)]. All ratings significantly decreased in the experimental group both from baseline and relative to the control group. Twelve participants in the experimental group responded to neurofeedback (defined as at least a 50% decrease in MADRS score), compared with two participants in the control group. Six participants in the experimental group and one in the control group met criteria for remission at study end (MADRS score > 10), resulting in a number needed to treat of four (95% confidence interval, 2–50). This remission rate is similar to rates seen with antidepressant medications (Arroll et al., 2005) and cognitive behavioral therapy (Cuijpers et al., 2010). Furthermore, there was a significant relationship between the ability to regulate the amygdala and the degree of improvement in clinical symptoms, providing additional support for the causal role between rt-fMRI-NF learning and clinical improvement.

Furthermore, autobiographical memory (AM) recall was improved and increased processing of positive stimuli was observed (Young et al., 2017a,b). It is a well-replicated finding in the literature that patients with MDD have AM deficits, characterized by overgeneral memory recall—defined as decreased recall of specific AM (a memory for an event that occurred at an identifiable time and place and which did not last over 24 h; e.g., "I went grocery shopping last Sunday") and increased recall of general, categorical AM (summaries or categories of events without reference to a single episode; e.g., "I go grocery shopping every weekend") (Williams et al., 2007). Following two rt-fMRI-NF sessions, participants in the experimental group had an increase in the percent of specific memories recalled and a decrease in the percent of overgeneral memories recalled (Young et al., 2017b). The effect was predominately attributable to changes in positive memories. Decreased reaction times to identify positive faces and to classify self-referential words as positive was also observed following neurofeedback in the experimental group (Young et al., 2017a). Finally, amygdala responses to implicitly presented emotional faces in a Backward Masking task normalized following amygdala neurofeedback training—amygdala activity increased to positive faces and decreased to negative (Young et al., 2017a). This finding suggests that training the amygdala response in one direction (upregulate to positive) at least partly generalized to the processing of other types of emotional stimuli in the amygdala and that patients learned to adaptively regulate their amygdala response rather than to increase it nonspecifically. Additional clinical trials are ongoing (NCT02709161; NCT03428828) to further develop this procedure into a standardized intervention for MDD.

To date, there has been only one study attempting to train participants with MDD to downregulate the brain response to emotional stimuli. Hamilton et al. (2016) trained participants with MDD to downregulate a region within the predefined salience network that was found to be most active when viewing negative pictures (Hamilton et al., 2016). As the salience network is overactive to negative stimuli in depression (Hamilton et al., 2012), this approach would be classified as a disturbed process approach. A yoked sham control group was employed where participants saw the signal from a participant in the experimental group instead of their own brain signal. The experimental group showed a significant decrease in emotional ratings of negative pictures and in self-relevance ratings of negative adjectives following neurofeedback that was not observed in the control group. This suggests that downregulating regions involved in emotional processing may also be clinically effective in MDD. It is likely that a combination of upregulation to positive and downregulation to negative stimuli will ultimately be the most effective intervention for MDD; however, this research has yet to be done.

1.2 Compensatory function as NF target in MDD

In contrast to the disturbed process approach, this approach focuses on training functional regions that can compensate for dysfunctional brain activity. For example, in order to compensate for low amygdala reactivity to positive stimuli, depressed participants were trained to enhance brain activity in regions found to be active while viewing positive stimuli or recalling positive experiences (Linden et al., 2012; Mehler et al., 2018). The theory behind this work was to train individuals to make the brain areas they typically recruit during positive experiences (such as the ventrolateral prefrontal cortex and insula) even more responsive to positive stimuli. This line of research has been conducted by Linden and colleagues and has produced mixed results. In their first study, a localizer scan identified which regions were most active while participants viewed positive images and then participants were trained to increase activity in these regions while engaging in positive imagery strategies. A control group performed the positive imagery without neurofeedback. Depressive symptoms (measured using the HDRS) decreased 29% in the experimental group and increased slightly in the control group (Linden et al., 2012). However, when the same procedure was repeated with a different control group that upregulated the parahippocampus using positive imagery and imagery of scenes, both groups improved to a similar degree (48% and 59% decrease on the HDRS for the experimental and control groups) (Mehler et al., 2018). While regulation success was not associated with clinical change, self-efficacy was. Participants in either group who improved clinically also reported increased self-efficacy, suggesting that it is enhancing feelings of self-efficacy and not gaining control over a particular signal driving the clinical effects observed in these studies. However, the control group in this study actually increased activity in the same regions as the experimental group (in addition to the parahippocampus) so it is possible that both groups' symptoms improved because they both ultimately regulated the same regions. Further research is needed to disentangle the effects of reward and increasing self-efficacy from gaining control over a brain signal.

2 fMRI neurofeedback for posttraumatic stress disorder

Posttraumatic stress disorder (PTSD) is a commonly occurring disorder with a lifetime prevalence ranging from 1.3% to 12.2% (Karam et al., 2014) that has a profound public health impact by virtue of its high prevalence, persistence, accompanying functional impairment, and elevated risk of other mental and physical disorders. Transient PTSD symptoms are frequently observed shortly after traumatic events, remit in most survivors, but leave approximately 30% of those who meet acute PTSD diagnostic criteria with chronic, unremitting PTSD (Koren et al., 2001; Perkonigg et al., 2005).

While exposure therapy is one of the most effective treatments for PTSD (Foa and Kozak, 1986; Schnurr et al., 2007), it involves exposure to trauma-related stimuli and is itself an excruciating process. In exchange for its effectiveness, the distress of exposure therapy renders the patients with difficulties in engagement and results in a considerable rate of early dropout (i.e., 20%–40% within the first 2 months of the treatment period). Unfortunately, there is an even higher rate of nonresponse [i.e., 30%–50% do not respond to exposure-based treatment (Bradley et al., 2005)]. Moreover, pharmacological interventions yield only partial success, mainly targeting symptoms of hypervigilance, but remain helpless in face of symptom clusters such as intrusiveness, avoidance, and cognitive and emotional changes (Jorge, 2015). Therefore from a clinical perspective a novel noninvasive yet mechanism-driven therapy for PTSD is vital.

Multiple functional neuroimaging studies point to limbic dysregulation as a **chief neural mechanism in PTSD**, exhibiting hyperactivation of the amygdala and dorsal anterior cingulate cortex (dACC), alongside hypoactivation of the ventromedial prefrontal cortex (vmPFC) and inferior frontal gyrus (IFG) (Fenster et al., 2018; Hayes et al., 2012; Shin et al., 2006). Prospective fMRI studies in stress-prone individuals suggest that amygdala hyperactivity prior to trauma exposure is a major risk factor for subsequent posttraumatic symptom development (Admon et al., 2009, 2013). Consequently, amygdala functionality is an effective target for brain-deficit guided intervention through neurofeedback in PTSD. Amygdala deactivation to negative stimuli is also regarded as a signal of enhanced emotion regulation and a marker of greater therapeutic effects following treatments. For example, individuals with borderline personality disorder (commonly comorbid with complex PTSD) that participated in dialectical behavioral therapy (an emotion regulation focused treatment) displayed decreased amygdala activation to unpleasant pictorial stimuli posttreatment. Moreover, they displayed improved amygdala habituation to repeated-unpleasant pictures, which was associated with improved overall self-reported emotional regulation capacities (Goodman et al., 2014).

2.1 Disturbed process as NF target in PTSD

Following the summary of evidence earlier, we suggest that the amygdala may serve as a promising disturbed-process target for NF in PTSD. Specifically, we propose that a personalized process-based characterization of the PTSD patient followed by a specific NF treatment protocol will be capable of accurately targeting the dysfunctional process (see perspective—Lubianiker et al., 2019). Importantly, the initial characterization as well as outcome measures will be based on behavioral as well as physiological assessment. Following such characterization, patients will modulate their amygdala activation by interacting with customized NF interfaces that will specifically target the most relevant impaired process. This model assumes that certain interfaces will provoke activity in designated brain circuitry, yielding specific modulation patterns of the circuit of interest via the amygdala. Such intervention will not only lead to more precise and individualized protocols, but will also result in a better mechanistic understanding of PTSD.

PTSD is a construct that has various underlying impairments in neurobehavioral processes, such as fear learning and extinction, threat detection, emotion regulation, and others (Misaki et al., 2018; Shalev et al., 2017). Importantly, when considering brain mechanisms, such a conceptualization emphasizes the pivotal role of the amygdala in different aspects of

PTSD. For example, altered fear learning, impaired extinction, and safety signal processing are crucial for PTSD symptomatology, but also depend on the amygdala functionality of its subnuclei and various cell types (Fanselow and LeDoux, 1999; Janak and Tye, 2015). Similarly, emotion dysregulation, resulting in intense emotional reactivity, irritability, and impulsivity (Lanius et al., 2010; Sripada et al., 2012), is known to be underlined by a lack of cortical control over amygdala reactivity, specifically manifested by impaired connectivity patterns between the amygdala and the vmPFC and dlPFC (Etkin et al., 2015). Further, maladjusted threat detection may give rise to increased attention and reactivity to threatening or salient stimuli and is accompanied by hypervigilance and related aggressive behavior, mediated by the amygdala as well as cortical regions such as the insula, vmPFC, dACC, as well as brain stem areas such as the PAG and locus coeruleus (Dileo et al., 2008; Gilam et al., 2017; Lanius et al., 2007). Taken together, the breakdown of PTSD to neurobehavioral processes and their accompanying neural bases exemplifies the extent to which the amygdala is involved in the various aspects of PTSD, but also the roles various networks and their interactions with the amygdala play in a context-dependent manner.

Identifying specific disturbed processes holds promise for tailoring NF interventions. For example, individuals suffering from dysfunctions in threat processing (PTSD, social anxiety disorders, etc.) could benefit from associating their experienced virtual environment with their neural state, such that gaining control over specific threat-related neural targets would result in a more tranquil simulated environment that corresponds with their specific avoidance (trauma or social related, etc.). Alternatively, an individual with disrupted processes of emotional reactivity or irritability manifested in PTSD hypervigilance might benefit from a neutral, serene NF interface that reinstates connectivity of amygdala and the vmPFC and dlPFC.

Real-time self-modulation of amygdala BOLD activity (rt-fMRI-NF) in PTSD has been explored in several small sampled studies without convincing control conditions. Gerin et al. (2016) performed an rt-fMRI-NF feasibility study with three PTSD patients trained to modulate their amygdala activity during a symptom provocation paradigm while receiving visual feedback. This protocol was based on the notion that training participants to volitionally control emotion-related brain activation during trauma recall could target neural circuits interrelated to their symptomatology. Following three amygdala rt-fMRI-NF sessions, participants showed increased amygdala-PFC connectivity and significant decrease in the Clinician-Administered PTSD Scale (CAPS) scores. Likewise, Nicholson et al. (2017) introduced three rt-fMRI-NF sessions to ten PTSD patients. In the test condition, patients were instructed to downregulate the amygdala while viewing personalized trauma words; while in the control condition they passively viewed trauma words. The NF training phase was followed by a transfer phase with no feedback. Following training, PTSD patients successfully downregulated amygdala activity (compared to viewing condition) both during

NF and transfer cycles. Zweerings et al. (2018) targeted upregulation of the anterior cingulate cortex (ACC), an integral part of the limbic system and core node of emotion regulation network which is underactive in patients with PTSD relative to healthy controls, as they experience trauma-related stimuli. They compared nine patients with PTSD after single trauma exposure and nine matched healthy controls following three rt-fMRI-NF sessions. Following NF training, self-regulation of the ACC was achieved in both groups, but the amplitude of regulation and learning was reduced in the PTSD group, and posttraumatic symptomatology (assessed by impact of event scale) was associated with a reduced learning effect. Interestingly, feedback of ongoing ACC activity was provided by a direct social reward. Specifically, a computer-generated male face avatar was displayed and responded to an increase in ACC activity with a rewarding smile that faded with decreasing ACC activity. This method recruited the benefits of social reinforcement and sets an example for ways to manipulate the interface on behalf of the disorder or targeted process.

Another approach to NF in PTSD includes Decoded Neurofeedback (DecNef) that has been recently developed as a novel procedure with potential clinical applications (Shibata et al., 2019; Watanabe et al., 2017). Instead of the average fMRI BOLD signals, feedback is derived from multivoxel pattern analysis (MVPA). This method analyzes brain activity from each participant to create an individualized brain signature associated with a specific mental or perceptual state, which is then regulated implicitly throughout DecNef training (Chiba et al., 2019; Watanabe et al., 2017; Yamada et al., 2017) (this method is described in more detail in Chapter 10). In short, DecNef targets neural patterns congruent with a specific mental state and for that reason, may serve as a good surrogate for process-based NF (Lubianiker et al., 2019).

This approach may especially benefit PTSD interventions since traumatic episodes and the related neural representations differ across individual patients. Theoretically, DecNef may enable patients to induce brain activation patterns associated specifically with their trauma (e.g. brain patterns that are observed during or after an effective exposure therapy) and thus directly reinforces therapeutic neural activity while bypassing the need for conscious exposure, and therefore might especially benefit the patients who cańt tolerate conscious trauma exposure. Despite such a potential advantage, it is yet to be determined whether DecNef is effective on diminishing actual PTSD symptoms. A preliminary study reported findings from four individuals with PTSD that were traumatized by "angry men" (i.e., victims of domestic violence or child abuse), during three DecNef sessions on consecutive days. Following DecNef training, participants displayed reductions in CAPS scores (Chiba et al., 2019).

Notwithstanding the above, process-based neural targeting may present several challenges. One issue involves the scalability of the process-based intervention. fMRI holds a critical advantage over other neuroimaging techniques for targeting defined neural mechanisms: its superior spatial resolution. Yet its expense, limited accessibility, and inconvenience especially to clinical populations (e.g., it might induce stress and anxiety) might hamper fMRI-NF clinical translation. Electroencephalograms (EEG), on the other hand, are cost-effective and mobile. However, due to poor spatial resolution, EEG's ability to target functional processes associated with distributed cortical as well as subcortical areas is severely limited. Hence, a measuring tool that offers both precise localization and high accessibility is greatly needed for the applicability of process-based NF, particularly in individuals suffering from psychopathology.

An innovative approach combined the strengths of EEG and fMRI, providing both high accessibility and precise spatial localization. This framework adopted signal-processing and machine learning techniques, based on temporal and frequency analyses. This approach, termed electrical fingerprint (EFP), successfully predicted fMRI BOLD activations in the amygdala and medial prefrontal cortex using only EEG data from single channels (Keynan et al., 2016; Meir-Hasson et al., 2016). This method was recently applied to healthy individuals undergoing a stressful military training program (Keynan et al., 2019), results indicated that repeated amygdala EFP training sessions for downregulating the amygdala had a beneficial effect on neural and behavioral indices of stress resilience.

Integrating neuroscientific understanding of PTSD and the low-cost mobile techniques of EFP is the focus of a randomized controlled trial among patients with chronic PTSD with amygdala-EFP neurofeedback (amyg-EFP-nf) (Fruchtman et al., 2019). This study included 40 individuals randomized into three groups: amyg-EFP-NF in a neutral context, amyg-EFP-NF exposed to trauma-related context, treatment as usual (control) group. Neutral context incorporated a visual and auditory interface in an interleaved manner while the trauma-related context also included exposure to a personalized auditory trauma narrative. Feasibility analyses confirmed that during training patients learned to volitionally downregulate their amyg-EFP signal and that this learning effect increased throughout the sessions. Moreover, greater reduction in amygdala-BOLD signal was demonstrated postintervention in the treatment arm compared to the control arm, supporting target engagement. Clinical measures postintervention indicated reduced PTSD symptoms (as measured by CAPS) in both active groups (compared to the control group), and this improvement increased over follow-up (as measured by Post Traumatic Checklist scores). It is worthy to note that the large clinical effect size (NNT of 2.7) found is comparable to similar clinical benefits in commonly used cognitive-behavioral therapies (Watts et al., 2013).

2.2 Compensatory function as NF target in PTSD

To date, there have not been any studies examining fMRI-NF training through compensatory function in PTSD. Nevertheless, training adjacent neural pathways that remain intact but are of relevance to PTSD process (e.g., mvPCF, dlPFC, striatum) might be of therapeutic potential and possibly a target easier to train.

3 fMRI NF for borderline personality disorder

BPD is a devastating psychiatric condition with severe deficits in patients' emotional processing and emotion regulation skills (Sanislow et al., 2002; Schmahl et al., 2014). A key neural feature of BPD is a hyperactivation of the amygdala in response to emotional stimuli (Schulze et al., 2016) as well as reduced lateral prefrontal cortex (PFC) activation in the processing of emotions (Krause-Utz et al., 2012; Lang et al., 2012; Schulze et al., 2011, 2016), which most likely reflects the emotion regulation deficits observed in BPD patients (Schmahl et al., 2014). Training aberrant neural patterns associated with emotion dysregulation falls in line with the disturbed processes approach. An initial study displayed aversive pictures and received feedback from a thermometer display, which showed the amygdala blood oxygenation level-dependent signal to eight BDP patients (Paret et al., 2016a). BPD patients downregulated right amygdala activation but there were no improvements over time. Nevertheless, dissociation, as well as subscale of emotion regulation difficulties decreased with training. A consecutive single arm trial (Zaehringer et al., 2019) included 24 patients with BPD who underwent four runs of amygdala neurofeedback. Following successful downregulation there was a decrease of BPD symptoms and a decrease in emotion-modulated startle to negative pictures after training. These initial findings suggest that amygdala NF may alter brain connectivity, as well as emotion regulation and BPD symptoms even in what is considered the ultimate and most stubborn diagnosis in emotion regulation disorders.

4 fMRI NF for phobia and other anxiety disorders

Anxiety disorders are the most common mental health condition, with specific phobia the most common subtype of anxiety experienced (Kessler et al., 2012). The neural substrates that underpin the enhanced fear response evident in phobia include increased activity in the amygdala and insula and decreased activity in prefrontal control regions (Etkin and Wager, 2007). Zilverstand et al. (2015) examined the effect of neurofeedback training in women with spider phobia. In line with the disturbed-processes approach, they aimed to increase the dlPFC and decrease the insula while engaging in cognitive reappraisal while viewing pictures of spiders. A control group was instructed to use the strategy of cognitive reappraisal while viewing spider pictures but did not receive feedback. Participants in both groups demonstrated increased dlPFC activity during regulate trials, but only the experimental group had decreased insula activity with training. Both groups experienced decreased anxiety both immediately after training and at a 3-month follow-up. The postintervention decrease in anxiety was qualitatively, but not significantly, greater in the experimental group. Furthermore, the degree of improvement was correlated with the decrease in insula activity in the experimental group. These results suggest that neurofeedback training may indeed be a viable intervention for phobias.

However, this type of neurofeedback shares the same problems as exposure therapy—it requires the participants to experience the object of which they are anxious. This tends to lead to high dropout rates in exposure therapy (Choy et al., 2007) that may also hinder neurofeedback interventions. To this end, decoded neurofeedback has been increasingly used as a way to treat phobia by allowing neurofeedback training to occur covertly, without the stimulus being presented to the participants. Decoded neurofeedback and its application in anxiety disorders is covered in more detail in Chapter 10.

5 Conclusions

Experiments repeatedly demonstrate that real-time fMRI neurofeedback allows individuals to modulate the BOLD signal from various regions and that learning to control these signals results in behavioral change and clinical improvement. This evidence suggests that fMRI neurofeedback may develop into a powerful biobehavioral intervention in psychiatry that may also serve as a promising path for the transdiagnostic RDoC perspective in treatment (Insel et al., 2010) as demonstrated in Fig. 1. However, for that to occur, more well-designed randomized clinical trials are needed, as are comparisons to currently available treatments. There are still several outstanding issues related to personalization and precision of the intervention, including determining the optimal number of sessions (dosing) and follow-up time points. Nevertheless, for some mental illnesses, particularly MDD and PTSD, neurofeedback is moving beyond the proof-of-concept state and toward robust, replicable, well-controlled designs.

From a broader perspective, neurofeedback interventions target dysfunctional neural processes and enhance functional processes related to emotion regulation disorders, therefore adopting a multidimensional approach toward understanding and intervening in mental disorders. Accordingly, the different aspects of the intervention (neural target selection, feedback interface etc.) should correspond with the target process to optimally ameliorate dysfunctions. Current neurofeedback practice of emotion regulation disorders can further develop toward process-specific interfaces with contextual cues and the enhancement of process engagement (i.e. via immersive virtual reality and/or augmented reality technologies, see Chapter 12). Employing neurofeedback interventions based on the psychological and neural substrates of maladaptive behaviors has the potential of improving the precision and efficacy of psychiatric interventions, and widening the horizon beyond current disorder-based classification and treatment.

Acknowledgments

TH acknowledges financial support by a number of funding resources which facilitated this work: Award number 602186 from the European Union—FP7, BrainTrain, award number W81XWH-16-C-0198 from the US DOD, "Emotional Brain Fitness via Limbic Targeted NeuroFeedback," and grant number 2107/17 from the Israel Science

Foundation, "Causal Modulation of Limbic Circuits in Post Traumatic Stress Disorder due to Childhood Sexual Abuse." KY acknowledges financial support from the National Institutes of Health/National Institute of Mental Health under Award Numbers R00MH101235 and R61MH115927.

References

Admon, R., Lubin, G., Stern, O., Rosenberg, K., Sela, L., Ben-Ami, H., Hendler, T., 2009. Human vulnerability to stress depends on amygdala's predisposition and hippocampal plasticity. Proc. Natl Acad. Sci. USA 106 (33), 14120–14125. https://doi.org/10.1073/pnas.0903183106.

Admon, R., Leykin, D., Lubin, G., Engert, V., Andrews, J., Pruessner, J., Hendler, T., 2013. Stress-induced reduction in hippocampal volume and connectivity with the ventromedial prefrontal cortex are related to maladaptive responses to stressful military service. Hum. Brain Mapp. 34 (11), 2808–2816. https://doi.org/10.1002/hbm.22100.

Aldao, A., Nolen-Hoeksema, S., Schweizer, S., 2010. Emotion-regulation strategies across psychopthaology: a meta-analytic review. Clin. Psychol. Rev. *30* (2), 217–237. https://doi.org/10.1016/j.cpr.2009.11.004.

Arroll, B., Macgillivray, S., Ogston, S., Reid, I., Sullivan, F., Williams, B., Crombie, I., 2005. Efficacy and tolerability of tricyclic antidepressants and SSRIs compared with placebo for treatment of depression in primary care: a meta-analysis. Ann. Fam. Med. 3 (5), 449–456. https://doi.org/10.1370/afm.349.

Bradley, R., Greene, J., Russ, E., Dutra, L., Westen, D., 2005. A multidimensional meta-analysis of psychotherapy for PTSD. Am. J. Psychiatry 162 (2), 214–227. https://doi.org/10.1176/appi.ajp.162.2.214.

Cain, R.A., 2007. Navigating the sequenced treatment alternatives to relieve depression (STAR*D) study: practical outcomes and implications for depression treatment in primary care. Prim. Care 34 (3), 505–519. vi https://doi.org/10.1016/j.pop.2007.05.006.

Caria, A., Veit, R., Sitaram, R., Lotze, M., Weiskopf, N., Grodd, W., Birbaumer, N., 2007. Regulation of anterior insular cortex activity using real-time fMRI. NeuroImage 35 (3), 1238–1246. https://doi.org/10.1016/j.neuroimage.2007.01.018.

Chiba, T., Kanazawa, T., Koizumi, A., Ide, K., Taschereau-Dumouchel, V., Boku, S., Kawato, M., 2019. Current status of neurofeedback for post-traumatic stress disorder: a systematic review and the possibility of decoded neurofeedback. Front. Hum. Neurosci. 13, 233. https://doi.org/10.3389/fnhum.2019.00233.

Choy, Y., Fyer, A.J., Lipsitz, J.D., 2007. Treatment of specific phobia in adults. Clin. Psychol. Rev. 27 (3), 266–286. https://doi.org/10.1016/j.cpr.2006.10.002.

Cuijpers, P., Smit, F., Bohlmeijer, E., Hollon, S.D., Andersson, G., 2010. Efficacy of cognitive-behavioural therapy and other psychological treatments for adult depression: meta-analytic study of publication bias. Br. J. Psychiatry J. Ment. Sci. 196 (3), 173–178. https://doi.org/10.1192/bjp.bp.109.066001.

Davis, M., Whalen, P.J., 2001. The amygdala: vigilance and emotion. Mol. Psychiatry 6 (1), 13–34.

deCharms, R.C., Maeda, F., Glover, G.H., Ludlow, D., Pauly, J.M., Soneji, D., Mackey, S.C., 2005. Control over brain activation and pain learned by using real-time functional MRI. Proc. Natl Acad. Sci. USA 102 (51), 18626–18631. https://doi.org/10.1073/pnas.0505210102.

Dileo, J.F., Brewer, W.J., Hopwood, M., Anderson, V., Creamer, M., 2008. Olfactory identification dysfunction, aggression and impulsivity in war veterans with post-traumatic stress disorder. Psychol. Med. 38 (4), 523–531. https://doi.org/10.1017/S0033291707001456.

Drevets, W.C., 2003. Neuroimaging abnormalities in the amygdala in mood disorders. Ann. NY Acad. Sci. 985, 420–444.

Etkin, A., Wager, T.D., 2007. Functional neuroimaging of anxiety: a meta-analysis of emotional processing in PTSD, social anxiety disorder, and specific phobia. Am. J. Psychiatry 164, 1476–1488. https://doi.org/10.1176/appi.ajp.2007.07030504.

Etkin, A., Buchel, C., Gross, J.J., 2015. The neural bases of emotion regulation. Nat. Rev. Neurosci. 16 (11), 693–700. https://doi.org/10.1038/nrn4044.

Fanselow, M.S., LeDoux, J.E., 1999. Why we think plasticity underlying Pavlovian fear conditioning occurs in the basolateral amygdala. Neuron 23 (2), 229–232. https://doi.org/10.1016/s0896-6273(00)80775-8.

Fenster, R.J., Lebois, L.A.M., Ressler, K.J., Suh, J., 2018. Brain circuit dysfunction in post-traumatic stress disorder: from mouse to man. Nat. Rev. Neurosci. 19 (9), 535–551. https://doi.org/10.1038/s41583-018-0039-7.

Foa, E.B., Kozak, M.J., 1986. Emotional processing of fear: exposure to corrective information. Psychol. Bull. 99 (1), 20–35.

Fruchtman, T., Cohen, A., Jaljuli, I., Keynan, J.N., Drori, G., Routledge, E., Hendler, T., 2019. Feasibility and effectiveness of personalized amygdala-related neurofeedback for post-traumatic stress disorder. PsyArXiv.

Fu, C.H., Williams, S.C., Cleare, A.J., Brammer, M.J., Walsh, N.D., Kim, J., Bullmore, E.T., 2004. Attenuation of the neural response to sad faces in major depression by antidepressant treatment: a prospective, event-related functional magnetic resonance imaging study. Arch. Gen. Psychiatry 61 (9), 877–889. https://doi.org/10.1001/archpsyc.61.9.87761/9/877.

Gerin, M.I., Fichtenholtz, H., Roy, A., Walsh, C.J., Krystal, J.H., Southwick, S., Hampson, M., 2016. Real-time fMRI neurofeedback with war veterans with chronic PTSD: a feasibility study. Front. Psych. 7, 111. https://doi.org/10.3389/fpsyt.2016.00111.

Gilam, G., Lin, T., Fruchter, E., Hendler, T., 2017. Neural indicators of interpersonal anger as cause and consequence of combat training stress symptoms. Psychol. Med. 47 (9), 1561–1572. https://doi.org/10.1017/S0033291716003354.

Goodman, M., Carpenter, D., Tang, C.Y., Goldstein, K.E., Avedon, J., Fernandez, N., Hazlett, E.A., 2014. Dialectical behavior therapy alters emotion regulation and amygdala activity in patients with borderline personality disorder. J. Psychiatr. Res. 57, 108–116. https://doi.org/10.1016/j.jpsychires.2014.06.020.

Greenberg, P.E., Fournier, A.A., Sisitsky, T., Pike, C.T., Kessler, R.C., 2015. The economic burden of adults with major depressive disorder in the United States (2005 and 2010). J. Clin. Psychiatry 76 (2), 155–162. https://doi.org/10.4088/JCP.14m09298.

Gross, J., 2007. Handbook of Emotion Regulation. The Gullford Press, New York.

Hamilton, J.P., Furman, D.L., Lemus, M.G., Johnson, R.F., Gotlib, I.H., 2012. Functional neuroimaging of major depressive disorder: a meta-analysis and new integration of baseline activation and neural response data. Am. J. Psychiatry 169 (7), 693–703.

Hamilton, J.P., Glover, G.H., Bagarinao, E., Chang, C., Mackey, S., Sacchet, M.D., Gotlib, I.H., 2016. Effects of salience-network-node neurofeedback training on affective biases in major depressive disorder. Psychiatry Res. 249, 91–96. https://doi.org/10.1016/j.pscychresns.2016.01.016.

Hayes, J.P., Vanelzakker, M.B., Shin, L.M., 2012. Emotion and cognition interactions in PTSD: a review of neurocognitive and neuroimaging studies. Front. Integr. Neurosci. 6, 89. https://doi.org/10.3389/fnint.2012.00089.

Insel, T., Cuthbert, B., Garvey, M., Heinssen, R., Pine, D.S., Quinn, K., Wang, P., 2010. Research domain criteria (RDoC): toward a new classification framework for research on mental disorders. Am. J. Psychiatry 167 (7), 748–751. https://doi.org/10.1176/appi.ajp.2010.09091379.

Janak, P.H., Tye, K.M., 2015. From circuits to behaviour in the amygdala. Nature 517 (7534), 284–292. https://doi.org/10.1038/nature14188.

Johnston, S.J., Boehm, S.G., Healy, D., Goebel, R., Linden, D.E., 2010. Neurofeedback: a promising tool for the self-regulation of emotion networks. NeuroImage 49 (1), 1066–1072. https://doi.org/10.1016/j.neuroimage.2009.07.056.

Jorge, R.E., 2015. Posttraumatic stress disorder. Continuum (Minneap. Minn.) 21 (3 behavioral neurology and neuropsychiatry), 789–805. https://doi.org/10.1212/01.CON.0000466667.20403.b1.

Karam, E.G., Friedman, M.J., Hill, E.D., Kessler, R.C., McLaughlin, K.A., Petukhova, M., Koenen, K.C., 2014. Cumulative traumas and risk thresholds: 12-month PTSD in the world mental health (WMH) surveys. Depress. Anxiety 31 (2), 130–142. https://doi.org/10.1002/da.22169.

Kessler, R.C., Petukhova, M., Sampson, N.A., Zaslavsky, A.M., Wittchen, H.U., 2012. Twelve-month and lifetime prevalence and lifetime morbid risk of anxiety and mood disorders in the United States. Int. J. Methods Psychiatr. Res. 21 (3), 169–184. https://doi.org/10.1002/mpr.1359.

Keynan, J.N., Meir-Hasson, Y., Gilam, G., Cohen, A., Jackont, G., Kinreich, S., Hendler, T., 2016. Limbic activity modulation guided by functional magnetic resonance imaging-inspired electroencephalography improves implicit emotion regulation. Biol. Psychiatry 80 (6), 490–496. https://doi.org/10.1016/j.biopsych.2015.12.024.

Keynan, J.N., Cohen, A., Jackont, G., Green, N., Goldway, N., Davidov, A., Hendler, T., 2019. Electrical fingerprint of the amygdala guides neurofeedback training for stress resilience. Nat. Hum. Behav. 3 (1), 63–73. https://doi.org/10.1038/s41562-018-0484-3.

Koren, D., Arnon, I., Klein, E., 2001. Long term course of chronic posttraumatic stress disorder in traffic accident victims: a three-year prospective follow-up study. Behav. Res. Ther. 39 (12), 1449–1458. https://doi.org/10.1016/s0005-7967(01)00025-0.

Krause-Utz, A., Oei, N.Y., Niedtfeld, I., Bohus, M., Spinhoven, P., Schmahl, C., Elzinga, B.M., 2012. Influence of emotional distraction on working memory performance in borderline personality disorder. Psychol. Med. 42 (10), 2181–2192. https://doi.org/10.1017/S0033291712000153.

Lang, S., Kotchoubey, B., Frick, C., Spitzer, C., Grabe, H.J., Barnow, S., 2012. Cognitive reappraisal in trauma-exposed women with borderline personality disorder. NeuroImage 59 (2), 1727–1734. https://doi.org/10.1016/j.neuroimage.2011.08.061.

Lanius, R.A., Frewen, P.A., Girotti, M., Neufeld, R.W., Stevens, T.K., Densmore, M., 2007. Neural correlates of trauma script-imagery in posttraumatic stress disorder with and without comorbid major depression: a functional MRI investigation. Psychiatry Res. 155 (1), 45–56. https://doi.org/10.1016/j.pscychresns.2006.11.006.

Lanius, R.A., Bluhm, R.L., Coupland, N.J., Hegadoren, K.M., Rowe, B., Theberge, J., Brimson, M., 2010. Default mode network connectivity as a predictor of post-traumatic stress disorder symptom severity in acutely traumatized subjects. Acta Psychiatr. Scand. 121 (1), 33–40. https://doi.org/10.1111/j.1600-0447.2009.01391.x.

LeDoux, J., 2003. The emotional brain, fear, and the amygdala. Cell. Mol. Neurobiol. 23 (4–5), 727–738.

Linden, D.E., Habes, I., Johnston, S.J., Linden, S., Tatineni, R., Subramanian, L., Goebel, R., 2012. Real-time self-regulation of emotion networks in patients with depression. PLoS One 7 (6), e38115. https://doi.org/10.1371/journal.pone.0038115.

Lubianiker, N., Goldway, N., Fruchtman-Steinbok, T., Paret, C., Keynan, J.N., Singer, N., Hendler, T., 2019. Process-based framework for precise neuromodulation. Nat. Hum. Behav. 3 (5), 436–445. https://doi.org/10.1038/s41562-019-0573-y.

Mehler, D.M.A., Sokunbi, M.O., Habes, I., Barawi, K., Subramanian, L., Range, M., Linden, D.E.J., 2018. Targeting the affective brain-a randomized controlled trial of real-time fMRI neurofeedback in patients with depression. Neuropsychopharmacology. https://doi.org/10.1038/s41386-018-0126-5.

Meir-Hasson, Y., Keynan, J.N., Kinreich, S., Jackont, G., Cohen, A., Podlipsky-Klovatch, I., Intrator, N., 2016. One-class FMRI-inspired EEG model for self-regulation training. PLoS One 11 (5), e0154968. https://doi.org/10.1371/journal.pone.0154968.

Misaki, M., Phillips, R., Zotev, V., Wong, C.K., Wurfel, B.E., Krueger, F., Bodurka, J., 2018. Connectome-wide investigation of altered resting-state functional connectivity in war veterans with and without posttraumatic stress disorder. Neuroimage Clin. 17, 285–296. https://doi.org/10.1016/j.nicl.2017.10.032.

Murray, E.A., 2007. The amygdala, reward and emotion. Trends Cogn. Sci. 11 (11), 489–497. https://doi.org/10.1016/j.tics.2007.08.013.

Namburi, P., Beyeler, A., Yorozu, S., Calhoon, G.G., Halbert, S.A., Wichmann, R., Tye, K.M., 2015. A circuit mechanism for differentiating positive and negative associations. Nature 520 (7549), 675–678. https://doi.org/10.1038/nature14366.

Nicholson, A.A., Rabellino, D., Densmore, M., Frewen, P.A., Paret, C., Kluetsch, R., Lanius, R.A., 2017. The neurobiology of emotion regulation in posttraumatic stress disorder: amygdala downregulation via real-time fMRI neurofeedback. Hum. Brain Mapp. 38 (1), 541–560. https://doi.org/10.1002/hbm.23402.

Paret, C., Hendler, T., 2020. Live from the "regulating brain": harnessing the brain to change emotion. Emotion 20 (1), 126–131. https://doi.org/10.1037/emo0000674.

Paret, C., Kluetsch, R., Zaehringer, J., Ruf, M., Demirakca, T., Bohus, M., Schmahl, C., 2016a. Alterations of amygdala-prefrontal connectivity with real-time fMRI neurofeedback in BPD patients. Soc. Cogn. Affect. Neurosci. 11 (6), 952–960. https://doi.org/10.1093/scan/nsw016.

Paret, C., Ruf, M., Gerchen, M.F., Kluetsch, R., Demirakca, T., Jungkunz, M., Ende, G., 2016b. fMRI neurofeedback of amygdala response to aversive stimuli enhances prefrontal-limbic brain connectivity. NeuroImage 125, 182–188. https://doi.org/10.1016/j.neuroimage.2015.10.027.

Perkonigg, A., Pfister, H., Stein, M.B., Hofler, M., Lieb, R., Maercker, A., Wittchen, H.U., 2005. Longitudinal course of posttraumatic stress disorder and posttraumatic stress disorder symptoms in a community sample of adolescents and young adults. Am. J. Psychiatry 162 (7), 1320–1327. https://doi.org/10.1176/appi.ajp.162.7.1320.

Phelps, E.A., LeDoux, J.E., 2005. Contributions of the amygdala to emotion processing: from animal models to human behavior. Neuron 48 (2), 175–187. https://doi.org/10.1016/j.neuron.2005.09.025.

Posse, S., Fitzgerald, D., Gao, K., Habel, U., Rosenberg, D., Moore, G.J., Schneider, F., 2003. Real-time fMRI of temporolimbic regions detects amygdala activation during single-trial self-induced sadness. NeuroImage 18 (3), 760–768.

Sah, P., Faber, E.S., Lopez De Armentia, M., Power, J., 2003. The amygdaloid complex: anatomy and physiology. Physiol. Rev. 83 (3), 803–834. https://doi.org/10.1152/physrev.00002.2003.

Sander, D., Grafman, J., Zalla, T., 2003. The human amygdala: an evolved system for relevance detection. Rev. Neurosci. 14 (4), 303–316.

Sanislow, C.A., Grilo, C.M., Morey, L.C., Bender, D.S., Skodol, A.E., Gunderson, J.G., McGlashan, T.H., 2002. Confirmatory factor analysis of DSM-IV criteria for borderline personality disorder: findings from the collaborative longitudinal personality disorders study. Am. J. Psychiatry 159 (2), 284–290. https://doi.org/10.1176/appi.ajp.159.2.284.

Schmahl, C., Herpertz, S.C., Bertsch, K., Ende, G., Flor, H., Kirsch, P., Bohus, M., 2014. Mechanisms of disturbed emotion processing and social interaction in borderline personality disorder: state of knowledge and research agenda of the German clinical research unit. Borderline Personal. Disord. Emot. Dysregul. 1, 12. https://doi.org/10.1186/2051-6673-1-12.

Schnurr, P.P., Friedman, M.J., Engel, C.C., Foa, E.B., Shea, M.T., Chow, B.K., Bernardy, N., 2007. Cognitive behavioral therapy for posttraumatic stress disorder in women: a randomized controlled trial. JAMA 297 (8), 820–830. https://doi.org/10.1001/jama.297.8.820.

Schulze, L., Domes, G., Kruger, A., Berger, C., Fleischer, M., Prehn, K., Herpertz, S.C., 2011. Neuronal correlates of cognitive reappraisal in borderline patients with affective instability. Biol. Psychiatry 69 (6), 564–573. https://doi.org/10.1016/j.biopsych.2010.10.025.

Schulze, L., Schmahl, C., Niedtfeld, I., 2016. Neural correlates of disturbed emotion processing in borderline personality disorder: a multimodal meta-analysis. Biol. Psychiatry 79 (2), 97–106. https://doi.org/10.1016/j.biopsych.2015.03.027.

Sergerie, K., Chochol, C., Armony, J.L., 2008. The role of the amygdala in emotional processing: a quantitative meta-analysis of functional neuroimaging studies. Neurosci. Biobehav. Rev. 32 (4), 811–830. https://doi.org/10.1016/j.neubiorev.2007.12.002.

Shalev, A., Liberzon, I., Marmar, C., 2017. Post-traumatic stress disorder. N. Engl. J. Med. 376 (25), 2459–2469. https://doi.org/10.1056/NEJMra1612499.

Shibata, K., Lisi, G., Cortese, A., Watanabe, T., Sasaki, Y., Kawato, M., 2019. Toward a comprehensive understanding of the neural mechanisms of decoded neurofeedback. NeuroImage 188, 539–556. https://doi.org/10.1016/j.neuroimage.2018.12.022.

Shin, L.M., Rauch, S.L., Pitman, R.K., 2006. Amygdala, medial prefrontal cortex, and hippocampal function in PTSD. Ann. NY Acad. Sci. 1071, 67–79. https://doi.org/10.1196/annals.1364.007.

Siegle, G.J., Steinhauer, S.R., Thase, M.E., Stenger, V.A., Carter, C.S., 2002. Can't shake that feeling: event-related fMRI assessment of sustained amygdala activity in response to emotional information in depressed individuals. Biol. Psychiatry 51 (9), 693–707.

Siegle, G.J., Ghinassi, F., Thase, M.E., 2007. Neurobehavioral therapies in the 21st century: summary of an emerging field and an extended example of cognitive control training for depression. Cogn. Ther. Res. 31, 235–262.

Sripada, R.K., King, A.P., Welsh, R.C., Garfinkel, S.N., Wang, X., Sripada, C.S., Liberzon, I., 2012. Neural dysregulation in posttraumatic stress disorder: evidence for disrupted equilibrium between salience and default mode brain networks. Psychosom. Med. 74 (9), 904–911. https://doi.org/10.1097/PSY.0b013e318273bf33.

Suslow, T., Konrad, C., Kugel, H., Rumstadt, D., Zwitserlood, P., Schoning, S., Dannlowski, U., 2010. Automatic mood-congruent amygdala responses to masked facial expressions in major depression. Biol. Psychiatry 67 (2), 155–160. https://doi.org/10.1016/j.biopsych.2009.07.023.

Victor, T.A., Furey, M.L., Fromm, S.J., Ohman, A., Drevets, W.C., 2010. Relationship between amygdala responses to masked faces and mood state and treatment in major depressive disorder. Arch. Gen. Psychiatry 67 (11), 1128–1138. https://doi.org/10.1001/archgenpsychiatry.2010.144.

Watanabe, T., Sasaki, Y., Shibata, K., Kawato, M., 2017. Advances in fMRI real-time neurofeedback. Trends Cogn. Sci. 21 (12), 997–1010. https://doi.org/10.1016/j.tics.2017.09.010.

Watts, B.V., Schnurr, P.P., Mayo, L., Young-Xu, Y., Weeks, W.B., Friedman, M.J., 2013. Meta-analysis of the efficacy of treatments for posttraumatic stress disorder. J. Clin. Psychiatry 74 (6), e541–e550. https://doi.org/10.4088/JCP.12r08225.

Williams, J.M., Barnhofer, T., Crane, C., Herman, D., Raes, F., Watkins, E., Dalgleish, T., 2007. Autobiographical memory specificity and emotional disorder. Psychol. Bull. 133 (1), 122–148. https://doi.org/10.1037/0033-2909.133.1.122.

World Health Organization, 2004. The World Health Report 2004—Changing History. World Health Organization. https://apps.who.int/iris/handle/10665/42891.

Yamada, T., Hashimoto, R.I., Yahata, N., Ichikawa, N., Yoshihara, Y., Okamoto, Y., Kawato, M., 2017. Resting-state functional connectivity-based biomarkers and functional MRI-based neurofeedback for psychiatric disorders: a challenge for developing theranostic biomarkers. Int. J. Neuropsychopharmacol. 20 (10), 769–781. https://doi.org/10.1093/ijnp/pyx059.

Young, K.D., Zotev, V., Phillips, R., Misaki, M., Yuan, H., Drevets, W.C., Bodurka, J., 2014. Real-time FMRI neurofeedback training of amygdala activity in patients with major depressive disorder. PLoS One 9 (2), e88785. https://doi.org/10.1371/journal.pone.0088785.

Young, K.D., Siegle, G.J., Bodurka, J., Drevets, W.C., 2016. Amygdala activity during autobiographical memory recall in depressed and vulnerable individuals: association with symptom severity and autobiographical Overgenerality. Am. J. Psychiatry 173 (1), 78–89. https://doi.org/10.1176/appi.ajp.2015.15010119.

Young, K.D., Misaki, M., Harmer, C.J., Victor, T., Zotev, V., Phillips, R., Bodurka, J., 2017a. Real-time fMRI amygdala neurofeedback changes positive information processing in major depressive disorder. Biol. Psychiatry. https://doi.org/10.1016/j.biopsych.2017.03.013.

Young, K.D., Siegle, G.J., Zotev, V., Phillips, R., Misaki, M., Yuan, H., Bodurka, J., 2017b. Randomized clinical trial of real-time fMRI amygdala neurofeedback for major depressive disorder: effects on symptoms and autobiographical memory recall. Am. J. Psychiatry 174 (8), 748–755.

Zaehringer, J., Ende, G., Santangelo, P., Kleindienst, N., Ruf, M., Bertsch, K., Paret, C., 2019. Improved emotion regulation after neurofeedback: a single-arm trial in patients with borderline personality disorder. Neuroimage Clin. 24, 102032. https://doi.org/10.1016/j.nicl.2019.102032.

Zilverstand, A., Sorger, B., Sarkheil, P., Goebel, R., 2015. fMRI neurofeedback facilitates anxiety regulation in females with spider phobia. Front. Behav. Neurosci. 9, 148. https://doi.org/10.3389/fnbeh.2015.00148.

Zilverstand, A., Sorger, B., Slaats-Willemse, D., Kan, C.C., Goebel, R., Buitelaar, J.K., 2017. fMRI neurofeedback training for increasing anterior cingulate cortex activation in adult attention deficit hyperactivity disorder. An exploratory randomized, single-blinded study. PloS One *12* (1), e0170795. https://doi.org/10.1371/journal.pone.0170795.

Zotev, V., Krueger, F., Phillips, R., Alvarez, R.P., Simmons, W.K., Bellgowan, P., Bodurka, J., 2011. Self-regulation of amygdala activation using real-time FMRI neurofeedback. PLoS One 6 (9), e24522. https://doi.org/10.1371/journal.pone.0024522.

Zotev, V., Phillips, R., Misaki, M., Wong, C.K., Wurfel, B.E., Krueger, F., Bodurka, J., 2018. Real-time fMRI neurofeedback training of the amygdala activity with simultaneous EEG in veterans with combat-related PTSD. Neuroimage Clin. 19, 106–121. https://doi.org/10.1016/j.nicl.2018.04.010.

Zweerings, J., Pflieger, E.M., Mathiak, K.A., Zvyagintsev, M., Kacela, A., Flatten, G., Mathiak, K., 2018. Impaired voluntary control in PTSD: probing self-regulation of the ACC with real-time fMRI. Front. Psych. 9, 219. https://doi.org/10.3389/fpsyt.2018.00219.

CHAPTER 9

The treatment and study of psychiatric disorders with fMRI neurofeedback[*]

Zhiying Zhao, Emma Romaker, and Michelle Hampson
Department of Radiology and Biomedical Imaging, Yale University School of Medicine, New Haven, CT, United States

The use of real-time fMRI neurofeedback (rt-fMRI NF) for therapeutic purposes in psychiatry is an extremely promising new avenue of research. Although in some respects similar to cognitive-behavioral therapy, neurofeedback differs in that neural rather than mental patterns are trained. Neurofeedback also depends less on explicit learning processes and has been shown to engage implicit learning mechanisms (e.g., Taschereau-Dumouchel et al., 2018 and see also Chapter 10). However, neurofeedback is similar to cognitive-behavioral therapy in that it attempts to harness natural learning mechanisms for therapeutic purposes. The clinical utility of neurofeedback thus depends on whether patient populations can learn the specific neural activity patterns trained, as well as whether the trained neural patterns translate into clinical improvement. In this chapter we review the work that has been done addressing these questions and more generally exploring the promise of fMRI neurofeedback for the treatment and study of psychiatric disorders. As other chapters have addressed the development of rt-fMRI NF for emotion regulation disorders (see Chapters 8 and 10), here we focus on other psychiatric conditions, including disorders of compulsive consumption, obsessive-compulsive disorder, neurodevelopmental disorders, schizophrenia, and psychopathy.

1 Addiction and eating disorders

The DSM-5 defines 11 main classes of substances of abuse (including, for example, alcohol, amphetamines, cocaine, opioids, and nicotine). A substance use disorder is not primarily defined by the amount consumed (this is often denoted by "harmful" or "hazardous" use, particularly of alcohol), but by the behavioral pattern and psychosocial consequences of the substance use. Substance abuse can persist for a long time, but often also progresses to substance dependence or addiction. Tolerance (increasing doses are needed to achieve the same physiological and psychological effects) and the development of withdrawal symptoms

---

[*] Excerpts of text first published in *The Biology of Psychological Disorders*, 2019, David Linden. Red Globe Press, London, have been included in this chapter with permission.

fMRI Neurofeedback. https://doi.org/10.1016/B978-0-12-822421-2.00016-8

when sufficient doses are not maintained are the key features of physiological dependence. The psychological side of substance dependence is characterized by compulsive consumption and almost exclusive cognitive focus on the substance of abuse. Addiction is commonly regarded to be a lifelong condition conferring vulnerability of uncontrolled consumption after reexposure. In this section, we will discuss rt-fMRI NF research on addiction and other disorders of compulsive consumption that share overlapping neural circuits related to craving and reward (Volkow et al., 2012).

1.1 Addiction

Addiction is a disorder that develops through natural learning processes acting on neural circuits (Heinz et al., 2019). Thus it is a particularly promising application for a learning-based intervention such as neurofeedback: hopefully, the plasticity that allows addiction to develop may also be harnessed to resolve the problem. However, a major challenge, as in all clinical applications of NF, is to identify an aspect of brain function that, if altered, may improve clinical outcome.

One common approach for psychiatric neurofeedback applications is to identify brain patterns associated with a symptomatic state, and to train patients to downregulate those brain patterns in the context of a situation that would normally activate the patterns. If participants can learn to control their symptom-relevant brain activity in provoking circumstances in the training session, the hope is that they will maintain that ability after the scan, and this will allow them to control their symptoms as they arise in their daily lives, and that this will translate into healthier mental function and behavior.

What are the symptoms of addiction that participants must learn to control in order to resist compulsive consumption? One promising candidate is craving, the strong desire an addict feels for the substance. This phenomenon has been the focus of the bulk of rt-fMRI NF studies of addiction.

For example, a group at the Medical University of South Carolina (MUSC) has done substantial work using fMRI neurofeedback to treat and study nicotine dependence by training participants to control their craving-related brain patterns. The series of studies they conducted provide an example of the iterative process of design, testing, and refinement involved in the development of a novel rt-fMRI application for treating psychiatric patients.

Based on existing literature regarding the neurobiological basis of craving, the group began with the theory that craving involves activity in the anterior cingulate cortex (ACC) and can be inhibited by engagement of the middle prefrontal cortex (mPFC). Thus, in their first two studies, they tested the hypothesis that nicotine users could learn to self-regulate these two brain areas via rt-fMRI NF, and that successful training would decrease their craving in response to smoking cues (Hanlon et al., 2013; Li et al., 2013). More specifically, participants were trained to decrease ACC activity (believed to be associated with the urge to smoke) and to increase mPFC activity (believed to play a role in resisting the urge), while viewing images designed to induce nicotine craving. Both studies found that participants learned to regulate activity in ACC but not mPFC, and that ACC activity during downregulation was correlated with self-reported craving ratings after downregulation blocks. The fact that participants did not demonstrate an improved ability to self-regulate the mPFC highlights one of the major challenges in rt-fMRI NF research: the efficacy of the intervention is limited by the ability of participants to learn to control the targeted brain pattern. When learning does not occur, there are two options for moving forward. One is to alter the training paradigm (using different parameters, longer training, more rewarding feedback, etc.) to see if learning can be more successfully induced. The second is to focus on a different target brain pattern that may be more easily trained.

Given their success in training regulation of the ACC, the MUSC group took the latter approach, and focused their next study on training on the ACC only (Canterberry et al., 2013). Participants underwent three fMRI sessions. Within each session, self-reported craving was significantly lower after neurofeedback training. In line with this behavioral finding, ACC activity was also found to decrease in the feedback runs when participants were trying to regulate the region (and their craving) compared with baseline runs when they were not. Although this regulation ability qualitatively increased across sessions, the change across sessions was not significant.

Nevertheless, the findings across these studies that ACC activity and craving were decreased during neurofeedback, and that craving levels were correlated with ACC activity, support the promise of neurofeedback training of the ACC for nicotine addiction. If this training is helpful in reducing craving in the short term, perhaps the training protocol can be optimized to get more persistent effects. However, it is important to note that the three initial studies just described did not involve a control group and the findings are based on within-subject changes occurring in a neurofeedback paradigm that involved trying to resist the urge to smoke while viewing smoking cue images. Thus it is impossible to tell whether the decreases in ACC activity and in craving during neurofeedback were driven by neurofeedback learning, or by some other aspect of the protocol, such as repeated practice controlling smoking urges, or repeated exposure to images designed to provoke nicotine craving.

This issue was addressed by a randomized controlled clinical trial with a larger sample of 33 completers (Hartwell et al., 2016). Participants recruited in this study were nicotine-dependent but not treatment-seeking. Half of them were allocated to a control group for which feedback was not provided during self-regulation. The study involved three neurofeedback sessions in which participants attempted to regulate their craving and were provided with intermittent feedback (the control group saw a blank thermometer). Of note, target region selection was functionally defined in a flexible manner, to include not only ACC but other prefrontal midline structures that had been previously been implicated in cue-related craving (Janes et al., 2010; McClernon et al., 2005) and that activated during provocation. During the feedback sessions, the experimental group displayed more activity reduction in their craving-related target regions than the control group and there was a difference of trend-level significance in the postscan craving scores between the groups (experimental < control). However, there were no significant effects across sessions on craving scores. Although the no-feedback control condition used in this study did not allow for subject blinding (and thus some nonspecific effects, such as placebo, cannot be ruled out as contributing to the within-session group differences), it did control for the potentially important effects of repeated practice in controlling craving and extended exposure to provocative images.

Thus the body of work conducted at MUSC has successfully identified a target region that nicotine users can learn to control, and has demonstrated a relationship between activity in the region and craving. Some preliminary data have also been obtained supporting the possibility that the neurofeedback training itself, rather than other aspects of the intervention, is driving a reduction in craving in the short term. Further work is needed to rule out placebo effects, and to explore whether more persistent effects on craving can be induced.

In addition to this work on nicotine dependence at MUSC, there have been two other rt-fMRI NF studies that have focused on regulating craving-related brain patterns in addiction, both of which have aimed to reduce alcohol cue-related neural responses in the brains of participants with alcohol addiction. Karch et al. (2015) conducted single sessions of neurofeedback training on patients with alcohol use disorder ($n=13$) as well as on a group of healthy controls ($n=14$). These subjects received feedback from functionally localized regions of cortex that activated to alcohol stimuli designed to induce craving. The patients were recruited from a clinical program for alcohol addiction after detoxification. Two patients and five healthy subjects were also recruited for an active control intervention that involved receiving feedback from regions believed to be unrelated to craving. During neurofeedback, participants were instructed to decrease the brain activity displayed by a thermometer while viewing alcohol cues. Craving measures decreased significantly after neurofeedback across experimental neurofeedback subjects (healthy subjects and patients), but were not significantly changed in the participants who received the control intervention, although this may be a power issue related to the limited sample sizes of the control groups. During the experimental NF intervention, brain activity in craving-related brain areas decreased across runs specifically in the patient group.

While the studies discussed before all trained patients to regulate cortical structures, the subcortex is also highly relevant to addiction, given its role in reward processing, cue reactivity, and drug seeking (Koob and Volkow, 2010). Kirsch et al. (2016) carried out a study to explore whether neurofeedback training of ventral striatum (VS) could decrease cue reactivity to alcohol cues and thus reduce craving. In this proof-of-concept study, 38 heavy but not addicted social drinkers were recruited and allocated to three groups (real NF/yoked feedback/passive control). The neurofeedback and yoked feedback control groups were instructed to bring the activity down with any strategies they thought potentially helpful. The control group was instructed to view the alcohol pictures without doing any regulation. Craving levels were assessed before and after the scanning session. Not surprisingly, given that they had been viewing images designed to induce craving without attempting to regulate that craving, craving was found to increase in the no-feedback control group. It was unchanged in the two feedback groups. Region of interest (ROI) analysis revealed greater decrease of VS activation over the neurofeedback runs in the real NF group comparing to the other two groups. In an exploratory whole-brain analysis, activity in rIFG was found to activate most strongly in the real NF group and was correlated with successful VS downregulation, suggesting this region may have been playing a regulatory role.

In summary, a number of rt-fMRI NF paradigms have been developed that aim to help individuals with nicotine or alcohol addiction to control their craving. This approach of training control over troublesome symptoms is common for rt-fMRI neurofeedback interventions. Another very promising avenue of development is to train individuals with psychiatric disorders to upregulate healthy brain function.

This alternative approach was used in a rt-fMRI NF study of cocaine abuse (Kirschner et al., 2018). As drug addiction is associated with a loss of pleasure to nondrug rewards, they reasoned that restoring sensitivity to nondrug rewards may enable individuals with addiction to focus on healthy priorities. Thus, rather than training participants to downregulate drug cue-related brain activity, they trained participants to upregulate neural activity in dopaminergic reward centers (ventral tegmental area and substantia nigra) in response to nondrug-related positive imagery. Neurofeedback was found to enhance ability to activate reward areas in both healthy subjects ($n=22$) and cocaine users ($n=26$) during positive mental imagery, but the effects did not persist in the posttraining transfer run.

This work suggests fMRI neurofeedback holds promise for balancing reward sensitivity in addiction (decreasing neural responses related to drug craving and increasing neural responses to nondrug rewards). However, many of the studies to date have only involved a single session of training and none have demonstrated persistent effects. Furthermore, most of the literature has focused on alcohol and nicotine use. Going forward, we expect the rt-fMRI NF literature on addiction will be expanded to include studies of addiction for other substances such as opioids and amphetamines, as well as behavioral addictions, such as gambling and video games.

1.2 Eating disorders

Real-time fMRI NF studies focused on eating disorders were designed with similar rationales as for addiction disorders, that is, to either reduce food craving by modulation of motivational circuitry, or to help obese individuals make healthier food choices by enhancing activity that support self-control.

Neuroimaging studies suggest a link between obesity and anterior insula cortex (AIC) activation to hedonic food stimuli. For example, after satiation, activity in the anterior insula was found to drop more in the brains of obese than lean individuals (Gautier et al., 2000, 2001). Furthermore, in the healthy brain, activity increase in AIC when viewing appetizing food was correlated with body mass index (BMI) (Batterink et al., 2010). Based on these data, it was hypothesized that obese individuals could better upregulate their AIC activity during neurofeedback training than lean individuals (Frank et al., 2012). This was tested in 11 lean and 10 obese males who were instructed to increase their AIC activity by thinking about something emotional during the training. No stimuli were presented during the training sessions. It was found that both groups were able to upregulate their bilateral AIC, but obese individuals were more successful at increasing their right AIC activity. Differences between groups in functional connectivity were also reported. The findings were interpreted as supporting the view that obese men are "more sensible to hedonic gustatory learning and can better shift their attention to emotional and body-related stimuli" (Frank et al., 2012). Although this may be informative for models of obesity, downregulation training of the AIC in obesity seems more relevant clinically.

Ihssen et al. (2017) later showed that rt-fMRI NF training of limbic regions could modulate food craving in healthy individuals. Ten healthy young females who had not eaten for 4 h participated in the study and received a single session of neurofeedback training on limbic regions that activated to palatable food stimuli. They received "motivational" neurofeedback, during which brain activity within the target region was indicated by the size of food pictures on the screen. Participants were instructed to reduce the size of pictures by self-regulation. This feedback form was designed to boost participants' motivation for self-regulation. Also, directly locking the size of the food stimuli to brain activity has the feature that it may alleviate the cognitive load compared to providing a separate feedback stimulus, such as a thermometer on the screen along with the food images. During self-regulation, activity decreased in the amygdala, insula, and prefrontal areas. Comparing subjective reports before and after neurofeedback runs, hunger was significantly reduced and craving was reduced at a trend level of significance. The reduction in hunger was also positively associated with activity decrease in right amygdala during neurofeedback. However, comparing measures collected after the study to before, state craving increased, likely due to the 1.5 additional hours without food. Interestingly, dorsolateral prefrontal cortex (dlPFC) and ventrolateral prefrontal cortex (vlPFC), previously indicated to be involved in top-down control, were not found to be activated in the self-regulation process. Thus the downregulation of food craving was speculated to be underpinned by implicit operant learning (Ihssen et al., 2017).

In another study on healthy subjects, the potential of neurofeedback targeting the functional coupling between two prefrontal regions, previously implicated in value encoding and food choices (Hare et al., 2009, 2011), was explored (Spetter et al., 2017). As functional connectivity between the two regions (dlPFC and ventromedial prefrontal cortex, vmPFC) was observed to increase during the exertion of self-control (Hare et al., 2009), the researchers hypothesized that upregulating the connectivity between them would help the individuals make healthier food choices. Four sessions of upregulation training were conducted, with a self-report based food choice task before and after each session. In addition, a covert calorie intake test was administered at the start and end of the study. Within each neurofeedback session, the targeted functional connection did increase significantly, but no session effects were seen. At the behavioral level, there was a trend of decrease in self-reported high-calorie food choices during each session. However, covert calorie intake increased across sessions (possibly due to changes in agitation and fear which decreased across sessions).

The same research group then trained overweight/obese individuals to upregulate their dlPFC activity with a single session of neurofeedback training (Kohl et al., 2019). They found that both the experimental group ($n = 16$) and the control group ($n = 21$), which received feedback from a visual area, were able to upregulate brain activity inside their trained regions, but their ability to regulate did not improve with training. During upregulation compared with passive viewing, both groups had increased activity in dlPFC and increased connectivity between dlPFC and vmPFC. In line with these findings, both groups reported healthier food choices after three runs of training. Given the similar pattern seen across groups, further work is needed to disentangle neurofeedback-specific effects from contributions of other factors such as repetitive exposure to stimuli and mental practice.

These studies have all focused on obesity and overeating. To our knowledge, rt-fMRI NF has yet to be applied to other eating disorders such as binge eating disorder (BED), anorexia nervosa (AN), and bulimia nervosa (BN). Sokunbi (2018) discusses potential targets and study designs for implementing NF with BED, AN, and BN patients. A more dimensional approach could also focus on emotional eating, a phenomenon that plays a role in multiple eating disorders. Emotional eating (sometimes known as hedonic feeding) involves over/ under eating in positive/negative mood states or experiences (Turton et al., 2017). Recent evidence suggests that deficits in emotion regulation contribute to emotional overeating, therefore emotion regulation training might be therapeutic for these patient populations (Gianini et al., 2013; Van Strien, 2018). Neurofeedback training has shown promise for individuals with emotion dysregulation; more on applications of rt-fMRI NF for emotion regulation can be found in Chapter 8.

2 Obsessive-compulsive disorder

Obsessive-compulsive disorder (OCD) involves obsessions, which are intrusive, anxiety-inducing thoughts, and compulsions, which are actions performed to reduce the anxiety caused by the obsessive thoughts. OCD is associated with abnormalities in the orbitofrontal cortex (OFC). These include abnormalities in glucose metabolism (Swedo et al., 1989), brain volume (Rotge et al., 2009), activity level (Chamberlain et al., 2008; Saxena et al., 1998), and functional connectivity (Beucke et al., 2013). In a metaanalysis of imaging studies of OCD, the OFC was the most consistently implicated region (Menzies et al., 2008), and hyperactivity in this region has been associated with symptom severity (Swedo et al., 1992). Thus the OFC is a candidate target region for real-time fMRI neurofeedback aimed at normalizing OCD symptoms.

Factor analyses have identified several common types of OCD symptoms (Bloch et al., 2008). One common symptom is contamination anxiety, which tends to be associated with washing compulsions. Interestingly, contamination anxiety in healthy subjects, as well as in OCD patients, has been found to be associated with hyperactivity in the OFC (Mataix-Cols et al., 2003, 2004). This supports a dimensional model of contamination anxiety and suggests that NF training of the OFC may have similar effects in healthy subjects as in OCD patients who have contamination anxiety. Therefore we decided to conduct a feasibility study training healthy individuals with subclinical contamination anxiety to control activity in the orbitofrontal cortex during exposure to provocative contamination stimuli. Our aim was to see if such training could improve their control over the region, and more importantly, to see if it could improve their control over their contamination anxiety as assessed via a behavioral measure outside of the scanner. For illustrative purposes, we describe this protocol, discuss a number of the design considerations involved, and explain how some aspects have evolved over time.

A flowchart for the study protocol is shown in Fig. 1A. Healthy subjects who reported experiencing contamination anxiety were recruited. Screening included a complete health history (to ensure they were healthy participants) as well as completion of the Padua Inventory (which measures different types of obsessive compulsive symptoms). Inclusion criteria required a score of equal to or greater than eight on the Contamination Subscale. In this manner, we ensured there was some level of contamination anxiety present prior to the intervention that could potentially be mitigated via neurofeedback. In the first Imaging Assessment session, a high resolution structural image (MPRAGE) was collected to be used for registration of images across sessions and subjects, resting state functional imaging data were collected and the functional localizer was run. During the functional localizer (3 runs), participants were exposed to provocative contamination imagery and neutral images in alternating blocks. The peak activation to the provocative imagery within their OFC (defined broadly to include adjacent areas of the frontal pole) was then identified in offline analysis to be used as the target region. Using a functionally localized target region improves power over a structurally defined region, because it is tailored to the neurobiology of the individual participant and is specific to their symptom-provoked state.

Subjects then participated in a Strategy Development Session in which they met with a clinical psychologist who helped them to develop strategies for controlling their OFC activity.

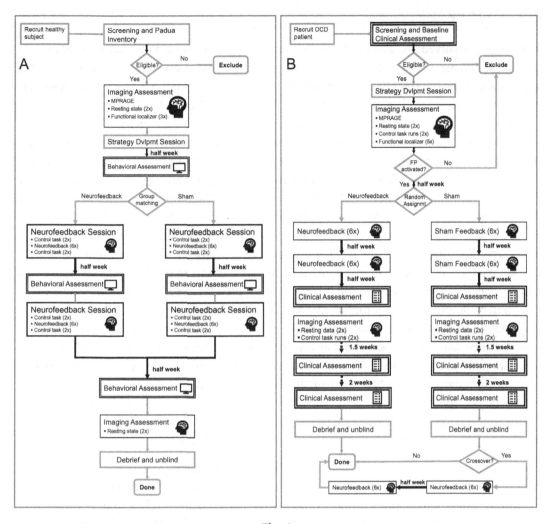

Fig. 1

Flowcharts of the study protocol for the feasibility study in healthy subjects (Panel A) and our current protocol for OCD patients (Panel B). In both flowcharts, the boxes with double outlines indicate the time points when the primary outcome measures are collected. In the feasibility study, the primary outcome measure is the behavioral measure of control over contamination anxiety (indicated with a monitor icon, described in text). In the study with OCD patients, the primary outcome measure (indicated with a paper icon) is the Yale-Brown Obsessive-Compulsive Symptom scale (Y-BOCS), a gold-standard clinical instrument for assessing OCD symptoms. In the feasibility study, the primary behavioral outcome measure is only collected once after the feedback training (half a week after). In contrast, in the OCD study, we collect the clinical assessments three times after the NF is completed (half a week, 2 weeks, and 4 weeks after), allowing us to follow symptom changes for a month. Note that control task scans were collected at the beginning and ending of the feedback sessions in the feasibility study (see details printed in the boxes labeled Neurofeedback session and Sham feedback session). In contrast, in the OCD protocol, these are collected in the Imaging Assessment sessions that occur on different days before and after feedback training. The neuroimaging sessions in both flowcharts are indicated by boxes with brain icons. Note, that after debriefing, the clinical protocol (B) additionally offers the option of real NF to those who were randomized to receive sham feedback. This is offered to the patients for ethical reasons so that every patient enrolling in the study has the potential to try real NF.

This session involved discussion of evidence-based cognitive behavioral therapy (CBT) strategies. The use of these strategies was optional, but the idea was to give them some initial strategies that the NF training could then help them to improve and optimize. The decision to include this session touches on a controversial issue in fMRI neurofeedback research: namely, is it advisable to provide conscious strategies to the subjects, or does providing conscious strategies only interfere with subconscious learning? A number of neurofeedback studies have successfully induced learning using implicit neurofeedback, that is, using paradigms where the subjects don't know what is trained, or sometimes even that training is occurring (Ramot et al., 2016; Shibata et al., 2018). The success of these implicit training studies demonstrates that subconscious learning plays a powerful role in neurofeedback learning paradigms. However, this does not rule out the possibility that conscious learning can also play an important role. If neurofeedback can help patients to consciously identify mental strategies that are more or less helpful in managing their symptoms, this in itself could yield substantial clinical benefit. In this case, providing participants with a toolset of strategies to try that are known to be helpful for controlling symptoms (such as those from evidence-based CBT) may enable subjects to identify effective strategies more quickly and thus may potentially optimize their learning. An argument against providing strategies, however, is that the suggestion of specific strategies for subjects may constrain the learning process and interfere with subconscious learning. Indeed, a small study that investigated the effects of providing strategies did report that the subjects who received instructions showed qualitatively (but not significantly) poorer performance (in terms of improvement in regulation of the target region) than those who did not receive instructions (Sepulveda et al., 2016).

One consideration relevant to this issue in studies using explicit neurofeedback training (that is, training in which subjects know what aspect of mental function is being targeted) in clinical populations is that a number of patients enrolled in the study will likely have been exposed to CBT previously. If prior CBT exposure is not matched across groups, this could create a confound. For example, if the NF group had substantially more CBT exposure than the sham group prior to entering the study, the NF group may show more clinical improvement simply because they spent time practicing a lot of useful CBT strategies, while the sham group did not (because they didn't know these strategies). In order to avoid this problem, we have chosen to give everyone a summary of accepted evidence-based CBT strategies. Whether these strategies help or hinder their NF learning is unclear, and this remains an interesting question in the field. In either case, our hope is that the effects will be matched across groups as we have provided them with a similar set of strategies to try. One thing to bear in mind if you choose to provide strategies to subjects is that this should be done in a standardized manner across real NF subjects and those in the control group. In our studies, the cognitive psychologist administering this session is blind to the group assignment of all participants.

After the Strategy Development Session, a behavioral task was administered to assess participants' baseline ability to control their anxiety while viewing contamination imagery. This behavioral measure involved instructing participants to try to control their anxiety, showing them contamination images, asking them to self-report how anxious each image made them feel on a scale of 1–5, and averaging their responses across all images. The images used before and after feedback training were balanced for how intensely provocative they were, and the change in control over anxiety over the course of the study was calculated as the difference in this behavioral measure from before to after training. This behavioral measure was the primary outcome measure for the study. In clinical studies, it is standard to use a validated clinical instrument to assess symptom severity changes. However, in feasibility studies of subclinical populations, clinical instruments are likely to have problematic floor effects and other options (such as behavioral measures) may need to be considered.

After this behavioral measure of control over contamination anxiety was collected, the participants received two sessions of feedback training spaced half a week apart: the experimental group received feedback from their target region while the yoked sham control group was shown feedback time courses taken from their matched subject in the experimental group (each sham subject was matched to a different NF subject, and the matches were assigned so that paired participants had a similar age and gender). As these were healthy subjects, they were not told there was a sham control condition, and all were led to believe they were receiving real NF. In the feedback scans, the timing of increase and decrease blocks was consistent across subjects, so sham subjects were given feedback indicating they were succeeding or failing to increase/decrease activity based on how successful their matched experimental subject was. A feature of this form of yoked sham is thus that the two groups receive identical levels of positive feedback indicating success during the feedback runs. To assess control over the target region, separate control task scans were collected where subjects were cued to alternately increase and decrease activity in the target region in the absence of feedback and their ability to modulate the region on cue was assessed (see Chapter 3 and also Chapter 6 for discussion of the varied ways in which control over the target region is assessed in neurofeedback studies). In our feasibility study, we collected control task data at the beginning and end of each of the two feedback scanning sessions.

Half a week after the feedback training was completed, the behavioral measure of control over anxiety was collected again, and resting state data were collected in a final Imaging Assessment session. Finally, subjects were debriefed, the deception in the study was revealed (that is, the fact that there was a control group that did not receive real NF), and they were told which group they had been assigned to. The protocol design is described in further detail in a methods paper (Hampson et al., 2012).

We obtained complete data on 20 adults with subclinical contamination anxiety in this feasibility study: 10 who were assigned to the experimental intervention and 10 who were assigned to the sham control intervention (Scheinost et al., 2013). The peak activation when localizing the target area consistently fell in a frontal polar region. Control over the target region was found to increase in the neurofeedback group and not in the sham group. Notably, the clinical potential of the intervention was supported by the finding that control over contamination anxiety (as measured by the behavioral task) increased after the neurofeedback training in the experimental group, but not in the control group (Fig. 2A). Changes in brain function were also explored by examining degree of centrality, a voxel-wise measure of global functional connectivity (Buckner et al., 2009; Rubinov and Sporns, 2010), in the resting state data collected several days before and after the training sessions. It was found that global functional connectivity was significantly decreased in nodes of emotion circuitry such as insula (para) hippocampal areas, thalamus, and amygdala, and was increased in prefrontal cortex, in the neurofeedback group. No significant alterations in resting-state functional connectivity were found in the control group. Interestingly, improvement in anxiety control in the experimental group correlated with changes in degree centrality in the frontal polar target region (Fig. 2B).

In a follow-up analysis of the same data, the global functional connectivity in the frontal pole in the baseline resting data (that is, the resting data collected prior to the neurofeedback

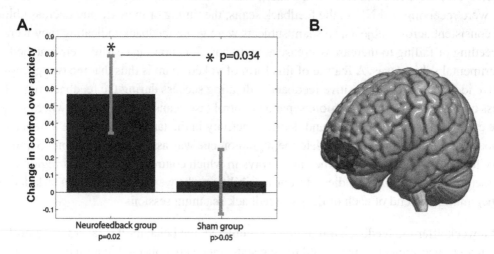

Fig. 2

Control over contamination was only increased in the experiment group but not in the control group (A). This change was significantly correlated (at a $P < .05$ whole-brain corrected level) with decreases in degree of connectivity in the frontal pole (B). *Reproduced with permission from Scheinost, D., Stoica, T., Saksa, J., Papademetris, X., Constable, R.T., Pittenger, C., Hampson, M., 2013. Orbitofrontal cortex neurofeedback produces lasting changes in contamination anxiety and resting-state connectivity. Transl. Psychiatry 3, e250.*

training) was found to predict response to the intervention (that is, improvement in control over anxiety from before to after training) (Scheinost et al., 2014). In summary, these data suggest that individuals with high baseline global connectivity in the frontal pole are the most likely to benefit from this intervention which yields improvements in control over contamination anxiety that are associated with decreases in global connectivity in the frontal polar target region.

Given the promising data from the subclinical population, this protocol was translated to an OCD sample and a double-blind, randomized trial in adult patients was initiated. A flowchart of the design in the OCD clinical trial is shown in Fig. 1B. Although many aspects are similar to the feasibility study, there are also notable differences. To highlight a few of these:

1. Note that the OCD protocol includes two time points at which participants can be screened out of the study—during the screening session and after the functional localizer was collected if they do not show activation in the target area. Although it did not occur to us until we had completed the feasibility study (and fortunately did not occur in that study), the possibility that a participant would not sufficiently activate the target region would prevent us from being able to include them and thus should be defined as exclusion criteria for the trial. Similar to other exclusion criteria, exclusion due to lack of activation in a functional localizer should be applied in a manner that is independent of the group assignment of the participant. Otherwise, neurophysiological differences across groups could arise due to the different sampling restrictions. Therefore our protocol design now includes these exclusion criteria prior to group assignment.

2. The use of our behavioral measure of control over contamination anxiety in the feasibility study has been replaced with a standard clinical assessment (Y-BOCS) in the clinical trial. The Y-BOCS is a validated measure of obsessive-compulsive symptoms that would have been used in the feasibility study, except that floor effects on this measure would be problematic in a healthy population. One consideration when using a clinical assessment like the Y-BOCS is the time window over which that assessment examines symptoms— this is a week in the case of the Y-BOCS. Thus, ideally, the assessments will be collected at least a week apart to get independent measures. For this reason, we did not conduct an assessment between the two neurofeedback scans, in contrast to the feasibility study, in which we did collect a midpoint behavioral measure between the two feedback scans.

3. Participants were age and gender matched across groups in the feasibility study as we felt these variables may not end up balanced in such a small sample with a randomized design. The clinical trial was larger in sample size so we adopted a randomized design.

4. The control task runs were shifted from the beginning and ending of each of the two feedback scanning sessions to separate imaging assessment sessions that occur prior to and after the training. This change was driven by our observation that the neurofeedback training was quite fatiguing for subjects and our desire to avoid confounds related to fatigue from corrupting our control task data.

5. While the feasibility study only assessed symptoms once after the NF was completed, the clinical trial includes three postintervention assessments at a half-week, 2 weeks, and 4 weeks posttraining. This follow-up data has proven very interesting. Although the trial is still running, in the interim data it is apparent that subjects who have symptom improvements during the intervention continue to improve over time for weeks after the intervention. After noticing this pattern, we examined data from another neurofeedback study we were running that was training a different brain area in a different patient population and we were surprised to see a similar pattern. The data were combined across studies to allow evaluation of the statistical significance of this pattern of symptom change. Results suggested that clinical symptoms can continue to improve for weeks following neurofeedback, highlighting the importance of including clinical follow-ups for weeks after neurofeedback even in very early stage trials, in order to ensure that the time point of greatest effect is sampled. This finding was published in NeuroImage (Rance et al., 2018) and other groups have reported similar patterns of symptom or behavioral changes following NF (Amano et al., 2016; Goldway et al., 2019; Mehler et al., 2018; Schnyer et al., 2015). This pattern of symptom change has important implications for NF study design that are discussed in detail in Rance et al. (2018). To summarize these implications briefly: (1) it is important to follow up all studies, even very early stage feasibility studies, (2) interleaving assessments with NF scans is a flawed approach to optimizing the number of sessions because it assumes changes in symptoms induced by a NF scan occur during (not after) that scan, and (3) cross-over designs are likely to have carryover effects contaminating the second leg.

6. Based on the literature highlighting the role of OFC in OCD symptoms including contamination anxiety, our feasibility study targeted the OFC. However, we soon noticed that the peak activation in the OFC in our functional localizer tended to spread into adjacent, more dorsal regions of the frontal pole, so we used a relaxed definition of the OFC to include this frontal polar area. In the clinical study, we have found that the peak activation is consistently in the frontal pole and not in other areas of the OFC. Also, the resting state functional connectivity analyses from our feasibility study highlighted the role of the frontal pole in symptom changes. Therefore, going forward in our next study, we will likely focus on the frontal pole as our target region. This includes anterior portions of the OFC as well as more dorsal parts of Brodmann's area 10. This capacity for trials designed to evaluate efficacy of a specific neurofeedback intervention to inform our models of mechanisms and thus potentially contribute to the development of improved training protocols is a feature of neurofeedback that amplifies its development potential.

In addition to the OFC/frontal pole, there are a number of other brain areas that have been implicated in contamination anxiety. These include anterior insula: hyperactivity in anterior insula has been shown to be linked with contamination-provoked disgust and was found to decrease after successful treatment (Wright et al., 2004). Based on this neural mechanism of contamination anxiety, a study from another group trained three adult OCD patients to downregulate their brain activity in the anterior insula during exposure to aversive pictures (Buyukturkoglu et al., 2015). Clinical improvements were assessed by ratings of disgusting pictures, as well as a novel ecological disgust test (EDT) that required participants to decide their physical distances to personalized disgusting objects. The researchers found that after 2 to 4 sessions of training, anterior insula activity in response to the aversive images was decreased (to varying degrees) in all three participants during the training runs, as well as during the posttraining transfer runs. For behavioral measures, two out of the three participants showed improvements in both the EDT and the picture rating task.

The use of novel behavioral outcome measures, such as the EDT described before, or the behavioral measure we used in our feasibility study, can be helpful when developing clinical applications for a variety of reasons. In the study described before (Buyukturkoglu et al., 2015), the behavioral tasks included multiple measurements in each subject before and after the intervention, allowing within-subject pre-to-post statistical analyses. This can be of interest in very small sample feasibility studies where group-level statistics are not possible. Another situation that arises in feasibility studies conducted in subclinical populations, such as our feasibility study described before, is that existing clinical instruments may not be appropriate for the population targeted as they are designed for and normed in the clinical groups. Finally, in some cases, the intervention may target a very specific aspect of the disorder that is believed to influence overall clinical state, but is not represented directly in standard clinical assessments. In early development of these interventions, where proof of concept remains to be demonstrated, researchers may hope to demonstrate promise in a small sample of subjects. Unfortunately, the small sample size may preclude identification of significant effects on clinical measures, because the training has only a small effect on the clinical symptoms although it may have a large effect on the specific aspect of mental function trained. In this case, sensitivity may be increased by using a measure tailored to the specific aspect of mental function targeted by the intervention. If successful, later and larger studies can then focus on whether significant clinical effects (as assessed with standard instruments) can also be induced.

Results from the studies described in this section suggest rt-fMRI NF can have promising neuromodulation effects on the neural circuitry that gives rise to contamination anxiety, as indicated by the activity and connectivity changes of the target areas demonstrated. Furthermore, these neurofeedback training protocols have also shown promise for reducing contamination anxiety. However, more work is needed to extend the protocols to treat obsessive-compulsive symptom dimensions other than contamination, such as checking or symmetry symptoms, and to test their efficacy in patient populations.

3 Neurodevelopmental disorders

Neurodevelopmental disorders emerge in childhood and adolescence. Although early intervention is often helpful, many families are reluctant to give their children pharmaceutical treatments. Neurofeedback can be an appealing option for families as it uses natural learning processes to reorganize brain function. Furthermore, the ability of the brain to reorganize via feedback learning depends on neural plasticity, which is high throughout childhood. If neurofeedback can steer children toward healthier development at an early stage, it could potentially have large impacts on their lifelong mental health trajectory. However, there is also substantial risk involved in altering normative developmental trajectories, as the full implications of such alterations are not yet known. In short, pediatric intervention has great promise, but also substantial risk. These issues are as discussed more thoroughly by Cohen Kadosh et al. (2016).

In this section we review the rt-fMRI NF research on neurodevelopmental disorders. Some of this work has been conducted in adult populations, and the translation of findings to pediatric populations in these cases remains to be demonstrated. However, an effective treatment, even if limited to the adult population, would still be clinically valuable.

3.1 Attention deficit hyperactivity disorder

Attention deficit hyperactivity disorder (ADHD) is characterized by two clusters of symptoms, related to inattention and hyperactivity-impulsivity. These symptoms have to exceed the behavioral problems normally observed at a comparable level of development, and for a DSM-5 diagnosis some of them have to be present before age 12, although the diagnosis may be made several years later based on retrospective appreciation of the child's development. Behavior is disturbed in more than one setting, normally at home and at school (or work, for adults) and interferes with family life, social contacts, and school or work performance. ADHD is a relatively common disorder with an estimated global prevalence of 5% of children meeting diagnostic criteria as well as substantial subclinical population (Sayal et al., 2018). The core cognitive symptoms of ADHD are believed to be associated with a dysfunctional frontostriatal network. This network involves lateral prefrontal regions, dorsal anterior cingulate cortex (dACC), and striatal regions such as the caudate nucleus and putamen (Cubillo et al., 2012; Emond et al., 2009).

The dACC is commonly implicated in ADHD. For example, during cognitive tasks that require effortful control of attention, patients with ADHD were found to demonstrate hypoactivity in dACC compared to healthy controls (Bush, 2011). Zilverstand et al. (2017) conducted a proof-of-concept randomized trial upregulating this region in a sample of 13 adults with ADHD. The efficacy of rt-fMRI NF was evaluated by comparing the change in ADHD symptoms and dACC activity after 4 weekly sessions between a neurofeedback group ($n=7$) and a no-feedback control group ($n=6$). During the training and transfer runs, participants in both groups were instructed to perform a mental calculation task in order to enhance dACC activation. In both groups, dACC activity during training and transfer runs was increased between the second and the third session. Although there were no significant improvements in ADHD symptoms as assessed with clinical scales, there were some improvements on the cognitive tasks. Both groups demonstrated improvements on a cognitive interference task after the four sessions of training relative to baseline. In addition, the neurofeedback group also improved on response inhibition and visual working memory performance, but there were no significant between-group differences in terms of improvements on these measures.

In another randomized rt-fMRI NF study (Alegria et al., 2017), the right inferior frontal gyrus (rIFG) was selected as the target region for boys with ADHD. Thirteen out of thirty-one subjects were allocated to an active control condition, which trained the participants to regulate the middle parahippocampal gyrus. Participants were instructed to upregulate the activity in the feedback region across multiple training sessions. To ensure high motivation, brain activity was displayed as a rocket and a monetary reward was provided based on performance. Examination of pre-to-post changes in ADHD symptoms revealed significant clinical improvements in both groups, which persisted 11 months later. However, there were no significant differences between the groups in terms of clinical change. On a neural level, each group successfully increased activity in their target region relative to the other group, indicating specific learning effects. During the fMRI stop signal tasks performed both before and after neurofeedback training, both groups showed a reduced standard deviation of reaction time to stimuli after training, while better adjustment of reaction time following errors was only found in the experimental group. The experimental group also had an increase in the error-monitoring related activity in inferior frontal cortex, extending into insula and putamen, which was correlated with improvements in ADHD symptoms (Criaud et al., 2020). In addition to the brain activity changes, the experimental group showed changes in functional connectivity with the rIFG that were associated with symptom improvements (Rubia et al., 2019). These included increased correlations within fronto-cingulo-striatal networks and increased anticorrelations to default mode regions.

The effect sizes of the behavioral improvements of ADHD participants in both these studies (Alegria et al., 2017; Zilverstand et al., 2017) were between medium and large. As these neurofeedback protocols required sustained attention to the feedback signal while also performing a cognitive task, multiple sessions of training may have played a role similar to cognitive therapies received by patients with attentional deficits. This idea is supported by the behavioral improvements in control groups of both studies in this section and highlights the challenges of disentangling the specific effect of neurofeedback from the effects of cognitive training.

3.2 Tourette syndrome

Tourette syndrome (TS) is a neurodevelopmental disorder characterized by motor and vocal tics with symptom severity often peaking in adolescence (Leckman, 2002). Dysfunction of motor cortico-striato-thalamo-cortical loops has been hypothesized to cause tics by driving hyperactivity in cortical motor areas, including the supplementary motor area, or SMA (Leckman, 2002). Evidence from neuroimaging studies has linked the motor and vocal tics of TS patients with aberrant activity in the SMA (Biswal et al., 1998; Bohlhalter et al., 2006; Braun et al., 1993; Hampson et al., 2009; Neuner et al., 2014; Stern et al., 2000) and electrical stimulation of this area has been shown to induce movements and urges to make movements that are strikingly similar to the symptoms of TS (Fried et al., 1991).

Based on these data, we conducted a proof-of-concept rt-fMRI NF study to investigate the feasibility of self-regulation of SMA activity (Hampson et al., 2011). The aim was to explore the promise of the technique for treating TS by first examining the feasibility of controlling this area in a healthy population. Eight healthy adults were recruited and underwent four sessions of neurofeedback training in which they were alternately cued with arrows to increase and decrease activity in their SMA and given feedback via a line graph. Up and downregulation strategies were discussed before beginning NF to provide a starting point for subjects. These strategies included, for example, imagining sports-related movements or cognitively demanding tasks to increase activity, and inducing a relaxed, clear mindset to decrease activity. Control over the SMA was evaluated by comparing SMA activity in the increase and the decrease blocks of the training runs. Although this analysis did not find a significant change in control over SMA across sessions, participants did develop significant control in the later sessions. Moreover, there were decreases in resting-state functional connectivity between the SMA and subcortical regions including the striatum and thalamus after neurofeedback training. These results support the potential of this training protocol to modulate SMA activity and possibly even normalize pathways in motor cortico-striato-thalamo-cortical (CSTC) loops.

A similar training procedure was then applied to a clinical sample of adolescents with TS ($n=21$) using a randomized, sham-controlled, cross-over study design (Sukhodolsky et al., 2020). In this clinical study, the SMA target region was functionally localized by imitation of tic movements in the scanner to allow identification (in a subject-specific manner) of the region of the SMA controlling tic-relevant musculature. After the localizer session, participants received two arms of intervention. In one of the arms, the brain signal from the SMA was provided as feedback (neurofeedback condition). In the other arm, feedback from a previous participant was displayed in order to control for perceived regulation success (i.e., a yoked sham control was used). Transfer/control task scans in which participants were instructed to perform up/down regulation without the aid of feedback were administered before and after the feedback trainings in each arm to assess self-regulation ability in the absence of feedback.

The results of the trial revealed significantly greater symptom improvement during neurofeedback than during sham feedback (Sukhodolsky et al., 2020). Because there was a suggestion of carryover effects across arms, data were then reanalyzed focusing solely on the first arm. This analysis also revealed greater symptom improvement during neurofeedback than during sham. Moreover, participants that received real neurofeedback in the first arm showed a clinically meaningful improvement in the mean Yale Global Tic Symptom Severity Scale (3.8-point difference).

Surprisingly, these clinical differences were found despite the fact that, on a neural level, no significant changes in SMA activity were seen in the transfer/control task scans. However, during publication of the results, the reviewers of the manuscript requested an exploratory analysis of the neurofeedback and sham feedback runs. This exploratory analysis did reveal that the SMA (as well as the striatum and dorsal frontal cortex) was more active during neurofeedback than during sham feedback. The data on control over the target brain area are thus mixed, with an exploratory measure suggesting NF did improve control, while the primary measure (based on changes in control task runs) did not support the view that NF improved control over the target region. The fact that there are multiple potential ways to assess whether the intervention affects control over the target brain area highlights the need for careful and detailed preregistration to reduce false positives resulting from multiple comparisons. In this particular instance, the preregistered measure of control over the target region was based on change in control in the transfer (control task) runs, and did not show any effects: thus it must be concluded that this trial did not provide evidence that the intervention worked by improving control over the SMA. However, the data from this study also illustrate how it can be helpful to look at exploratory measures that were not preregistered, as findings can inform future research decisions. For example, if some measures appear more sensitive than others, they may be better options to choose for registration in future studies.

Overall, the results of this trial suggest SMA neurofeedback training may be clinically helpful for individuals with TS although more data are needed to establish efficacy and to clarify the mechanism of action.

3.3 Autism spectrum disorders

Autism spectrum disorders (ASD) is the overarching DSM-5 category for a group of disorders characterized by deficits in social communication and social interaction, restricted interests, and repetitive behaviors. They have significant comorbidity with intellectual disability but also occur in patients with average or above-average intelligence. Although individuals with ASD are highly heterogeneous in terms of developmental trajectories, a number of neuroimaging studies have linked some of the typical symptoms with aberrant activity (Ecker and Murphy, 2014), anatomy (Courchesne et al., 2011), and functional connectivity (Maximo et al., 2014) in the brain.

Based on the findings from previous studies (Khan et al., 2015) and their own data (Gotts et al., 2012) on an underconnected pathway between superior temporal sulcus (STS) and somatosensory cortex, and a hyperconnection between STS and inferior parietal lobule in ASD, Ramot et al. (2017) conducted a study to investigate whether neurofeedback could be used to successfully modulate these pathways. They trained male ASD patients ages 15–25 toward more a typical connectivity pattern. Compared to neurofeedback training on brain activity, functional connectivity NF suffers from longer delays in feedback due to the number of time points necessary for calculating the connectivity measurements (Spetter et al., 2017; Zhao et al., 2019; Zilverstand et al., 2014). To tackle this problem, Ramot et al. used a novel index to approximate the functional connectivity, with which positive connectivity was defined as the same trend of signal change in the two target regions over two adjacent time points. In their training paradigm, participants were unaware of the purpose of the study. They were simply instructed to unveil the puzzle picture shown on the screen. When STS was changing in the same direction with somatosensory cortex and in the opposite direction as the inferior parietal lobule, an upbeat sound was played to the participant and a piece of the picture revealed. Seventeen ASD participants received four sessions of this covert neurofeedback training. To control for nonspecific effects of training, a typically developing (TD) control group was trained toward a different network configuration of the same three regions. Effects of neurofeedback training were evaluated by examining the changes in functional connectivity between the target regions from day 1 to follow-up. The findings reveal that the target connectivity during training increased over the course of training and follow-up sessions for the ASD group, while the TD group did not show a change in connectivity in the trained network. On an individual level, 15 of the 17 ASD patients showed the targeted pattern of connectivity change. A similar pattern of change was also observed in resting-state data collected in each of the training sessions for the patient group. The changes in connectivity in resting state were correlated with changes in the neurofeedback runs. Finally, change in resting-state functional connectivity of the ASD group (first NF session vs last NF session) was correlated with the improvements in Social Responsiveness Scale score, although the ASD group did not show a significant improvement on this scale overall.

More work is needed examining the potential of real-time fMRI neurofeedback for treating and studying ASD. The study described before incorporates several promising design decisions. First, functional connectivity training is particularly relevant for ASD, as aberrant connectivity has long been implicated in ASD symptoms (Muller et al., 2011). Second, the network of regions comprising the "social brain," of which STS is a key locus, are of particular interest (Gotts et al., 2012). Third, a novel puzzle-based feedback interface may amplify engagement for young participants.

However, as discussed in Chapter 14, care must be taken when using implicit NF in clinical studies. Participants may not want their symptoms reduced. Some individuals with psychiatric disorders embrace their symptoms as a welcome form of neurodiversity. Even those who struggle with or dislike their symptoms may still feel the symptoms are an integral part of their personal identity. Thus any study aiming to reduce symptoms in a psychiatric population should carefully consider this issue.

4 Schizophrenia

Schizophrenia is a severe and highly heterogeneous mental disorder involving many different types of symptoms: two patients with schizophrenia could easily have nonoverlapping symptom profiles. A commonly used distinction is that between psychotic or "positive" (addition or distortion of normal function) and "negative" (diminished normal function) symptoms. Hallucinations, for example, can be defined as perceptual experience in the absence of an adequate external stimulus, and thus represent an addition to normal perception. Conversely, some core negative symptoms—diminished emotional expression and avolition (inability to initiate goal-directed actions)—consist in a reduction of normal functioning. Because of the symptom heterogeneity in this disorder, most rt-fMRI NF studies of schizophrenia have taken a dimensional approach targeting a specific type of symptom. The bulk of the research has focused on auditory verbal hallucinations, a distinctive positive symptom of the disorder. We summarize this work first, followed by work on the negative symptoms (specifically, social and cognitive deficits) associated with schizophrenia.

4.1 Positive symptoms: AVHs

Auditory verbal hallucinations (AVHs) involve hearing voices in the absence of an auditory verbal stimulus. This symptom is experience by more than 60% percent of patients with schizophrenia (Lim et al., 2016). Consistent with the auditory-verbal nature of this phenomenon, neuroimaging studies have linked AVHs with aberrant neural function in the language network including language regions in the superior temporal (STG) and inferior frontal gyrus (IFG) (Allen et al., 2012; Hoffman et al., 2011a,b; Jardri et al., 2011).

Three recent rt-fMRI neurofeedback studies have trained these regions in patients with schizophrenia who suffer from AVHs (Okano et al., 2020; Orlov et al., 2018; Zweerings et al., 2019). First, an open-label study trained 12 patients to downregulate their STG activity and found a significant decrease of STG activity over the course of the training and a significant decrease in hallucination-related symptoms (Orlov et al., 2018). Seed-based functional connectivity maps between STG and the rest of the brain were compared between the first and last neurofeedback run and revealed network-wide changes induced by the neurofeedback training. These promising data suggest a larger randomized controlled study of this protocol would be worthwhile. Second, a study training average activity across IFG and STG used a double-blind cross-over design to compare the effects of upregulation and downregulation training (conducted on separate days with a randomly assigned order) (Zweerings et al., 2019). The study involved training 21 patients and 35 healthy subjects. Offline analyses confirmed significantly lower activity during the downregulation training than during the upregulation training, and confirmed that participants had increasing regulation success across sessions on each scanning day. Connectivity changes across the upregulate and downregulate conditions were also examined and compared across groups. This revealed changes in functional connectivity between the language network and the default mode network (DMN) that were more pronounced in the patient group. Moreover, the connectivity increase between the target regions and the inferior parietal lobule (seen to emerge during downregulation) was associated with symptom improvements. The effects of STG modulation have been recently replicated by another group with a single session of intermittent neurofeedback training (Okano et al., 2020). In this group of participants, only training on STG, but not control training on somatosensory cortex, resulted in reductions of auditory hallucination symptoms. Moreover, there was a significant correlation between symptom reduction and STG activity change, directly linking symptom improvement with neurofeedback training.

DMN is another promising target for neurofeedback training in patients with AVH. In addition to its hyperconnectivity with STG, previous work has linked failure in DMN deactivation as well as weakened anticorrelation between DMN and the central executive network (CEN) to AVH symptoms (Chai et al., 2011; Shim et al., 2010; Whitfield-Gabrieli et al., 2009). Based on these findings, in a companion study to their STG training (Okano et al., 2020), 10 out of 11 of the same cohort of patients were trained to use neurofeedback-guided meditation to modulate their DMN. Specifically, the neurofeedback signal provided was the difference in activity between the CEN and the DMN after normalizing each relative to a baseline period. The training shifted DMN resting-state connectivity patterns in the desired direction (Fig. 3) and resulted in a significant reduction in AVH scores a week after the training (Bauer et al., 2020). These findings suggest neurofeedback-supported meditation may have therapeutic potential for AVH.

Finally, a small study explored the clinical potential of training patients with AVHs to upregulate their ACC activity (Dyck et al., 2016). Three patients were trained with mixed clinical responses.

Although the positive symptoms of schizophrenia include delusions as well as hallucinations (Andreasen et al., 1995), real-time fMRI neurofeedback studies to date have focused exclusively on hallucinations. This is likely due to a greater understanding of the neural substrate of hallucinations than of other psychotic symptoms. However, neuroimaging research is beginning to reveal neural patterns relevant to delusions and passivity experiences that may provide neurofeedback researchers with biomarkers to target (e.g., Limongi et al., 2020; Schnell et al., 2008), so the development of interventions targeting these positive symptoms is a promising future direction.

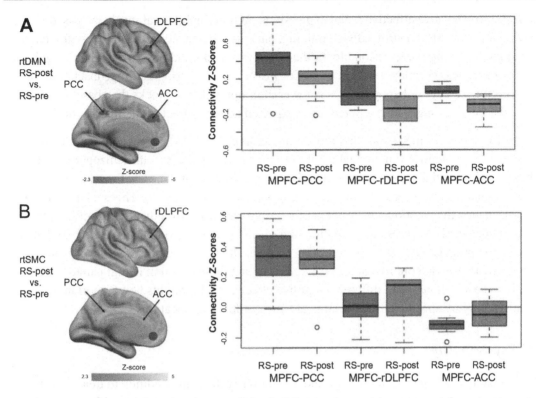

Fig. 3   Resting state functional connectivity (rsFC) was changed (pre vs post) for posterior cingulate cortex (PCC), right dorsolateral prefrontal cortex (rDLPFC), and anterior cingulate cortex (ACC) with medial prefrontal cortex (MPFC, *dark circle*) as the seed region after the neurofeedback session (A) but not after the control session (B) in which the participants received feedback from motor cortex during finger tapping tasks. Results shown in the figure survived correction at $P < .05$ FWE, cluster level. *Figure reproduced with minor adaptation from Bauer, C.C.C., Okano, K., Gosh, S.S., Lee, Y.J., Melero, H., Angeles, C.L., Nestor, P.G., Del Re, E.C., Northoff, G., Niznikiewicz, M.A., Whitfield-Gabrieli, S., 2020. Real-time fMRI neurofeedback reduces auditory hallucinations and modulates resting state connectivity of involved brain regions: part 2: default mode network -preliminary evidence. Psychiatry Res. 284, 112770. https://doi.org/10.1016/j.psychres.2020.112770.*

4.2 Negative symptoms: Social and cognitive deficits

Dysfunction in facial emotion perception has been linked to symptom severity in schizophrenia patients (Kohler et al., 2000). Insula cortex plays a key role in processing of negative facial expressions (Singer et al., 2009), and a previous study of emotion regulation found hypoactivation of insula in patients with schizophrenia comparing with their nonaffected siblings (van der Meer et al., 2014). Based on these data, Ruiz et al. (2013) trained nine schizophrenia patients to upregulate their bilateral anterior insula with rt-fMRI neurofeedback and investigated whether the training enhanced their capacity to recognize negative affective facial expressions. Activity in bilateral insula increased during training. After neurofeedback training, patients recognized disgust faces with higher accuracy following upregulation blocks than baseline blocks and this differential recognition performance was correlated with left anterior insula activity during neurofeedback training. However, accuracy for happy faces was lower after upregulation blocks than baseline blocks after the training, suggesting a potential unexpected adverse effect of the intervention.

Apart from its roles in salience and reward processing, ACC also plays an important role in supporting cognitive function which is compromised in patients with schizophrenia. The therapeutic potential of neurofeedback training upregulation of the ACC for schizophrenia was examined using a social feedback paradigm (Cordes et al., 2015). This social feedback approach uses the emotional expression of a virtual character, from neutral to smiling, to indicate the level of success in regulation of a given brain area (Mathiak et al., 2010). Patients tended to upregulate the ACC by activating a dorsal subdivision while the control group tended to activate a more rostral subregion. Given that these different neural patterns are likely to be associated with different cognitive effects, this highlights how important it is to identify a highly specific target for clinical neurofeedback applications.

5 Psychopathy

Psychopathy is a huge social problem and a notoriously difficult condition to treat (Olver, 2016). Although psychopathy is not included in the Diagnostic and Statistical Manual of Mental Disorders (DSM), it overlaps closely with the DSM definition of antisocial personality disorder, and is of high clinical relevance. To explore whether neurofeedback can effectively alter the neural substrates underlying psychopathy, a study trained upregulation of the insula during aversive memory recall in four individuals with psychopathy (Sitaram et al., 2014). The insula was targeted based on findings of insular hypoactivity in psychopaths during the processing of negative emotions (Birbaumer et al., 2005; Veit et al., 2002). Importantly, the participants were paid based on their regulation success, to ensure motivation on the regulation task. One of the four participants demonstrated an improved ability to upregulate the insula during neurofeedback and changes in emotion processing and brain connectivity in the successful participant were identified (Sitaram et al., 2014). This study indicates that upregulation of insula may be difficult to train in psychopaths, but appears to be possible for some individuals.

6 Conclusion

This chapter has reviewed current literature on applications of fMRI neurofeedback for a number of psychiatric disorders and discussed some of the challenges and design decisions that arise in the context of psychiatric intervention development. Given the rapid advancement of this field, the work reviewed here must be seen as a snapshot in time. Researchers embarking on new studies are advised to search the literature for relevant work. In order to avoid duplication and to maximize the impact of any new study, it is also worth investing time to explore ongoing research. A simple search of https://clinicaltrials.gov/ (and other large clinical trial registration sites) can be very helpful in this respect. For example, before beginning a new study for alcohol addiction, a current search of https://clinicaltrials.gov/ for neurofeedback studies would reveal two potentially relevant studies: one examining whether fMRI neurofeedback can modulate socioemotional cue processing (NCT03535129) and another examining if functional near-infrared spectroscopy neurofeedback can reduce relapse (NCT03595293). Summary information about the major aims of the studies are provided on the trial registration site, as well as contact information for the research groups in case more information is needed.

Although the research reviewed here on psychiatric applications of rt-fMRI NF has supported the promise of the technique, the field is still at an early stage of development and faces daunting challenges. Many of the studies conducted to date have not included control groups. Even when control groups are included, they cannot control for all nonspecific effects of the intervention. Furthermore, there are a wide array of variables that can potentially modulate the efficacy of neurofeedback interventions, making optimization difficult. In short, the field faces challenges associated with the development and evaluation of complex interventions.

On the positive side, an exciting aspect of clinical neurofeedback research is the closed-loop potential for target development: each neurofeedback study yields data on the changes in brain function associated with symptom improvement, providing useful information for evolving refinement of targets to maximize therapeutic relevance. Furthermore, in theory, brain patterns associated with undesirable side effects can be identified in one study and then trained down in future studies. Thus the potential for precise therapeutic development is extremely promising if patients prove able to learn the targeted neural activity patterns. Hopefully, this closed-loop approach to optimizing neurofeedback targets will be leveraged in the coming years to advance and refine the development of more clinically useful interventions.

To address the challenges intrinsic to development of these complex interventions, as well as to harness the potential benefits of closed-loop target refinement, a flexible and iterative approach is required for neurofeedback intervention development. As discussed in Chapter 7, intervention development for complex interventions is not a linear path through a fixed set of stages. Instead the potential for each development stage to inform all other stages should be embraced and optimized. For example, an evaluation trial testing efficacy can identify a potentially more effective target and thus inform a feasibility study using that new target. Or an implementation study may identify the brain pattern associated with a long-term adverse side effect and thus motivate development of new model of brain-behavior relationships. In this way, the rich information in neurofeedback studies can be used most effectively to further both research and clinical treatment.

Acknowledgments

This work was supported by the National Institute of Mental Health (R01 MH100068 and R61 MH115110), and the American Endowment Foundation (project titled "A neurofeedback booster for emotion regulation therapy").

References

Alegria, A.A., Wulff, M., Brinson, H., Barker, G.J., Norman, L.J., Brandeis, D., Stahl, D., David, A.S., Taylor, E., Giampietro, V., Rubia, K., 2017. Real-time fMRI neurofeedback in adolescents with attention deficit hyperactivity disorder. Hum. Brain Mapp. 38, 3190–3209.

Allen, P., Modinos, G., Hubl, D., Shields, G., Cachia, A., Jardri, R., Thomas, P., Woodward, T., Shotbolt, P., Plaze, M., Hoffman, R., 2012. Neuroimaging auditory hallucinations in schizophrenia: from neuroanatomy to neurochemistry and beyond. Schizophr. Bull. 38, 695–703.

Amano, K., Shibata, K., Kawato, M., Sasaki, Y., Watanabe, T., 2016. Learning to associate orientation with color in early visual areas by associative decoded fMRI neurofeedback. Curr. Biol. 26, 1861–1866.

Andreasen, N.C., Arndt, S., Alliger, R., Miller, D., Flaum, M., 1995. Symptoms of schizophrenia. Methods, meanings, and mechanisms. Arch. Gen. Psychiatry 52, 341–351.

Batterink, L., Yokum, S., Stice, E., 2010. Body mass correlates inversely with inhibitory control in response to food among adolescent girls: an fMRI study. NeuroImage 52, 1696–1703.

Bauer, C.C.C., Okano, K., Gosh, S.S., Lee, Y.J., Melero, H., Angeles, C.L., Nestor, P.G., Del Re, E.C., Northoff, G., Niznikiewicz, M.A., Whitfield-Gabrieli, S., 2020. Real-time fMRI neurofeedback reduces auditory hallucinations and modulates resting state connectivity of involved brain regions: part 2: default mode network -preliminary evidence. Psychiatry Res. 284, 112770.

Beucke, J.C., Sepulcre, J., Talukdar, T., Linnman, C., Zschenderlein, K., Endrass, T., Kaufmann, C., Kathmann, N., 2013. Abnormally high degree connectivity of the orbitofrontal cortex in obsessive-compulsive disorder. JAMA Psychiat. 70, 619–629.

Birbaumer, N., Veit, R., Lotze, M., Erb, M., Hermann, C., Grodd, W., Flor, H., 2005. Deficient fear conditioning in psychopathy: a functional magnetic resonance imaging study. Arch. Gen. Psychiatry 62, 799–805.

Biswal, B., Ulmer, J.L., Krippendorf, R.L., Harsch, H.H., Daniels, D.L., Hyde, J.S., Haughton, V.M., 1998. Abnormal cerebral activation associated with a motor task in Tourette syndrome. Am. J. Neuroradiol. 19, 1509–1512.

Bloch, M.H., Landeros-Weisenberger, A., Rosario, M.C., Pittenger, C., Leckman, J.F., 2008. Meta-analysis of the symptom structure of obsessive-compulsive disorder. Am. J. Psychiatr. 165, 1532–1542.

Bohlhalter, S., Goldfine, A., Matteson, S., Garraux, G., Hanakawa, T., Kansaku, K., Wurzman, R., Hallet, M., 2006. Neural correlates of tic generation in Tourette syndrome: an event-related functional MRI study. Brain 129, 2029–2037.

Braun, A.R., Stoetter, B., Randolph, C., Hsiao, J.K., Vladar, K., Gernert, J., Carson, R.E., Herscovitch, P., Chase, T.N., 1993. The functional neuroanatomy of Tourette's syndrome: an FDG-PET study. I. Regional changes in cerebral glucose metabolism differentiating patients and controls. Neuropsychopharmacology 9, 277–291.

Buckner, R.L., Sepulcre, J., Talukdar, T., Krienen, F.M., Liu, H., Hedden, T., Andrews-Hanna, J.R., Sperling, R.A., Johnson, K.A., 2009. Cortical hubs revealed by intrinsic functional connectivity: mapping, assessment of stability, and relation to Alzheimer's disease. J. Neurosci. 29, 1860–1873.

Bush, G., 2011. Cingulate, frontal, and parietal cortical dysfunction in attention-deficit/hyperactivity disorder. Biol. Psychiatry 69, 1160–1167.

Buyukturkoglu, K., Roettgers, H., Sommer, J., Rana, M., Dietzsch, L., Arikan, E.B., Veit, R., Malekshahi, R., Kircher, T., Birbaumer, N., Sitaram, R., Ruiz, S., 2015. Self-regulation of anterior insula with real-time fMRI and its behavioral effects in obsessive-compulsive disorder: a feasibility study. PLoS One 10, e0135872.

Canterberry, M., Hanlon, C.A., Hartwell, K.J., Li, X., Owens, M., LeMatty, T., Prisciandaro, J.J., Borckardt, J., Saladin, M.E., Brady, K.T., George, M.S., 2013. Sustained reduction of nicotine craving with real-time neurofeedback: exploring the role of severity of dependence. Nicotine Tob. Res. 15, 2120–2124.

Chai, X.J., Whitfield-Gabrieli, S., Shinn, A.K., Gabrieli, J.D., Nieto Castanon, A., McCarthy, J.M., Cohen, B.M., Ongur, D., 2011. Abnormal medial prefrontal cortex resting-state connectivity in bipolar disorder and schizophrenia. Neuropsychopharmacology 36, 2009–2017.

Chamberlain, S.R., Menzies, L., Hampshire, A., Suckling, J., Fineberg, N.A., del Campo, N., Aitken, M., Craig, K., Owen, A.M., Bullmore, E.T., Robbins, T.W., Sahakian, B.J., 2008. Orbitofrontal dysfunction in patients with obsessive-compulsive disorder and their unaffected relatives. Science 321, 421–422.

Cohen Kadosh, K., Lisk, S., Lau, J.Y.F., 2016. The ethics of (neuro) feeding back to the developing brain. AJOB Neurosci. 7, 132–133.

Cordes, J.S., Mathiak, K.A., Dyck, M., Alawi, E.M., Gaber, T.J., Zepf, F.D., Klasen, M., Zvyagintsev, M., Gur, R.C., Mathiak, K., 2015. Cognitive and neural strategies during control of the anterior cingulate cortex by fMRI neurofeedback in patients with schizophrenia. Front. Behav. Neurosci. 9, 169.

Courchesne, E., Campbell, K., Solso, S., 2011. Brain growth across the life span in autism: age-specific changes in anatomical pathology. Brain Res. 1380, 138–145.

Criaud, M., Wulff, M., Alegria, A.A., Barker, G.J., Giampietro, V., Rubia, K., 2020. Increased left inferior fronto-striatal activation during error monitoring after fMRI neurofeedback of right inferior frontal cortex in adolescents with attention deficit hyperactivity disorder. Neuroimage Clin. 27, 102311.

Cubillo, A., Halari, R., Smith, A., Taylor, E., Rubia, K., 2012. A review of fronto-striatal and fronto-cortical brain abnormalities in children and adults with attention deficit hyperactivity disorder (ADHD) and new evidence for dysfunction in adults with ADHD during motivation and attention. Cortex 48, 194–215.

Dyck, M.S., Mathiak, K.A., Bergert, S., Sarkheil, P., Koush, Y., Alawi, E.M., Zvyagintsev, M., Gaebler, A.J., Shergill, S.S., Mathiak, K., 2016. Targeting treatment-resistant auditory verbal hallucinations in schizophrenia with fMRI-based neurofeedback–exploring different cases of schizophrenia. Front. Psych. 7, 37.

Ecker, C., Murphy, D., 2014. Neuroimaging in autism—from basic science to translational research. Nat. Rev. Neurol. 10, 82–91.

Emond, V., Joyal, C., Poissant, H., 2009. Structural and functional neuroanatomy of attention-deficit hyperactivity disorder (ADHD). Encephale 35, 107–114.

Frank, S., Lee, S., Preissl, H., Schultes, B., Birbaumer, N., Veit, R., 2012. The obese brain athlete: self-regulation of the anterior insula in adiposity. PLoS One 7, e42570.

Fried, I., Katz, A., McCarthy, G., Sass, K.J., Williamson, P., Spencer, S.S., Spencer, D.D., 1991. Functional organization of human supplementary motor cortex studied by electrical stimulation. J. Neurosci. 11, 3656–3666.

Gautier, J.F., Chen, K., Salbe, A.D., Bandy, D., Pratley, R.E., Heiman, M., Ravussin, E., Reiman, E.M., Tataranni, P.A., 2000. Differential brain responses to satiation in obese and lean men. Diabetes 49, 838–846.

Gautier, J.F., Del Parigi, A., Chen, K., Salbe, A.D., Bandy, D., Pratley, R.E., Ravussin, E., Reiman, E.M., Tataranni, P.A., 2001. Effect of satiation on brain activity in obese and lean women. Obes. Res. 9, 676–684.

Gianini, L.M., White, M.A., Masheb, R.M., 2013. Eating pathology, emotion regulation, and emotional overeating in obese adults with binge eating disorder. Eat. Behav. 14, 309–313.

Goldway, N., Ablin, J., Lubin, O., Zamir, Y., Keynan, J.N., Or-Borichev, A., Cavazza, M., Charles, F., Intrator, N., Brill, S., Ben-Simon, E., Sharon, H., Hendler, T., 2019. Volitional limbic neuromodulation exerts a beneficial clinical effect on Fibromyalgia. NeuroImage 186, 758–770.

Gotts, S.J., Simmons, W.K., Milbury, L.A., Wallace, G.L., Cox, R.W., Martin, A., 2012. Fractionation of social brain circuits in autism spectrum disorders. Brain 135, 2711–2725.

Hampson, M., Tokoglu, F., King, R.A., Constable, R.T., Leckman, J.F., 2009. Brain areas coactivating with motor cortex during chronic motor tics and intentional movements. Biol. Psychiatry 65, 594–599.

Hampson, M., Scheinost, D., Qiu, M., Bhawnani, J., Lacadie, C.M., Leckman, J.F., Constable, R.T., Papademetris, X., 2011. Biofeedback of real-time functional magnetic resonance imaging data from the supplementary motor area reduces functional connectivity to subcortical regions. Brain Connect. 1, 91–98.

Hampson, M., Stoica, T., Saksa, J., Scheinost, D., Qiu, M., Bhawnani, J., Pittenger, C., Papademetris, X., Constable, T., 2012. Real-time fMRI biofeedback targeting the orbitofrontal cortex for contamination anxiety. J. Vis. Exp. 59, e3535.

Hanlon, C.A., Hartwell, K.J., Canterberry, M., Li, X., Owens, M., Lematty, T., Prisciandaro, J.J., Borckardt, J., Brady, K.T., George, M.S., 2013. Reduction of cue-induced craving through realtime neurofeedback in nicotine users: the role of region of interest selection and multiple visits. Psychiatry Res. 213, 79–81.

Hare, T.A., Camerer, C.F., Rangel, A., 2009. Self-control in decision-making involves modulation of the vmPFC valuation system. Science 324, 646–648.

Hare, T.A., Schultz, W., Camerer, C.F., O'Doherty, J.P., Rangel, A., 2011. Transformation of stimulus value signals into motor commands during simple choice. Proc. Natl. Acad. Sci. USA 108, 18120–18125.

Hartwell, K.J., Hanlon, C.A., Li, X., Borckardt, J.J., Canterberry, M., Prisciandaro, J.J., Moran-Santa Maria, M.M., LeMatty, T., George, M.S., Brady, K.T., 2016. Individualized real-time fMRI neurofeedback to attenuate craving in nicotine-dependent smokers. J. Psychiatry Neurosci. 41, 48–55.

Heinz, A., Beck, A., Halil, M.G., Pilhatsch, M., Smolka, M.N., Liu, S., 2019. Addiction as learned behavior patterns. J. Clin. Med. 8, 1086.

Hoffman, R.E., Fernandez, T., Pittman, B., Hampson, M., 2011a. Elevated functional connectivity along a corticostriatal loop and the mechanism of auditory/verbal hallucinations in patients with schizophrenia. Biol. Psychiatry 69, 407–414.

Hoffman, R.E., Pittman, B., Constable, R.T., Bhagwagar, Z., Hampson, M., 2011b. Time course of regional brain activity accompanying auditory verbal hallucinations in schizophrenia. Br. J. Psychiatry 198, 277–283.

Ihssen, N., Sokunbi, M.O., Lawrence, A.D., Lawrence, N.S., Linden, D.E.J., 2017. Neurofeedback of visual food cue reactivity: a potential avenue to alter incentive sensitization and craving. Brain Imaging Behav. 11, 915–924.

Janes, A.C., Pizzagalli, D.A., Richardt, S., De, B.F.B., Chuzi, S., Pachas, G., Culhane, M.A., Holmes, A.J., Fava, M., Evins, A.E., Kaufman, M.J., 2010. Brain reactivity to smoking cues prior to smoking cessation predicts ability to maintain tobacco abstinence. Biol. Psychiatry 67, 722–729.

Jardri, R., Pouchet, A., Pins, D., Thomas, P., 2011. Cortical activations during auditory verbal hallucinations in schizophrenia: a coordinate-based meta-analysis. Am. J. Psychiatry 168, 73–81.

Karch, S., Keeser, D., Hummer, S., Paolini, M., Kirsch, V., Karali, T., Kupka, M., Rauchmann, B.S., Chrobok, A., Blautzik, J., Koller, G., Ertl-Wagner, B., Pogarell, O., 2015. Modulation of craving related brain responses using real-time fMRI in patients with alcohol use disorder. PLoS One 10, e0133034.

Khan, S., Michmizos, K., Tommerdahl, M., Ganesan, S., Kitzbichler, M.G., Zetino, M., Garel, K.L., Herbert, M.R., Hamalainen, M.S., Kenet, T., 2015. Somatosensory cortex functional connectivity abnormalities in autism show opposite trends, depending on direction and spatial scale. Brain 138, 1394–1409.

Kirsch, M., Gruber, I., Ruf, M., Kiefer, F., Kirsch, P., 2016. Real-time functional magnetic resonance imaging neurofeedback can reduce striatal cue-reactivity to alcohol stimuli. Addict. Biol. 21, 982–992.

Kirschner, M., Sladky, R., Haugg, A., Stampfli, P., Jehli, E., Hodel, M., Engeli, E., Hosli, S., Baumgartner, M.R., Sulzer, J., Huys, Q.J.M., Seifritz, E., Quednow, B.B., Scharnowski, F., Herdener, M., 2018. Self-regulation of the dopaminergic reward circuit in cocaine users with mental imagery and neurofeedback. EBioMedicine 37, 489–498.

Kohl, S.H., Veit, R., Spetter, M.S., Gunther, A., Rina, A., Luhrs, M., Birbaumer, N., Preissl, H., Hallschmid, M., 2019. Real-time fMRI neurofeedback training to improve eating behavior by self-regulation of the dorsolateral prefrontal cortex: a randomized controlled trial in overweight and obese subjects. NeuroImage 191, 596–609.

Kohler, C.G., Bilker, W., Hagendoorn, M., Gur, R.E., Gur, R.C., 2000. Emotion recognition deficit in schizophrenia: association with symptomatology and cognition. Biol. Psychiatry 48, 127–136.

Koob, G.F., Volkow, N.D., 2010. Neurocircuitry of addiction. Neuropsychopharmacology 35, 217–238.

Leckman, J.F., 2002. Tourette's syndrome. Lancet 360, 1577–1586.

Li, X., Hartwell, K.J., Borckardt, J., Prisciandaro, J.J., Saladin, M.E., Morgan, P.S., Johnson, K.A., Lematty, T., Brady, K.T., George, M.S., 2013. Volitional reduction of anterior cingulate cortex activity produces decreased cue craving in smoking cessation: a preliminary real-time fMRI study. Addict. Biol. 18, 739–748.

Lim, A., Hoek, H.W., Deen, M.L., Blom, J.D., Investigators, G., 2016. Prevalence and classification of hallucinations in multiple sensory modalities in schizophrenia spectrum disorders. Schizophr. Res. 176, 493–499.

Limongi, R., Mackinley, M., Dempster, K., Khan, A.R., Gati, J.S., Palaniyappan, L., 2020. Understanding the effect of left prefrontal stimulation on positive symptoms of schizophrenia: a dynamic causal modeling study of ultra-high field (7-Tesla) resting state fMRI. BioRxiv.

Mataix-Cols, D., Cullen, S., Lange, K., Zelaya, F., Andrew, C., Amaro, E., Brammer, M.J., Williams, S.C., Speckens, A., Phillips, M.L., 2003. Neural correlates of anxiety associated with obsessive-compulsive symptom dimensions in normal volunteers. Biol. Psychiatry 53, 482–493.

Mataix-Cols, D., Wooderson, S., Lawrence, N., Brammer, M.J., Speckens, A., Phillips, M.L., 2004. Distinct neural correlates of washing, checking, and hoarding symptom dimensions in obsessive-compulsive disorder. Arch. Gen. Psychiatry 61, 564–576.

Mathiak, K.A., Koush, Y., Dyck, M., Gaber, T.J., Alawi, E., Zepf, F.D., Zvyagintsev, M., Mathiak, K., 2010. Social reinforcement can regulate localized brain activity. Eur. Arch. Psychiatry Clin. Neurosci. 260 (Suppl. 2), S132–S136.

Maximo, J.O., Cadena, E.J., Kana, R.K., 2014. The implications of brain connectivity in the neuropsychology of autism. Neuropsychol. Rev. 24, 16–31.

McClernon, F.J., Hiott, F.B., Huettel, S.A., Rose, J.E., 2005. Abstinence-induced changes in self-report craving correlate with event-related FMRI responses to smoking cues. Neuropsychopharmacology 30, 1940–1947.

Mehler, D.M.A., Sokunbi, M.O., Habes, I., Barawi, K., Subramanian, L., Range, M., Evans, J., Hood, K., Luhrs, M., Keedwell, P., Goebel, R., Linden, D.E.J., 2018. Targeting the affective brain-a randomized controlled trial of real-time fMRI neurofeedback in patients with depression. Neuropsychopharmacology 43, 2578–2585.

Menzies, L., Chamberlain, S.R., Laird, A.R., Thelan, S.M., Sahakian, B.J., Bullmore, E.T., 2008. Integrating evidence from neuroimaging and neuropsychological studies of obsessive-compulsive disorder: the orbitofrontal-striatal model revisited. Neurosci. Biobehav. Rev. 32, 525–549.

Muller, R.A., Shih, P., Keehn, B., Deyoe, J.R., Leyden, K.M., Shukla, D.K., 2011. Underconnected, but how? A survey of functional connectivity MRI studies in autism spectrum disorders. Cereb. Cortex 21, 2233–2243.

Neuner, I., Werner, C.J., Arrubla, J., Stocker, T., Ehlen, C., Wegener, H.P., Schneider, F., Shah, N.J., 2014. Imaging the where and when of tic generation and resting state networks in adult Tourette patients. Front. Hum. Neurosci. 8, 362.

Okano, K., Bauer, C.C., Ghosh, S.S., Lee, Y.J., Melero, H., de los Angeles, C., Nestor, P.G., del Re, E.C., Northoff, G., Whitfield-Gabrieli, S., 2020. Real-time fMRI feedback impacts brain activation, results in auditory hallucinations reduction: part 1: superior temporal gyrus-preliminary evidence. Psychiatry Res. 286, 112862.

Olver, M.E., 2016. Treatment of psychopathic offenders: evidence, issues, and controversies. J. Community Saf. Well-Being 1, 75–82.

Orlov, N.D., Giampietro, V., O'Daly, O., Lam, S.L., Barker, G.J., Rubia, K., McGuire, P., Shergill, S.S., Allen, P., 2018. Real-time fMRI neurofeedback to down-regulate superior temporal gyrus activity in patients with schizophrenia and auditory hallucinations: a proof-of-concept study. Transl. Psychiatry 8, 46.

Ramot, M., Grossman, S., Friedman, D., Malach, R., 2016. Covert neurofeedback without awareness shapes cortical network spontaneous connectivity. Proc. Natl. Acad. Sci. USA 113, E2413–E2420.

Ramot, M., Kimmich, S., Gonzalez-Castillo, J., Roopchansingh, V., Popal, H., White, E., Gotts, S.J., Martin, A., 2017. Direct modulation of aberrant brain network connectivity through real-time neurofeedback. eLife 6, 1–23.

Rance, M., Walsh, C., Sukhodolsky, D.G., Pittman, B., Qiu, M., Kichuk, S.A., Wasylink, S., Koller, W.N., Bloch, M., Gruner, P., Scheinost, D., Pittenger, C., Hampson, M., 2018. Time course of clinical change following neurofeedback. NeuroImage 181, 807–813.

Rotge, J.Y., Guehl, D., Dilharreguy, B., Tignol, J., Bioulac, B., Allard, M., Burbaud, P., Aouizerate, B., 2009. Meta-analysis of brain volume changes in obsessive-compulsive disorder. Biol. Psychiatry 65, 75–83.

Rubia, K., Criaud, M., Wulff, M., Alegria, A., Brinson, H., Barker, G., Stahl, D., Giampietro, V., 2019. Functional connectivity changes associated with fMRI neurofeedback of right inferior frontal cortex in adolescents with ADHD. NeuroImage 188, 43–58.

Rubinov, M., Sporns, O., 2010. Complex network measures of brain connectivity: uses and interpretations. NeuroImage 52, 1059–1069.

Ruiz, S., Lee, S., Soekadar, S.R., Caria, A., Veit, R., Kircher, T., Birbaumer, N., Sitaram, R., 2013. Acquired self-control of insula cortex modulates emotion recognition and brain network connectivity in schizophrenia. Hum. Brain Mapp. 34, 200–212.

Saxena, S., Brody, A.L., Schwartz, J.M., Baxter, L.R., 1998. Neuroimaging and frontal-subcortical circuitry in obsessive-compulsive disorder. Br. J. Psychiatry 173, 26–37.

Sayal, K., Prasad, V., Daley, D., Ford, T., Coghill, D., 2018. ADHD in children and young people: prevalence, care pathways, and service provision. Lancet Psychiatry 5, 175–186.

Scheinost, D., Stoica, T., Saksa, J., Papademetris, X., Constable, R.T., Pittenger, C., Hampson, M., 2013. Orbitofrontal cortex neurofeedback produces lasting changes in contamination anxiety and resting-state connectivity. Transl. Psychiatry 3, e250.

Scheinost, D., Stoica, T., Wasylink, S., Gruner, P., Saksa, J., Pittenger, C., Hampson, M., 2014. Resting state functional connectivity predicts neurofeedback response. Front. Behav. Neurosci. 8, 338.

Schnell, K., Heekeren, K., Daumann, J., Schnell, T., Schnitker, R., Moller-Hartmann, W., Gouzoulis-Mayfrank, E., 2008. Correlation of passivity symptoms and dysfunctional visuomotor action monitoring in psychosis. Brain 131, 2783–2797.

Schnyer, D.M., Beevers, C.G., deBettencourt, M.T., Sherman, S.M., Cohen, J.D., Norman, K.A., Turk-Browne, N.B., 2015. Neurocognitive therapeutics: from concept to application in the treatment of negative attention bias. Biol. Mood Anxiety Disord. 5, 1.

Sepulveda, P., Sitaram, R., Rana, M., Montalba, C., Tejos, C., Ruiz, S., 2016. How feedback, motor imagery, and reward influence brain self-regulation using real-time fMRI. Hum. Brain Mapp. 37, 3153–3171.

Shibata, K., Lisi, G., Cortese, A., Watanabe, T., Sasaki, Y., Kawato, M., 2018. Toward a comprehensive understanding of the neural mechanisms of decoded neurofeedback. NeuroImage 188, 539–556.

Shim, G., Oh, J.S., Jung, W.H., Jang, J.H., Choi, C.H., Kim, E., Park, H.Y., Choi, J.S., Jung, M.H., Kwon, J.S., 2010. Altered resting-state connectivity in subjects at ultra-high risk for psychosis: an fMRI study. Behav. Brain Funct. 6, 58.

Singer, T., Critchley, H.D., Preuschoff, K., 2009. A common role of insula in feelings, empathy and uncertainty. Trends Cogn. Sci. 13, 334–340.

Sitaram, R., Caria, A., Veit, R., Gaber, T., Ruiz, S., Birbaumer, N., 2014. Volitional control of the anterior insula in criminal psychopaths using real-time fMRI neurofeedback: a pilot study. Front. Behav. Neurosci. 8, 344.

Sokunbi, M.O., 2018. Using real-time fMRI brain-computer interfacing to treat eating disorders. J. Neurol. Sci. 388, 109–114.

Spetter, M.S., Malekshahi, R., Birbaumer, N., Luhrs, M., van der Veer, A.H., Scheffler, K., Spuckti, S., Preissl, H., Veit, R., Hallschmid, M., 2017. Volitional regulation of brain responses to food stimuli in overweight and obese subjects: a real-time fMRI feedback study. Appetite 112, 188–195.

Stern, E., Silbersweig, D.A., Chee, K.-Y., Holmes, A., Robertson, M.M., Trimble, M., Frith, C.D., Frackowiak, R.S.J., Dolan, R.J., 2000. A functional neuroanatomy of tics in Tourette syndrome. Arch. Gen. Psychiatry 57, 741–748.

Swedo, S.E., Schapiro, M.B., Grady, C.L., Cheslow, D.L., Leonard, H.L., Kumar, A., Friedland, R., Rapoport, S.I., Rapoport, J.L., 1989. Cerebral glucose metabolism in childhood-onset obsessive-compulsive disorder. Arch. Gen. Psychiatry 46, 518–523.

Sukhodolsky, D.G., Walsh, C., Koller, W.N., Eilbott, J., Rance, M., Fulbright, R.K., Zhao, Z., Bloch, M.H., King, R., Leckman, J.F., Scheinost, D., Pittman, B., Hampson, M., 2020. Randomized, sham-controlled trial of real-time functional magnetic resonance imaging neurofeedback for tics in adolescents with Tourette syndrome. Biol. Psychiatry 87 (12), 1063–1070.

Swedo, S.E., Pietrini, P., Leonard, H.L., Schapiro, M.B., Rettew, D.C., Goldberger, E.L., Rapoport, S.I., Rapoport, J.L., Grady, C.L., 1992. Cerebral glucose metabolism in childhood-onset obsessive-compulsive disorder. Revisualization during pharmacotherapy. Arch. Gen. Psychiatry 49, 690–694.

Taschereau-Dumouchel, V., Cortese, A., Chiba, T., Knotts, J.D., Kawato, M., Lau, H., 2018. Towards an unconscious neural reinforcement intervention for common fears. Proc. Natl. Acad. Sci. USA 115, 3470–3475.

Turton, R., Chami, R., Treasure, J., 2017. Emotional eating, binge eating and animal models of binge-type eating disorders. Curr. Obes. Rep. 6, 217–228.

van der Meer, L., Swart, M., van der Velde, J., Pijnenborg, G., Wiersma, D., Bruggeman, R., Aleman, A., 2014. Neural correlates of emotion regulation in patients with schizophrenia and non-affected siblings. PLoS One 9, e99667.

Van Strien, T., 2018. Causes of emotional eating and matched treatment of obesity. Curr. Diab. Rep. 18, 35.

Veit, R., Flor, H., Erb, M., Hermann, C., Lotze, M., Grodd, W., Birbaumer, N., 2002. Brain circuits involved in emotional learning in antisocial behavior and social phobia in humans. Neurosci. Lett. 328, 233–236.

Volkow, N.D., Wang, G.J., Fowler, J.S., Tomasi, D., Baler, R., 2012. Food and drug reward: overlapping circuits in human obesity and addiction. Curr. Top. Behav. Neurosci. 11, 1–24.

Whitfield-Gabrieli, S., Thermenos, H.W., Milanovic, S., Tsuang, M.T., Faraone, S.V., McCarley, R.W., Shenton, M.E., Green, A.I., Nieto-Castanon, A., LaViolette, P., Wojcik, J., Gabrieli, J.D., Seidman, L.J., 2009. Hyperactivity and hyperconnectivity of the default network in schizophrenia and in first-degree relatives of persons with schizophrenia. Proc. Natl. Acad. Sci. USA 106, 1279–1284.

Wright, P., He, G., Shapira, N.A., Goodman, W.K., Liu, Y., 2004. Disgust and the insula: fMRI responses to pictures of mutilation and contamination. Neuroreport 15, 2347–2351.

Zhao, Z., Yao, S., Li, K., Sindermann, C., Zhou, F., Zhao, W., Li, J., Luhrs, M., Goebel, R., Kendrick, K.M., Becker, B., 2019. Real-time functional connectivity-informed neurofeedback of amygdala-frontal pathways reduces anxiety. Psychother. Psychosom. 88, 5–15.

Zilverstand, A., Sorger, B., Zimmermann, J., Kaas, A., Goebel, R., 2014. Windowed correlation: a suitable tool for providing dynamic fMRI-based functional connectivity neurofeedback on task difficulty. PLoS One 9, e85929.

Zilverstand, A., Sorger, B., Slaats-Willemse, D., Kan, C.C., Goebel, R., Buitelaar, J.K., 2017. fMRI neurofeedback training for increasing anterior cingulate cortex activation in adult attention deficit hyperactivity disorder. An exploratory randomized, single-blinded study. PLoS One 12, e0170795.

Zweerings, J., Hummel, B., Keller, M., Zvyagintsev, M., Schneider, F., Klasen, M., Mathiak, K., 2019. Neurofeedback of core language network nodes modulates connectivity with the default-mode network: a double-blind fMRI neurofeedback study on auditory verbal hallucinations. NeuroImage 189, 533–542.

CHAPTER 10

Implicit decoded neurofeedback training as a clinical tool

Ai Koizumi[a,b,c] **and Mitsuo Kawato**[a,d]

[a]Department of Decoded Neurofeedback, Computational Neuroscience Laboratories, Advanced Telecommunications Research Institute International (ATR), Kyoto, Japan, [b]Sony Computer Science Laboratories, Inc., Tokyo, Japan, [c]Graduate School of Media and Governance, Keio University, Minato City, Japan, [d]RIKEN Center for Advanced Intelligence Project (AIP), Tokyo, Japan

1 Implicit nature of decoded neurofeedback (DecNef)

Decoded neurofeedback (DecNef) is a relatively novel type of neurofeedback which allows real-time neurofeedback based on spatial activation patterns in targeted brain areas (Watanabe et al., 2018). Combined with fMRI multivoxel decoding techniques to dissociate different neural representations (e.g., Yamashita et al., 2008), DecNef provides feedback regarding the likelihood that a certain representation is activated in a given brain area. For example, it provides feedback to a participant based on whether his or her visual cortex is likely to be representing a red rather than a green target stimulus (Amano et al., 2016; Koizumi et al., 2016) or whether their prefrontal areas are likely to be representing a high rather than a low state of perceptual confidence (Cortese et al., 2017).

One of the features which makes DecNef distinguishable from many other neurofeedback techniques is its implicitness (Watanabe et al., 2018). That is, participants remain unaware of what neural representation is being induced throughout DecNef training sessions (Fig. 1). They are generally instructed to somehow manipulate their brain activation in order to receive better feedback (e.g., a circle size on a screen) through trial-and-error. Yet, they are never provided with any explicit instruction, e.g., to imagine a red stimulus. Despite the fact that participants generally learn to successfully induce the targeted brain activation patterns, posttraining questionnaires and/or forced-choice questions have consistently revealed that participants do remain unaware of the identity of targeted neural activation patterns (Amano et al., 2016; Cortese et al., 2017; Koizumi et al., 2016; Shibata et al., 2011; Taschereau-Dumouchel et al., 2018; Shibata et al., 2019 for review).

fMRI Neurofeedback. https://doi.org/10.1016/B978-0-12-822421-2.00013-2

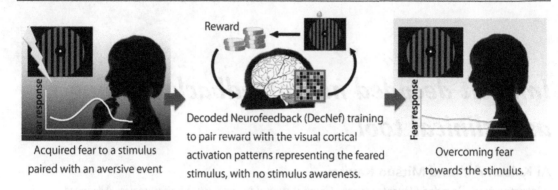

Reward

Decoded Neurofeedback (DecNef) training
to pair reward with the visual cortical
activation patterns representing the feared
stimulus, with no stimulus awareness.

Acquired fear to a stimulus
paired with an aversive event

Overcoming fear
towards the stimulus.

Fig. 1
Schematics of the implicit DecNef training to help overcome fear and anxiety.

The fact that participants remain unaware of the induced neural representations may sound surprising to some. However, it is in line with a large body of literature on consciousness: Neural representations in confined brain areas need to be connected with wider parts of the brain to reach conscious awareness (Brown et al., 2019), although the exact mechanisms involved in consciousness remain a matter of active debate. Previous studies with DecNef have shown that the neural representation induced in a targeted brain area is highly localized (Shibata et al., 2011). For example, even when an intended stimulus representation of a right tilted grating is successfully induced in the early visual cortex targeted during DecNef training, activation patterns in other brain areas often fail to corepresent the right tilted grating (Shibata et al., 2011). Because the induced representation is generally confined to the targeted brain area, this representation may remain outside of conscious awareness.

2 DecNef may benefit the treatment of fear-related disorders with its implicit nature

Its implicit nature makes DecNef a unique tool to potentially treat anxiety disorders such as posttraumatic stress disorder and phobias. One of the common treatments for anxiety disorders is exposure therapy. During exposure therapy, a patient often experiences strong aversive emotions because he or she needs to observe or imagine the scenes and objects related to their disorders, e.g., an image of a car that reminds them of a traumatic car accident. Exposure therapy is thought to rely on a fear extinction process through which a patient eventually learns that the feared objects are no longer associated with pain or trauma. Despite its effectiveness, the distress of therapy leads to a nonnegligible rate of dropouts, with an estimated range from 0 to as high as 70% (Loerinc et al., 2015; Zayfert et al., 2005).

DecNef, with its implicitness, may help overcome such issue of distress and benefit the treatment of anxiety disorders. Specifically, instead of explicitly viewing or imagining a feared object, a patient could unknowingly induce a neural representation of the feared object through DecNef training. Repeated implicit reactivation of the neural representation of a feared object, when paired with reward as described later, may eventually alleviate fear toward the object in a manner similar to explicit exposure therapy. Here we describe a few studies that have directly examined this possibility.

3 Progressive development of DecNef as a clinical tool

The first study examined the effectiveness of DecNef for reducing fear-like responses among healthy participants (Fig. 2; Koizumi et al., 2016). In this study, participants initially underwent a fear conditioning session to obtain fear-like response to two colored stimuli, red and green gratings, both of which were paired with uncomfortable electric shocks. Participants then went through a 3-day DecNef session in which they were provided

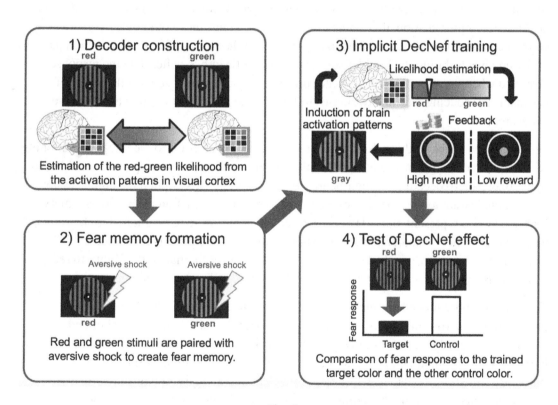

Fig. 2

Schematics of the procedure in Koizumi et al. (2016). In this study, healthy participants went through a fear conditioning session to form two fear memories to *red* and *green* colored gratings. They then underwent DecNef training (with *gray* gratings) to reduce one of these fear memories. In this example, the *red* memory is targeted during training, and the fear response to the *red* stimulus is reduced relative to the control (*green*) stimulus.

with rewarding feedback when their early visual cortices (V1/V2) were more likely to be representing either the red or green stimulus. Which color served as their target stimulus was counterbalanced across participants and was fixed throughout the session. Better induction of the activation patterns representing the target stimulus was followed by a larger disc presented on the monitor, whose size was proportional to the actual monetary reward provided to the participants at the end of each day.

After the 3-day DecNef session, participants underwent a test session in which they were explicitly presented with the fear conditioned red and green stimuli. In the test session, participants showed reduced skin conductance responses and amygdala activation to the stimulus that served as target and had its neural representation paired with reward during the DecNef training, compared to the control stimulus whose neural representation was not paired with reward during DecNef training.

Importantly, when participants were asked to guess which color, red or green, served as their target neural representation after completing all the sessions, they could only guess the target color at chance level. Moreover, fear-like responses to the neurally induced activation patterns of feared objects during the DecNef session were significantly smaller than the responses observed when the stimuli were explicitly presented. These results suggest that DecNef is capable of reducing fear-like responses to feared objects without explicit and aversive exposure.

One limitation of the study by Koizumi et al. (2016) was that, prior to the threat-conditioning session, the red and green stimuli were explicitly presented to the participants to enable the multivoxel pattern decoding of their neural representations. This explicit decoding session was not unpleasant to the participants as it was prior to the formation of aversive memory for the decoded representations. However, if the procedure were to be applied to the actual treatment of anxiety disorders, aversive exposure to the feared objects for the sake of decoding would undermine the key advantage of this approach, that is, the ability to reduce fear associations via the implicit and nonaversive nature of DecNef training.

To make the entire procedure implicit, it is necessary to also render the decoding process implicit. To achieve this, Taschereau-Dumouchel et al. (2018) has elaborated the aforementioned DecNef training procedure by integrating another novel technique, hyperalignment (Guntupalli et al., 2016; Haxby et al., 2011). With hyperalignment, this study aimed to alleviate fear-like responses to feared animals among subclinically phobic participants. Briefly, hyperalignment enabled the construction of a decoder for the representation of a feared animal in each participant's brain that was based on, or "borrowed from," the brain activation patterns of surrogate participants.

The first stage of the study involved learning how to align the neural activation patterns of surrogate participants to the activation patterns of a participant with a subclinical level of phobia. This first stage was achieved using activation patterns obtained while the surrogates as well as phobic participants explicitly observed various images of animals that did not include the feared animals. For example, if the phobic participant is fearful of both snakes and spiders, the first stage used the activation patterns in ventral temporal cortex for various animals such as butterflies, dolphins, etc., but did not involve those for snakes or spiders. Data from this stage allowed computation of a mapping that could translate arbitrary activation patterns in ventral temporal cortex from the surrogate group to the participant's brain. In the second stage, the activation patterns obtained while the surrogate participants explicitly observed the feared animals (e.g., snakes and spiders) were aligned to the neural space of the phobic-participant using this mapping.

Since this study involved only subclinically phobic participants, the accuracy of this "borrowed" decoder could be tested with the actual neural activation patterns obtained while they explicitly observed their feared animals. The decoding accuracy was as high as 82.4%, which was better than the accuracy of the decoder (71.7%) built directly from the neural data of the phobic participant. This relatively high accuracy may be because the benefit of using a larger data set from surrogate participants ($N=29$) outperforms the potential information loss that occurs when aligning the activation patterns between the participants. Even with the borrowed decoder, this study showed that fear-like response could be reduced through DecNef training. Importantly, the effect of DecNef was selective to one of the feared animals that went through the DecNef training as a target (e.g., snakes) and did not generalize to the other, control feared animal (e.g., spiders) that never underwent the training. We here highlight that this was a double-blind, placebo controlled, randomized trial, where neither the experimenters nor the participants were aware of which of the animals served as a target of DecNef and which was the control animal. Thus the effect of DecNef training could not be accounted for by potential placebo effects, experimenter effects, and/or voluntary strategies of participants. Critically, decoding with hyperalignment can render the entire procedure of DecNef training implicit (and thus not aversive), while maintaining the effectiveness of training for reducing fear responses.

Another way to render the decoding process implicit is to use subliminal presentation of feared objects. When only weak sensory inputs are presented, such inputs are processed in the brain to some extent but often fail to evoke conscious awareness of their presence. One of the established procedures to present visual stimuli subliminally is to use continuous flash suppression (CFS; Tsuchiya and Koch, 2005). With CFS, a target visual stimulus is presented to a nondominant eye while dynamic Mondrian patterns are continuously presented to the other, dominant eye. When the stimulus properties such as contrast and duration are carefully manipulated, the target stimulus is often rendered unconscious.

Currently, Chiba et al. (2019) are developing a DecNef training protocol that integrates implicit decoding using CFS. This work targets a clinical sample of female PTSD patients who are fearful of aggressive men because of their traumatic experiences of male violence. Instead of explicitly presenting the visual images of angry male faces, this study implicitly presents such images with CFS for decoding purposes. The study then builds a decoder which can estimate the likelihood that the target of an angry man is being represented in a high-level visual area, i.e., superior-temporal sulcus. Although the data collection is still in progress and thus the sample size is currently small, this DecNef training has so far shown success in alleviating PTSD symptoms (Chiba et al., 2019). The effectiveness of this implicit DecNef procedure will be reported in the future after testing has been completed on the full preplanned sample size.

4 Potential mechanisms behind DecNef training

The mechanisms by which DecNef training alleviates fear remain to be further examined. One potential mechanism is similar to the mechanism of a typical fear extinction procedure or exposure therapy. That is, repetitive reactivation of the neural representation of a feared object in the absence of threat forms a new association memory between the object and safety (Bouton, 2004). Another potential mechanism of the DecNef training is counterconditioning induced when an aversive object is repetitively reinforced with positive rewards (Newall et al., 2017). The DecNef training provides monetary reward which is proportional to the success in inducing the target neural representation. Thus the representation of a feared object is not only repeated in the absence of threat but is also repetitively paired with reward.

To dissociate the two possible mechanisms, Chiba et al. (2019) examined whether the trial-by-trial progress of the DecNef induction success (i.e., likelihood of target stimulus) was better fit by a model based on fear extinction learning or by a model based on counterconditioning. The study revealed that the fear extinction model fit the DecNef performance of the previous two studies (Koizumi et al., 2016; Taschereau-Dumouchel et al., 2018) better than the counterconditioning model. This result suggests that DecNef training may rely more on a mechanism similar to fear extinction.

This modeling result, however, may need to be elaborated further, and more data on brain activity are needed to better elucidate the mechanisms underlying this form of DecNef training. For example, Koizumi et al. (2016) showed that the striatum, which is involved in reward-related learning (Cox and Witten, 2019), was activated during DecNef training in a manner related to the trial-wise success in inducing the feared object representation in visual cortices. Meanwhile, the involvement of the ventromedial prefrontal cortex, which is widely implicated in fear extinction (Milad et al., 2007; Phelps et al., 2004), was not seen in the data from Koizumi et al. (2016). These neuroimaging results suggest at least some additional role of reward and/or involvement of a nontypical extinction process in DecNef training. Better understanding of the neural mechanisms of DecNef training may help to optimize the training for more effective alleviation of fear and anxiety.

5 Alleviating both implicit and explicit symptoms of anxiety disorders with DecNef

The implicit nature of the DecNef training is beneficial in reducing the aversiveness of exposure when treating anxiety disorders. Given its implicit nature, however, one concern is that the effect of the training might be confined to more implicit symptoms of the disorders (Schiller, 2016). That is, participants might still feel a subjective experience of fear that is as strong as in the pretraining phase, even when they show reduced autonomic responses to the feared objects. Such dissociations between implicit and explicit measurements of fear have been demonstrated in the past (Ledoux, 2019).

Indeed, the earlier study with DecNef training (Koizumi et al., 2016) only demonstrated the effects on objective measurements of fear-like responses, such as skin conductance response and amygdala activation. Results on the additional effect of DecNef training on the subjective fear are still scarce and mixed, and thus such an effect needs to be further investigated. For example, the aforementioned study in progress (Chiba et al., 2019) has so far been successful in reducing PTSD symptoms, which are assessed through explicit, subjective reports by the patients. Meanwhile, more explicit, subjective experiences of fear with animals were shown to remain unchanged after DecNef training with the hyperalignment technique (Taschereau-Dumouchel et al., 2018, 2020).

Further investigations may more directly examine the effects of DecNef training on both implicit and explicit components of fear- and anxiety-related symptoms, in order to improve the training to better treat them both. For example, the DecNef training may be improved by directly targeting the neural activation patterns related to each component of symptoms. One recent study (Taschereau-Dumouchel et al., 2019) has demonstrated that while the degree of fear-like response measured via skin conductance could be decoded from the activation patterns in the amygdala, the degree of explicit reporting of experiencing fear could be decoded from the prefrontal areas. Based on this dissociation, DecNef training may target the neural activation patterns in the amygdala and/or its associated areas such as sensory cortices to reduce implicit fear-like responses, while simultaneously targeting the patterns in the prefrontal areas to additionally alleviate the subjective experience of fear.

6 Summary and future directions

Implicit DecNef training may prove beneficial for the treatment of other disorders involving anxiety besides phobias and PTSD. One example may be obsessive-compulsive disorder (OCD). OCD is a disorder which involves *obsessions* with certain unwanted and intrusive thoughts inducing anxiety (e.g., I may have left the house unlocked) and/or *compulsions* to repetitively perform certain behaviors to neutralize such obsessions (e.g., repeated checking) (Stein et al., 2019). One of the common treatments for OCD is Exposure Response Prevention

(ERP, Wheaton et al., 2016), in which patients need to face their fear through exposure to images and situations related to their symptoms (e.g., viewing a door) while inhibiting their urge to respond (e.g., refraining from checking the lock). As one potential new application, DecNef training may elaborate on this ERP procedure. Specifically, DecNef training may help patients to implicitly induce the neural activation patterns representing the symptom-provoking stimuli. Because of the implicit nature of the activated representations, compulsive responses may be less likely to be evoked and cannot be executed within MRI scanners during the training. Thus inhibition of such responses during DecNef training may be less effortful and stressful than during standard ERP.

The procedure of DecNef training has been progressively modified across studies, and future studies may further customize the training in a flexible manner to meet the needs of targeted disorders. Our hope is not to replace the existing clinical practice with DecNef training, but rather to provide some additional treatment options to patients so that they can more flexibly choose how they would like to overcome their disorders.

References

Amano, K., Shibata, K., Kawato, M., Sasaki, Y., Watanabe, T., 2016. Learning to associate orientation with color in early visual areas by associative decoded fMRI neurofeedback. Curr. Biol. 26, 1861–1866.

Bouton, M.E., 2004. Context and behavioral processes in extinction. Learn. Mem. 11, 485–494.

Brown, R., Lau, H., Ledoux, J.E., 2019. Understanding the higher-order approach to consciousness. Trends Cogn. Sci. 23, 754–768.

Chiba, T., Kanazawa, T., Koizumi, A., Ide, K., Taschereau-Dumouchel, V., Boku, S., Hishimoto, A., Shirakawa, M., Sora, I., Lau, H., Yoneda, H., Kawato, M., 2019. Current status of neurofeedback for post-traumatic stress disorder: a systematic review and the possibility of decoded neurofeedback. Front. Hum. Neurosci. 13, 233.

Cortese, A., Amano, K., Koizumi, A., Lau, H., Kawato, M., 2017. Decoded fMRI neurofeedback can induce bidirectional confidence changes within single participants. NeuroImage 149, 323–337.

Cox, J., Witten, I.B., 2019. Striatal circuits for reward learning and decision-making. Nat. Rev. Neurosci. 20, 482–494.

Guntupalli, J.S., Hanke, M., Halchenko, Y.O., Connolly, A.C., Ramadge, P.J., Haxby, J.V., 2016. A model of representational spaces in human cortex. Cereb. Cortex 26, 2919–2934.

Haxby, J.V., Guntupalli, J.S., Connolly, A.C., Halchenko, Y.O., Conroy, B.R., Gobbini, M.I., Hanke, M., Ramadge, P.J., 2011. A common, high-dimensional model of the representational space in human ventral temporal cortex. Neuron 72, 404–416.

Koizumi, A., Amano, K., Cortese, A., Shibata, K., Yoshida, W., Seymour, B., Kawato, M., Lau, H., 2016. Fear reduction without fear through reinforcement of neural activity that bypasses conscious exposure. Nat. Hum. Behav. 1, 0006 (2017).

Ledoux, J.E., 2019. The Deep History of Ourselves: The Four-Billion-Year Story of How We Got Conscious Brains. Penguin Group (USA) LLC, New York.

Loerinc, A.G., Meuret, A.E., Twohig, M.P., Rosenfield, D., Bluett, E.J., Craske, M.G., 2015. Response rates for CBT for anxiety disorders: need for standardized criteria. Clin. Psychol. Rev. 42, 72–82.

Milad, M.R., Wright, C.I., Orr, S.P., Pitman, R.K., Quirk, G.J., Rauch, S.L., 2007. Recall of fear extinction in humans activates the ventromedial prefrontal cortex and hippocampus in concert. Biol. Psychiatry 62, 446–454.

Newall, C., Watson, T., Grant, K.A., Richardson, R., 2017. The relative effectiveness of extinction and counter-conditioning in diminishing children's fear. Behav. Res. Ther. 95, 42–49.

Phelps, E.A., Delgado, M.R., Nearing, K.I., Ledoux, J.E., 2004. Extinction learning in humans: role of the amygdala and vmPFC. Neuron 43, 897–905.

Schiller, D., 2016. Neuroscience: hacking the brain to overcome fear. Nat. Hum. Behav. 1, 0010 (2017).

Shibata, K., Watanabe, T., Sasaki, Y., Kawato, M., 2011. Perceptual learning incepted by decoded fMRI neurofeedback without stimulus presentation. Science 334, 1413–1415.

Shibata, K., Lisi, G., Cortese, A., Watanabe, T., Sasaki, Y., Kawato, M., 2019. Toward a comprehensive understanding of the neural mechanisms of decoded neurofeedback. NeuroImage 188, 539–556.

Stein, D.J., Costa, D.L.C., Lochner, C., Miguel, E.C., Reddy, Y.C.J., Shavitt, R.G., Van Den Heuvel, O.A., Simpson, H.B., 2019. Obsessive-compulsive disorder. Nat Rev Dis Primers 5, 52.

Taschereau-Dumouchel, V., Cortese, A., Chiba, T., Knotts, J.D., Kawato, M., Lau, H., 2018. Towards an unconscious neural reinforcement intervention for common fears. Proc. Natl. Acad. Sci. USA 115, 3470–3475.

Taschereau-Dumouchel, V., Kawato, M., Lau, H., 2019. Multivoxel pattern analysis reveals dissociations between subjective fear and its physiological correlates. Mol. Psychiatry 25, 2342–2354.

Taschereau-Dumouchel, V., Chiba, T., Koizumi, A., Kawato, M., Lau, H., 2020. Multivoxel neural reinforcement changes resting-state functional connectivity within the threat regulation network. BioRxiv. https://doi.org/10.1101/2020.04.03.021956.

Tsuchiya, N., Koch, C., 2005. Continuous flash suppression reduces negative afterimages. Nat. Neurosci. 8, 1096–1101.

Watanabe, T., Sasaki, Y., Shibata, K., Kawato, M., 2018. Advances in fMRI real-time neurofeedback: (trends in cognitive sciences 21, 997-1010, 2017). Trends Cogn. Sci. 22, 738.

Wheaton, M.G., Galfalvy, H., Steinman, S.A., Wall, M.M., Foa, E.B., Simpson, H.B., 2016. Patient adherence and treatment outcome with exposure and response prevention for OCD: which components of adherence matter and who becomes well? Behav. Res. Ther. 85, 6–12.

Yamashita, O., Sato, M.A., Yoshioka, T., Tong, F., Kamitani, Y., 2008. Sparse estimation automatically selects voxels relevant for the decoding of fMRI activity patterns. NeuroImage 42, 1414–1429.

Zayfert, C., Deviva, J.C., Becker, C.B., Pike, J.L., Gillock, K.L., Hayes, S.A., 2005. Exposure utilization and completion of cognitive behavioral therapy for PTSD in a "real world" clinical practice. J. Trauma. Stress. 18, 637–645.

CHAPTER 11

Hemodynamic neurofeedback in neurorehabilitation*

David Linden

School for Mental Health and Neuroscience, Faculty of Health, Medicine and Life Sciences, Maastricht University, Maastricht, Netherlands

1 Rationale for hemodynamic neurofeedback in neurorehabilitation and proof of concept

This chapter provides an overview of the use of hemodynamic neurofeedback in neurorehabilitation (Linden and Turner, 2016). In the context of this book, the focus is on the hemodynamic signals acquired through fMRI or fNIRS although some of the much larger EEG-neurofeedback literature will also be discussed. With "neurorehabilitation" I refer to all efforts to restore or retain function after the onset of a brain disease, thus including both acute events such as stroke and chronic neurodegenerative disorders such as Parkinson's or Alzheimer's disease.

Applications of hemodynamic neurofeedback in neurorehabilitation are still in their infancy. Their development has been motivated by the need to boost conventional approaches in neurorehabilitation (e.g., physiotherapy) and the disappointing results of pharmacological efforts to boost neuroplasticity and thus recovery of function, especially after stroke. Conceptually the development of neurofeedback paradigms for neurorehabilitation was encouraged by the increasing interest in mental imagery/mental practice therapies (Park et al., 2018; Malouin et al., 2013) and some promising results of transcranial stimulation studies in stroke (Plow et al., 2015) and movement disorders (Benninger and Hallett, 2015). Because these techniques have only had limited clinical utility so far there is still considerable scope for analogous developments in neurofeedback, which can be conceptualized as a combination of guided imagery and targeted (self-)stimulation of the brain.

Mental imagery-based practice is an attractive addition to rehabilitation programs because it allows for repeated exercises of motor programs without fatigue and in a safe setting. It also has a good neurophysiological and neuropsychological rationale because of the homologies between actual

---

* Excerpts of text first published in *The Biology of Psychological Disorders*, 2019, David Linden. Red Globe Press, London, have been included in this chapter with permission.

fMRI Neurofeedback. https://doi.org/10.1016/B978-0-12-822421-2.00003-X

and imagined movements both at the level of chronometry and at the level of neural activations. For example, mental imagery of a movement generally takes roughly as long as the actual movement. Moreover, a large body of functional imaging studies has demonstrated considerable overlap of neural activations although it is still a matter of debate whether this also applies to primary motor cortex, where imagery-related activation has been observed inconsistently (Mehler et al., 2019).

However, mental imagery training faces practical challenges such as patient selection and motivation and long-term adherence to an intervention that does not provide immediate success measures (in contrast to physical exercise). Correspondingly, clinical effects have been moderate at best, and regardless of its safety and ease of administration mental imagery protocols have not yet entered routine clinical practice. Might the addition of neurofeedback—which can provide immediate feedback on the success of imagery training if we can assume a tight correspondence between mental imagery and activation levels in (higher) motor areas—be a solution to this motivation problem? Initial data suggest that neurofeedback can significantly enhance the efficiency of mental imagery, at least as measured by the consistency of neural activation patterns (Bagarinao et al., 2018; Lee et al., 2019).

Neurofeedback also has analogies with brain stimulation approaches that aim to restore function or rebalance brain networks. In Plow's taxonomy, recovery of function after stroke can be achieved by ipsilesional plasticity, improvement of interhemispheric balance (generally meaning suppression of contralesional activity), or recruitment of synergistic/compensatory areas (Plow et al., 2015). This taxonomy can be applied to neurofeedback just as it has been to noninvasive brain stimulation. For example, hemodynamic neurofeedback studies in stroke have used the ipsilesional activation (Mihara et al., 2013) and compensatory approach (Mehler et al., 2020). Furthermore, a study piloting stroke NF methods in healthy individuals (with concurrent motor execution) has focused on lateralization of motor cortex activity (Neyedli et al., 2018). Of course, the distinction between these approaches is not clear cut. For example, activation training of ipsilesional premotor cortex can be regarded both as a method to reactivate damaged cortex and recruit compensatory circuits (Sitaram et al., 2012).

2 Hemodynamic neurofeedback studies in neurodegenerative diseases

2.1 Parkinson's disease

Parkinson's disease (PD) is a neurodegenerative disease that affects primarily the dopaminergic neurons of the pars compacta of the substantia nigra. Clinical symptoms start when ca. 60% of these neurons are lost. With disease progression, serotonergic neurons in the raphe nuclei, noradrenergic nuclei in the locus coeruleus, and cholinergic neurons in the basal nucleus of Meynert also degenerate. Most cases are sporadic, but about one-third of patients have other affected family members and about 1% are inherited in autosomal dominant or recessive fashion. Age of onset of symptoms is normally between 60 and 80 in sporadic cases, but can be much earlier, especially in inherited cases. The cellular pathology is characterized by abnormal accumulation of the protein alpha-synuclein, which forms the cytoplasmic inclusions first described by the German neurologist Friedrich Lewy (1885–1950) and hence called "Lewy bodies." The lack of dopaminergic input to the striatum leads to changes in the balance between excitatory and inhibitory input into the direct and indirect basal ganglia pathways, which have increased inhibition of the thalamus by the internal globus pallidus as a net result (see Fig. 1). Because the thalamus is an important pacemaker for cortical motor

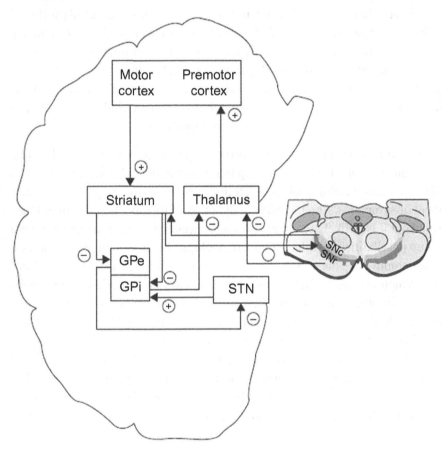

Fig. 1

The direct and indirect pathways of the basal ganglia are important for the understanding of Parkinson's disease: The basal ganglia [striatum: putamen and caudate nucleus; globus pallidus, external and internal parts (GPe, GPi), subthalamic nucleus (STN) and thalamus] form an important loop for motor control (in addition to other sensory and homoeostatic functions not shown here). The striatum is the main input station of the basal ganglia and receives excitatory (glutamatergic) input from motor cortex. The main output station is the (ventrolateral/ventral anterior) thalamus, which sends excitatory projections to (pre-)motor cortex. The striatum regulates the thalamic motor nuclei through a direct (through the GPi) and an indirect (through GPe, STN and GPi) loop and further loops through the substantia nigra, pars reticulata (SNr). The striatal function is modulated by dopaminergic input from the substantia nigra, pars compacta (SNc), which is disrupted in Parkinson's disease.*Modified from Linden, D., 2019. The Biology of Psychological Disorders, second ed. Red Globe Press, London.*

regions, the symptoms of PD are largely hypokinetic, such as the characteristic shuffling gait or difficulty initiating movements. Tremor and rigidity are other characteristic signs. Neuropsychiatric consequences such as depression or dementia develop in up to 50% of patients after several years of disease progression. The dementia is characterized by psychomotor slowing, slow thinking, apathy and deficits in memory recall, which has been termed a "subcortical pattern" because "cortical" functions such as memory encoding and language are relatively preserved. The cognitive symptoms of PD generally follow the motor symptoms by several years. Behavioral abnormalities such as pathological gambling and paranoid psychosis are a rare but important side effect of dopaminergic medication, which is the mainstay of treatment. In patients who do not respond well to treatment with dopamine agonists and/or levodopa (a dopamine precursor that passes through the blood-brain barrier), modulation of the basal ganglia pathways through deep brain stimulation may improve motor function but can also increase neuropsychiatric complications.

Parkinson's disease is conceptually a very attractive target for new neuromodulatory treatments because the great success of deep brain stimulation, particularly of the subthalamic nucleus, demonstrates the ability of modulation of neural circuits to provide considerable improvement of symptoms. The mechanism of action of therapeutic DBS in PD has not yet been clarified but it is unlikely to operate through regeneration of dopaminergic neurons. This opens up possibilities for other nonpharmacological neuromodulatory treatments, possibly even noninvasive ones such as neurofeedback. Although DBS is very effective for some motor symptoms, particularly tremor, rigidity, and bradykinesia (motor slowing), it works less well for others and has little benefit for nonmotor symptoms. Furthermore, it is an invasive technique that requires neurosurgical intervention and follow-up and thus has so far been confined to relatively advanced cases of PD. If fMRI-NF could establish itself as a noninvasive add-on treatment that improves motor (and possibly also nonmotor) functions it would thus respond to a real clinical need. One added bonus might be the possibility to reduce dosage of dopaminergic drugs which would reduce the side effects, such as the uncontrolled jerky movements called hyperkinesia, that arise from the sensitization of dopamine receptors after long-term treatment.

fMRI neurorehabilitation in PD was piloted by our group (Subramanian et al., 2011) and then evaluated in an randomized controlled trial (RCT) (Subramanian et al., 2016). As target we selected the supplementary motor area (SMA) based on its direct connections with the subthalamic nucleus and its role in movement planning and initiation. The choice of this target region also had pragmatic reasons in terms of protocol design. Firstly, it is generally easier to obtain robust single-trial signal, needed for neurofeedback, from cortical than subcortical regions. Secondly, whereas neuropsychological models suggested relatively clearly that upregulation of SMA should be a sensible therapeutic strategy, it was less clear in which direction the regulation of a subcortical area such as the STN should go.

Our initial study showed the basic feasibility of SMA upregulation in PD (Subramanian et al., 2011). Although this was not a randomized study we had a control group that engaged in the same mental imagery processes while in the MRI, but without neurofeedback. This control group had less activation in the SMA during the imagery runs than the active group during imagery plus neurofeedback, and also less clinical improvement after two sessions (separated by 2–6 months) than the NF group. Of course, these clinical results were only preliminary considering the small size (10 patients in total) and pilot design of the study, but it was important to see that this type of training is feasible and leads to recruitment of a wider network of cortico-subcortical motor areas.

In the subsequent RCT (see Fig. 2) we compared the same fMRI-NF protocol with an active non-MRI-based control intervention, physical exercise on the WiiFit system (Subramanian et al., 2016). Because physical exercise-based interventions generally have a higher frequency than fMRI-NF we added homework sessions, and subsequently also WiiFit to the fMRI-NF protocol. This relatively complex design served two purposes, to keep the intensity (in terms of time spent on intervention and assessments) even between groups, and to introduce elements of mental training and transfer technology into the fMRI-NF protocol. We considered the latter point to be important because ultimately it might be difficult (in terms of resources and logistics) to obtain the required intensity of training for sustained neurorehabilitative effects through fMRI-NF alone, and a combination with exercises that can be done without or with low-key technology at patients' homes would be desirable. This combined fMRI-NF, mental imagery, and WiiFit protocol had very good feasibility and also achieved a clinically significant clinical improvement on the UPDRS motor scale, but effects were not significantly different than for the control intervention, possibly because of lack of power of this study with 30 patients (26 of whom completed the trial). Because of the small relative improvements on clinical scales that can be achieved (or at least have been achieved so far) with neurofeedback in neurodegenerative disorders and the small effect sizes for improvement over control interventions the sample sizes needed for properly powered trials will be even larger than those needed for depression or other mental disorders. The difficulty of resourcing such trials, and the added challenge of running multicenter trials of fMRI-NF, which needs implementation of standardization procedures across scan sites, have so far hindered the further development of fMRI-NF for Parkinson's disease and will likely also apply to other neurodegenerative diseases. A possible alternative to much larger RCTs might be the use of novel assessment tools, such as ecological momentary assessments or advanced sensing technology (Heijmans et al., 2019). However, we do not know whether these types of assessments, which are only just beginning to enter clinical practice in movement disorders, will be more sensitive to the specific clinical effects that can be brought about by neurofeedback.

Another interesting recent development is invasive NF. This is a unique opportunity in PD because of the widespread use of DBS, which provides access to signals from the targeted

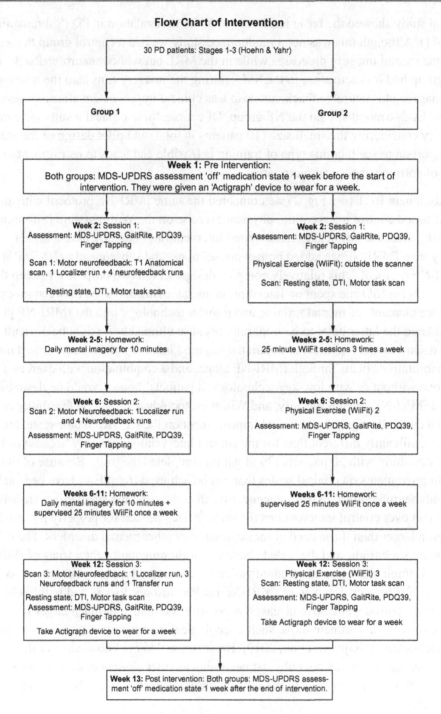

Flow Chart of Intervention

30 PD patients: Stages 1-3 (Hoehn & Yahr)

Group 1

Group 2

Week 1: Pre Intervention:
Both groups: MDS-UPDRS assessment 'off' medication state 1 week before the start of intervention. They were given an 'Actigraph' device to wear for a week.

Week 2: Session 1:
Assessment: MDS-UPDRS, GaitRite, PDQ39, Finger Tapping

Scan 1: Motor neurofeedback: T1 Anatomical scan, 1 Localizer run + 4 neurofeedback runs

Resting state, DTI, Motor task scan

Week 2: Session 1:
Assessment: MDS-UPDRS, GaitRite, PDQ39, Finger Tapping

Physical Exercise (WiiFit): outside the scanner

Scan: Resting state, DTI, Motor task scan

Week 2-5: Homework:
Daily mental imagery for 10 minutes

Weeks 2-5: Homework:
25 minute WiiFit sessions 3 times a week

Week 6: Session 2:
Scan 2: Motor Neurofeedback: 1Localizer run and 4 Neurofeedback runs
Assessment: MDS-UPDRS, GaitRite, PDQ39, Finger Tapping

Week 6: Session 2:
Physical Exercise (WiiFit) 2
Assessment: MDS-UPDRS, GaitRite, PDQ39, Finger Tapping

Weeks 6-11: Homework:
Daily mental imagery for 10 minutes + supervised 25 minutes WiiFit once a week

Weeks 6-11: Homework:
supervised 25 minutes WiiFit once a week

Week 12: Session 3:
Scan 3: Motor Neurofeedback: 1 Localizer run, 3 Neurofeedback runs and 1 Transfer run
Resting state, DTI, Motor task scan
Assessment: MDS-UPDRS, GaitRite, PDQ39, Finger Tapping
Take Actigraph device to wear for a week

Week 12: Session 3:
Physical Exercise (WiiFit) 3
Scan: Resting state, DTI, Motor task scan
Assessment: MDS-UPDRS, GaitRite, PDQ39, Finger Tapping
Take Actigraph device to wear for a week

Week 13: Post intervention: Both groups: MDS-UPDRS assessment 'off' medication state 1 week after the end of intervention.

Fig. 2
See the legend on opposite page

areas while electrodes are externalized (in the initial postimplantation phase before the stimulator is implanted and connected, or during operations to change the stimulator). There are also efforts to integrate continuous recording capabilities into commercially available DBS systems, which would even make regular NF sessions possible. In a proof-of-concept study from Osaka, Japan, four patients each trained up or downregulation of beta-band power during an operation for stimulator change. Downregulation was achieved by all four patients, but upregulation was more difficult, possibly because of heightened baseline beta power in PD (Fukuma et al., 2018; Carney, 2019). We cannot infer anything about possible clinical effects from this brief single session but it might be interesting to explore whether NF can help more specifically suppress pathological oscillations in PD than DBS, or whether the two ways of modulating neural activity can work synergistically. One of the putative neurophysiological mechanisms of DBS in PD is the "desynchronization" or reduction of beta-band activity in the subthalamic nucleus (Rosa et al., 2012), which might open up interesting potential for combination between this (invasive) brain stimulation technique and a noninvasive self-regulation technique (neurofeedback).

2.2 Huntington's disease

Huntington's disease (HD) is an autosomally inherited neurodegenerative disorder that starts in the caudate nucleus and results in chorea, irregular jerky movements that can lead to loss of balance and severely interfere with regular motor actions, and dystonia, uncontrollable muscle contractions. At later stages visceral movements such as swallowing can also be impaired. Affective symptoms include both depression and mania, and obsessive-compulsive symptoms are also common. Because of the relentless course of the disorder, resulting in disability and dementia, and its impact on family planning, the associated psychosocial stress is considerable. Estimates for the prevalence of HD range between 1 and 5/100,000. HD has no known disease-modifying treatment although several trials, for example with gene silencing therapies, are planned or in progress. Currently the clinical management consists of psychosocial support and symptomatic treatment. Chorea can often be reduced

---

Fig. 2

Protocol of the trial reported in Subramanian et al. (2016). This protocol demonstrates the complexity of developing a NF-based intervention that involves elements that can be transferred to patients' homes, and comparing it with a control intervention. It also demonstrates the different layers of potential assessments and outcome measures—clinical scales, questionnaires, automated gait assessment, motor tasks, and ambulatory physiological and motor assessments using wearable technology. *From Subramanian, L., Morris, M.B., Brosnan, M., Turner, D.L., Morris, H.R., Linden, D.E., 2016. Functional magnetic resonance imaging neurofeedback-guided motor imagery training and motor training for Parkinson's disease: randomized trial. Front. Behav. Neurosci. 10, 111, under CC-BY license.*

with antidopaminergic drugs, such as antipsychotics blocking dopamine receptors or with tetrabenazine, an antagonist at the vesicular monoamine transporter that reduces dopamine release (Linden, 2019). Dystonia can be controlled to some extent through benzodiazepines, and the psychiatric symptoms are managed with conventional antidepressants or antipsychotics, but there is a clear need for new, add-on treatments to improve both motor and nonmotor symptoms. One very active area of intervention development is centered on physical activities (Quinn et al., 2016). Neurofeedback does not yet play a major role in such efforts but a first study with fMRI-NF, using the SMA as target area similar to the PD protocols presented in the previous section, has shown the basic feasibility of this approach (Papoutsi et al., 2018).

2.3 Alzheimer's disease

Alzheimer's disease (AD) is the most common form of dementia. AD alone or combined with vascular dementia accounts for 75% of dementia cases. Its prevalence increases with increasing age, from 1% in the 60–65 age group to 40% in the over 85 age group. AD was first described by the German psychiatrist and neuropathologist Alois Alzheimer (1864–1915) in 1905. Alzheimer already noted the characteristic histopathological features, the extracellular plaques and intracellular neurofibrillary tangles. We now know that the plaques are accumulations of beta-amyloid protein, and that the tangles are formed of tau protein. Postmortem studies sampling different stages of the disease have revealed a progressive loss of neurons in the brainstem, basal nucleus of Meynert, entorhinal cortex and hippocampus, followed by association areas of the neocortex. Primary sensory and motor areas are affected last, except in the posterior cortical atrophy form, where occipital and posterior parietal areas degenerate early, leading to visual and visuo-spatial dysfunction.

AD has several characteristic neuropsychological features. Declarative memory is affected first, and semantic knowledge is often better preserved than autobiographical information. The latter tends to be lost with a temporal gradient, with information that was encoded earlier being preserved until later stages of the disease. There is often a profound short-term memory deficit at relatively early stages as well. Language problems arise at variable stages, but visuo-spatial problems often arise early. Conversely, visual and tactile recognition may be preserved until later stages, probably because sensory cortices are affected last by the pathological process (except in the posterior cortical atrophy form mentioned before). Psychotic symptoms and behavioral abnormalities normally start several years into the progression of cognitive decline, but a more dramatic course is possible as well.

Loss of cholinergic neurons in the basal forebrain is one of the pathological hallmarks of AD. Inhibition of the acetylcholine-esterase (AChE), the main acetylcholine-degrading enzyme, increases synaptic acetylcholine levels and may partly remediate the loss of cholinergic innervation. The three AChE inhibitors (AChEI) in clinical use for AD and other dementias are donepezil, rivastigmine, and galantamine. Their clinical effect is best documented in mild to moderate dementia, where the drugs may delay cognitive decline, or even produce temporary improvement of cognitive function. The other main drug used for delaying cognitive decline in AD is memantine, an antagonist at the NMDA glutamate receptor with putative neuroprotective effects. The AChEIs are aimed at restoring cholinergic function that is lost as a consequence of cell death, and memantine is supposed to prevent excitotoxicity in already damaged neurons. These pharmacological strategies are therefore symptomatic rather than causal. Various causal treatment strategies are also under development, most prominently into drugs preventing or reversing the accumulation of amyloid plaques although progress over the last decade has been disappointing (Mehta et al., 2017).

Although lifetime levels of cognitive activity may be protective against or delay the onset of dementia, a beneficial effect of cognitive training after the onset of clinical symptoms has not been shown. Cognitive rehabilitation, which differs from cognitive training in that it helps patients pursue individually selected cognitive or everyday goals rather than training on standardized test batteries, may be more promising and has shown preliminary benefits on subjective ratings (Clare et al., 2010). There is no specific treatment for mild cognitive impairment, the state of subjective or objective cognitive decline considered to be a precursor or "at risk" stage for AD. There is no evidence that specific cognitive intervention or physical exercise programs are beneficial, although general cognitive and physical activity may usefully be promoted as part of a healthy lifestyle.

Because of the limited efficacy of existing symptomatic treatments and the evidence for neuromodulatory effects of the two main classes of antidementia drugs (on the cholinergic and glutamatergic systems, respectively, see earlier) there may be a good rationale for the development of neurofeedback interventions, similar to parallel efforts in direct invasive neuromodulation (Aldehri et al., 2018). Recent work has demonstrated feasibility of fMRI-NF of the parahippocampal gyrus, one of the areas implicated in relatively early AD pathology, in both MCI and AD, but it is too early to make any predictions of its potential clinical utility (Hohenfeld et al., 2017, 2020).

3 Hemodynamic neurofeedback studies in stroke

Strokes are brain lesions caused by damage to the cerebral circulation. About 90% of strokes are ischemic, meaning that they are caused by blocked blood supply to the brain, and the remainder are hemorrhagic (bleeds). Ischemic strokes can result from cerebrovascular or cardiac disease, but also from other diseases affecting blood coagulation and blood vessel integrity. High blood pressure, high cholesterol, diabetes, smoking, and high levels of uric acid are all common risk factors for atherosclerosis (buildup of plaques inside arteries), which explains their association with stroke (as well as heart attack and other vascular problems). Stroke is a medical emergency associated with high mortality and morbidity. The functional impairment and level of disability is determined by the size and location of the brain damage and associated brain edema. Brainstem strokes affecting the respiratory centers in the medulla oblongata can lead to respiratory failure, and thalamic damage often leads to disturbed consciousness. Compression of the ventricles by large hemispheric strokes denotes poor prognosis, and if the edema compresses the midbrain or cerebellar tonsils the outcome is almost invariably fatal. In ischemic strokes, it may be possible to dissolve the thrombus early in order to open the blood vessel again and thus prevent most of the damage to the perfused tissue. Thrombolytic agents that reverse blood clotting can be injected into a vein and will then be transported to the desired site of action through the blood stream, or they can be injected locally by moving a catheter through the arterial system to the site of the thrombus. These procedures are still confined to specialized centers and have a number of side effects, particularly bleeding. A recent major advance in the treatment of ischemic stroke has been the development of procedures for mechanical thrombectomy, which entails the removal of the clot by a device that is inserted through the arterial system. Strokes from bleeds (hemorrhagic strokes) can sometimes be treated by surgery in order to reduce compression and tissue damage.

The classic location for intracerebral hemorrhages associated with high blood pressure is the basal ganglia region. This often results in compression of the internal capsule and damage to the pyramidal tract, resulting in paralysis (total loss of motor function) or paresis (weakness) on the contralesional side. The middle cerebral artery (MCA) supplies the lateral frontal and parietal lobes, the anterior cerebral artery (ACA) supplies the medial surface of the frontal lobe, and the posterior cerebral artery (PCA) supplies the visual cortex. MCA strokes can thus result in aphasia, if the dominant hemisphere is affected, contralesional motor deficits and neglect, ACA strokes can lead to apathy, and PCA strokes to contralateral hemianopia. Depending on the exact extent of the lesion, a wide variety of neuropsychological deficits and syndromes have been described, which are discussed in detail in textbooks of neuropsychology.

Regardless of the considerable advances in the acute treatment of stroke and the associated improved functional outcome, little progress has been made in neuroprotective or neurorehabilitative therapies beyond the acute window. Although combination of conventional behavioral training and exercises (e.g., physiotherapy, speech-and-language therapy, occupational therapy, depending on the nature of the deficits) with methods targeting relevant neural circuits would be attractive, not much dependable evidence has come out of such developments, whether this concerns the addition of drugs, external brain stimulation, or indeed neurofeedback. Nevertheless, refinements of these approaches, especially on the neural side, remain a priority for neurorehabilitation research (Page et al., 2015).

EEG neurofeedback has been applied for several decades to enhance motor training and promote recovery of motor and cognitive functions after stroke (Jeunet et al., 2019; Carvalho et al., 2019; Renton et al., 2017). The main target for motor rehabilitation is the sensorimotor rhythm (SMR), which is generally described as a low beta (12–15 Hz) oscillation recorded over the motor cortex that increases with both motor activity and imagery. EEG-NF training has targeted both up and downregulation of the SMR, which makes interpretation of clinical effects (which have so far been inconsistent) difficult. Nevertheless, because of the large literature on changes in SMR and related EEG rhythms after stroke and their tight association with motor functions, EEG-NF remains an attractive possibility for investigation and enhancement of neuroplasticity after stroke. The first hemodynamic NF studies in stroke were conducted with fNIRS, with promising results (Mihara and Miyai, 2016) that yet have to be confirmed in larger clinical trials. FMRI-NF for stroke is still in its infancy. One study in nine stroke patients with visuo-spatial deficits provided proof of concept of upregulation of visual cortex in the lesioned hemisphere (or self-regulation of the interhemispheric balance between the visual areas) (Robineau et al., 2019), which could become a training tool for visual hemineglect. Another small proof-of-concept study demonstrated that stroke patients with aphasia could upregulate their language network, but did not find clinical benefits compared to a control group (Sreedharan et al., 2019). For motor rehabilitation, ventral premotor cortex (Sitaram et al., 2012), SMA (Mehler et al., 2020), and cortico-subcortical functional connectivity (Liew et al., 2016) have been tried as targets but so far even the feasibility of this kind of approach in relatively acute patients is uncertain. There is thus a mismatch between the clear attractiveness of hemodynamic neurofeedback as a tool to promote the (re-)use of lesioned tissue or recruitment of compensatory networks and its practical implementation.

4 FMRI-neurofeedback studies in tinnitus

Tinnitus is a condition of continuous or intermittent sound perception in the absence of external stimuli. Patients often describe these sounds as "ringing," "buzzing," or "clicking," and they may be severely distressed by them, sometimes even leading to suicidality. In some cases a cause can be found (for example vessel abnormalities in the ear) but in most cases the cause remains unknown although hyperactivity in the brainstem hearing pathways and/or the auditory cortex has been suspected. Although tinnitus co-occurs with hearing loss, it is also reported by people with otherwise normal hearing. Its estimated prevalence in the population is around 10%, and it increases with age. Corresponding to the putative mechanism of (auditory) cortical hyperactivity, neurofeedback paradigms for the attenuation of auditory cortex activity have been developed and some of them have been piloted in patients with tinnitus (Emmert et al., 2017b; Haller et al., 2010; Sherwood et al., 2018, 2019). Feasibility appears to be good but it is still too early for an assessment of the potential clinical efficacy. A similar concept has been applied to the downregulation of auditory cortex in schizophrenia patients suffering from auditory hallucinations (Orlov et al., 2018).

5 FMRI-neurofeedback studies in chronic pain

Pain was the target of the first clinical fMRI-neurofeedback study, in which it was demonstrated that patients with chronic pain could obtain control over the activation of their anterior cingulate cortex (ACC), a key component of the "pain matrix" of central processing of noxious stimuli, and healthy participants managed to modulate pain levels with such a self-regulation training (deCharms et al., 2005). Further work has demonstrated feasibility of downregulation of other parts of the pain matrix (Emmert et al., 2017a).

Although it has taken some time for follow-up work in clinical populations to be published, two recent studies have investigated the feasibility of hemodynamic (-inspired) neurofeedback for chronic pain conditions. One study, in fibromyalgia, used an EEG-neurofeedback paradigm modeled on amygdala activation as measured by fMRI ("electrical fingerprint" of fMRI activity, see Chapters 8 and 12; Goldway et al., 2019). The other, in postherpetic neuralgia, used the ACC self-regulation paradigm, with some promising clinical effects (Guan et al., 2015).

6 Outlook

We have seen in the previous sections that, regardless of our fairly good understanding of pathophysiological processes and the good rationale for neural targets, particularly in PD and stroke, clinical outcomes of neurofeedback studies have so far been meager. Obstacles include basic feasibility, especially in patients with multimorbidity (common in stroke) and cognitive decline, and small clinical effect sizes necessitating large sample sizes for RCTs. In this final section of the chapter I will therefore consider future pathways for the further development of neurofeedback tools for neurorehabilitation.

Feasibility of an intervention that involves a certain degree of concentration and motivation, as well as understanding of the procedure and intact learning mechanisms, is inevitably going to be linked to a minimum degree of cognitive functioning. Although patients with mild dementia may still be able to learn self-regulation through neurofeedback there will be a boundary—yet to be determined—below which neurofeedback that utilizes cognitive models and/or operant conditioning is unlikely to be feasible. It may then still be possible to condition neural activity with implicit or direct neurofeedback, which implies that certain neuronal patterns are directly reinforced without the requirement of the patient's active involvement (note that this terminology is by necessity imprecise because it assumes an artificial separation between mind/self and brain/neural activation). Such reinforcement of neural patterns that is not even noticed by participants has been piloted in the DECNEF methodology (see Chapter 10) and but so far not been extended to neurorehabilitation scenarios.

Feasibility can also be improved by using more mobile/bedside technologies such as NIRS, already successfully piloted in stroke (Mihara and Miyai, 2016), or EEG. Interesting work is currently looking at the combination of fMRI and EEG in multimodal or "hybrid" neurofeedback systems (Perronnet et al., 2017; Mano et al., 2017). A group in Rennes, France, is currently conducting a trial of "Neurofeedback for Upper-limb Recovery After Stroke (NeuroFB-AVC)" with such a hybrid system in patients with subacute and chronic stroke (ClinicalTrials.gov: NCT03766113).

The challenge of small clinical effect sizes (and consequently large sample sizes) can be addressed by either increasing the clinical effects or increasing the sample sizes of the clinical trials. The latter is largely a matter of resources and logistics, including the standardization of protocols (both in terms of MR acquisition and processing and instruction manuals for neurofeedback) for multicenter studies. The former may be limited by the clinical and neuroplastic effects achievable in patients with structural damage to their brain but higher intensity protocols and combination with other exercises such as online movement (Neyedli et al., 2018) or offline WiiFit training (Subramanian et al., 2016) could have synergistic effects.

7 Summary

In summary, hemodynamic neurofeedback remains an attractive tool for the development of new neurorehabilitation strategies especially for diseases that have well-supported pathophysiological models such as PD and stroke. It can benefit from parallel developments in the study of targets and neuroplastic effects of other neuromodulation techniques such as transcranial magnetic stimulation. The promising clinical effects in PD have so far been too small to show superiority over a semiactive control intervention in an RCT, and work in other areas of neurology (HD, AD, stroke) is still in the feasibility stage. We can reasonably expect that with increasing investment in this type of research and combination of neurofeedback with other types of (physical, cognitive) training, progress will be made toward an ultimate clinical application.

References

Aldehri, M., Temel, Y., Alnaami, I., Jahanshahi, A., Hescham, S., 2018. Deep brain stimulation for Alzheimer's disease: an update. Surg. Neurol. Int. 9, 58.

Bagarinao, E., Yoshida, A., Ueno, M., Terabe, K., Kato, S., Isoda, H., Nakai, T., 2018. Improved volitional recall of motor-imagery-related brain activation patterns using real-time functional MRI-based neurofeedback. Front. Hum. Neurosci. 12, 158.

Benninger, D.H., Hallett, M., 2015. Non-invasive brain stimulation for Parkinson's disease: current concepts and outlook 2015. NeuroRehabilitation 37 (1), 11–24.

Carney, R.S., 2019. Neurofeedback training enables voluntary alteration of β-band power in the subthalamic nucleus of individuals with Parkinson's disease. eNeuro 6 (2). https://doi.org/10.1523/ENEURO.0144-19.2019.

Carvalho, R., Dias, N., Cerqueira, J.J., 2019. Brain-machine interface of upper limb recovery in stroke patients rehabilitation: a systematic review. Physiother. Res. Int. 24 (2), e1764.

Clare, L., Linden, D.E.J., Woods, R.T., Whitaker, R., Evans, S.J., Parkinson, C.H., van Paasschen, J., Nelis, S.M., Hoare, Z., Yuen, K.S.L., Rugg, M.D., 2010. Goal-oriented cognitive rehabilitation for people with early-stage Alzheimer disease: a single-blind randomized controlled trial of clinical efficacy. Am. J. Geriatr. Psychiatry 18 (10), 928–939.

deCharms, R., Maeda, F., Glover, G., Ludlow, D., Pauly, J., Soneji, D., Gabrieli, J., Mackey, S., 2005. Control over brain activation and pain learned by using real-time functional MRI. Proc. Natl Acad. Sci. USA 102 (51), 18626–18631.

Emmert, K., Breimhorst, M., Bauermann, T., Birklein, F., Rebhorn, C., Van De Ville, D., Haller, S., 2017a. Active pain coping is associated with the response in real-time fMRI neurofeedback during pain. Brain Imaging Behav. 11 (3), 712–721.

Emmert, K., Kopel, R., Koush, Y., Maire, R., Senn, P., Van De Ville, D., Haller, S., 2017b. Continuous vs. intermittent neurofeedback to regulate auditory cortex activity of tinnitus patients using real-time fMRI—a pilot study. Neuroimage Clin. 14, 97–104.

Fukuma, R., Yanagisawa, T., Tanaka, M., Yoshida, F., Hosomi, K., Oshino, S., Tani, N., Kishima, H., 2018. Real-time neurofeedback to modulate β-band power in the subthalamic nucleus in Parkinson's disease patients. eNeuro 5 (6). https://doi.org/10.1523/ENEURO.0246-18.2018.

Goldway, N., Ablin, J., Lubin, O., Zamir, Y., Keynan, J.N., Or-Borichev, A., Cavazza, M., Charles, F., Intrator, N., Brill, S., Ben-Simon, E., Sharon, H., Hendler, T., 2019. Volitional limbic neuromodulation exerts a beneficial clinical effect on Fibromyalgia. NeuroImage 186, 758–770.

Guan, M., Ma, L., Li, L., Yan, B., Zhao, L., Tong, L., Dou, S., Xia, L., Wang, M., Shi, D., 2015. Self-regulation of brain activity in patients with postherpetic neuralgia: a double-blind randomized study using real-time FMRI neurofeedback. PLoS One 10 (4), e0123675.

Haller, S., Birbaumer, N., Veit, R., 2010. Real-time fMRI feedback training may improve chronic tinnitus. Eur. Radiol. 20 (3), 696–703.

Heijmans, M., Habets, J.G.V., Herff, C., Aarts, J., Stevens, A., Kuijf, M.L., Kubben, P.L., 2019. Monitoring Parkinson's disease symptoms during daily life: a feasibility study. NPJ Parkinsons Dis. 5, 21.

Hohenfeld, C., Nellessen, N., Dogan, I., Kuhn, H., Müller, C., Papa, F., Ketteler, S., Goebel, R., Heinecke, A., Shah, N.J., Schulz, J.B., Reske, M., Reetz, K., 2017. Cognitive improvement and brain changes after real-time functional MRI neurofeedback training in healthy elderly and prodromal Alzheimer's disease. Front. Neurol. 8, 384.

Hohenfeld, C., Kuhn, H., Müller, C., Nellessen, N., Ketteler, S., Heinecke, A., Goebel, R., Shah, N.J., Schulz, J.B., Reske, M., Reetz, K., 2020. Changes in brain activation related to visuo-spatial memory after real-time fMRI neurofeedback training in healthy elderly and Alzheimer's disease. Behav. Brain Res. 381, 112435.

Jeunet, C., Glize, B., McGonigal, A., Batail, J.M., Micoulaud-Franchi, J.A., 2019. Using EEG-based brain computer interface and neurofeedback targeting sensorimotor rhythms to improve motor skills: theoretical background, applications and prospects. Neurophysiol. Clin. 49 (2), 125–136.

Lee, D., Jang, C., Park, H.J., 2019. Neurofeedback learning for mental practice rather than repetitive practice improves neural pattern consistency and functional network efficiency in the subsequent mental motor execution. NeuroImage 188, 680–693.

Liew, S.L., Rana, M., Cornelsen, S., Fortunato de Barros Filho, M., Birbaumer, N., Sitaram, R., Cohen, L.G., Soekadar, S.R., 2016. Improving motor corticothalamic communication after stroke using real-time fMRI connectivity-based neurofeedback. Neurorehabil. Neural Repair 30 (7), 671–675.

Linden, D., 2019. The Biology of Psychological Disorders, second ed. Red Globe Press, London.

Linden, D.E., Turner, D.L., 2016. Real-time functional magnetic resonance imaging neurofeedback in motor neurorehabilitation. Curr. Opin. Neurol. 29 (4), 412–418.

Malouin, F., Jackson, P.L., Richards, C.L., 2013. Towards the integration of mental practice in rehabilitation programs. A critical review. Front. Hum. Neurosci. 7, 576.

Mano, M., Lécuyer, A., Bannier, E., Perronnet, L., Noorzadeh, S., Barillot, C., 2017. How to build a hybrid neurofeedback platform combining EEG and fMRI. Front. Neurosci. 11, 140.

Mehler, D.M.A., Williams, A.N., Krause, F., Lührs, M., Wise, R.G., Turner, D.L., Linden, D.E.J., Whittaker, J.R., 2019. The BOLD response in primary motor cortex and supplementary motor area during kinesthetic motor imagery based graded fMRI neurofeedback. NeuroImage 184, 36–44.

Mehler, D.M.A., Williams, A.N., Whittaker, J.R., Krause, F., Lührs, M., Kunas, S., Wise, R.G., Shetty, H.G.M., Turner, D.L., Linden, D.E.J., 2020. Graded fMRI neurofeedback training of motor imagery in middle cerebral artery stroke patients: a preregistered proof-of-concept study. Front. Hum. Neurosci. 14, 226.

Mehta, D., Jackson, R., Paul, G., Shi, J., Sabbagh, M., 2017. Why do trials for Alzheimer's disease drugs keep failing? A discontinued drug perspective for 2010-2015. Expert Opin. Investig. Drugs 26 (6), 735–739.

Mihara, M., Miyai, I., 2016. Review of functional near-infrared spectroscopy in neurorehabilitation. Neurophotonics 3 (3), 031414.

Mihara, M., Hattori, N., Hatakenaka, M., Yagura, H., Kawano, T., Hino, T., Miyai, I., 2013. Near-infrared spectroscopy-mediated neurofeedback enhances efficacy of motor imagery-based training in poststroke victims: a pilot study. Stroke 44 (4), 1091–1098.

Neyedli, H.F., Sampaio-Baptista, C., Kirkman, M.A., Havard, D., Lührs, M., Ramsden, K., Flitney, D.D., Clare, S., Goebel, R., Johansen-Berg, H., 2018. Increasing lateralized motor activity in younger and older adults using real-time fMRI during executed movements. Neuroscience 378, 165–174.

Orlov, N.D., Giampietro, V., O'Daly, O., Lam, S.L., Barker, G.J., Rubia, K., McGuire, P., Shergill, S.S., Allen, P., 2018. Real-time fMRI neurofeedback to down-regulate superior temporal gyrus activity in patients with schizophrenia and auditory hallucinations: a proof-of-concept study. Transl. Psychiatry 8 (1), 46.

Page, S.J., Cunningham, D.A., Plow, E., Blazak, B., 2015. It takes two: noninvasive brain stimulation combined with neurorehabilitation. Arch. Phys. Med. Rehabil. 96 (4 Suppl), S89–S93.

Papoutsi, M., Weiskopf, N., Langbehn, D., Reilmann, R., Rees, G., Tabrizi, S.J., 2018. Stimulating neural plasticity with real-time fMRI neurofeedback in Huntington's disease: a proof of concept study. Hum. Brain Mapp. 39 (3), 1339–1353.

Park, S.W., Kim, J.H., Yang, Y.J., 2018. Mental practice for upper limb rehabilitation after stroke: a systematic review and meta-analysis. Int. J. Rehabil. Res. 41 (3), 197–203.

Perronnet, L., Lécuyer, A., Mano, M., Bannier, E., Lotte, F., Clerc, M., Barillot, C., 2017. Unimodal versus bimodal EEG-fMRI neurofeedback of a motor imagery task. Front. Hum. Neurosci. 11, 193.

Plow, E.B., Cunningham, D.A., Varnerin, N., Machado, A., 2015. Rethinking stimulation of the brain in stroke rehabilitation: why higher motor areas might be better alternatives for patients with greater impairments. Neuroscientist 21 (3), 225–240.

Quinn, L., Trubey, R., Gobat, N., Dawes, H., Tudor Edwards, R., Jones, C., Townson, J., Drew, C., Kelson, M., Poile, V., Rosser, A., Hood, K., Busse, M., 2016. Development and delivery of a physical activity intervention for people with Huntington disease: facilitating translation to clinical practice. J. Neurol. Phys. Ther. 40 (2), 71–80.

Renton, T., Tibbles, A., Topolovec-Vranic, J., 2017. Neurofeedback as a form of cognitive rehabilitation therapy following stroke: a systematic review. PLoS One 12 (5), e0177290.

Robineau, F., Saj, A., Neveu, R., Van De Ville, D., Scharnowski, F., Vuilleumier, P., 2019. Using real-time fMRI neurofeedback to restore right occipital cortex activity in patients with left visuo-spatial neglect: proof-of-principle and preliminary results. Neuropsychol. Rehabil. 29 (3), 339–360.

Rosa, M., Giannicola, G., Marceglia, S., Fumagalli, M., Barbieri, S., Priori, A., 2012. Neurophysiology of deep brain stimulation. Int. Rev. Neurobiol. 107, 23–55.

Sherwood, M.S., Parker, J.G., Diller, E.E., Ganapathy, S., Bennett, K., Nelson, J.T., 2018. Volitional down-regulation of the primary auditory cortex via directed attention mediated by real-time fMRI neurofeedback. AIMS Neurosci. 5 (3), 179–199.

Sherwood, M.S., Parker, J.G., Diller, E.E., Ganapathy, S., Bennett, K.B., Esquivel, C.R., Nelson, J.T., 2019. Self-directed down-regulation of auditory cortex activity mediated by real-time fMRI neurofeedback augments attentional processes, resting cerebral perfusion, and auditory activation. NeuroImage 195, 475–489.

Sitaram, R., Veit, R., Stevens, B., Caria, A., Gerloff, C., Birbaumer, N., Hummel, F., 2012. Acquired control of ventral premotor cortex activity by feedback training: an exploratory real-time FMRI and TMS study. Neurorehabil. Neural Repair 26 (3), 256–265.

Sreedharan, S., Chandran, A., Yanamala, V.R., Sylaja, P.N., Kesavadas, C., Sitaram, R., 2019. Self-regulation of language areas using real-time functional MRI in stroke patients with expressive aphasia. Brain Imaging Behav. 14 (5), 1714–1730.

Subramanian, L., Hindle, J.V., Johnston, S., Roberts, M.V., Husain, M., Goebel, R., Linden, D., 2011. Real-time functional magnetic resonance imaging neurofeedback for treatment of Parkinson's disease. J. Neurosci. 31 (45), 16309–16317.

Subramanian, L., Morris, M.B., Brosnan, M., Turner, D.L., Morris, H.R., Linden, D.E., 2016. Functional magnetic resonance imaging neurofeedback-guided motor imagery training and motor training for Parkinson's disease: randomized trial. Front. Behav. Neurosci. 10, 111.

CHAPTER 12

Translation to the clinic and other modalities

Jessica Elizabeth Taylor[a,*], Itamar Jalon[b,c,*], Toshinori Chiba[a,*],
Tomokazu Motegi[a], Mitsuo Kawato[d], and Talma Hendler[c,e,f,g]

[a]Advanced Telecommunications Research Institute International (ATR), Kyoto, Japan, [b]Sagol Brain Institute, Tel Aviv Sourasky Medical Center, Tel Aviv, Israel, [c]School of Psychological Sciences, Tel Aviv University, Tel Aviv, Israel, [d]Department of Decoded Neurofeedback, Computational Neuroscience Laboratories, Advanced Telecommunications Research Institute International (ATR), Kyoto, Japan [e]Faculty of Medicine, Tel Aviv University, Tel Aviv, Israel, [f]Department of Psychiatry and Neuroscience, Sagol School of Neuroscience, Tel Aviv University, Tel Aviv, Israel, [g]Sagol Brain Institute, Imaging Section, Tel Aviv Sourasky Medical Center (Ichilov), Tel Aviv, Israel

The translation of neurofeedback (NF) into legitimate, tangible, clinical applications requires focusing on three elements in the procedure (see Fig. 1): **1. Improved precision** of neural targeting through activity decoders, network functional connectivity, and/or feedback context. For example, data-driven NF, where the targeted neural signal is selected using AI/machine learning algorithms, has already demonstrated promising implications for "precision" in neuromodulation (see Chapter 10 for clinical applications). By using such an approach, the specific neural circuit related to a psychiatric disorder or the specific pattern of neural activity an individual has to symptom-provoking stimuli can be determined and targeted. **2. Increased scaling** of application through EEG informed by fMRI and the use of mobile devices. For example, using AI to develop common EEG "electrical fingerprints" to predict fMRI BOLD activity in the target region of interest (Meir-Hasson et al., 2014, 2016). NF targets selected by this approach have been successfully used for self-regulation (see Chapter 8 for clinical applications). The advantage of this technique is that, relative to fMRI-NF, EEG-NF is cheaper and more accessible, thus allowing for the potential application of NF to a much greater range of patients. In the future, EEG-NF is likely to become even less costly, potentially to the point where it may be run through mobile interfaces such as cellphones. **3. Enhanced personalization** of the training procedure. This can be achieved by employing mobile technology to cue training based on state indices, by improving individual targeting through disorder-specific content in the feedback, and by using adaptive feedback based on

---

*Equally contributing first authors.

fMRI Neurofeedback. https://doi.org/10.1016/B978-0-12-822421-2.00002-8

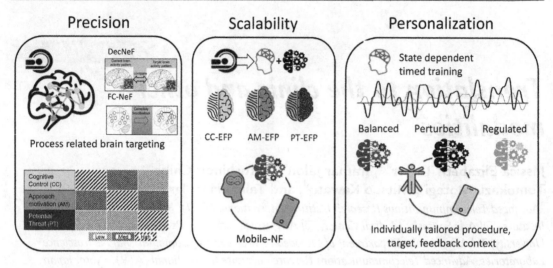

Fig. 1

The chapter's overview of how to best translate NF into clinically effective interventions while considering precision, scalability, and personalization aspects *(from left to right)*. Aspects are framed around the idea that psychiatric diagnoses can be decomposed into different weights of disturbed mental processes. For example, here *(lower table on left panel)*: cognitive control (CC), approach motivation (AM), and potential threat (PT). These mental processes can be associated to known brain-networks and provide **precision** in fMRI-NF, either by DecNef or by FC-Nef. For **scalability**, process related fMRI networks (CC, AM and PT) could inspire computational modeling of EEG into process-related Electrical Finger Prints (EFPs) and be used in EEG-NF via mobile devices. Lastly, **personalization** can be achieved by continuous daily monitoring and computing of process-related electrical modulations (represented here for the potential threat process (PT)). Such monitoring could identify balanced versus perturbed neural states of the process that could then be used for individually tailored brain training. *Elements of the figures are adapted from the following website: https://bicr.atr.jp/decnefpro/ (Accessed 01 June 2020).*

on-line predicted success or monitored state. For example, using trauma-related individual content as feedback was proven more effective for NF in Posttraumatic Stress Disorder (PTSD) than using neutral content (see Chapter 8). Likewise, pictures of individual phobia objects (e.g., snake or mice) have been successfully used to decode personal brain targets (see Chapter 10). In this chapter we will discuss the aforementioned developments, with the aim to best guide the way forward for the adaption of NF into real-life usage.

1 Precision of the neuromodulation target

Recent NF techniques have begun to borrow from AI approaches when selecting neural signals to be targeted. In comparison to experimental designs that aim to manipulate hypothesized neural signals (hypothesis driven), these recent techniques allow for experimental designs that aim to manipulate neural signals that are inherent in the data itself (data driven). When NF is applied based on neural signals that were selected in a data-driven manner, the concerns that these signals were selected due to human bias or bias in the literature can be ruled out. In terms of clinical applications, the targeting of "dysfunctional" neural signals that were selected in a data-driven manner should allow NF to directly influence the specific neural circuits related to a specific disorder. This is an advantage over more traditional symptom-based treatments for psychiatric disorders, which are blunter and less specific; for example, SSRIs, which are given to patients who are diagnosed with a range of disorders from depression to anorexia, inhibit serotonin reuptake receptors across the whole brain and even in other parts of the body such as the dietary tract. Because data-driven NF aims to manipulate neural activity in more localized regions of interest (ROIs), the side effects are expected to be greatly reduced when compared to traditional treatments such as medication. Depending on the exact technique selected, the related NF can be individualized with a high degree of precision and/or it can be used to train individual patients to induce healthier network-level brain activity. Two such data-driven NF techniques—Decoded Neurofeedback and Functional Connectivity Neurofeedback—will be described later in terms of current status and future promise. In addition, the use of immersive virtual reality technology and the use of context appropriate interfaces to more precisely induce the neural activity of interest will be discussed.

1.1 Decoded NeuroFeedback (DecNeF)

Conventional fMRI NF paradigms are usually employed with the goal of training participants to either up- or down-regulate average fMRI signals from specific brain ROIs in a univariate way. Instead of being trained to regulate average fMRI BOLD signals, participants in a DecNef paradigm are trained to implicitly regulate multivoxel patterns (MVP) of BOLD signals (see Chapter 2 for details). Recent advancements in decoding techniques have allowed for the MVP decoding of individual subjects' neural patterns of activity to specific stimuli. This means that disease-relevant stimuli, for example stimuli that evoke phobic responses, can be decoded and this can be used as a target for NF. As a consequence, DecNef has recently grown rapidly as a novel neurofeedback procedure with many potential basic science, as well as clinical, applications (Watanabe et al., 2018; Shibata et al., 2019; Chapters 4, 10, 13, and 14).

Importantly, DecNef does not require trainees to understand what mental state or neural representation is associated with brain activation manipulation success (Chapters 4, 10, and 13). This is especially beneficial for clinical purposes, as it can bypass the distress induced by conventional therapies, such as exposure therapy. Not only does DecNef appear to hold much promise in clinical settings, but additionally it may prove helpful in the clarification of the causative effects of the induction of different neural activity patterns within predetermined ROIs on whole-brain neural activity, symptoms, and/or behavior.

There are two possible approaches to designing DecNef experiments in a clinical setting. First, one can design a DecNef experiment where the "to-be-induced" brain activity is similar to that which is induced during more conventional treatments. For example, by the implicit DecNef induction of brain activity patterns corresponding to feared stimuli, it has been shown that objective fear to these stimuli can be reduced (Koizumi et al., 2016; Taschereau-Dumouchel et al., 2018). This is comparable to exposure therapy without conscious awareness (Fig. 2).

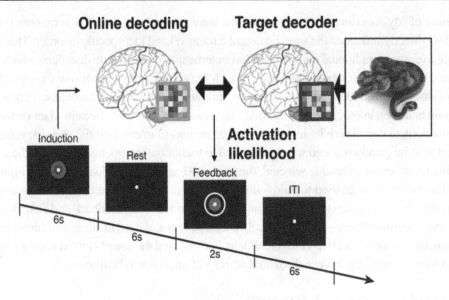

Fig. 2

The DecNef task used by Taschereau-Dumouchel et al. (2018). After a participant's multivoxel pattern of activity to their phobic-specific stimulus was decoded, they completed this task. On each trial, during the "induction" phase, the likelihood that the current multivoxel pattern of activity was that to the participant's phobic-specific stimulus was calculated online. The greater the likelihood the bigger the feedback circle that was presented in the "feedback" phase and the greater the reward on that trial. *Adapted from Taschereau-Dumouchel, V., Cortest, A., Chiba, T., Knotts, J.D., Kawato, M., Lau, H., 2018. Towards an unconscious neural reinforcement intervention for common fears. Proc. Natl. Acad. Sci. U. S. A. 115, 3470–3475.*

DecNef might also be used to reproduce the effects of treatments that involve Transcranial magnetic stimulation (TMS) or Transcranial direct-current stimulation (tDCS). TMS and tDCS can be used to activate or deactivate neural activity in a ROI by an electromagnet or a low electric current, respectively. There are cases in which the mechanism behind the disease might not reside in the TMS-stimulated ROI itself. Instead the therapeutic effects may occur as a result of the TMS-stimulated ROI *modulating* neural activity in other "disease-related" regions of the brain (e.g., see Fonzo et al., 2017). Using MVPA, the "disease-related" patterns of neural activity could be directly decoded from these "disease-related" regions and then directly targeted with DecNef. DecNef targeting of these "disease-related patterns" in the "disease-related" regions should be less invasive than TMS, and since it would be more direct it might also prove more effective. Second, one can design DecNef experiments to "normalize" disease-specific abnormal brain activity patterns. By comparing brain activity patterns between patients and healthy controls, or by comparing those between pre- and posteffective treatment, we can define "normal" brain activity patterns. Subsequently, by the use of DecNef procedures in which "normal" patterns of brain activity are induced, patients (including potentially those who are resistant to standard therapies) may find a reduction in symptomatology.

DecNef comes with its own list of considerations required for clinical application. First, target patterns of neural activity must be decoded in advance. The procedure itself can sometimes induce distress (e.g., the decoding of a fearful object may require repeated presentation of this object to the patient). Solving this problem requires originality and ingenuity. Several lines of research have attempted to solve this, for example via the unconscious stimuli presentation method (Chiba et al., 2019) and the hyperalignment technique (Taschereau-Dumouchel et al., 2018; Haxby et al., 2011) (see Chapter 10). In addition to the considerations that arise from clinical demand, technical matters must be taken into consideration. The design of decoder construction experiments must be well thought out so that the decoder will correctly decode the categories of interest, rather than other irrelevant information. For example, if one wished to construct a decoder that classified between angry and happy faces, then one would need to ensure that the stimuli being presented to participants only differed in this feature of interest (face emotionality). Otherwise one might accidentally construct a decoder that classified features of no interest (e.g., backgrounds, genders of the faces, luminance, etc.). Second, decoding MVPA for specific stimuli requires a large number of data points, which isn't always possible due to time/financial constraints. To decode useful information from an ROI, which may contain hundreds to thousands of voxels, a large number of data points are required. This problem might be solved by the use of hyperalignment (Taschereau-Dumouchel et al., 2018; Haxby et al., 2011), which allows for the concatenation of data from multiple different individuals. Third, the target pattern of neural activity and ROI must be carefully considered with regard to the target psychiatric disease. For example, in DecNef targeting Obsessive-Compulsive Disorder (OCD), one may predict that repeated induction of brain activity for symptom-provocative images may reduce OCD symptoms, because participants in the DecNef procedure are rewarded for correct induction and so this neural pattern of activity may become associated with reward. Alternatively, however, one may predict that the exact same paradigm could lead to increased OCD symptoms, because the participants learn to induce the symptom-provocative brain activity more often. Therefore the potential effects of the "to-be-induced" brain activity must be considered very carefully. Because of these considerations, a deep understanding of both psychiatry and machine learning is required for effective DecNef design. Basic researchers and clinical experts should design DecNef experiments together.

Overall, DecNef is a promising method for dealing with various disease-based processes, as shown by previous findings. In addition, DecNef may help in the elucidation of mechanisms driving disease. However, so far, mainly due to its reliance on fMRI, DecNef has not yet been formally established in a clinical setting.

1.2 Functional connectivity NeuroFeedback (FCNef)

During FCNef training, a participant's real-time BOLD activity is measured using fMRI and used to calculate measures of the functional connectivity (FC) between predetermined neural ROIs. The connectivity level is then converted to a form of feedback that is presented to the participants so that they may attempt to subsequently increase or decrease the desired connectivity pattern. Depending on the task design, participants may be instructed to perform a specific task to increase feedback scores or they may be given no explicit instruction except that their goal is to increase the feedback scores "somehow." The goal is usually to directly change the participants' connectivity between these ROIs and thereby induce related changes in resting-state connectivity, behavior, cognitive performance, and/or clinical symptomatology. A fundamental study showed that, via FCNef training, one group of participants learned to upregulate and another group of participants learned to downregulate the FC between their primary motor and lateral parietal cortices (Yamashita et al., 2017). This indicates that (at least with the right ROIs) people can successfully learn to regulate their own FC. In this study, cognitive performance was also found to change depending on the direction of FC regulation, which indicates that changes in FC engendered by FCNef training can have real-life consequences.

FCNef is beginning to be applied to various diseases with the aim of ameliorating their clinical symptoms. Preliminary evidence suggests that FCNef may be an effective way to treat various psychiatric symptoms such as state (Koush et al., 2017) and trait (Zhao et al., 2019) anxiety, nicotine cravings (Kim et al., 2015), ASD symptoms (Ramot et al., 2017), and depressive symptoms (Yamada et al., 2017). Recent studies have begun to identify generalizable FC neural "biomarkers" for different psychiatric diseases. Using whole-brain resting-state fMRI data and machine learning algorithms, these biomarkers are created in a data-driven manner to identify FCs that can be used to discriminate between patient groups and healthy controls. For example, FC biomarkers have been made for autism spectrum disorder (Yahata et al., 2016), schizophrenia spectrum disorder (Yoshihara et al., 2020), major depressive disorder (Yamashita et al., 2020), and OCD (Takagi et al., 2017).

Because they are data driven, FC biomarkers can further be used to identify and target disease subtypes. For example, Drysdale et al. (2017) demonstrated that patients with therapy-resistant depression can be subdivided into four neurophysiological subtypes defined by distinct patterns of dysfunctional connectivity in limbic and frontostriatal networks. Another study identified three subtypes of depression that can be characterized using a biomarker which incorporates FC between the right angular gyrus and other default mode ROIs, as well as scores from the Child Abuse Trauma Scale (Tokuda et al., 2018). The advantage of this is that it may allow for more precision than traditional symptom-based diagnoses, which are often very heterogeneous in terms of symptoms and treatment response.

After a FC biomarker has been identified (whether for a disease in general or for a disease subtype), it may then be targeted in FCNef to try to alleviate the clinical symptoms of patients. For example, the FCNef study by Yamada et al. (2017) targeted a FC that was identified as a melancholic depression biomarker by Ichikawa et al. (2020). In Yamada et al.'s study, subclinically and clinically depressed participants whose FC became more similar to that of healthy controls after FCNef training displayed a reduction in their depressive symptoms. This result indicates that FC biomarkers might provide relevant targets for the clinical applications of FCNef training.

When compared to traditional activation-based NF, or even to DecNef, another big advantage of FCNef is that it may affect more global-network patterns of neural activity. NF, in general, is not expected to affect the brain in the same blunt global way as, for example, an SSRI does. It is expected to affect more than just the small ROIs being targeted because the brain works in intrinsic functional networks. FCNef might be particularly effective at changing global-network function because activity in multiple ROIs, that are known to be functionally connected, is targeted for feedback. The study by Megumi et al. (2015) showed that the upregulation of FC between the primary motor and lateral parietal cortices during FCNef training led not only to a greater FC between these two ROIs, but also to a subsequent greater FC between the two intrinsic networks to which these ROIs belonged (the motor/visuospatial network and the default mode network, respectively). This indicates that FCNef training may be used to induce broad network-level changes in neural plasticity.

One potential limitation of biomarker targeted FCNef is that biomarkers need to be constructed for each disease or collection of symptoms which will be targeted with FCNef. Given the number of participants required using current methodology to build these biomarkers, this is highly expensive in terms of time and cost. Nonetheless, this work has already begun and so a range of biomarkers have already been discovered (e.g., Yahata et al., 2016; Ichikawa et al., 2020; Yoshihara et al., 2020; Yamashita et al., 2019; Yamashita et al., 2020; Takagi et al., 2017; Drysdale et al., 2017; Tokuda et al., 2018).

Compared to DecNef, one potential disadvantage of FCNef is that FCNef does not utilize individual-specific multivoxel patterns of neural activity within ROIs. Therefore the feedback that is provided in FCNef training is less tailored to the individual participant (Yamashita et al., 2019) or patient than that which would be provided via DecNef training. Attempts can be made, however, to make FCNef training as individually tailored as possible. Some ways in which this may be achieved are discussed in Section 3 later.

While initial studies using FCNef have proven promising, there still remains a lot to be determined. What different parameters may influence FCNef "success" and how can these parameters be optimized? For example, is it better to give a continuous or intermittent form of feedback? How long should each participant spend on each FCNef trial trying to manipulate their own neural activity? How many sessions of FCNef are required for optimal long-term effects? Furthermore, it needs to yet be determined whether the optimal parameters differ dramatically for each type of FCNef paradigm (e.g., FCNef to reduce depressive symptoms versus FCNef to reduce nicotine craving), or if there is some acceptable "one-fits-all" set of parameters. Preliminary studies addressing some of these questions have been conducted (e.g., Oblak et al., 2017); however, much is still unknown and the parameters used in most FCNef studies to date have been arbitrarily set and thus are potentially not optimal. Future research to address these questions is imperative for the evolution of optimal FCNef.

It remains undetermined whether, but seems unlikely that, FC between all pairs of ROIs in the brain can be equally and volitionally self-regulated. As is the case with all sciences, null results are not often published in the NF domain, and so as publications increase we are likely to learn more about which ROIs can have their FC self-regulated, but not about which ROIs cannot. As the literature showing which ROIs can have their FC self-regulated increases, different outcomes—behavioral, psychological, and neural—are likely to be found to be related to these FCs, which should open the way for newer treatments. However, it is important that studies showing which ROIs cannot have their FC self-regulated are also published, so that future researchers do not waste time and money testing something that has already been shown not to work. Even if a functional connection is selected by a data-driven biomarker as relevant, FCNef targeting this functional connection will be of no use if it cannot be self-regulated by the patients.

Whether or not the use of FCNef will be of advantage to practitioners and researchers depends on the goals of their intervention and/or experiment. This has to be determined on an individual basis. However, overall, if the goal is to train participants to induce a specific pattern of activity to a given stimulus within a specific ROI, then a more individual-specific multivoxel pattern targeted NF approach, such as DecNef, will more likely be of use than a FCNef approach. On the other hand, if the goal is to induce long-term changes in global neural-network level function, then a FCNef approach will more likely be of use than an activity-based NF or DecNef approach.

Given that DecNef and FCNef both have their own advantages, the next logical step might be to design a NF paradigm which combines these. Rather than measuring connectivity as the simple correlation between the averaged activity of two ROIs, the weights for how much each voxel from each ROI contributes to the overall connectivity could be determined using MVPA. Then the MVPA weighted connectivity could be used as a target for NF. Like DecNef, the use of MVPA would mean that this paradigm could be tailored to be specific to the individual participant or patient. However, because this paradigm would target the connectivity (weighted by MVPA) between ROIs, rather than just the activity within one ROI, like FCNef this paradigm should be able to affect long-term changes in neural-network plasticity in a more targeted manner. In the future, this type of new NF paradigm may provide a more precise, individualized, form of NF that could target network-level changes in plasticity.

1.3 Process-specific feedback context

Another way to increase target precision is by using context specific feedback-interface, presumably activating a disorder relevant network. The majority of NF studies, to date, have used an abstract meter as a feedback interface. This type of feedback does nothing to specifically provoke the neuro-mental processes targeted during NF training. There are, however, two promising ways in which process precision during NF might be improved (see Lubianiker et al., 2019 for a detailed account). One is via the use of immersive environments and the other is through contextual interfaces. The use of immersive virtual reality (VR) technologies that simulate highly naturalistic environments can facilitate improved learning, generalizability, and process specificity. A study comparing abstract versus animated feedback showed that animated feedback resulted in more engagement and longer sustainability of the learning (Cohen et al., 2016). Contextual interfaces, likewise, may aid participants in inducing the neural process of interest, especially if these are disease related. A revealing example for this is the NF study by Paret et al. (2016), where aversive images were presented on-screen alongside a meter which individuals were trying to regulate with their neural activity. This approach assumes that exposing trainees to the emotional stimuli while they were attempting to self-regulate activity in their amygdala would aid them in inducing the targeted emotion-related neural activation. A different approach was applied by Young et al. (2017) in a randomized controlled trial in depression. Trainees (patients with depression) were asked to recall positive memories while trying to upregulate their amygdala activity. They showed increases in positive mood after training. Future research, using different types of context induction, should try to determine the conditions under which activation of neural hubs (that are involved in multiple processes) can be provoked. Furthermore, other feedback interface factors may also be harnessed for process induction. These include the utilization of different feedback protocols for process targeting, as well as NF task instructions (i.e., providing participants with suggestions for specific process-related imageries).

2 Scaling up the neuromodulation procedure

fMRI NF has proven promising for modulating well-defined brain functionality for basic research and clinical use. Yet, its high cost and immobility stand in its way to broadly being applied for clinical purposes in psychiatry and neurology. In addition, being dependent on hospital technology, such as MR scanners, precludes the hope of integrating NF into daily life. To better scale fMRI NF, different brain recording methods as well as the use of mobile interfaces must be considered. These will be described in this section.

2.1 Electrical Finger Print NF (EFP-NF)

EEG is an accessible and widely used neural monitoring device, both for NF and for other uses. Yet, its spatial resolution is much inferior to that of fMRI, making it less useful for the guiding of precise NF. Computational advancements in AI and machine learning could assist in overcoming this issue by injecting spatial information into the EEG recordings. This could be done, for example, by using low-resolution electromagnetic tomography (LORETA; Grech et al., 2008) or its variants (Congedo et al., 2004). However, these computationally estimated solutions necessitate the use of a dense grid of electrodes. This limits mobility and accessibility, and at the same time makes recording highly sensitive to noise, particularly when from deep subcortical areas (Yao and Dewald, 2005). Other approaches have used fMRI to improve EEG inverse localization models (Sato et al., 2004; Valdes-Sosa et al., 2009; Aihara et al., 2012), while relying on critical a-priori assumptions regarding the biophysical origins of the EEG and fMRI signals. Yet, this type of approach again requires high density recording sites and thus hampers scalability. To overcome this, data-driven statistical approaches have been applied to associate EEG and fMRI signals (Laufs et al., 2008), using either simple correlations between EEG frequency bands and localized BOLD activity (Emmert et al., 2017; Ben-Simon et al., 2008; de Munck et al., 2007) or machine learning tools to predict BOLD activity from EEG frequency bands (Mantini et al., 2007). In the context of NF, the latter approach, termed Electrical Finger-Print (EFP), has repeatedly been used to successfully predict fMRI BOLD activations in the amygdala and medial prefrontal cortex from EEG data, even from a single EEG channel (Meir-Hasson et al., 2014, 2016). Of importance to this chapter, the amygdala EFP model has been successfully used as a modulation target in NF, yielding evidence that EEG-NF training can be successfully used for precise modulation of a deeply located limbic region (Keynan et al., 2016, 2019; Meir-Hasson et al., 2016).

Results from validation experiments have demonstrated that participants who were trained outside the fMRI scanner to downregulate their amygdala-EFP model not only successfully decreased amygdala BOLD activity during fMRI-NF in a following session, but also showed reduced amygdala reactivity to threatening visual stimuli and improved performance in an emotion regulation task (Keynan et al., 2016). The efficacy of the amygdala-EFP method was further demonstrated in several NF studies in both healthy and patient cohorts, e.g., stress resilience in combat soldiers (Keynan et al., 2019), and emotion regulation in chronic pain patients with fibromyalgia (Goldway et al., 2019). EFP-NF combines the strengths of EEG and fMRI, providing both high accessibility and more precise spatial localization of the neuromodulation. From a clinical perspective, it paves the way for the development of additional "fingerprints" for various target regions (for example, see Klovatch-Podlipsky et al., 2016, which presents the development of a right inferior frontal gyrus EFP model), for network-level metrics, for multivoxel-based patterns (like the ones utilized in DecNef) and/or for FC networks (like in FCNef). Furthermore, since it relies on EEG only, neuromodulation can be performed in relatively naturalistic and/or virtual/augmented environments, allowing for more process-specific targeting (see review Lubianiker et al., 2019).

The EFP approach contains some limitations. First, it does not uniquely monitor a specific brain region, but rather a set of regions that are coactivated along with the target region. Indeed, when examining the BOLD correlates of the amygdala EFP in an EEG–fMRI experiment on a new group, it was found that the EFP was associated not only with the signal fluctuations within the amygdala but also with additional functionally related regions such as the insula and higher-order visual areas (Keynan et al., 2016). Second, even though EFP models were developed and validated for BOLD activations in single regions, fingerprinting more complex neural indices (i.e., MVPA, network connectivity, etc.) might prove to be more challenging in terms of susceptibility to movement and/or physiological artifacts and/or other factors influencing signal to noise ratios. Future empirical work is required in order to demonstrate whether reliable fingerprint models for such complex network indices are feasible. Third, it is assumed that an EFP index is a *general* correlate of BOLD activations in a specific target region. However, it remains to be determined whether an EFP model that is created in one MRI acquisition context can generalize to other contexts to reflect brain modulation beyond NF (for example, clinical outcome tasks, resting-state scans, etc.). Future studies should provide evidence for the generalizability of models across various datasets and contexts. Lastly, the EFP was developed as a common model (Meir-Hasson et al., 2016), yet its application to clinical populations might require further optimization and possibly more personal calibration due to the large interindividual variability among patients. One way to deal with this issue, without requiring an fMRI scan for each trainee (thus impairing scalability), is by establishing a library of EFP subclasses, each depicting different parts of the whole model variance (Jacobs et al., 1991). Previous work has shown that, while the common amygdala-EFP model has reasonable predictive power across individuals (r Pearson=0.4), predictive power is highest ($r=0.5–0.8$) when an individual's own amygdala-EFP model is used to predict their amygdala activity (Meir-Hasson et al., 2016). This calls for a computational approach that allows some level of individualization, without having to conduct an fMRI scan for each individual. Close examination of the common amygdala-EFP model performance suggests that this performance is affected by other individual characteristics such as EEG frequency bands distribution and the correlation of the common amygdala-EFP model with alpha and theta power. Thus creating subtypes of the common amygdala-EFP model may improve the model performance. Consistently, preliminary testing conducted on previous data has revealed that assigning different models to different individuals according to the characteristics mentioned before may improve the model performance by up to 20% percent (Meir-Hasson, 2016).

In addition to the approach described before, it is possible to test the performance of other data-driven approaches when trying to associate EEG and fMRI data. From a machine learning perspective, the above is a problem of learning a mapping between two continuous signals. In the nomenclature of deep learning, this is known as sequence to sequence modeling (Sutskever et al., 2014). The spatiotemporal nature of these signals, and their high dimensionality, make the problem challenging, but state-of-the-art methods like LSTM (Graves and Jaitly, 2014) have the potential for achieving satisfactory accuracy on this task. Additionally, the mappings will need to take into account the intrinsic statistics of both the fMRI and EEG signals (namely, irrespective of their correlations). This is handled within the framework of structured prediction, which can be used to elegantly represent statistical properties in prediction (Meshi et al., 2010) (see recent work in this direction by Simões et al., 2020).

2.2 Harness mobile technology toward increasing NF accessibility

Recent years have seen consumer electronics gain many abilities and become widely accessible. These include cheap and easy-to-use devices for physiological measurements, such as EEG headsets (Ratti et al., 2017), heart rate monitors (Wang et al., 2017), and sleep monitors (Kang et al., 2017). Fortuitously, the reported data quality for many of these is of acceptable levels. At the same time, virtual and augmented reality glasses, as well as internet-connected mobile phones, have become virtually ubiquitous. The clearest utility of this progress for NF is the accessibility of affordable, consumer-oriented EEG headsets, which could allow patients to practice NF anywhere. This change can be thought of as bringing the clinic into the patient's natural environment. This is in line with prevalent psychotherapy protocols, such as Cognitive Behavioral Therapy and Dialectical Behavioral Therapy (Hofmann and Smits, 2008; Dimeff and Koerner, 2007), which augment in-clinic treatment with teaching patients skills and techniques that they can use in their day-to-day lives. Bridging the gap between the clinic and patient environment is likely to improve both treatment efficacy and accessibility. Patients' ability to practice NF in their own homes should help disseminate the treatment, as well as allow for exploration of protocols that are more frequent than clinic conditions usually allow for. It would be worthwhile to consider mobile phones as a feedback instrument. If mobile phones can be used to deliver feedback, then, coupled with a mobile EEG headset, this would mean that patients are not limited to practicing NF at home or in a clinic, but that they could do it practically anywhere. As this aim is realized, however, it is also important to bear in mind the potential that widely disseminated NF has for social influence and to guard against abuse (for example, by those marketing NF systems). Please see Chapter 14 for further discussion of ethical considerations.

3 Personalizing the neuromodulation effect

The need for personalization in the diagnosis and treatment of psychiatric disorders has been largely acknowledged in the last decade. This has led to large-scale neurocognitive studies looking for potential biomarkers that can assign patients to clinical subtypes or objectively defined biotypes (Buckholtz and Meyer-Lindenberg, 2012; Lubianiker et al., 2019). The personalization of NF training should focus on the training target (when and what to train) and on improving training protocols (how to train). Both aspects require further technological developments along the following considerations.

3.1 Timing of training

While current NF protocols involve training in a clinic or a lab, moving NF to the home (as described before) could allow for training to be completed at the time points which are most clinically efficient and needed. This could be done by timing NF practice according to environmental aspects or physiological aspects. Behavioral factors that are associated with psychiatric disease, such as sustained attention, working memory, and attentional bias, can fluctuate dynamically even within a single behavioral experiment that lasts 5–10 min (Naim et al., 2018; DeBettencourt et al., 2019). Recent research has shown that, when BOLD signal is used to determine trial onset, resulting behavioral outcomes can differ to some extent (Chew et al., 2019). Therefore the efficacy of NF (and conventional) treatments might likewise dynamically fluctuate and it is worth examining if such fluctuations could be decoded using MVPA and/or physiological measurements. If so, then decoder outputs (that estimate whether or not the effect is likely to be maximum) and/or physiological indices could be used to inform the timing of feedback. For example, patients suffering from alcohol abuse could induce the relevant neural activity in a NF training procedure to reduce their desire for alcohol when the neural and/or physiological indices indicate the desire is the largest. Real-time decoding methods might also be useful for modifying feedback threshold. Since the NF success in each regulation block fluctuates dynamically, it may not be reasonable to use the same feedback threshold throughout the session (see for example recent work by Osin et al., 2020). On-line prediction of the next regulation block's success may allow continuous modification of the feedback threshold accordingly, and increase the effectiveness of NF protocol overall.

Many psychological treatment protocols attempt to give patients tools that can be used in situations that patients find difficult to handle, commonly referred to as guided self-help (GSH; Bennett et al., 2019). GSH has been shown effective in disorders such as eating disorders (Wilson and Zandberg, 2012), anxiety, depression (van't Hof et al., 2009; Haug et al., 2012), and PTSD (Lewis et al., 2017). These difficult to handle situations are often highly context dependent. In explicit NF, patients normally practice the induction of a mental strategy to be used in difficult situations and then have to try and apply their strategy in real life in the absence of external feedback. Using a mobile setup, where NF is monitored using an affordable EEG headset and feedback is delivered by a mobile phone application (mobile-NF) would allow patients to receive feedback in real-life challenging situations. Potential use cases could include social anxiety (e.g., practicing NF prior to giving a public speech or attending an important meeting), Attention deficit hyperactivity disorder (ADHD, e.g., practicing inside a classroom, or while trying to concentrate at home), and specific phobias (e.g., practicing when encountering the phobic object). Another alternative is to time NF practice according to the patient's state. NF could utilize the high recent accessibility of wearable physiological monitors (including heart rate and skin conductance) to time NF sessions according to a patient's physiological state (heart rate, skin conductance, pupil dilation). This could be highly relevant in disorders that are characterized by high physiological arousal states (Chalmers et al., 2014; Imeraj et al., 2011), such as general anxiety, PTSD, or even ADHD. Furthermore, this could also be beneficial in major psychiatric disorders such as depression and schizophrenia, where stress can exacerbate core symptoms. Decreased heart rate variability is an established marker of high arousal modulation (Thayer et al., 2012) and could serve as the relevant physiological marker for stress. Data from a heart rate monitor could be used to alert a patient that their arousal levels are rising, and suggest that it might be time to practice NF. Such practice could also be highly valuable to healthy individuals under especially demanding situations (e.g., pilots) for improvement of their performance.

3.2 Individually tailored disorder-specific interface content

In some psychopathologies, symptoms are often triggered by a specific external stimulus. These include disorders such as specific phobias (e.g., fear of spiders or heights), social anxiety disorder (social criticism), substance abuse (smoking, drugs), PTSD (traumatic content and its reminders), and OCD (washing, checking). Indeed, prevalent cognitive-behavioral therapy protocols have long demonstrated that using a controlled exposure to the patient's specific stressors could be beneficial for treatment (Foa et al., 2007; Choy et al., 2007). This concept has recently been demonstrated in PTSD patients (Fruchtman et al., 2019, see Chapter 8) by combining amygdala EFP-NF and trauma-related content as feedback in a gradual manner. It has likewise been demonstrated for OCD and phobia, where the MVP for disorder-related stimuli were targeted using DecNef (see Chapter 10). The next step may be combining NF with immersive technologies (e.g., Virtual/Augmented Reality; VR/AR) to allow personal specificity of the scenario's content used for feedback. This could be based on work already performed using VR-based exposure therapy in anxiety disorders (Carl et al., 2019).

While existing 2D computerized applications allow high controllability, they provide low ecological validity and thus hamper generalizability to daily life experience and/or to dynamics in the mental state of an individual. In this regard, immersive 3D technologies such as VR/AR can provide a middle ground with both high controllability and strong contextuality (Bohil et al., 2011; Sanchez-Vives and Slater, 2005). Since the experience induced via these technologies is entirely programmable, different types of feedback cues can communicate continuously with behavioral (e.g., eye-tracking and movement) and biological (e.g., skin conductance, ECG, EEG, respiration, heat maps) signals. Importantly for psychiatric interventions, the VR/AR experience is predominantly mediated by highly engaging sensory-perceptual processes, which may circumvent resistance to treatment and increase adherence. The fundamental idea is that in each disorder, particular situations induce maladaptive behaviors (Schmitz and Grillon, 2012; Sjoerds et al., 2013; Domsalla et al., 2014). Therefore the VR scenario can be designed to reward each participant for acting appropriately in the specific situations that best simulate their real-life difficulties (e.g., lowering the height of an elevator or decreasing traumatic story intensity). Continued eye-tracking, behavioral monitoring, and physiological measures will constitute domain-specific readouts for better characterizing the experience in association to neuromodulation.

Averaged activity in predefined ROIs can capture crucial ingredients of a disorder and in some cases thereby work as effective targets for NF. For example, NF targeting average activity in a left amygdala ROI has been shown to influence emotional processing in patients with major depressive disorder (Young et al., 2014). However, in other cases it might be of benefit to more precisely define the target ROI for the individual patient. This may particularly be the case for patients whose symptoms are provoked by specific stimuli, such as those suffering from addiction, OCD, and PTSD. In patients with these disorders, neural representations for these symptom-provoking stimuli are thought to be abnormally wired within their reward and/or fear circuitry. This means that predefined ROIs might not capture the relevant circuitry well for these patients. Functional localizers are often used in such cases, so that the neural regions active in response to symptom-provoking stimuli can be determined for each individual patient and targeted in NF (e.g., see Gerin, 2016; Hampson et al., 2012; Rance et al., 2018; Scheinost et al., 2014; Subramanian et al., 2011). Taking this one step further, the exact multivoxel patterns of activity a patient displays to symptom-provoking stimuli can be used to define ROIs, which thereby capture even more fine-grained representations. These are the type of ROIs that are targeted in DecNef (see Chapter 2). For example, the pattern of activity a phobic person has to the specific stimulus that they are scared of can be determined (either straight from their own neural activity or by inferences based on the neural patterns of activity of surrogates, see Taschereau-Dumouchel et al., 2018). Then on each trial of DecNef, the likelihood that the current multivariate pattern of activation is related to the phobic-specific stimulus can be determined and feedback given accordingly (see Fig. 2). DecNef using this design (where for each participant, induction of the multivariate pattern of activation related to their phobic-specific stimulus was counterconditioned with reward) has been shown to reduce participants' fear of phobia-specific stimuli (Taschereau-Dumouchel et al., 2018). DecNef and other approaches involving functional localization of target regions or patterns can thus be utilized for personalized treatment by targeting (in the case of DecNef individual patterns of) brain activity of an individual patient to a specific stimulus.

FCNef, particularly when the target is determined by a biomarker, is less personalized than DecNef. However, some attempts have been made to personalize FCNef as much as possible. FC is often calculated as the coefficient for the correlation between the ongoing BOLD activity in two ROIs. In FCNef, feedback is often given depending on the sign and absolute value of this correlation coefficient. Rather than using absolute correlation coefficients to determine feedback, the correlation coefficient representing FC on each trial of FCNef can be compared to that of an individually determined baseline to calculate feedback. For example, in the study by Yamada et al. (2017), each participant's baseline correlation coefficient was determined during a SHAM session. During the SHAM session, each participant completed the exact same task as that which they would complete on

FCNef sessions, but with random feedback. Then during subsequent FCNef sessions, each participant's feedback was calculated based on how much more positive or negative the correlation coefficient calculated for the current trial was relative to that measured during that participant's SHAM session. This allowed each participant to try to improve on their own specific FC, rather than try to attain some predetermined "ideal level" of FC. Another way in which FCNef can be somewhat tailored to the individual is by determining the ROIs in a functional localizer task, rather than by simple anatomical parcellation. This method of ROI selection may not be pertinent, however, if the FC of interest was determined from a biomarker that was created using anatomical parcellation. Nonetheless, biomarker targeted FCNef, itself, has the potential to become very personalized. If researchers continue to make new FC biomarkers then one day we could reach the stage that a patient comes into the clinic and is diagnosed based on their resting-state brain activity, rather than on self-reported symptoms. Based on this data-driven approach, the likelihood of factors such as which FCs in this individual patient differ the most from healthy controls; how likely this individual patient is to respond well to FCNef; and whether FCNef, medication, or a combination of these is most likely to be of benefit for this individual patient could be easily and quickly determined. Once we reach this stage, then FCNef based on such diagnoses could be considered well personalized.

4 Conclusion

In this chapter we have highlighted several strategies we believe could be beneficial for the dissemination of NF as an effective treatment for varied psychopathologies. These strategies include translation of state-of-the-art imaging and computational approaches into neuroscientifically precise treatments (Dec-NF, FCNeF), as well as strategies for integrating imaging techniques with computational and consumer-electronics advances to enhance scalability and personalization of treatment (EFP, mobile- and VR-NF). Regarding precision, we presented evidence for the utility of advanced image analysis tools to depict distributed activation or functional connectivity, as well as interfaces tailored for relevant processes. The need for scalability was discussed with respect to accessible signal probing and mobility of application through EEG rather than fMRI. Lastly, personalization was highlighted with regard to timing of treatment and individually tailored indications for brain probes and feedback interface. Table 1 summarizes how well a number of currently popular NF approaches implement these three strategies.

Achievement of the ideas put forth in this chapter can be pursued through collaboration between clinical and basic/methodological scientists, as well as by trying to improve the accessibility of tools which are currently only available to highly technically oriented research groups. This challenge could be overcome by publishing toolboxes, which could make these technical processes accessible to clinical scientists, for example, by producing

Table 1: Comparing the challenges and promise of different NF strategies.

Method	Precision	Scalability	Personalization	
Single region fMRI NF	Based on limited, highly localized, accounts of psychopathologies.	High cost, low accessibility. fMRI based. The target is generalized; a relevant ROI can be used transdiagnostically (e.g Amygdala NF used in PTSD and Depression).	Individual ROIs can be localized.	Alternatively, the same anatomically parcellated ROI can be used for all subjects.
DecNef	Neural target patterns are matched per individual per process and therefore provide high precision.	High cost, low accessibility. fMRI based. Matching target patterns to patients requires a preliminary scan, technical expertise, and sometimes personalized stimuli. Hyperalignment enables more generalizability.	Each patient receives a personalized neural target.	
FC-Nef	Can target FC of multiple ROIs. FC selected based on existing literature or disorder biomarker.	High cost, low accessibility. fMRI based. Currently disorder specific, but could be also process driven and more transdiagnostic.	Based on disorder categorization. Can be improved by targeting disorder subclasses or processes that fit each patient.	
EFP NF	Currently based on limited ROIs, but captures the related network. In the future models can be developed for precise process-related functions.	Low cost, high accessibility. EEG based. Currently done in the clinic, but in the future could be mobile and home based.	Current generation is based on a common model; same probe for all participants. In the future, the signature could be calibrated to each individual, either through a library of signatures or a single fMRI/EEG test. When mobile, patients could practice anywhere and at the times deemed most clinically beneficial.	

= low

= high

EFPs, performing hyperalignment, or by creating a cloud computing interface for EEG-NF through mobile phones. Unlike pharmacological treatments, if these steps are taken, NF has the potential to become a highly "open source" treatment protocol—highly accessible and modifiable for specific individuals, disorders, or subdisorders. Ethical considerations and perils of ease of access should not be neglected (see Chapter 14 for an in-depth consideration), but, in our view, improving accessibility for patients and clinicians could highly advance the field.

Acknowledgments

TH acknowledges financial support by a number of funding resources which facilitated this work: Award number 602186 from the European Union-FP7, BrainTrain, award number W81XWH-16-C-0198 from the US DOD, "Emotional Brain Fitness via Limbic Targeted NeuroFeedback," and grant number 2107/17 from the Israel Science Foundation, "Causal Modulation of Limbic Circuits in Post Traumatic Stress Disorder due to Childhood Sexual Abuse." JT, TC, TM, and MK are supported by the contract research "Brain/MINDS Beyond" Grant Number JP18dm0307008, supported by the Japan Agency for Medical Research and Development (AMED),"Development of BMI Technologies for Clinical Application" of the Strategic Research Program for Brain Sciences JP17dm0107044 (AMED), the Innovative Science and Technology Initiative for Security (JPJ004596), ATLA, and KDDI collaborative research contract.

References

Aihara, T., et al., 2012. Cortical current source estimation from electroencephalography in combination with near-infrared spectroscopy as a hierarchical prior. NeuroImage 59 (4), 4006–4021.

Bennett, S.D., et al., 2019. Practitioner review: unguided and guided self-help interventions for common mental health disorders in children and adolescents: a systematic review and meta-analysis. J. Child Psychol. Psychiatry 60 (8), 828–847.

Ben-Simon, E., Podlipsky, I., Arieli, A., Zhdanov, A., Hendler, T., 2008. Never resting brain: simultaneous representation of two alpha related processes in humans. PLoS One 3 (12), e3984.

Bohil, C.J., Alicea, B., Biocca, F.A., 2011. Virtual reality in neuroscience research and therapy. Nat. Rev. Neurosci. 12 (12), 752–762.

Buckholtz, J.W., Meyer-Lindenberg, A., 2012. Psychopathology and the human connectome: toward a transdiagnostic model of risk for mental illness. Neuron 74 (6), 990–1004.

Carl, E., et al., 2019. Virtual reality exposure therapy for anxiety and related disorders: a meta-analysis of randomized controlled trials. J. Anxiety Disord. 61, 27–36.

Cavazza, M., et al., 2014. Integrating virtual agents in BCI neurofeedback systems. In: Proceedings of the 2014 Virtual Reality International Conference, Laval, France, April (ACM, 2014).

Chalmers, J.A., Quintana, D.S., Abbott, M.J., Kemp, A.H., 2014. Anxiety disorders are associated with reduced heart rate variability: a meta-analysis. Front. Psychiatry 11 (5), 80.

Chew, B., et al., 2019. Endogenous fluctuations in the dopaminergic midbrain drive behavioral choice variability. Proc. Natl. Acad. Sci. U. S. A. 116 (37), 18732–18737.

Chiba, T., et al., 2019. Current status of Neurofeedback for post-traumatic stress disorder: a systematic review and the possibility of decoded neurofeedback. Front. Hum. Neurosci. 13, 233.

Choy, Y., Fyer, A.J., Lipsitz, J.D., 2007. Treatment of specific phobia in adults. Clin. Psychol. Rev. 27 (3), 266–286.

Cohen, A., et al., 2016. Multi-modal virtual scenario enhances neurofeedback learning. Front. Robot. AI 3, 52.

Congedo, M., Lubar, J.F., Joffe, D., 2004. Low-resolution electromagnetic tomography neurofeedback. IEEE Trans. Neural Syst. Rehabil. Eng. 12 (4), 387–397.

de Munck, J.C., et al., 2007. The hemodynamic response of the alpha rhythm: an EEG/fMRI study. NeuroImage 35 (3), 1142–1151.

DeBettencourt, M.T., Keene, P.A., Awh, E., Vogel, E.K., 2019. Real-time triggering reveals concurrent lapses of attention and working memory. Nat. Hum. Behav. 3 (8), 808–816.

Dimeff, L.A., Koerner, K.E., 2007. Dialectical Behavior Therapy in Clinical Practice: Applications across Disorders and Settings. Guilford Press.

Domsalla, M., et al., 2014. Cerebral processing of social rejection in patients with borderline personality disorder. Soc. Cogn. Affect. Neurosci. 9 (11), 1789–1797.

Drysdale, A.T., et al., 2017. Resting-state connectivity biomarkers define neurophysiological subtypes of depression. Nat. Med. 23 (1), 28–38.

Emmert, K., et al., 2017. Continuous vs. intermittent neurofeedback to regulate auditory cortex activity of tinnitus patients using real-time fMRI – a pilot study. Neuroimage Clin. 14, 97–104.

Foa, E., Hembree, E., Rothbaum, B.O., 2007. Prolonged Exposure Therapy for PTSD: Emotional Processing of Traumatic Experiences Therapist Guide. Oxford University Press.

Fonzo, G.A., et al., 2017. PTSD psychotherapy outcome predicted by brain activation during emotional reactivity and regulation. Am. J. Psychiatry 174 (12), 1163–1174.

Fruchtman, T., et al., 2019. Feasibility and effectiveness of personalized amygdala-related neurofeedback for post-traumatic stress disorder. Psyarxiv. https://doi.org/10.31234/osf.io/qmsz3.

Gerin, M.I., 2016. Real-time fMRI Neurofeedback with war veterans with chronic PTSD: a feasibility study. Front. Psychiatry 7, 111.

Goldway, N., et al., 2019. Volitional limbic neuromodulation exerts a beneficial clinical effect on fibromyalgia. NeuroImage 186, 758–770.

Graves, A., Jaitly, N., 2014. Towards end-to-end speech recognition with recurrent neural networks. In: Proceedings of the 31st International Conference on Machine Learning (ICML-14), pp. 1764–1772.

Grech, R., et al., 2008. Review on solving the inverse problem in EEG source analysis. J. Neuroeng. Rehabil. 5 (1), 25.

Hampson, M., et al., 2012. Real-time fMRI biofeedback targeting the orbitofrontal cortex for contamination anxiety. J. Vis. Exp. 59, 3535.

Haug, T., Nordgreen, T., Öst, L.G., Havik, O.E., 2012. Self-help treatment of anxiety disorders: a meta-analysis and meta-regression of effects and potential moderators. Clin. Psychol. Rev. 32 (5), 425–445.

Haxby, J.V., et al., 2011. A common, high-dimensional model of the representational space in human ventral temporal cortex. Neuron 72 (2), 404–416.

Hofmann, S.G., Smits, J.A., 2008. Cognitive-behavioral therapy for adult anxiety disorders: a meta-analysis of randomized placebo-controlled trials. J. Clin. Psychiatry 69 (4), 621–632.

Ichikawa, N., et al., 2020. Primary functional brain connections associated with melancholic major depressive disorder and modulation by antidepressants. Sci. Rep. 10 (1), 3542.

Imeraj, L., et al., 2011. Diurnal variations in arousal: a naturalistic heart rate study in children with ADHD. Eur. Child Adolesc. Psychiatry 20 (8), 381–392.

Jacobs, R.A., Jordan, M.I., Nowlan, S.J., Hinton, G.E., 1991. Adaptive mixtures of local experts. Neural Comput. 3 (1), 79–87.

Kang, S.G., et al., 2017. Validity of a commercial wearable sleep tracker in adult insomnia disorder patients and good sleepers. J. Psychosom. Res. 97, 38–44.

Keynan, J.N., et al., 2016. Limbic activity modulation guided by functional magnetic resonance imaging-inspired electroencephalography improves implicit emotion regulation. Biol. Psychiatry 80 (6), 490–496.

Keynan, J.N., et al., 2019. Electrical fingerprint of the amygdala guides neurofeedback training for stress resilience. Nat. Hum. Behav. 3 (1), 63–73.

Kim, D.Y., et al., 2015. The inclusion of functional connectivity information into fMRI-based neurofeedback improves its efficacy in the reduction of cigarette cravings. J. Cogn. Neurosci. 27 (8), 1552–1572.

Klovatch-Podlipsky, I., Or-Borichev, A., Sar-El, R., Lubianiker, N., Hendler, T., 2016. Towards fMRI Informed EEG neurofeedback for ADHD. Front. Hum. Neurosci. https://www.frontiersin.org/10.3389/conf.fnhum.2016.220.00018/event_abstract.

Koizumi, A., et al., 2016. Fear reduction without fear through reinforcement of neural activity that bypasses conscious exposure. Nat. Hum. Behav. 1, 0006.

Koush, Y., et al., 2017. Learning control over emotion networks through connectivity-based neurofeedback. Cereb. Cortex 27 (2), 1193–1202.

Laufs, H., Daunizeau, J., Carmichael, D.W., Kleinschmidt, A., 2008. Recent advances in recording electrophysiological data simultaneously with magnetic resonance imaging. NeuroImage 40 (2), 515–528.

Lewis, C.E., et al., 2017. Internet-based guided self-help for posttraumatic stress disorder (PTSD): randomized controlled trial. Depress Anxiety 34 (6), 555–565.

Lubianiker, N., et al., 2019. Process-based framework for precise neuromodulation. Nat. Hum. Behav. 3 (5), 537.

Mantini, D., Perrucci, M.G., Del Gratta, C., Romani, G.L., Corbetta, M., 2007. Electrophysiological signatures of resting state networks in the human brain. Proc. Natl. Acad. Sci. U. S. A. 104 (32), 13170–13175.

Megumi, F., et al., 2015. Functional MRI neurofeedback training on connectivity between two regions induces long-lasting changes in intrinsic functional network. Front. Hum. Neurosci. 30 (9), 160.

Meir-Hasson, Y., 2016. Integration of different modalities to improve spatio-temporal resolution. Doctoral dissertation, Tel Aviv University.

Meir-Hasson, Y., Kinreich, S., Podlipsky, I., Hendler, T., Intrator, N., 2014. An EEG finger-print of fMRI deep regional activation. NeuroImage 102, 128–141.

Meir-Hasson, Y., et al., 2016. One-class FMRI-inspired EEG model for self-regulation training. PLoS One 11 (5), e0154968.

Meshi, O., Sontag, D., Globerson, A., Jaakkola, T.S., 2010. Learning efficiently with approximate inference via dual losses. In: Proceedings of the 27th International Conference on Machine Learning (ICML-10), pp. 783–790.

Naim, R., Kivity, Y., Bar-Haim, Y., Huppert, J.D., 2018. Attention and interpretation bias modification treatment for social anxiety disorder: a randomized clinical trial of efficacy and synergy. J. Behav. Ther. Exp. Psychiatry 59, 19–30.

Oblak, E.F., et al., 2017. Self-regulation strategy, feedback timing and hemodynamic properties modulate learning in a simulated fMRI neurofeedback environment. PLoS Comput. Biol. 13 (7), e1005681.

Osin, J., Wolf, L., Gurevitch, G., Keynan, J.N., Fruchtman-Steinbok, T., Or-Borichev, A., Hendler, T., 2020. Learning personal representations from fMRI by predicting neurofeedback performance. In: Martel, A.L., et al. (Eds.), Medical Image Computing and Computer Assisted Intervention – MICCAI 2020. Lecture Notes in Computer Science, vol 12267. Springer, Cham. https://doi.org/10.1007/978-3-030-59728-3_46

Paret, C., Ruf, M., Gerchen, M.F., Kluetsch, R., Demirakca, T., Jungkunz, M., et al., 2016. fMRI neurofeedback of amygdala response to aversive stimuli enhances prefrontal–limbic brain connectivity. NeuroImage 125, 182–188.

Ramot, M., et al., 2017. Direct modulation of aberrant brain network connectivity through real-time NeuroFeedback. elife 6, e28974.

Rance, M., et al., 2018. Time course of clinical change following neurofeedback. NeuroImage 181, 807–813.

Ratti, E., Waninger, S., Berka, C., Ruffini, G., Verma, A., 2017. Comparison of medical and consumer wireless EEG systems for use in clinical trials. Front. Hum. Neurosci. 3 (11), 398.

Sanchez-Vives, M.V., Slater, M., 2005. From presence to consciousness through virtual reality. Nat. Rev. Neurosci. 6 (4), 332–339.

Sato, M., et al., 2004. Hierarchical bayesian estimation for MEG inverse problem. NeuroImage 23 (3), 806–826.

Scheinost, D., et al., 2014. Resting state functional connectivity predicts neurofeedback response. Front. Behav. Neurosci. 8, 338.

Schmitz, A., Grillon, C., 2012. Assessing fear and anxiety in humans using the threat of predictable and unpredictable aversive events (the NPU-threat test). Nat. Protoc. 7 (3), 527–532.

Shibata, K., et al., 2019. Toward a comprehensive understanding of the neural mechanisms of decoded neurofeedback. NeuroImage 188, 539–556.

Simões, M., Abreu, R., Direito, B., Sayal, A., Castelhano, J., Carvalho, P., Castelo-Branco, M., 2020. How much of the BOLD-fMRI signal can be approximated from simultaneous EEG data: relevance for the transfer and dissemination of neurofeedback interventions J. Neural Eng. 17(4), 046007.

Sjoerds, Z., et al., 2013. Behavioral and neuroimaging evidence for overreliance on habit learning in alcohol-dependent patients. Transl. Psychiatry 3 (12), e337.

Subramanian, L., et al., 2011. Real-time functional Magnestic resonance imaging neurofeedback for treatment of Parkinson's disease. J. Neurosci. 31 (45), 16309–16317.

Sutskever, I., Vinyals, O., Le, Q.V., 2014. Sequence to sequence learning with neural networks. In: Ghahramani, Z., Welling, M., Cortes, C., Lawrence, N.D., Weinberger, K.Q. (Eds.), Advances in Neural Information Processing Systems. 27. Curran Associates Inc, pp. 3104–3112.

Takagi, T., et al., 2017. A neural marker of obsessive-compulsive disorder from whole-brain functional connectivity. Sci. Rep. 7 (1), 7538.

Taschereau-Dumouchel, V., Cortest, A., Chiba, T., Knotts, J.D., Kawato, M., Lau, H., 2018. Towards an unconscious neural reinforcement intervention for common fears. Proc. Natl. Acad. Sci. U. S. A. 115, 3470–3475.

Thayer, J.F., et al., 2012. A meta-analysis of heart rate variability and neuroimaging studies: implications for heart rate variability as a marker of stress and health. Neurosci. Biobehav. Rev. 36 (2), 747–756.

Tokuda, T., et al., 2018. Identification of depression subtypes and relevant brain regions using a data-driven approach. Sci. Rep. 8, 14082.

Valdes-Sosa, P.A., et al., 2009. Model driven EEG/fMRI fusion of brain oscillations. Hum. Brain Mapp. 30 (9), 2701–2721.

van't Hof, E., Cuijpers, P., Stein, D.J., 2009. Self-help and Internet-guided interventions in depression and anxiety disorders: a systematic review of meta-analyses. CNS Spectr. 14 (2 Suppl 3), 34–40.

Wang, R., et al., 2017. Accuracy of wrist-worn heart rate monitors. JAMA Cardiol. 2 (1), 104–106.

Watanabe, T., et al., 2018. Advances in fMRI real-time Neurofeedback: (trends in cognitive sciences 21, 997-1010, 2017). Trends Cogn. Sci. 22 (8), 738.

Wilson, G.T., Zandberg, L.J., 2012. Cognitive–behavioral guided self-help for eating disorders: effectiveness and scalability. Clin. Psychol. Rev. 32 (4), 343–357.

Yahata, N., et al., 2016. A small number of abnormal brain connections predicts adult autism spectrum disorder. Nat. Commun. 7, 11254.

Yamada, T., et al., 2017. Resting-state functional connectivity-based biomarkers and functional MRI-based neurofeedback for psychiatric disorders: a challenge for developing theranostic biomarkers. Int. J. Neuropsychopharmacol. 20 (10), 769–781.

Yamashita, A., et al., 2017. Connectivity neurofeedback training can differentially change functional connectivity and cognitive performance. Cereb. Cortex 27 (10), 4960–4970.

Yamashita, A, et al., 2019. Harmonization of resting-state functional MRI data acrossmultiple imaging sites via the separation of site differences intosampling bias and measurement bias. PLoS Biol. 17 (4). https://doi.org/10.1371/journal.pbio.3000042, e3000042.

Yamashita, A., et al., 2020. Generalizable brain network markers of major depressive disorder across multiple imaging sites. PLoS Biol. 18 (12). https://doi.org/10.1371/journal.pbio.3000966, e3000966.

Yao, J., Dewald, J.P., 2005. Evaluation of different cortical source localization methods using simulated and experimental EEG data. NeuroImage 25 (2), 369–382.

Yoshihara, Y., et al., 2020. Overlapping but asymmetrical relationships between schizophrenia and autism revealed by brain connectivity. Schizophr. Bull. 46 (5), 1210–1218. https://doi.org/10.1093/schbul/sbaa021.

Young, K.D., Zotev, V., Phillips, R., Misaki, M., Yuan, H., Drevets, W.C., Bodurka, J., 2014. Real-time FMRI neurofeedback training of amygdala activity in patients with major depressive disorder. PLoS One 9 (2), e88785.

Young, K.D., et al., 2017. Randomized clinical trial of real-time fMRI amygdala neurofeedback for major depressive disorder: effects on symptoms and autobiographical memory recall. Am. J. Psychiatry 174 (8), 748–755.

Zhao, Z., et al., 2019. Real-time functional connectivity-informed Neurofeedback of amygdala-frontal pathways reduces anxiety. Psychother. Psychosom. 88 (1), 5–15.

CHAPTER 13

Mechanisms of fMRI neurofeedback

Kazuhisa Shibata
Lab for Human Cognition and Learning, Center for Brain Science, RIKEN, Wako, Saitama, Japan

1 Introduction

What is changed in the brain as a result of fMRI neurofeedback training? Neural mechanisms of fMRI neurofeedback training have been controversial (Birbaumer et al., 2013; Hampson et al., 2019; Sitaram et al., 2017; Watanabe et al., 2017). One reason for this controversy is that there are different types of fMRI neurofeedback methods, each of which may involve different neural mechanisms. As outlined later, this chapter focuses on these mechanisms and discusses possible brain architectures that enable the induction of plastic changes at the neuronal level, which in turn manifest as changes in behavior.

First, we introduce two mechanistic models that describe how changes in brain function can yield changes in behavior as a result of fMRI neurofeedback training. The first model proposes that behavioral changes occur due to experience-dependent neural plasticity within a target brain area chosen for fMRI neurofeedback training. We call this model the targeted neural plasticity (TNP) model. The second model postulates that behavioral changes occur due to changes in modulation on a target area by other brain areas that are not used for fMRI neurofeedback training. We call this model the learned modulation (LM) model.

Second, we discuss how training using conventional fMRI neurofeedback methods leads to changes in fMRI signals and behavior. A significant characteristic of the conventional methods is the use of explicit strategies that allow participants to induce desired changes in fMRI signals of a target area (deCharms et al., 2004, 2005; Scharnowski et al., 2012; Scheinost et al., 2013). After summarizing findings about mechanisms of learning involved in conventional neurofeedback training, we conclude that behavioral changes in these explicit neurofeedback studies are likely accounted for by a combination of the TNP and LM models. However, some research groups have argued that these changes can be explained by other accounts, including the placebo effect, experimenter effect, and physiological artifacts (Thibault et al., 2016, 2017, 2018). Overall, further work is needed to narrow down the neural mechanisms that underlie fMRI neurofeedback learning in conventional training paradigms.

fMRI Neurofeedback. https://doi.org/10.1016/B978-0-12-822421-2.00004-1

Third, we describe recent methodological advances in fMRI neurofeedback and discuss how these advances have helped researchers clarify one neural mechanisms involved in fMRI neurofeedback learning. In particular, we describe a new method termed decoded neurofeedback (DecNef) (Shibata et al., 2011) that integrates three recent methodological features, including external reward, implicit neurofeedback, and fMRI multivariate analysis (Watanabe et al., 2017). DecNef allows researchers to induce a specific fMRI signal pattern in a target area without participants' awareness of the purpose of the experiment. The TNP model better explains findings by DecNef than the LM model and the other accounts, including the placebo effect, experimenter effect, and physiological artifacts. This work thus provides evidence that neurofeedback can induce learning via plasticity in the targeted area.

Fourth, we propose a neural architecture that enables synaptic plasticity at the neuronal level within a target brain area to be trained in a targeted manner by DecNef. The proposed architecture of targeted neural plasticity has the following three potential problems (Shibata et al., 2019; Watanabe et al., 2017). The first potential problem is a one-to-many correspondence between the voxel signal level (a voxel is the spatial unit of fMRI) and neuronal activity patterns. Each voxel typically represents the net activity of millions of neurons. Thus the same fMRI signal pattern can be generated from a large number of different patterns of neuronal activity. This one-to-many correspondence may prevent participants from learning to induce a desired pattern of activity at the neuronal level based on feedback of fMRI signals. The second potential problem is the limited expression of the targeted pattern during DecNef training. While target activity patterns occur in response to the presentation of specific stimuli or performance of certain tasks, during DecNef training, which does not involve these stimuli or tasks, different patterns of activity may be expressed. Such differences between the target and spontaneous activity patterns may make it difficult to train up the target activity pattern during DecNef training. The third potential problem is the computational difficulty of learning to induce a target pattern of fMRI signals within a practical number of trials during DecNef training. This problem is often called the curse of dimensionality. In a DecNef procedure, target areas typically contain hundreds of voxels, resulting in vast number of possible fMRI signal patterns. Such a number would be too large for participants to complete a search for inducing the target fMRI signal pattern within a period of DecNef training (Huang, 2016). We argue that these potential problems become unlikely by introducing biologically plausible assumptions, which are based on previous findings in neuroscience, to the proposed architecture of targeted neural plasticity (Shibata et al., 2019; Watanabe et al., 2017). We also discuss empirical and theoretical evidence that supports these assumptions.

2 Models of plasticity underlying fMRI neurofeedback training

This section aims to describe the details of two models of plasticity in association with fMRI neurofeedback training. First, we outline the closed-loop system that consists of a neurofeedback task, neural activity, and fMRI signals during training. Second, we describe the details of each of the two models.

2.1 Closed-loop neurofeedback system

Fig. 1 represents a standard closed-loop fMRI neurofeedback system. A participant engages in a neurofeedback task. In response to the task, corresponding neural activity patterns in the participant's brain should occur. Although these activity patterns at the neuronal level are not measured during fMRI neurofeedback training, the neural activity patterns are reflected in measured fMRI signals. A neurofeedback score is calculated based on the fMRI signals within a target brain area or a difference in fMRI signals between the target area and a control area outside of the target. The participant is asked to learn to regulate his/her neural activity so that induction of a desired fMRI signal is achieved. Researchers typically examine what brain areas are involved in this learning and whether a specific behavior is changed as a result of the induction of the desired fMRI signal level in the target brain area.

It is important to emphasize that a particular type of plasticity at the neuronal level should underlie the changes in behaviors after fMRI neurofeedback training. Since activity patterns at the neuronal level are not observed during fMRI neurofeedback training, there is always room for discussion regarding what is changed at the neuronal level as a result of training based on feedback calculated at the voxel level.

2.2 Two models of plasticity

Here, we introduce two models of plasticity as a result of fMRI neurofeedback training (Fig. 2). Assume that changes in neuronal activity patterns of a target brain area lead to corresponding behavioral changes. Such neuronal changes, if any, can occur due to plasticity

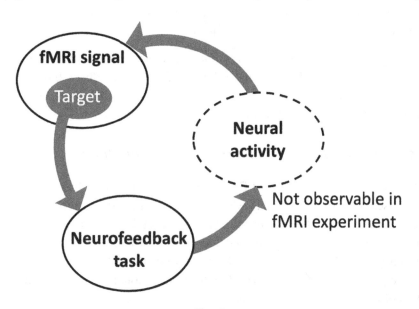

Fig. 1
Closed-loop fMRI neurofeedback system.

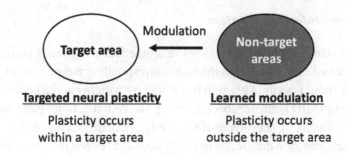

Fig. 2
Two models of plasticity underlying fMRI neurofeedback learning.

of the neurons within the area. However, the same changes can occur without any plasticity within the area; changes in modulation on the target area by other nontarget areas should be able to lead to the same changes. Thus there are at least two different models that account for behavioral changes due to fMRI neurofeedback training.

The first model proposes that fMRI neurofeedback training results in experience-dependent synaptic plasticity at the neuronal level within a target area (Fig. 2, left). Changes in behavior are observed as a result of this synaptic plasticity in the target area. We call this model the targeted neural plasticity (TNP) model. The TNP model does not consider neural plasticity outside the target area.

On the other hand, the second model assumes neural plasticity in other areas outside the target area, but not in the target area (Fig. 2, right). In this model, changes in behaviors are accounted for by changes in modulation on the target area by the other nontarget areas. We call this model the learned modulation (LM) model.

Note that the TNP and LM models are not mutually exclusive. Thus either or a combination of the two models can be used to explain results of fMRI neurofeedback training. In the subsequent two sections, we summarize the existing results of fMRI neurofeedback studies and describe how the TNP and LM models capture the results.

3 Plasticity mechanisms based on conventional methods

In this section, we summarize results of fMRI neurofeedback studies based on conventional methods and discuss how the TNP and LM models account for the results. First, we outline the common characteristics of the conventional methods and major findings based on the methods. Second, we review studies that addressed how learning to induce desired fMRI signals is achieved during training. Third, we argue that TNP and LM models comprehensively explain the findings based on the conventional methods. Finally, we mention the limitation of the conventional methods.

3.1 Common characteristics of conventional methods and findings

One major characteristic of the conventional methods is the use of explicit strategy (Watanabe et al., 2017). Explicit strategy refers to guidance or instructions for participants to improve performance on a neurofeedback task. In a typical study, participants are informed of the purpose of training, what the neurofeedback score represents, what brain function is to be trained, and/or what behavioral changes are expected to occur (deCharms et al., 2004, 2005; Scharnowski et al., 2012; Scheinost et al., 2013).

Another major characteristic of the conventional methods is that a neurofeedback score reflects the mean fMRI signal amplitude across voxels in a target brain area. Some studies calculated the mean change in the fMRI signal amplitudes during a neurofeedback task (Scharnowski et al., 2012). Other studies calculated a difference of the mean changes in fMRI signal amplitudes between a target area and a control area (Bray et al., 2007; deCharms et al., 2004, 2005; Scheinost et al., 2013).

Here we review the study by deCharms and colleagues (deCharms et al., 2005) since this is a pioneering fMRI neurofeedback experiment that showed changes in both fMRI signals and behavior by fMRI neurofeedback training. The experiment aimed to alter pain sensation by fMRI neurofeedback training. Mean fMRI signal amplitude within a target area was trained and explicit strategies were employed in the experiment. During training, neurofeedback scores represented the mean fMRI signal amplitude of voxels within the rostral anterior cingulate cortex (rACC). rACC is known to be involved in pain perception and regulation.

With the aim of effective control of fMRI signals in rACC during training, specific types of explicit strategies were given to participants. These explicit strategies included attentional control and voluntary facilitation/suppression of pain sensation. During training, each participant was presented with nociceptive stimuli that evoked a certain level of pain sensation. Participants were asked to use these strategies during a neurofeedback task and achieve better control of the feedback signals that reflected the mean fMRI signal amplitude of rACC.

The neurofeedback task was to increase and decrease neurofeedback scores based on a time course of neurofeedback scores presented on a visual display. Participants were asked to learn to regulate their neural activity so that the difference of the neurofeedback scores between the increase and decrease periods would be enhanced. The effects of this training on fMRI signals were evaluated by comparing the differences in signal amplitudes between the last phase of training and the initial phase of training.

Participants were also asked to rate a perceived level of pain evoked by the nociceptive stimuli during each of the increase and decrease periods. The effects of fMRI neurofeedback training on pain ratings were evaluated by comparing the difference of the ratings between the increase and decrease periods in the final phase with that in the initial phase.

deCharms and colleagues found significant effects of fMRI neurofeedback training on both fMRI signal amplitudes within rACC and participants' pain sensation in the final run of training. In addition to rACC, significant effects on mean fMRI signal amplitudes were found in other nontarget areas, including the secondary somatosensory cortex, insula, supplementary motor cortex, superior temporal gyrus, and cerebellum, possibly representing engagement of other regions that were being used more to modulate the target area, as would be hypothesized by the LM model. Consistent with the successful learning of control over the mean fMRI signal amplitude in rACC, effects of training on the pain ratings were also significant at the final run of training. They also reported that a similar fMRI neurofeedback training on rACC resulted in a decrease in chronic pain in patients.

It is important to note that proper neurofeedback scores were necessary to obtain the significant effects of training on both fMRI signals and pain ratings. Similar training without fMRI signals, using fMRI signals from a nontarget area, or using sham fMRI signals derived from a different participant failed to lead to such effects. The results of the control experiments suggest that the neurofeedback scores calculated based on the mean fMRI signal amplitude of voxels in rACC play a crucial role in the successful control of rACC activations and changes in pain sensation.

Many studies using the conventional methods have found similar results (Scharnowski et al., 2012; Subramanian et al., 2011). Among these studies, the following common findings have been observed. First, some areas other than target areas showed activation changes during fMRI neurofeedback training. Second, changes were observed in behavioral and cognitive functions which were related to explicit strategies used during training. Third, the use of pseudo neurofeedback scores failed to lead to changes in behavior and fMRI signals. More recently, significant behavioral and fMRI activation changes were reported by experiments that employed a double-blind procedure in which both participants and experimenters who did clinical ratings (or had other critical interactions with patients) had no information about what experimental condition and/or group each participant was assigned to (Hamilton et al., 2016; Sukhodolsky et al., 2020; Young et al., 2017). These findings refute the possibility that effects of fMRI neurofeedback training simply reflect experimental artifacts such as the placebo effect (Thibault et al., 2017) and experimenter effect (Kennedy and Taddonio, 1976).

3.2 Mechanisms of activation induction in the conventional neurofeedback studies

Recent fMRI neurofeedback studies have reported that various brain areas are implicated in activation induction based on conventional neurofeedback training (Emmert et al., 2016; Skottnik et al., 2019). These brain areas have been implicated in different aspects of activation induction, including feedback monitoring, control of activation, and learning. During feedback monitoring in which a neurofeedback signal or reward is given to participants, multiple brain areas including the thalamus, ventromedial prefrontal cortex (PFC), rostral

PFC, insula, cingulate cortices, and striatum are engaged (Paret et al., 2018; Radua et al., 2018; Ramot et al., 2016; Sitaram et al., 2017). When participants are exerting effort to control their brain activations, the lateral PFC, posterior parietal cortex, insula, anterior cingulate cortex (ACC), and ventral striatum often show increased activations (Paret et al., 2018; Sitaram et al., 2017). These findings suggest that activation induction via conventional neurofeedback training is supported by neural mechanisms that involve distributed brain networks including both cortical and subcortical areas.

What is a computational principle that underlies induction learning based on the conventional methods? A variety of principles have been proposed (Birbaumer et al., 2013; Sitaram et al., 2017). Here, we specifically focus on the following two principles which are related to discussions in the later sections (see Sitaram et al., 2017 for a detailed summary). First, induction learning can occur based on operant conditioning or reinforcement learning of certain fMRI signals shaped by neurofeedback scores or reward (Bray et al., 2007; Caria, 2016; Radua et al., 2018). Second, neurofeedback scores can be used to find a better explicit strategy that leads to desired fMRI signals in a target area (Lee et al., 2019). These two principles are not mutually exclusive, but give different predictions. The former predicts that mere pairing of a certain brain activation and reward is sufficient for induction learning to occur (and indeed it is sufficient; see Ramot et al., 2016). The latter requires awareness of being trained during fMRI neurofeedback and an active search for an explicit strategy which gives a better outcome to the participant. It is likely that both play a role in the learning induced in conventional neurofeedback studies.

In the next section, we discuss how behavioral changes in conventional neurofeedback studies are accounted for by the TNP and LM models.

3.3 How TNP and LM models explain the findings in conventional neurofeedback studies

Behavioral changes in conventional neurofeedback studies are consistent with the LM and TNP models, and may involve a combination of both forms of learning. As previously described, the LM model assumes changes in modulation on a target area by other nontarget areas at the neuronal level. The TNP model postulates that neural plasticity in a target area is manifested as changes in fMRI signal patterns over the course of training that are localized within the target area.

In the LM model, behavioral changes can be accounted for by learned modulation on a target function (e.g., pain sensation in deCharms et al., 2005) by other functions, including attention and imagery (Lee et al., 2019), rather than direct alteration of the target function itself. Thus the LM model predicts changes in activation and connectivity in nontarget areas as a result of the fMRI neurofeedback training. Such changes in the nontarget areas have been observed in some neurofeedback studies based on the conventional methods (deCharms et al., 2005; Scheinost et al., 2013; Yoo et al., 2008). However, this is not definitive evidence for the LM model: the changes in the nontarget areas are not inconsistent with the TNP model as changes in the target area activity patterns could result in downstream alterations of other areas. Thus it seems likely, but has not been definitively demonstrated, that in conventional neurofeedback training studies, participants learn to use areas outside the target region to exert better cognitive control based on neurofeedback scores calculated from fMRI signals in a target area.

Since TNP and LM models are not mutually exclusive, neural plasticity in the target region may occur in addition to learned modulation of the region by other nontarget areas in conventional neurofeedback studies. However, additional evidence is necessary to support TNP models. In the example of deCharms et al. (2005), participants employed explicit strategies related to attentional control and voluntary facilitation/suppression of pain sensation. Thus one cannot tell whether changes in pain sensation derived from stronger suppression by attention (consistent with the LM model) or changes in the representation of pain within rACC (consistent with the TNP model).

How can we test the contributions of TNP and LM learning in the context of the conventional methods? One potentially promising way is to introduce pre- and posttraining stages in which fMRI signals are measured without the involvement of the explicit strategies used during fMRI neurofeedback training. In the case of deCharms et al. (deCharms et al., 2005), if representation of pain sensation within rACC is indeed changed by training, these changes should be reflected in fMRI responses of rACC voxels to passive exposure to the nociceptive stimuli without the involvement of the explicit strategies in the posttest stage, compared to the those in the pretest stage. Such addition of the passive condition has successfully dissociated fMRI signal changes related to sensory representation from those changes due to improved processing of a trained task in the field of perceptual learning (Shibata et al., 2012, 2016a). One may argue that participants come to use the trained strategies unconsciously after enough training on fMRI neurofeedback. If this is the case, the LM model may still account for behavioral changes. However, such unconscious cognitive control likely involves certain brain areas related to the cognitive control (van Gaal et al., 2010). Thus the implicit use of the trained strategy may induce activation changes in some areas outside a target area that should be apparent in the imaging data collected during the passive posttest condition. For these reasons, the introduction of the passive condition should help researchers test the TNP and LM models in studies based on the conventional methods.

3.4 Limitations of the conventional methods

One limitation of the conventional method arises from the use of the mean fMRI signal amplitude within a target area. It has been found that each of the different fMRI signal patterns of voxels within a visual area can represent individual perceptual features such as specific orientations and motion directions (Haynes and Rees, 2006; Kamitani and Tong, 2005, 2006). At the same time, the mean response amplitudes of the region as a whole to the individual features are highly similar or the same. In these situations, feedback based on the mean amplitude of a region cannot be used to train specific perceptual features. A similar issue may exist when training cognitive or emotional traits: if the desired traits are represented by the pattern of activity within a region rather than the mean activity of the region, then training mean activity cannot alter the desired traits.

Another major limitation of the conventional methods is the ambiguity of the relationships between changes in fMRI signals of a target area and behavior. It is unclear whether observed behavioral changes, if any, reflect plastic changes within the area and/or changes in modulation on the area by other nontarget areas. This limitation arises mainly from the use of explicit strategies, as described before. This limitation of the conventional method may be less crucial if the purpose of a study is to induce changes in behavior. As long as one can obtain robust and reliable outcomes, the underlying mechanisms may not be of particular interest. On the other hand, the limitation becomes a serious shortcoming for studies that aim to clarify the function of a target area based on fMRI neurofeedback.

We discuss next recent methods that potentially deal with these limitations.

4 Plasticity mechanisms based on recent methods

This section aims to review recent methods in fMRI neurofeedback and discuss how training based on these methods leads to neural plasticity in a target area. First, we describe three recent methodological advances, namely implicit neurofeedback, fMRI multivariate analysis, and external reward (Watanabe et al., 2017). Second, we introduce a new method, termed decoded neurofeedback (DecNef), that integrates the three methodological advances (Shibata et al., 2011). Third, we argue that changes in behavior and fMRI signals in DecNef studies are explained by the TNP model but not by the LM model or by placebo effects, experimenter effects, or physiological artifacts.

4.1 Recent methodological advances

4.1.1 Implicit neurofeedback

Implicit neurofeedback is a method that provides participants with no explicit instructions to improve performance in a neurofeedback task (Watanabe et al., 2017). This implicit neurofeedback is different from the conventional way in which participants are provided with explicit strategies to regulate their fMRI signals effectively. In fMRI neurofeedback training, participants are expected to learn to induce fMRI signals that match a predetermined criterion. In the case of implicit neurofeedback, participants received no explicit instruction or guidance. They are merely asked to make efforts to achieve better neurofeedback scores, without being informed of the purpose of the experiment, how the criterion has been determined, or how to match induced fMRI signals to the criterion. Recent studies have indicated that fMRI neurofeedback training using implicit neurofeedback leads to significant changes in fMRI signals in target areas and specific behaviors (Amano et al., 2016; Cortese et al., 2016, 2017; Koizumi et al., 2016; Ramot et al., 2016; Sepulveda et al., 2016; Shibata et al., 2011, 2016b; Taschereau-Dumouchel et al., 2018).

Implicit neurofeedback has several advantages and/or novel features compared to the conventional neurofeedback methods (Watanabe et al., 2017). First, implicit neurofeedback reduces or eliminates the possibility that the changes in behavior and fMRI activity patterns occur due to neural plasticity involved in the specific intention of participants to improve the behavior. In implicit neurofeedback, while participants are aware of the presence of neurofeedback scores, they are unaware of what the feedback scores represent. Thus the modified behavior can be more confidently attributed to a target area during training. Second, implicit neurofeedback decreases the possibility of the so-called experimenter effect in which participants consciously or unconsciously learn how to produce results that they think would meet the expectations of the experimenter (see Section 4.3 for more details).

Although studies using implicit neurofeedback have demonstrated robust effects (Amano et al., 2016; Cortese et al., 2016, 2017; Koizumi et al., 2016; Shibata et al., 2011, 2016b; Taschereau-Dumouchel et al., 2018), it remains unclear whether implicit neurofeedback is more effective than training with explicit strategies. One study showed a case in which implicit neurofeedback was qualitatively (although not significantly) more effective than neurofeedback training with relevant explicit strategies at enabling regulation of fMRI signals in a brain area (Sepulveda et al., 2016). However, this study did not investigate resultant behavioral measures. Systematic comparisons of the effects of implicit and explicit neurofeedback training approaches on fMRI signals and behaviors will be necessary to clarify this issue.

4.1.2 fMRI multivariate analysis

An fMRI multivariate analysis enables one to extract or decode certain information from fMRI signal patterns (Watanabe et al., 2017). For example, a multivariate analysis allowed researchers to identify a visual grating orientation that was presented to a participant among different orientations based on fMRI signal patterns in the visual cortex with high accuracy (Haynes and Rees, 2006; Kamitani and Tong, 2005). The introduction of multivariate analysis to fMRI neurofeedback has made it possible to obtain information about fMRI signal patterns in a target area in real time (deBettencourt et al., 2015; La Conte et al., 2007). One advantage of the use of multivariate analysis is that multivariate analysis enables neurofeedback scores to contain increased and more spatially sensitive information regarding fMRI signal patterns than the mean fMRI signal amplitude of the area does, as in the conventional methods (Section 3.1).

4.1.3 External reward

In most conventional fMRI neurofeedback studies, neurofeedback scores are provided to participants in the form of visual or auditory stimuli that are not associated with any external reward (deCharms et al., 2004, 2005; Johnson et al., 2012; Scharnowski et al., 2012; Subramanian et al., 2011; Weiskopf et al., 2003). In this case, feedback scores may work as a signal which provides information for better control of fMRI signals in a target area and gives an internal sense of achievement or internal reward (Gaume et al., 2016).

In addition to the neurofeedback scores, it has been shown that external reward is effective for induction learning to occur (Bray et al., 2007; Shibata et al., 2011). In particular, one fMRI neurofeedback study showed that repetitive pairing of an external reward such as money and specific patterns of fMRI signals can lead to modification of brain networks (Ramot et al., 2016). Importantly, during this neurofeedback experiment participants had no awareness of being trained. Thus the network changes cannot be accounted for by the internal sense of achievement or internal reward. These results demonstrate that external reward is another driving force for neurofeedback learning.

Does the combined use of neurofeedback scores and external reward make fMRI neurofeedback training more efficient than either one does? Recent fMRI neurofeedback studies provided participants with both neurofeedback scores and monetary reward (Watanabe et al., 2017). These studies have robustly caused changes in behaviors and fMRI signals in target areas. It is possible that a combination of neurofeedback scores and external rewards enhances the effects of fMRI neurofeedback training to a greater degree than neurofeedback scores or external rewards alone. A previous study (Sepulveda et al., 2016) reported that participants were better at regulating when neurofeedback scores were paired with monetary rewards than during fMRI neurofeedback training with feedback scores alone. Thus an external reward can work as an additional reinforcing factor during fMRI neurofeedback training.

4.2 Decoded neurofeedback

We have reviewed the three methodological advances in fMRI neurofeedback: implicit neurofeedback, fMRI multivariate analysis, and external rewards (Shibata et al., 2019; Watanabe et al., 2017). Recently, these methodological advances have been integrated into a new method, termed decoded neurofeedback (or DecNef) (Shibata et al., 2011). DecNef enables the induction of a target fMRI signal pattern associated with a specific behavioral function without participants' awareness of the purpose of an experiment or what the target fMRI signal pattern represents. In this section, we describe a typical procedure for DecNef studies and common results that have been obtained based on DecNef.

4.2.1 An example procedure of DecNef

In general, fMRI experiments in DecNef studies consist of the following two stages: decoder construction and induction stages (Fig. 3A). Following, each of the two stages will be described by taking the first DecNef study (Shibata et al., 2011) as an example.

The first DecNef study aimed to test whether the early visual cortex is capable of leading to visual perceptual learning of a primary visual feature such as orientation. Hereafter, we call this study "orientation DecNef study." In the orientation DecNef study, the early visual cortex (including primary and secondary visual areas), which is known to be involved in the processing of orientation (Hubel et al., 1978), was selected as a target area. During DecNef training, one specific orientation among three different orientations was selected as a target orientation for each participant. Before and after DecNef training, performance in a discrimination task on each of the three orientations was measured to test if perceptual learning of the target orientation occurred as a result of DecNef training.

The purpose of the decoder construction stage (Fig. 3B) was to construct a decoder that classifies an fMRI signal pattern of the early visual cortex to one of the three orientations based on an fMRI multivariate analysis. Participants were exposed to each of the three orientations in an MRI scanner, and fMRI signal patterns in the early visual cortex were measured. Based on the measured fMRI signal patterns and corresponding orientations, a

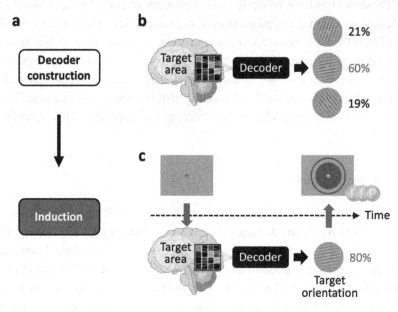

Fig. 3

A typical fMRI procedure for DecNef studies. (A) Two stages in fMRI experiments for DecNef studies. (B) Schematic of the decoder construction stage in Shibata et al. (2011). (C) Schematic of the induction stage in Shibata et al. (2011).

machine learning algorithm (Yamashita et al., 2008) computed a set of decoder weights for voxels in the early visual cortex to classify the fMRI signal patterns into one of the three orientations. After the decoder weights were computed, an output of the decoder represented a likelihood of each of the three orientations given an fMRI signal pattern in the early visual cortex. An fMRI signal pattern corresponding to the target orientation was defined as the target fMRI signal pattern.

In the induction stage (Fig. 3C), participants underwent ten days of DecNef training to increase the neurofeedback score. In this stage, a measured fMRI signal pattern in the early visual cortex was input to the orientation decoder constructed in the prior decoder construction stage in real time. The decoder output represented a likelihood of the target orientation. A disk was presented to participants, and the size of the disk reflected the likelihood. Participants were instructed to make the size of the disk as large as possible. They were also told that an additional amount of monetary reward would be provided based on the mean size of the disk on each day of DecNef training.

After the entire DecNef procedure, a questionnaire was administered. This questionnaire aimed to test if participants were aware of the purpose of the study and what the target pattern represented during the DecNef training.

4.2.2 Common results of DecNef studies

Following, we summarize four common results of DecNef studies (Shibata et al., 2019; Watanabe et al., 2017).

First, participants successfully learned to induce a target fMRI signal pattern in a target area (Amano et al., 2016; Cortese et al., 2016, 2017; Koizumi et al., 2016; Shibata et al., 2011, 2016b; Taschereau-Dumouchel et al., 2018). In the orientation DecNef study (Shibata et al., 2011), DecNef training significantly increased the likelihood of the target orientation in the early visual cortex. As described in Section 3.2, induction learning by the conventional methods can be accounted for by at least two different principles: reinforcement learning and search for a better explicit strategy. However, the latter is not able to explain induction learning with DecNef because participants are unaware of the purpose of the experiment and not provided with explicit strategies during DecNef training (see the later part of this section for more details). Thus induction learning with DecNef most likely occurs via reinforcement learning (see Shibata et al., 2019 for detailed discussion).

Second, the induction of a target fMRI signal pattern was mostly confined to the target area (Amano et al., 2016; Cortese et al., 2016, 2017; Koizumi et al., 2016; Shibata et al., 2011, 2016b; Taschereau-Dumouchel et al., 2018). To test whether induction of the target pattern occurred in a location-specific manner, researchers have used a method termed leak analysis based on the following logic. During DecNef training, the size of a disk is based on the similarity between a current fMRI signal pattern and the target fMRI signal pattern in a target area. However, this procedure alone does not ensure that the induction of the target fMRI signal pattern is confined to the target area. In concert with the successful induction of the target pattern in the target area, fMRI signal patterns representing a target stimulus or internal state may occur in some other areas outside the target area during DecNef training. If the target pattern in the target area "leaked out" and induced the patterns representing the target stimulus or state in other areas, the fMRI signal pattern in those areas should be able to reconstruct the information related to the target patterns in the target area. In the orientation DecNef study (Shibata et al., 2011), the results of the leak analysis showed that fMRI signal patterns outside the early visual cortex during DecNef training were not informative to estimate the likelihood of a target orientation computed from fMRI signal patterns within the early visual cortex. This result suggests that orientation-related information did not leak from the early visual cortex to other areas outside the early visual cortex during DecNef training.

Third, DecNef training induces a specific behavioral change (Amano et al., 2016; Cortese et al., 2016, 2017; Koizumi et al., 2016; Shibata et al., 2011, 2016b; Taschereau-Dumouchel et al., 2018). In the orientation DecNef study (Shibata et al., 2011), participants' sensitivity was specifically improved for the target orientation, but not for the other nontarget orientations.

Fourth, participants are primarily unaware of the purpose of experiments and what neurofeedback scores represent during DecNef training (Amano et al., 2016; Cortese et al., 2016, 2017; Koizumi et al., 2016; Shibata et al., 2011, 2016b; Taschereau-Dumouchel et al., 2018). In the orientation DecNef study (Shibata et al., 2011), the following results of the postexperiment questionnaire revealed that participants were unaware of the target orientation. First, strategies that participants employed during DecNef training were not related to orientation. Second, even after participants were informed of the general purpose of the experiment, their performance in the identification of the target orientation among the three orientations was not significantly different from chance. These results demonstrate that DecNef changes participants' behavior in a targeted fashion without participants' knowledge of what is being learned.

4.3 Mechanisms of behavioral changes by DecNef

We argue that the TNP model explains the behavioral changes based on DecNef, but the LM model does not. We also refute other accounts, including the placebo effect, experimenter effect, and physiological artifacts as possible explanations for the results of DecNef studies.

The characteristics and results of DecNef studies are best explained by the TNP model (Shibata et al., 2019). As described in Section 4.2, DecNef provides the experimental framework to induce a specific fMRI signal pattern within a target area without participants' awareness of what is being learned. The results of DecNef have shown that participants indeed succeeded in learning to induce such fMRI signal patterns. As a result of repetitive induction of the target fMRI signal pattern, specific behavioral changes corresponding to the induced fMRI signal patterns occurred. The induction of the target fMRI signal pattern was largely confined to the target area. All of these procedures and results are consistent with the TNP model in which neural plasticity within the target area due to fMRI neurofeedback training is manifested as corresponding behavioral changes.

On the other hand, the LM model is not supported by the characteristics and results of DecNef studies for the following reasons (Shibata et al., 2019). First, the results of DecNef consistently showed location-specific induction of a target fMRI signal pattern confined to a target area. This location specificity is inconsistent with the LM model's prediction of the involvement of nontarget areas. Second, participants did not employ a specific explicit strategy to improve neurofeedback scores during DecNef training. Thus it is unlikely that changes in behavior occurred due to changes in cognitive control, including attention and imagery.

The other accounts, such as the placebo effect, experimenter effect, and physiological artifacts, do not explain the DecNef results (Shibata et al., 2019). A research group has suggested that changes in behaviors and fMRI signals reported in conventional fMRI neurofeedback studies may be explained by placebo effects (Schabus et al., 2017; Thibault et al., 2017, 2018). In conventional fMRI neurofeedback studies, participants were provided with explicit strategies that enabled them to effectively regulate fMRI signals in a target area (deCharms et al., 2004, 2005; Scharnowski et al., 2012; Scheinost et al., 2013). Under such experimental settings, various factors, including the placebo effect, may influence behaviors and fMRI signals (Schabus et al., 2017; Thibault et al., 2017, 2018). However, the placebo effect is unlikely to occur in DecNef studies as participants remain unaware of the purpose of the experiments. They are also unlikely to consciously or unconsciously learn how to produce results that would meet their perceived expectations of what the experimenter wants as they have no idea what the experimenter intends. More recently, it has been shown that DecNef findings can be replicated with a double-blind procedure (Taschereau-Dumouchel et al., 2018). This result further decreases the possibility that the placebo and experimenter effects account for the results of DecNef.

Do physiological artifacts such as respiration, which influences fMRI signals (Thibault et al., 2018), account for the results of DecNef? Cardiorespiratory changes are known to cause a global increase or decrease in fMRI signal amplitudes (Abbott et al., 2005; Kastrup et al., 1999) and connectivity changes among brain areas (Weiss et al., 2020). However, the cardiorespiratory artifact is highly unlikely to explain the DecNef results (Shibata et al., 2019). DecNef induces a fine-grained fMRI signal pattern in a target area. The induction of such fine-grained and localized fMRI signal patterns cannot be caused by cardiorespiratory regulation that leads to global changes in fMRI signal amplitudes. Besides, a cardiorespiratory artifact is unlikely to cause precise behavioral changes, including the increased sensitivity to a specific target orientation (Shibata et al., 2011).

5 Proposed neural mechanisms of targeted neural plasticity

What are the neural architectures that enable targeted neural plasticity? In Section 4, we argued that the results of DecNef are best explained by the TNP model in which synaptic plasticity at the neuronal level in a target area is manifested as behavioral changes. However, the neural architectures of the TNP model are yet to be elucidated (Shibata et al., 2019). In this section, we first introduce a possible neural architecture of targeted neural plasticity. Second, we describe three potential problems involved in the architecture. Third, we argue that these problems are resolved by two assumptions derived from previous findings in neuroscience. Finally, we review recent empirical and computational evidence that supports the validity of the proposed architecture.

5.1 Neuronal-level architecture of the TNP model

A possible architecture of the TNP model is shown in Fig. 4 (Shibata et al., 2019). According to the TNP model, behavioral and fMRI signal changes in a target area occur as a result of DecNef training, as follows. First, a specific pattern of activity at the neuronal level is induced within the target area in response to a neurofeedback task. The induced activity pattern is reflected in fMRI signal pattern at the voxel level in the area. A decoder calculates

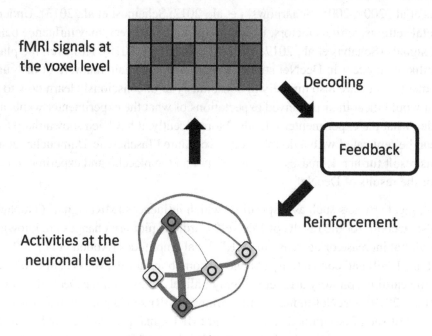

Fig. 4

A proposed architecture of targeted neural plasticity. *Adapted with permission from Shibata, K., Lisi, G., Cortese, A., Watanabe, T., Sasaki, Y., Kawato, M., 2019. Toward a comprehensive understanding of the neural mechanisms of decoded neurofeedback. NeuroImage 188, 539–556.*

a likelihood of a target stimulus/internal state of participants, and the likelihood is converted into a feedback score which is in turn fed back to the participants. The feedback score and corresponding external reward generate a reinforcement signal in the brain, which modulates synaptic plasticity of neurons involved in the target activity pattern at the neuronal level.

5.2 Three potential problems and solutions

There are three potential problems involved in this architecture (Shibata et al., 2019; Watanabe et al., 2017). The first potential problem is a one-to-many correspondence between voxel-level signal level and neuronal activity patterns in the voxel. The second potential problem is the differences between evoked and spontaneous neural activities. The third potential problem is the computational difficulty of learning to induce a target fMRI signal pattern within a practical number of trials during DecNef training. This problem is often called the curse of dimensionality. Following, we describe the details and solutions to these problems.

5.2.1 One-to-many correspondence

Fig. 5 illustrates a one-to-many correspondence between the voxel and neuronal levels (Watanabe et al., 2017). Each voxel typically represents the net activity of hundreds of thousands of neurons. Thus the same fMRI signal pattern can be generated from a large number of different patterns of neuronal activity. This potential one-to-many correspondence leads to a serious concern in DecNef training for the following reasons.

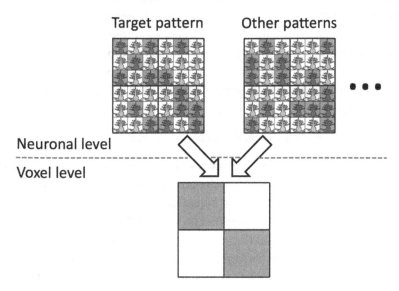

Fig. 5

Schematic of one-to-many correspondence between the neuronal and voxel levels. *Adapted with permission from Watanabe, T., Sasaki, Y., Shibata, K., Kawato, M., 2017. Advances in fMRI real-time neurofeedback. Trends Cogn. Sci. 21, 997–1010.*

In the orientation DecNef study (Shibata et al., 2011), a target fMRI signal pattern which represents a target orientation was identified during the decoder construction stage (see Section 4.2.1). In the decoder construction stage, the target fMRI signal pattern should reflect a target neuronal activity pattern that represents the target orientation since the target fMRI signal pattern occurred in response to the presentation of the orientation (Fig. 5, left). On the other hand, during the induction stage no orientation stimulus was presented. In this case, the induction of the target fMRI signal pattern may not reflect the target neuronal activity pattern, but some other patterns related to nonorientation processing (Fig. 5, right). This potential ill-posed problem has prompted some researchers to postulate that induction of a target fMRI signal pattern at the voxel level does not induce a specific target activity pattern at the neuronal level (Huang, 2016).

However, this potential ill-posed problem caused by the one-to-many correspondence is unlikely to occur (Watanabe et al., 2017). Some principles of brain processing have recently shown to function as constraints to resolve or loosen the one-to-many correspondence issue. Neuronal activity patterns do not occur randomly because of abundant synaptic connections among neurons (Blumenfeld et al., 2006; Goldberg et al., 2004). Physiological studies have shown that spontaneous activities of neurons in a brain area are strongly correlated, and therefore, activity patterns are constrained on a low-dimensional manifold (Berkes et al., 2011; Kenet et al., 2003; Luczak et al., 2009; Mochol et al., 2015; Oby et al., 2019; Renart et al., 2010; Ringach, 2009; Sadtler et al., 2014). If activities at the neuronal level are constrained on such low-dimensional manifold, fMRI signal patterns should also be constrained on a low-dimensional manifold at the voxel level. This is because the relationship between signals at the neuronal and voxel levels is almost linear, at least under a certain environment (Logothetis and Wandell, 2004; Logothetis et al., 2001). These constraints would make the ill-posed problem due to the one-to-many correspondence unlikely. The assumption of the low dimensionality enables the induction of target activities at the neuronal level based on neurofeedback scores computed at the voxel level.

5.2.2 Differences between evoked and spontaneous activity patterns

Another potential problem is possible differences between neuronal activity patterns evoked by specific stimuli and tasks during the decoder construction stage and neuronal activity induced by a neurofeedback task during the induction stage in a target area (Shibata et al., 2019). According to the DecNef procedure (Section 4.2.1), target activity patterns at the neuronal level in the target area should be determined based on specific events such as exposure to sensory stimuli and the performance of tasks during the decoder construction stage. On the other hand, during DecNef training in the induction stage, participants are not presented with the stimuli or asked to perform the tasks. If the target neuronal activity patterns do not overlap with neuronal activity patterns that initially occur in the induction stage, the brain should not easily be able to increase the contributions of the target neuronal activity patterns in the target area during DecNef training (Sadtler et al., 2014). Thus the target activity patterns must be already present in the activities of neurons in a target area from the beginning of the induction stage.

Importantly, the results of recent physiological studies suggest an overlap between spontaneous neuronal activity patterns and activity patterns evoked by the presentation of sensory stimuli or performance of certain tasks (Luczak et al., 2009; Sadtler et al., 2014). Fig. 6 outlines the relationship between spontaneous and evoked activity patterns at the neuronal level (Luczak et al., 2009). This figure has the following two important implications. First, activity patterns at the neuronal level are constrained to a low dimensional manifold, as discussed in Section 5.2.1. A space that spontaneous activity patterns account for (spont in Fig. 6) is much smaller than an activity space in which correlational structures among neurons are artificially removed (shuffled in Fig. 6). Second, evoked activity patterns are included in the spontaneous activity space. Sadtler et al. have reported that animals more effectively learn to induce target activity patterns at the neuronal level when the target activity patterns are included in a repertoire of activity patterns of those neurons at the beginning of training (Sadtler et al., 2014). Thus to enable efficient learning to induce target neuronal activity patterns, it is reasonable to assume that those patterns are included in the repertoire of spontaneous activity patterns present at the beginning of DecNef training.

5.2.3 Curse of dimensionality

The curse of dimensionality in DecNef is the problem that a space of potential fMRI signal patterns of voxels in a target area is too large for the brain to discover an efficient solution

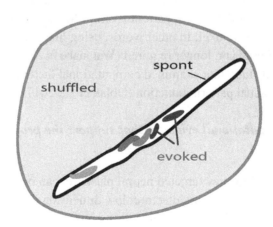

Fig. 6

Schematic relationships between spontaneous and evoked activity patterns at the neuronal level.
Adapted with permission from Luczak, A., Barthó, P., Harris, K.D., 2009. Spontaneous events outline the realm of possible sensory responses in neocortical populations. Neuron 62, 413–425.

within a practical number of trials during training because the search space is excessively high dimensional (Huang, 2016). Target areas for DecNef training typically contained a few hundreds of voxels. Assume that a target area contains 100 voxels, and each voxel takes a value of zero (inactivated) or one (activated). In this case, the maximum number of fMRI signal patterns would become 2^{100}. However, in the DecNef studies, participants often showed significant induction learning within a few hundred trials (Amano et al., 2016; Shibata et al., 2011, 2016b), indicating DecNef far outperforms expected learning for a scenario where the full space of patterns must be explored. In short, the curse of dimensionality does not appear to apply to DecNef.

How is it possible to circumvent the curse of dimensionality in the framework of the proposed architecture of the TNP model? The above-mentioned low-dimensionality assumption can address this issue. If activities at the neuronal level are constrained on a low-dimensional manifold, fMRI signal patterns should also be constrained on a low-dimensional manifold. Then, the curse of dimensionality should not be a problem since the number of possible fMRI signal patterns is substantially reduced (Watanabe et al., 2017).

In addition to the low dimensionality assumption, another reason why the curse of dimensionality should not apply to DecNef has been identified (Watanabe et al., 2017). In DecNef studies, outputs of decoders are calculated based on either a linear summation of voxel activations multiplied by weights (Shibata et al., 2016b) or a linear summation plus an additional transformation using a sigmoid function (Amano et al., 2016; Cortese et al., 2016, 2017; Koizumi et al., 2016; Shibata et al., 2011; Taschereau-Dumouchel et al., 2018). Thus the decoders have monotonically increasing functions for each voxel as that voxel approaches its target activity level. Therefore it is possible to calculate an appropriate error signal for each voxel from the decoder output. Thus, using these decoders, reinforcement learning to induce a specific fMRI signal pattern is simplified to learning to induce a certain fMRI signal amplitude in each voxel. In other words, using linear decoders, the search for inducing the specific pattern is no longer required (Watanabe et al., 2017). This argument has been validated in a recent study that examined computational factors that impact successful learning of target fMRI signal pattern induction (Oblak et al., 2017).

5.3 Empirical and computational evidence that support the proposed architecture of the TNP model

As discussed before, it is clear how targeted neural plasticity can occur if we make two assumptions regarding the neuronal architecture: low dimensionality of activity patterns and the inclusion of target activity patterns in spontaneous activity profiles. These two characteristics of the neural architecture collectively deal with the three potential problems we discussed for the learning of targeted neural plasticity: the one-to-many correspondence between voxel signal level and neuronal activity patterns, the differences between evoked and spontaneous activities, and the curse of dimensionality.

However, the proposed architecture of the TNP model needs to be validated. In the subsequent sections, we describe recent empirical and computational evidence that supports the architecture.

5.3.1 Empirical evidence

Shibata and colleagues (Shibata et al., 2019) reanalyzed fMRI datasets obtained from five previous DecNef studies (Amano et al., 2016; Cortese et al., 2016, 2017; Koizumi et al., 2016; Shibata et al., 2011, 2016b) and tested the validity of the proposed architecture of the TNP model. The following three predictions were particularly tested. The results of the reanalyses were consistent with all predictions.

The first prediction is derived from the assumption of the low dimensionality at the neuronal level. If the assumption is correct, fMRI signal patterns in a target area should not be random, but highly structured, and therefore, low dimensional. To test this prediction, Shibata and colleagues applied the principal component analysis (PCA) to fMRI signal patterns of target areas measured during the induction stage. Approximately 30% of principal components (PCs) accounted for 80% of the variance of the fMRI signal patterns across the five DecNef studies (Shibata et al., 2019). The result of PCA is consistent with the prediction that fMRI signal patterns in a target area are not random, but low dimensional.

The second prediction was designed to test the assumption of the inclusion of target activity patterns in spontaneous activity patterns at the neuronal level. If the assumption is true, fMRI signal pattern should also hold a similar structure. In a DecNef experiment, a target fMRI signal pattern is identified in the decoder construction stage and participants are trained to express the target pattern in the induction stage via rewarding feedback to target pattern expression. Thus it is expected that there is a significant overlap between fMRI signal patterns of a target area measured in the decoder construction and induction stages. Shibata and colleagues applied PCA to fMRI signals obtained in the two stages (see Shibata et al., 2019 for details). According to the assumption, it is expected that PCs calculated based on fMRI signals in the decoder construction stage should account for a certain degree of variance of fMRI signals in the induction stage. The result of this across-stage PCA showed that approximately 60% of PCs computed based on fMRI signal patterns in the decoder construction stage accounted for 80% of the variance of the fMRI signal patterns in the induction stage across the five DecNef studies (Shibata et al., 2019). These results are consistent with the prediction of the overlap between fMRI signal patterns of a target area in the decoder construction and induction stages.

The third prediction was made by, again, the assumption of the inclusion of target activity patterns in spontaneous activity profiles. As discussed in Section 5.2.2, to enable efficient learning of induction of target neuronal activity patterns, it is reasonable to assume that the target neuronal activity patterns are included in neuronal activity patterns present at the beginning of DecNef training. Thus it was expected that a target fMRI signal pattern measured in the decoder construction stage is already included in fMRI signal patterns existing from the beginning of the induction stage. This prediction was validated by applying the above-mentioned across-stage PCA to fMRI signal patterns of a target area in each day of DecNef training in the orientation DecNef study and confirming overlap even on the first training day (Shibata et al., 2019).

5.3.2 Computational evidence

Is it indeed possible to induce target activity patterns at the neuronal level with the proposed architecture of the TNP model (Fig. 4)? To examine the computational plausibility of the architecture, Shibata and colleagues tested whether induction of target activities at the neuronal level occurs with DecNef by performing a biologically plausible neural network simulation based on the proposed architecture under a computational environment that mimicked the orientation DecNef study (Shibata et al., 2019).

A well-established neural network (Blumenfeld et al., 2006; Goldberg et al., 2004) was applied to the neuronal-level layer. This network consisted of a number of neurons interconnected with each other through synapses. Each neuron had unique orientation selectivity, analogous to neurons in the early visual cortex (Hubel et al., 1978). In this network, neurons that have similar orientation selectivities shared strong positive bidirectional synaptic weights, while synaptic weights between neurons with different types of orientation selectivity were weakly positive or negative (Blumenfeld et al., 2006; Goldberg et al., 2004). Due to this synaptic weight pattern, neuronal activities were constrained on a low-dimensional manifold, termed a ring attractor (Blumenfeld et al., 2006; Goldberg et al., 2004). After initial random activities were assigned to the neurons, an activity pattern of the neurons converged to one of the points on the ring-shaped attractor composed of activity patterns evoked by orientation stimuli.

Neurofeedback scores were computed based on fMRI signal patterns at the voxel-level layer. The model proposed by Kamitani and Tong (Kamitani and Tong, 2005) was employed. Each voxel in the early visual cortex had a weak orientation selectivity that presumably reflects a nonuniform distribution of orientation columns in the voxel. As in the orientation DecNef study, an orientation decoder was made based on fMRI signal patterns evoked by the presentation of real orientations.

Based on the feedback scores, synaptic weights among the neurons at the neuronal-level layer were updated. This update followed the Hebbian rule modulated by reinforcement learning signals driven by the feedback.

In this simulation, after DecNef training, activities at the neuronal-level layer became more likely to converge to the activity pattern corresponding to the target orientation than other nontarget orientations (Shibata et al., 2019). Thus orientation-related activity patterns at the neuronal-level layer can be efficiently enhanced by neurofeedback based on signal patterns at the voxel-level layer. Although this simulation focused on orientation processing in the early visual cortex, a similar computational simulation should work for other brain areas where activities of neurons are constrained on a low-dimensional manifold. Previous physiological studies have found these types of low-dimensional manifolds in the visual, auditory, motor, and prefrontal cortices (Berkes et al., 2011; Kenet et al., 2003; Luczak et al., 2009; Mochol et al., 2015; Oby et al., 2019; Renart et al., 2010; Ringach, 2009; Sadtler et al., 2014).

6 Summary and outstanding questions

In this chapter, we discussed plasticity mechanisms that underlie behavioral changes as a result of fMRI neurofeedback training. In particular, we proposed two models: the targeted neural plasticity (TNP) model and the learned modulation (LM) model. The behavioral changes due to fMRI neurofeedback training in conventional training paradigms are best explained by a combination of the LM and TNP models. On the other hand, the behavioral changes induced by the recent fMRI neurofeedback methods (i.e., DecNef) are best explained by the TNP model alone. The hypothesis that a low-dimensional functional architecture enables DecNef learning, supported by the empirical and computational evidence provided before (Section 5.3), can be tested via new investigations that directly measure activity changes at the neuronal level as a result of DecNef training in an animal brain. Such research is needed to conclusively validate the two assumptions at the neuronal level that allow us to explain DecNef learning: the low dimensionality of activity patterns and the inclusion of target activity patterns in spontaneous activity profiles.

The findings in this chapter have the following two important implications for future fMRI neurofeedback studies. First, a choice of fMRI neurofeedback methods for a study should be determined in light of the purpose of the study. Some studies aim to induce robust behavioral modifications while the underlying brain mechanisms are not of primary interest. In this case, one can choose the method that gives the highest effect size among the conventional and recent fMRI neurofeedback methods. On the other hand, if a study is conducted to gain knowledge about the relationship between a certain brain area and a specific aspect of behavior, one should use an fMRI neurofeedback method that enables the induction of target fMRI signals that are confined to the specific brain area trained. Such a method allows us to draw solid conclusions about the brain-behavior relationships.

Second, learning to induce desired fMRI signals and subsequent behavioral changes can occur based on implicit neurofeedback (Amano et al., 2016; Cortese et al., 2016, 2017; Koizumi et al., 2016; Shibata et al., 2011, 2016b; Taschereau-Dumouchel et al., 2018). These results indicate that implicit neurofeedback can effectively lead to changes in behaviors, despite the inherent temporal delay of fMRI signals due to neurovascular coupling (Logothetis and Wandell, 2004; Logothetis et al., 2001). The implicit nature of this method is potentially suitable for patients whose cognitive ability does not allow them to understand complicated training instructions (Watanabe et al., 2017) and can enable training paradigms that have therapeutic benefit while avoiding aversive experiences that often occur during conventional therapeutic treatments (Koizumi et al., 2016; Taschereau-Dumouchel et al., 2018).

One open question is whether fMRI neurofeedback training enables one to learn the induction of a new neuronal activity pattern, which is not originally included in the set of neuronal activity patterns spontaneously expressed by the individual. The TNP model assumes that a target neuronal activity pattern is already included in spontaneous activity patterns expressed at the beginning of DecNef training. This assumption is consistent with physiological findings that animals more effectively learn to induce target activity patterns at the neuronal level when the target activity patterns are included in a repertoire of spontaneous activities of those neurons (Sadtler et al., 2014). However, a recent study has reported that long-term training based on a brain-computer interface allowed monkeys to learn to generate new neuronal activity patterns that are not included in a repertoire of neural activities before training (Oby et al., 2019). Thus it would be essential to ask if fMRI neurofeedback is also capable of inducing new neuronal activity patterns, and if so, what methodological approach is required to achieve this. One potentially encouraging finding has been made by an fMRI neurofeedback study in individuals with autism spectrum disorder (ASD) (Ramot et al., 2017). It has been well established that connectivity patterns among brain areas are different between ASD and typically developed individuals (Yahata et al., 2016). In Ramot et al., a specific set of aberrant connectivity patterns, which had been shown to correlate with symptom severity, were used as a target for connectivity-based fMRI neurofeedback. The authors found that training based on the connectivity-based fMRI neurofeedback led to connectivity changes mainly in these aberrant connectivity patterns, which were correlated to changes in behavior after training. These findings are encouraging since they demonstrated the case that fMRI neurofeedback training can induce a certain fMRI signal pattern which rarely occurs in the brain of ASD individuals.

In summary, this chapter discussed the brain mechanisms underlying fMRI neurofeedback training. The existing findings indicate that there are multiple types of learning and plasticity potentially involved in different types of fMRI neurofeedback training. Further systematic investigations of the learning induced by different types of training protocols will lead to better understanding of the neural mechanisms of fMRI neurofeedback.

Acknowledgment

This work was partially supported by Japan Society for the Promotion of Science KAKENHI Grant Number 19H01041 and 20H05715.

References

Abbott, D.F., Opdam, H.I., Briellmann, R.S., Jackson, G.D., 2005. Brief breath holding may confound functional magnetic resonance imaging studies. Hum. Brain Mapp. 24, 284–290.

Amano, K., Shibata, K., Kawato, M., Sasaki, Y., Watanabe, T., 2016. Learning to associate orientation with color in early visual areas by associative decoded fMRI neurofeedback. Curr. Biol. 26, 1861–1866.

Berkes, P., Orbán, G., Lengyel, M., Fiser, J., 2011. Spontaneous cortical activity reveals hallmarks of an optimal internal model of the environment. Science 331, 83–87.

Birbaumer, N., Ruiz, S., Sitaram, R., 2013. Learned regulation of brain metabolism. Trends Cogn. Sci. 17, 295–302.

Blumenfeld, B., Bibitchkov, D., Tsodyks, M., 2006. Neural network model of the primary visual cortex: from functional architecture to lateral connectivity and back. J. Comput. Neurosci. 20, 219–241.

Bray, S., Shimojo, S., O'Doherty, J.P., 2007. Direct instrumental conditioning of neural activity using functional magnetic resonance imaging-derived reward feedback. J. Neurosci. 27, 7498–7507.

Caria, A., 2016. Self-regulation of blood oxygenation level dependent response: primary effect or epiphenomenon? Front. Neurosci. 10, 117.

Cortese, A., Amano, K., Koizumi, A., Kawato, M., Lau, H., 2016. Multivoxel neurofeedback selectively modulates confidence without changing perceptual performance. Nat. Commun. 7, 13669.

Cortese, A., Amano, K., Koizumi, A., Lau, H., Kawato, M., 2017. Decoded fMRI neurofeedback can induce bidirectional confidence changes within single participants. NeuroImage 149, 323–337.

deBettencourt, M.T., Cohen, J.D., Lee, R.F., Norman, K.A., Turk-Browne, N.B., 2015. Closed-loop training of attention with real-time brain imaging. Nat. Neurosci. 18, 470–475.

deCharms, R.C., Christoff, K., Glover, G.H., Pauly, J.M., Whitfield, S., Gabrieli, J.D.E., 2004. Learned regulation of spatially localized brain activation using real-time fMRI. NeuroImage 21, 436–443.

deCharms, R.C., Maeda, F., Glover, G.H., Ludlow, D., Pauly, J.M., Soneji, D., Gabrieli, J.D.E., Mackey, S.C., 2005. Control over brain activation and pain learned by using real-time functional MRI. Proc. Natl. Acad. Sci. U. S. A. 102, 18626–18631.

Emmert, K., Kopel, R., Sulzer, J., Brühl, A.B., Berman, B.D., Linden, D.E.J., Horovitz, S.G., Breimhorst, M., Caria, A., Frank, S., et al., 2016. Meta-analysis of real-time fMRI neurofeedback studies using individual participant data: how is brain regulation mediated? NeuroImage 124, 806–812.

Gaume, A., Vialatte, A., Mora-Sánchez, A., Ramdani, C., Vialatte, F.B., 2016. A psychoengineering paradigm for the neurocognitive mechanisms of biofeedback and neurofeedback. Neurosci. Biobehav. Rev. 68, 891–910.

Goldberg, J.A., Rokni, U., Sompolinsky, H., 2004. Patterns of ongoing activity and the functional architecture of the primary visual cortex. Neuron 42, 489–500.

Hamilton, J.P., Glover, G.H., Bagarinao, E., Chang, C., Mackey, S., Sacchet, M.D., Gotlib, I.H., 2016. Effects of salience-network-node neurofeedback training on affective biases in major depressive disorder. Psychiatry Res. Neuroimaging 249, 91–96.

Hampson, M., Ruiz, S., Ushiba, J., 2019. Neurofeedback. NeuroImage 218, 116473.

Haynes, J.-D., Rees, G., 2006. Decoding mental states from brain activity in humans. Nat. Rev. Neurosci. 7, 523–534.

Huang, T.-R., 2016. Hebbian Plasticity for Improving Perceptual Decisions. ArXiv:1612.03270.

Hubel, D.H., Wiesel, T.N., Stryker, M.P., 1978. Anatomical demonstration of orientation columns in macaque monkey. J. Comp. Neurol. 177, 361–380.

Johnson, K.A., Hartwell, K., LeMatty, T., Borckardt, J., Morgan, P.S., Govindarajan, K., Brady, K., George, M.S., 2012. Intermittent "real-time" fMRI feedback is superior to continuous presentation for a motor imagery task: a pilot study. J. Neuroimaging 22, 58–66.

Kamitani, Y., Tong, F., 2005. Decoding the visual and subjective contents of the human brain. Nat. Neurosci. 8, 679–685.

Kamitani, Y., Tong, F., 2006. Decoding seen and attended motion directions from activity in the human visual cortex. Curr. Biol. 16, 1096–1102.

Kastrup, A., Krüger, G., Glover, G.H., Moseley, M.E., 1999. Assessment of cerebral oxidative metabolism with breath holding and fMRI. Magn. Reson. Med. 42, 608–611.

Kenet, T., Bibitchkov, D., Tsodyks, M., Grinvald, A., Arieli, A., 2003. Spontaneously emerging cortical representations of visual attributes. Nature 425, 954–956.

Kennedy, J.E., Taddonio, J.L., 1976. Experimenter effects in parapsychological research. J. Parapsychol. 40, 1–33.

Koizumi, A., Amano, K., Cortese, A., Shibata, K., Yoshida, W., Seymour, B., Kawato, M., Lau, H., 2016. Fear reduction without fear through reinforcement of neural activity that bypasses conscious exposure. Nat. Hum. Behav. 1, 0006.

La Conte, S.M., Peltier, S.J., Hu, X.P., 2007. Real-time fMRI using brain-state classification. Hum. Brain Mapp. 28, 1033–1044.

Lee, D., Jang, C., Park, H.-J., 2019. Neurofeedback learning for mental practice rather than repetitive practice improves neural pattern consistency and functional network efficiency in the subsequent mental motor execution. NeuroImage 188, 680–693.

Logothetis, N.K., Wandell, B.A., 2004. Interpreting the BOLD signal. Annu. Rev. Physiol. 66, 735–769.

Logothetis, N.K., Pauls, J., Augath, M., Trinath, T., Oeltermann, A., 2001. Neurophysiological investigation of the basis of the fMRI signal. Nature 412, 150–157.

Luczak, A., Barthó, P., Harris, K.D., 2009. Spontaneous events outline the realm of possible sensory responses in neocortical populations. Neuron 62, 413–425.

Mochol, G., Hermoso-Mendizabal, A., Sakata, S., Harris, K.D., de la Rocha, J., 2015. Stochastic transitions into silence cause noise correlations in cortical circuits. Proc. Natl. Acad. Sci. U. S. A. 112, 3529–3534.

Oblak, E.F., Lewis-Peacock, J.A., Sulzer, J.S., 2017. Self-regulation strategy, feedback timing and hemodynamic properties modulate learning in a simulated fMRI neurofeedback environment. PLoS Comput. Biol. 13, e1005681.

Oby, E.R., Golub, M.D., Hennig, J.A., Degenhart, A.D., Tyler-Kabara, E.C., Yu, B.M., Chase, S.M., Batista, A.P., 2019. New neural activity patterns emerge with long-term learning. Proc. Natl. Acad. Sci. U. S. A. 116, 15210–15215.

Paret, C., Zähringer, J., Ruf, M., Gerchen, M.F., Mall, S., Hendler, T., Schmahl, C., Ende, G., 2018. Monitoring and control of amygdala neurofeedback involves distributed information processing in the human brain. Hum. Brain Mapp. 39, 3018–3031.

Radua, J., Stoica, T., Scheinost, D., Pittenger, C., Hampson, M., 2018. Neural correlates of success and failure signals during neurofeedback learning. Neuroscience 378, 11–21.

Ramot, M., Grossman, S., Friedman, D., Malach, R., 2016. Covert neurofeedback without awareness shapes cortical network spontaneous connectivity. Proc. Natl. Acad. Sci. U. S. A. 113, E2413–E2420.

Ramot, M., Kimmich, S., Gonzalez-Castillo, J., Roopchansingh, V., Popal, H., White, E., Gotts, S.J., Martin, A., 2017. Direct modulation of aberrant brain network connectivity through real-time NeuroFeedback. elife 6.

Renart, A., de la Rocha, J., Bartho, P., Hollender, L., Parga, N., Reyes, A., Harris, K.D., 2010. The asynchronous state in cortical circuits. Science 327, 587–590.

Ringach, D.L., 2009. Spontaneous and driven cortical activity: implications for computation. Curr. Opin. Neurobiol. 19, 439–444.

Sadtler, P.T., Quick, K.M., Golub, M.D., Chase, S.M., Ryu, S.I., Tyler-Kabara, E.C., Yu, B.M., Batista, A.P., 2014. Neural constraints on learning. Nature 512, 423–426.

Schabus, M., Griessenberger, H., Gnjezda, M.-T., Heib, D.P.J., Wislowska, M., Hoedlmoser, K., 2017. Better than sham? A double-blind placebo-controlled neurofeedback study in primary insomnia. Brain 140, 1041–1052.

Scharnowski, F., Hutton, C., Josephs, O., Weiskopf, N., Rees, G., 2012. Improving visual perception through neurofeedback. J. Neurosci. 32, 17830–17841.

Scheinost, D., Stoica, T., Saksa, J., Papademetris, X., Constable, R.T., Pittenger, C., Hampson, M., 2013. Orbitofrontal cortex neurofeedback produces lasting changes in contamination anxiety and resting-state connectivity. Transl. Psychiatry 3, e250.

Sepulveda, P., Sitaram, R., Rana, M., Montalba, C., Tejos, C., Ruiz, S., 2016. How feedback, motor imagery, and reward influence brain self-regulation using real-time fMRI. Hum. Brain Mapp. 37, 3153–3171.

Shibata, K., Watanabe, T., Sasaki, Y., Kawato, M., 2011. Perceptual learning incepted by decoded fMRI neurofeedback without stimulus presentation. Science 334, 1413–1415.

Shibata, K., Chang, L.-H., Kim, D., Náñez Sr., J.E., Kamitani, Y., Watanabe, T., Sasaki, Y., 2012. Decoding reveals plasticity in V3A as a result of motion perceptual learning. PLoS One 7, e44003.

Shibata, K., Sasaki, Y., Kawato, M., Watanabe, T., 2016a. Neuroimaging evidence for 2 types of plasticity in association with visual perceptual learning. Cereb. Cortex 26, 3681–3689.

Shibata, K., Watanabe, T., Kawato, M., Sasaki, Y., 2016b. Differential activation patterns in the same brain region led to opposite emotional states. PLoS Biol. 14, e1002546.

Shibata, K., Lisi, G., Cortese, A., Watanabe, T., Sasaki, Y., Kawato, M., 2019. Toward a comprehensive understanding of the neural mechanisms of decoded neurofeedback. NeuroImage 188, 539–556.

Sitaram, R., Ros, T., Stoeckel, L., Haller, S., Scharnowski, F., Lewis-Peacock, J., Weiskopf, N., Blefari, M.L., Rana, M., Oblak, E., et al., 2017. Closed-loop brain training: the science of neurofeedback. Nat. Rev. Neurosci. 18, 86–100.

Skottnik, L., Sorger, B., Kamp, T., Linden, D., Goebel, R., 2019. Success and failure of controlling the real-time functional magnetic resonance imaging neurofeedback signal are reflected in the striatum. Brain Behav. 9, e01240.

Subramanian, L., Hindle, J.V., Johnston, S., Roberts, M.V., Husain, M., Goebel, R., Linden, D., 2011. Real-time functional magnetic resonance imaging neurofeedback for treatment of Parkinson's disease. J. Neurosci. 31, 16309–16317.

Sukhodolsky, D.G., Walsh, C., Koller, W.N., Eilbott, J., Rance, M., Fulbright, R.K., Zhao, Z., Bloch, M.H., King, R., Leckman, J.F., Scheinost, D., Pittman, B., Hampson, M., 2020. Randomized, sham-controlled trial of real-time functional magnetic resonance imaging neurofeedback for tics in adolescents with Tourette syndrome. Biol. Psychiatry 87, 1063–1070.

Taschereau-Dumouchel, V., Cortese, A., Chiba, T., Knotts, J.D., Kawato, M., Lau, H., 2018. Towards an unconscious neural reinforcement intervention for common fears. Proc. Natl. Acad. Sci. U. S. A. 115, 3470–3475.

Thibault, L., van den Berg, R., Cavanagh, P., Sergent, C., 2016. Retrospective attention gates discrete conscious access to past sensory stimuli. PLoS One 11, e0148504.

Thibault, R.T., Lifshitz, M., Raz, A., 2017. Neurofeedback or neuroplacebo? Brain 140, 862–864.

Thibault, R.T., MacPherson, A., Lifshitz, M., Roth, R.R., Raz, A., 2018. Neurofeedback with fMRI: a critical systematic review. NeuroImage 172, 786–807.

van Gaal, S., Ridderinkhof, K.R., Scholte, H.S., Lamme, V.A.F., 2010. Unconscious activation of the prefrontal no-go network. J. Neurosci. 30, 4143–4150.

Watanabe, T., Sasaki, Y., Shibata, K., Kawato, M., 2017. Advances in fMRI real-time neurofeedback. Trends Cogn. Sci. 21, 997–1010.

Weiskopf, N., Veit, R., Erb, M., Mathiak, K., Grodd, W., Goebel, R., Birbaumer, N., 2003. Physiological self-regulation of regional brain activity using real-time functional magnetic resonance imaging (fMRI): methodology and exemplary data. NeuroImage 19, 577–586.

Weiss, F., Zamoscik, V., Schmidt, S.N.L., Halli, P., Kirsch, P., Gerchen, M.F., 2020. Just a very expensive breathing training? Risk of respiratory artefacts in functional connectivity-based real-time fMRI neurofeedback. NeuroImage 210, 116580.

Yahata, N., Morimoto, J., Hashimoto, R., Lisi, G., Shibata, K., Kawakubo, Y., Kuwabara, H., Kuroda, M., Yamada, T., Megumi, F., et al., 2016. A small number of abnormal brain connections predicts adult autism spectrum disorder. Nat. Commun. 7, 11254.

Yamashita, O., Sato, M.-A., Yoshioka, T., Tong, F., Kamitani, Y., 2008. Sparse estimation automatically selects voxels relevant for the decoding of fMRI activity patterns. NeuroImage 42, 1414–1429.

Yoo, S.S., Lee, J.H., O'Leary, H., Panych, L.P., Jolesz, F.A., 2008. Neurofeedback fMRI-mediated learning and consolidation of regional brain activation during motor imagery. Int. J. Imaging Syst. Technol. 18, 69–78.

Young, K.D., Siegle, G.J., Zotev, V., Phillips, R., Misaki, M., Yuan, H., Drevets, W.C., Bodurka, J., 2017. Randomized clinical trial of real-time fMRI amygdala neurofeedback for major depressive disorder: effects on symptoms and autobiographical memory recall. Am. J. Psychiatry 174, 748–755.

CHAPTER 14

Ethical considerations for fMRI neurofeedback

Mouslim Cherkaoui[a], Jesse Rissman[a], Hakwan Lau[a,b], and Michelle Hampson[c]
[a]*Department of Psychology, University of California, Los Angeles (UCLA), Los Angeles, CA, United States,* [b]*State Key Laboratory of Brain and Cognitive Sciences, The University of Hong Kong, Hong Kong,* [c]*Department of Radiology and Biomedical Imaging, Yale University School of Medicine, New Haven, CT, United States*

1 Introduction

Ask students enrolled in higher education whether it would be convenient to learn a new skill unconsciously, without effort or concentration. The answer will likely be "yes." And how about erasing the memory of a difficult breakup? To some people, such possibilities might constitute a violation of their ethical principles. To others, such possibilities might be appealing.[a]

Market trends have witnessed an increased interest from the general public in technologies that claim to read brain signals or stimulate the brain. There is now a significant "do-it-yourself" movement in which consumers self-administer brain stimulation (Zuk et al., 2018). According to one estimate, the neurointervention industry is expected to reach about $13 billion in 2022.[b]

Neurointervention technologies remain controversial, as many companies make unsubstantiated claims about their products. This has led to calls for regulation and oversight (Coates McCall et al., 2019; Wexler and Thibault, 2019). Additionally, the advent of novel neurotechnologies has led to calls for reconceptualization and updating of ethics guidelines (Yuste et al., 2017) and human rights (Ienca and Andorno, 2017) to consider these emerging technologies.

Although science fiction often portrays neurotechnology as a powerful tool for enhancement of mental function (e.g., *Limitless*) and memory editing (e.g., *Eternal Sunshine of the Spotless Mind*), current tools have relatively limited capabilities (Westbrook et al., 2020). Even so, newly emerging neurotechnologies can be used to attain meaningful behavioral and neural changes. Functional magnetic resonance imaging (fMRI)-based neurofeedback is one such powerful method.[c]

---

a https://www.npr.org/sections/health-shots/2018/09/18/646251015/this-rapper-tried-to-use-neuroscience-to-get-over-her-ex.

b https://www.prnewswire.com/news-releases/global-neurotechnology-market-2018-2022-largest-segment-is-currently-neuromodulation-followed-by-neuroprosthetics-and-neurosensing-300775578.html.

c fMRI neurofeedback will hereby be referred to as "neurofeedback" unless stated otherwise.

fMRI Neurofeedback. https://doi.org/10.1016/B978-0-12-822421-2.00007-7

Some neurofeedback methods are particularly controversial because they are able to attain changes in brain function without the participant's knowledge of the purpose of the training or awareness that they are being trained at all (Ramot et al., 2016). *Implicit neurofeedback*, in particular, can be used to change a participant's preferences (Shibata et al., 2016) or potentially to incept memories (Amano et al., 2016; see deBettencourt and Norman (2016) for discussion on using implicit neurofeedback to implant memories for associations that were never consciously experienced). Press articles covering neurofeedback studies have noted that neurofeedback "sounds [..] like brainwashing,"[d] and that "if neurofeedback is to reach its potential, it demands we think carefully about the scientific and philosophical basis of human agency."[e] As technology advances, it is expected that this method will become more powerful. Thus neurofeedback's yet unleashed potential requires serious ethical consideration for researchers and clinicians. Indeed, the United States Presidential Commission for the Study of Bioethical Issues concluded in its 2015 report: "We should be open to the possibilities that neuroscience can bring, while ensuring the progress and responsible application of neuroscience to the legal system and policymaking." The goal of this chapter is to discuss the ethical issues surrounding the use, and potential abuse, of fMRI neurofeedback.

Some of the issues are not entirely new or unique to neurofeedback as they overlap with other types of neurointervention technologies (hereby collectively referred to as *neurotechnologies*). Indeed, the debate as it pertains to other forms of neurotechnologies is very active. For an extended discussion of these issues, we refer readers to Linden (2014). It is not possible to do full justice to all the details and subtleties here, but our aim will be to highlight some of the main lines for argumentation as far as they are also relevant to fMRI neurofeedback. Identifying parallel problems will allow researchers and practitioners to get insight into how to best handle problems using existing theoretical resources before the problems arise, and will also help to identify issues that are unique to fMRI neurofeedback.

2 Ethical issues in common with other neurotechnologies

To understand what makes neurofeedback different from other neurotechnologies we first have to discuss what neurofeedback has in common with other neurotechnologies. Our focus here will be on ethical issues that also arise for so-called smart drugs (pharmaceuticals that putatively confer cognition-enhancing properties) and neurostimulation devices.

---

d https://spectrum.ieee.org/the-human-os/biomedical/imaging/dont-like-his-face-brain-train-the-feeling-to-be-more-positive.

e https://aeon.co/essays/neurofeedback-can-zap-your-fears-without-you-even-knowing.

2.1 Cognitive liberty

The notion that individuals' preferences and memories should not be altered without their consent is a central ethical concept. The right to control one's own consciousness and thought process has been argued to be fundamental to just about every other freedom (Lavazza, 2018; Sententia, 2006). Sententia (2006) defined cognitive liberty as "every person's fundamental right to think independently, to use the full spectrum of his or her mind, and to have autonomy over his or her own brain chemistry" (p. 223). Bublitz (2013, p. 251) argued that cognitive liberty requires both the liberty to change one's mind and the protection of mental integrity. Cognitive liberty is an updated notion of "freedom of thought" that takes into account the ability to monitor and manipulate cognitive function *by means other than one's own* (Bublitz, 2013; Sententia, 2006). As we will see later, what is meant by "by means other than one's own" is itself subject to a person's *perception* of their mental processes as truly being "their own."

To begin to understand the importance of cognitive liberty, let us consider a study in which researchers collected end-user data of people that had undergone deep brain stimulation (DBS) to treat their depression (Klein et al., 2016). Some of these patients reported that after surgery they had begun to wonder whether the device produced emotions artificially. The patients also reported that they worried about lost agency over their actions and whether the way they interacted with others was actually due to the DBS device. As one patient recounted "your feelings do not get attributed to you, they are all due to the device" (Klein et al., 2016, p. 5). This study showed that neurotechnology can profoundly disrupt people's sense of identity.

Of course, DBS treatments are invasive and therefore often the option of last resort for depression treatment. However, while neurofeedback is much safer from the perspective of physical risk, it shares with DBS a risk to cognitive liberty. That is, it is possible that by efficiently manipulating some emotions or preferences, or incepting memories, neurofeedback could cause participants to begin to question their autonomy and agency. It might also be possible that long-lasting mental and behavioral changes could be instilled in participants through neurofeedback. This may lead to compromised selective expression, and exemplifies that cognitive liberty may be relinquished to some extent for patients and participants undergoing neurofeedback. One review of the ethics of neurotechnologies and artificial intelligence by Yuste et al. (2017) noted that existing ethics guidelines are insufficient to address concerns such as these. Indeed, they assert that the Declaration of Helsinki, a statement of ethical principles involving human subjects, and the Belmont Report, a statement by the US National Commission of the Protection for Human Subjects of Biomedical and Behavioral Research, are both deficient in this regard.

Cognitive liberty concerns whether the participants *perceive* their own mental process as their own. The related concept of mental integrity is slightly different because it is not so much concerned with how a person perceives their mental processes. Mental integrity refers to the right of an individual's neural computation to be protected. Mental integrity is considered by the European Convention of Human Rights and the European Union Charter of Fundamental rights as a right to mental health that is understood more broadly as part of physical health by the World Health Organization. Given that the aim of neurofeedback is to alter neural and thereby mental function, issues of mental integrity and cognitive liberty are raised even when the induced alterations in mental function are desirable, as discussed next.

2.2 Enhancement

There are many neurotechnologies that aim to enhance cognition. Enhancement refers to a biomedical intervention that is meant to improve or reform the body or mind above physical or mental capacities (President's Council of Bioethics, 2003). Such technologies include noninvasive neurostimulation devices such as transcranial magnetic stimulation (TMS) and transcranial direct current stimulation (tDCS). Noninvasive brain stimulation has been used with some success to enhance complex cognitive processes such as source memory retrieval and arithmetic ability (Snowball et al., 2013; Westphal et al., 2019). Pharmacological drugs for neuroenhancement were originally developed to ameliorate neuropsychiatric disorders but subsequently reappropriated to improve focus, attention, and emotion recognition in healthy people (Brühl et al., 2019; Buyx, 2015). Examples of these "smart drugs" include Methylphenidate (sold under the trade name Ritalin), Amphetamines (sold under the trade name Adderall, for example), and Modafinil (sold under the trade name Provigil).

Similar to these other neurotechnologies, neurofeedback has successfully been used to improve attention during a sustained attention task and to boost recall of specific positive autobiographical memories (deBettencourt et al., 2015; Young et al., 2017). While the neurofeedback effects demonstrated to date are relatively focal, in contrast to the domain general effects typically seen from smart drugs or neurostimulation, this does not mean that more pervasive effects will not prove feasible as neurofeedback development proceeds.

Although some forms of neurofeedback may eventually provide effective cognitive enhancement, there is concern that the efficacy of neurofeedback technologies that are publicly available will be overstated and marketed in a misleading way. This is a concern shared by other neurotechnologies. The potency of smart drugs and neurostimulation devices has sometimes been criticized as "hyped up" or exaggerated in the media (Brühl et al., 2019; Zuk et al., 2018). Actual evidence for positive effects of smart drugs remains mixed (Battleday and Brem, 2015; Brühl et al., 2019; Ilieva et al., 2015; Partridge et al., 2011). Nevertheless, public interest has been encouraged by media reports (Zuk et al., 2018). According to one estimate the widespread use of smart drugs is increasing (Maier et al., 2018). Overall, studies have suggested that the public view neurotechnologies both with promise and concern (Bard et al., 2018; Medaglia et al., 2019). As with other neurotechnologies, it is important that researchers engage in discussion with the media and regulatory agencies about the potential uses and misuses of neurofeedback, and work to minimize the impact of misleading media coverage. Clear communication with the public regarding the capabilities and risks of neurofeedback is critical to minimizing the potential for unethical application or marketing.

2.2.1 The enhancement/treatment and authenticity debate

One philosophical question that is relevant for all neuroenhancement is: How do we distinguish between enhancement and treatment? The assumption inherent in any answer to such a question is that a clear border *exists* between enhancement for nontherapeutic purposes and treatment of a medical condition. It is assumed that this border can be used to determine when neurotechnologies are regarded as treatment for an illness and or an intervention that is mainly for personal interest, which is not deemed to be absolutely necessary. But it is difficult to draw this border in absolute terms because it would depend on the elusive concepts of health and "disease" (Boorse, 2011; Schermer, 2015).

The President's Council on Bioethics (2003) evaluated smart drugs negatively because of fears that users would exhibit changes to their personalities and thus become less authentic. The authenticity argument states that for a person to be authentic, they have to be true to oneself and feel that their feelings are their own. By altering cognitive states through smart drugs, people may become alienated from their own experiences and feelings, and have a distorted perception of the world from what it *truly* is (President's Council, 2003). On this view, the consequence of a society-wide dissemination of smart drugs would be that by taking smart drugs as a "quick fix" one can no longer claim one's own efforts and experiences as truly *one's own* (Buyx, 2015). And some have argued that memory-editing drugs may pose a particular threat to one's authenticity by deceiving oneself about the content of past experiences and influencing our "natural disposition" to respond to life events in a certain way (Erler, 2011).

However, for some people, using enhancement neurotechnologies may allow them to *attain* a sense of authenticity because they feel a detachment between their current self and their true self. Furthermore, another counterargument to those who view enhancement technologies as a violation of authenticity is that enhancement interventions exist on a continuum starting from coffee, to exercise, to brain surgery. It is not necessarily the case that just because these interventions are also used to treat illnesses that they cannot be ethical for enhancement purposes.

2.3 Safety and efficacy

Like any medical intervention, neurofeedback, smart drugs, and neurostimulation devices have faced questions of safety and efficacy. For example, because smart drugs were originally developed for and trialed on clinical populations with diagnosed diseases, evidence is lacking on the risks of use in those that have not been diagnosed. Fortunately, due in part to its value as a basic science research tool, early development of fMRI neurofeedback has involved extensive research in cognitively healthy as well as patient populations. Including careful adverse events monitoring in these basic science neurofeedback studies, as well as the clinical studies, could ensure that knowledge regarding the safety and efficacy advance together for both patient and healthy populations.

Of particular ethical concern is the theoretical possibility that one could implement neurofeedback to *worsen* symptoms or impair cognition and behavior. Given our limited understanding of brain function, this can happen even when researchers have the best intentions. For instance, Ruiz et al. (2013) trained schizophrenia patients to achieve control of bilateral anterior insula cortex to improve facial emotion recognition (a common deficit in schizophrenia). While patients increased their ability to recognize disgust faces, their ability to recognize happy faces declined. As neurofeedback and our understanding of brain function develops, the capacity to target specific emotions and memories will increase, and accidental downstream effects will hopefully be minimized. There will, however, always be a potential for abuse. One can imagine a scenario in which neurofeedback originally developed to influence face preferences (Shibata et al., 2016) could instead be used by a malicious experimenter to try to make themselves more attractive to the subject. Similarly, neurofeedback could be used to influence preferences for specific brands of expensive products. Indeed, such a scheme could be accomplished if companies "sponsor" neuroimaging studies in return for a short neurofeedback scan that influences the subject without their knowledge. While this might seem unlikely, the research community needs to take such a possibility seriously and be prepared to thwart any insidious applications of neurofeedback technology. Doing so will involve proactively engaging with the public, regulators, and other researchers to create a dialogue around what types of interventions are considered ethically acceptable in which contexts.

One important distinction between neurofeedback and pharmacological drugs is that while the cognitive and behavioral impact of pharmacological drugs is continuously diminished by metabolic processes, neurofeedback can likely have more long-lasting effects. Recent studies have suggested that only a few neurofeedback sessions can induce effects that may last up to months or years (Megumi et al., 2015; Amano et al., 2016; Ramot et al., 2016, 2017; Rance et al., 2018; Robineau et al., 2017), but further work is needed to clarify the persistence of effects (both desired and undesired) across applications (Paret et al., 2019; Rance et al., 2018; Thibault et al., 2018). This is relevant to both the clinical efficacy of a neurofeedback-based intervention and the potential risks it engenders. More data on persistence of effects are necessary from an ethical perspective to evaluate the costs and benefits of neurofeedback interventions.

2.3.1 Enhancing the developing brain

Cohen-Kadosh et al. (2012) pointed out that great caution should be taken with regard to neurostimulation of the developing brain. Enhancing some abilities through neurostimulation may come at a cost for some other modalities, which may cause interference with normal brain development (Doruk Camsari et al., 2018; Hameed et al., 2017; Maslen et al., 2014). This reasoning has led to the suggestion that brain stimulation for enhancement purposes should be delayed until "the child has reached a state of maturity" (Maslen et al., 2014, p. 2). Similar concerns have been raised against shaping not-yet-mature brain networks of children through neurofeedback (Cohen-Kadosh et al., 2016). On the other hand, early intervention has potential to yield the greatest lifelong benefits by harnessing the high plasticity of childhood, and steering development at an early stage onto a more positive trajectory. Thus developmental applications of fMRI neurofeedback are potentially valuable but also potentially dangerous, and the need for careful monitoring of long-term outcomes is particularly acute in pediatric populations.

2.4 Reversibility of effect

The reversibility of the effect is directly related to Bublitz's first dimension of cognitive liberty, namely the liberty to change one's mind. Just as it is important to demonstrate that neurofeedback can induce an effect, it is important to determine if the effect can be suppressed or eliminated entirely with reverse feedback. This is especially relevant given reports that just a few training sessions can have lasting effects (Amano et al., 2016; Megumi et al., 2015; Ramot et al., 2017). There is also practical value in being able to "cancel out" any negative behavioral side effects of neurofeedback, should these occur.

Very little is known regarding the reversibility of neurofeedback effects. Cortese et al. (2017) demonstrated that it is possible, by training brain patterns in the opposite direction, to reverse to some extent the behavioral changes induced by neurofeedback within single participants. Participants were first trained, via decoded neurofeedback, to either up-regulate or down-regulate their level of confidence in a perceptual task, and then they were trained to modulate confidence in the opposite direction. The results showed evidence for "anterograde interference" such that previous learning interfered with subsequent learning. Indeed, once participants had been trained to up-regulate their confidence, retraining in the opposite direction only canceled out 20% of this effect, indicating that 80% of the original effect size persisted despite the experimenters' efforts to override it. Of course, the efficacy of cancellation is likely dependent on the number of induction training and reverse training days. Furthermore, reversibility is likely to be highly context dependent, varying depending on the circuitry trained and the timing between training and reverse training sessions. More studies are needed that investigate reversibility of neurofeedback effects. In particular, such work will be valuable for neurofeedback interventions that are demonstrated to be effective before they are considered/adapted for widespread application.

3 Distinct ethical issues raised by fMRI neurofeedback

In comparison with other noninvasive neurointerventions (pharmaceutical and transcranial stimulation-based approaches), neurofeedback effects on the brain can be targeted much more flexibly. That is, detailed and complex spatial patterns of brain activity (or functional connectivity) corresponding to biomarkers of the mental functions of interest can be trained to be induced by participants via fMRI neurofeedback. Although invasive neurostimulation (e.g., intracranial recordings) can achieve superior spatial specificity, fMRI neurofeedback is unique in that it may have the potential to effectively mold very precise spatial patterns of brain activity/connectivity in a completely noninvasive manner, and even without awareness of training occurring (Ramot et al., 2016; Taschereau-Dumouchel et al., 2018a). To the extent that this capacity translates into a powerful tool for mental control, existing ethical concerns may be amplified, and unique ethical issues may be raised.

For the purposes of this discussion, it is helpful to distinguish two types of ethical concerns associated with fMRI neurofeedback. One is concerned with the social impact of mental influence if exerted broadly across a large population of people. Even a small influence, of little note to an individual neurofeedback participant, could have dramatic repercussions on society if leveraged across large numbers of people. The second concerns the well-being of the trained individuals, and potential violations of their individual autonomy due to substantial influence over their personal mental, emotional, or perceptual function. These two possible concerns are described in more detail below, after which we discuss implicit neurofeedback, a form of neurofeedback that highlights these ethical challenges.

3.1 The potential for broad social impacts of neurofeedback

We believe that fMRI neurofeedback itself is extremely unlikely to be used for broad social influence, given the expense and inconvenience of MRI scanning. However, the advances it provides in terms of identifying neurofeedback targets that can be trained to influence specific aspects of mental function, if translated to other neuroimaging modalities, could pose risks of this nature. This concern is thus based heavily on speculation regarding the development and translation of neurofeedback. However, it is important to note that translation of neurofeedback to other modalities is currently a research area of great interest (Keynan et al., 2016, 2019; Meir-Hasson et al., 2014, 2016). In this current age where technical developments can sweep through society more quickly than ethical frameworks can develop, some thoughtful speculation and discussion is healthy for ensuring socially responsible development.

In a talk in 2019 at Harvard University, Mark Zuckerberg reported that Facebook is working on developing a portable headset for monitoring brain function. To quote from a *Wired* article reporting on this talk "The technology that Zuckerberg described is a shower-cap-looking device that surrounds a brain and discovers connections between particular thoughts and particular blood flows or brain activity, presumably to assist the glasses or headsets manufactured by Oculus VR, which is part of Facebook."[f] It's conceivable the public would embrace this new technology when marketed for its convenience and entertainment value. However, the linking of a device that monitors brain function to a feedback display via glasses or headsets would provide the full technological setup for neurofeedback. Successful dissemination of such a device to large numbers of people (presumably, the goal of Facebook) would create a science fiction-like scenario with frightening potential for social influence and control. Of course, the ability of the device to accurately measure complex brain patterns of relevance to mental function would be a critical limiting factor over its ability to influence people's thoughts and behaviors. However, even a small influence in a critical direction applied to large numbers of people can be very dangerous. Apparently, the device already "can distinguish when a person is thinking of a giraffe or an elephant based on neural activity."[f] In short, the potential for development along these lines is concerning. Communication with the public and government regulatory agencies regarding these risks, and the development of guidelines for preventing abuse of such technologies are needed.

3.2 Potential risks to individual subjects

The origins of neurofeedback trace back to operant autonomic conditioning. During the early days of electroencephalography (EEG) neurofeedback, many enthusiasts hailed EEG neurofeedback as a technology that could allow "mind-expansion" (Kimmel, 1986). While research in this area has progressed, in reality, EEG neurofeedback applications have to date proven more limited. It is similarly difficult to foresee how potent fMRI neurofeedback will prove to be as a tool for molding mental function. Although recent coverage has noted that fMRI neurofeedback "sounds... like brainwashing"[d] it has not been demonstrated as enabling effective control over the complex thought patterns of an individual to the degree typically associated with brainwashing, that is, to the degree that an individual's strongly held views can be reversed or specific thoughts can be introduced against their will. However, it has been demonstrated that learned associations can be trained into an individual via neurofeedback (Amano et al., 2016), that preferences can be altered (Shibata et al., 2016), and perceptions can be biased (Shibata et al., 2011). Thus fMRI neurofeedback can be used to alter some aspects of mental function, and an important question is whether further development will lead to a more powerful tool for mind control.

---

f https://www.wired.com/story/zuckerberg-wants-facebook-to-build-mind-reading-machine/.

To place this issue in context, it is important to note that the ability to influence mental function is not unique to neurofeedback, as basic psychological methods can also mold mental function. For example, researchers have demonstrated the ability to create a "false memory" simply by using suggestive techniques (Loftus, 2005). In one study, researchers falsely suggested to their participants that the participants had become ill after eating an egg salad as a child (Geraerts et al., 2008). This led some participants to confidently believe that they indeed had experienced this childhood event at a 4-month follow-up, even though they had previously denied having experienced it. What is more, the 4-month follow-up found that believers' eating behaviors and preferences reflected an intent to avoid egg salad. Geraerts et al. (2008) comment in their discussion that researchers should consider that they may induce lasting false beliefs in their participants that "have consequences not only for attitudes, but also behavior" (p. 752). We note that this is very similar to concerns that have been raised for neurofeedback protocols (Nakazawa et al., 2016; Sadato et al., 2019; see also Horstkötter, 2016).

Given that neurofeedback appears capable of inducing long-lasting behavioral, perceptual, and cognitive changes, researchers should give ethical consideration to the ways in which they develop and implement this technology. Important questions to answer include: Should neurofeedback be allowed to "enhance" cognitive capacity in healthy humans (e.g., to boost one's ability to flexibly shift or sustain attentional focus, maintain and manipulate information in working memory, form and retrieve long-term memories, make more rational decisions, etc.)? Should researchers be allowed to create artificial memories (e.g., to help people replace fearful associations with safer ones) and change preferences (e.g., to promote healthier eating habits or diminish harmful addictions)? Should researchers be allowed to manipulate emotions, and if so, which ones and in what contexts (e.g., to reduce sadness in depressed patients or worry in patient's anxiety disorders)? What are the long-term effects of such manipulations? What could constitute an adverse effect? What impacts could wide dissemination of neurofeedback have on societal norms and values? And how could neurofeedback be abused in the wrong hands? These are all important ethical questions that have yet to be fully explored and answered for modern fMRI neurofeedback.

3.3 Implicit neurofeedback

As discussed before, some forms of neurofeedback involve keeping the participant unaware of the precise nature of the intervention (e.g., Shibata et al., 2011). Implicit neurofeedback studies are important because they prevent participants from knowing the experimenters' goals and having expectations regarding the outcome of the training. In this way, implicit neurofeedback protocols can avoid potential confounds such as demand bias (participants reporting what they think the experimenter is hoping they will report) and placebo effects (participants experiencing effects consistent with their expectations). Theoretically, implicit neurofeedback may also be more efficient for some applications, by allowing subconscious learning to proceed without the interference of conscious effort (see, e.g., Sepulveda et al., 2016). Finally, implicit neurofeedback can be used in populations that cannot follow complex instructions or as an alternative for populations that find explicit therapeutic training aversive (Watanabe et al., 2017).

Implicit protocols have been demonstrated to induce effects with high degrees of behavioral and neural specificity (Ramot et al., 2016, 2017; Shibata et al., 2016, 2019). For example, using implicit neurofeedback, Shibata et al. (2016) showed that preferences for faces can be manipulated unconsciously with a high degree of specificity (i.e. by modulating different patterns of neural activity representing opposite directions of facial preferences *within* a brain region) and other studies have demonstrated implicit neurofeedback can be used to unconsciously manipulate perceptual confidence (Cortese et al., 2016) and physiological threat responses toward animals and objects (Taschereau-Dumouchel et al., 2018a). Emerging neurofeedback capabilities will be able to target more complex neural systems (Bassett and Khambhati, 2017), albeit within the limits to which the brain is robust to perturbations introduced through neurofeedback. Implicit neurofeedback can thus have nontrivial effects on mental function, and researchers who wish to use implicit neurofeedback are faced with unique challenges in obtaining informed consent from participants.

Informed consent is the process by which a researcher or clinician gets permission from a participant or patient before conducting an intervention. The Belmont Report specifies informed consent as part of a fundamental ethical principle for human subjects' research. Most, if not all, institutions consider the Belmont Report an essential reference for the institutional review board (IRB). Informed consent can only be obtained if the participant is of sound cognitive capacity and is provided with sufficient information to understand the potential risks and benefits of participation. Of course, implicit neurofeedback complicates the underlying assumption that the participant has sufficient information to evaluate the potential risks and benefits.

Given that many research studies rely on a degree of deception or secrecy of purpose, there is some allowance for this in the informed consent process. Deceptive instructions or omissions of information during the consent process can be authorized if it is deemed that the value and importance of a study can justify it, if the results cannot be obtained in some other way. However, sufficient information must still be provided to the participant to allow them to assess the risks and benefits of participation. In a situation involving deception or omission, it is important to consider that information that is sufficient for most people may not be sufficient for everyone.

For example, in the egg salad study discussed before, if a participant recently became vegetarian and disliked beans and dairy products, eggs could be a critical source of protein and the vitamin B12 for them. Inducing an aversion to egg salad in this case could actually result in a nontrivial dietary limitation. In short, the more information that is withheld, and the more deception that is used, the more risk there is that some participants may be unable to accurately assess risk of participation.

It is important to note that the degree to which implicit neurofeedback involves withholding information from participants can be considered as a continuum. On one end of the continuum are studies where participants do not even know that they are receiving neurofeedback. For example, Ramot et al. (2016) led participants to believe that they were participating in a neuroimaging study of reward responses in the brain, so participants had no idea that the reward they were receiving was dependent on their brain activity. More often, in implicit neurofeedback studies, participants are made aware of the fact that mental function is being trained by neurofeedback, but they are given no information about what aspect of mental function is trained (Amano et al., 2016; Cortese et al., 2016; Shibata et al., 2011, 2016). In some cases, participants may be given information regarding multiple possible types of mental function that may be trained, but are blinded to which type of training they will receive. Note that this approach involves a similar level of deception/omission as so-called explicit neurofeedback protocols that involve blinded control groups. This highlights that the explicit/implicit distinction may be less relevant from the perspective of ethical considerations than the degree of withheld information which varies in a dimensional sense across all neurofeedback protocols from those with full disclosure to those where participants do not even know they are being trained.

The more information is withheld during the consent process, the more responsibility falls on researchers and clinicians to avoid unwanted outcomes (Nakazawa et al., 2016). Extreme caution should be taken to ensure that the potential for any adverse effect is kept at minimum. One way to enhance informed consent but keep the participant unaware of the precise nature of the intervention is to let the participant know that the experiment involves placebo-controlled groups or conditions. This is a common procedure in clinically oriented neurofeedback experiments (Taschereau-Dumouchel et al., 2018a; Young et al., 2017; Zweerings et al., 2019).

Standards and guidelines set by IRBs and professional associations will often require that researchers debrief their study participants after completing the study. In the research context, a debriefing following participation is often included that provides more information to the subject regarding their training and its purpose. In cases of double-blind experiments, debriefing takes place once blinding is no longer critical for scientific purposes. In a nonresearch context, the mental aspects trained, and the purpose of that training should also be disclosed.

4 Conclusion

The goal of neurofeedback is to train participants to control specific aspects of brain activity. This technology is still in its infancy but holds much promise. It has potential as a personalized intervention tool for mental disorders which can be tested in double-blind and placebo-controlled settings (Chiba et al., 2019; Taschereau-Dumouchel et al., 2018b; Zahn et al., 2019). The ability to make causal inferences allows researchers the capacity to better study the relationship between the brain and behavior. Neurofeedback is only limited by how effectively its brain activity targets can be trained and how causally related those targets are to the mental functions of interest.

With new opportunities come new ethical challenges. The potential of neurofeedback to mold mental function raises concerns regarding threats to cognitive liberty that may be amplified over other noninvasive neurotechnologies if neurofeedback training proves capable of more effectively targeting specific mental processes. As fMRI neurofeedback is translated to more portable, accessible modalities, concerns arise regarding its potential social impact. Evidence for the efficacy of implicit neurofeedback amplifies these risks as well as risks to individual participants. Furthermore, the risk-benefit ratio of different neurofeedback protocols is not well understood given the limited data currently available on the longevity and reversibility of effects. In short, fMRI neurofeedback involves complex ethical concerns that deserve attention from the researchers who are developing its capacities for scientific and clinical application, and that should be communicated clearly to participants and to the public more generally.

The aim of this chapter is not to provide guidelines for the ethical conduct of fMRI neurofeedback research, which in our opinion, should be developed with input from the broader community. However, we can propose a few simple steps that could be helpful in fostering positive development. These include the collection of more follow-up data, not only monitoring persistence of the intended effects on mental function, but also incorporating broad screening of adverse events in both basic science and clinical studies. Careful management of prospective participants' expectations before neurofeedback training is also important. Fortunately, this is generally well managed at present due to existing regulatory frameworks governing human subjects' research. Finally, greater communication is needed on ethical issues between researchers, regulators, and the public.

As acknowledged early on, this is not intended as a comprehensive review of all the relevant ethical issues. Ethical issues are at risk of being overlooked as researchers often fail to imagine the personal impacts on participants or the potentially far-reaching consequences of increased dissemination in the context of technological development. However, it is important that we anticipate and reflect upon these issues before they become problematic. We hope this will provide a starting point for fruitful discussions on the ethics of fMRI neurofeedback.

Acknowledgments

MH was supported by the National Institute of Mental Health (R01 MH100068 and R61 MH115110), and the American Endowment Foundation (project titled "A neurofeedback booster for emotion regulation therapy").

References

Amano, K., Shibata, K., Kawato, M., Sasaki, Y., Watanabe, T., 2016. Learning to associate orientation with color in early visual areas by associative decoded fMRI neurofeedback. Curr. Biol. 26 (14), 1861–1866. https://doi.org/10.1016/j.cub.2016.05.014.

Bard, I., Gaskell, G., Allansdottir, A., da Cunha, R.V., Eduard, P., Hampel, J., et al., 2018. Bottom up ethics – neuroenhancement in education and employment. Neuroethics 11 (3), 309–322. https://doi.org/10.1007/s12152-018-9366-7.

Bassett, D.S., Khambhati, A.N., 2017. A network engineering perspective on probing and perturbing cognition with neurofeedback. Ann. N. Y. Acad. Sci. 1396, 126–143. https://doi.org/10.1111/nyas.13338.

Battleday, R.M., Brem, A.K., 2015. Modafinil for cognitive neuroenhancement in healthy non-sleep-deprived subjects: a systematic review. Eur. Neuropsychopharmacol. 25 (11), 1865–1881. https://doi.org/10.1016/j.euroneuro.2015.07.028.

Boorse, C., 2011. Concepts of Health and Disease. Philosophy of Medicine. Vol. 16 Elsevier B.V., https://doi.org/10.1016/B978-0-444-51787-6.50002-7.

Brühl, A.B., d'Angelo, C., Sahakian, B.J., 2019. Neuroethical issues in cognitive enhancement: modafinil as the example of a workplace drug? Brain and Neurosci. Adv. 3. https://doi.org/10.1177/2398212818816018, 239821281881601.

Bublitz, J.-C., 2013. My Mind Is Mine!? Cognitive Liberty as a Legal Concept. Springer, pp. 233–264, https://doi.org/10.1007/978-94-007-6253-4_19.

Buyx, A., 2015. Smart drugs: ethical issues. In: Handbook of Neuroethics, pp. 1192–1204, https://doi.org/10.1007/978-94-007-4707-4.

Chiba, T., Kanazawa, T., Koizumi, A., Ide, K., Taschereau-Dumouchel, V., Boku, S., et al., 2019. Current status of neurofeedback for post-traumatic stress disorder: a systematic review and the possibility of decoded neurofeedback. Front. Hum. Neurosci. 13 (July), 1–13. https://doi.org/10.3389/fnhum.2019.00233.

Coates McCall, I., Lau, C., Minielly, N., Illes, J., 2019. Owning ethical innovation: claims about commercial wearable brain technologies. Neuron 102 (4), 728–731. https://doi.org/10.1016/j.neuron.2019.03.026.

Cohen-Kadosh, R.C., Levy, N., O'Shea, J., Shea, N., Savulescu, J., 2012. The neuroethics of non-invasive brain stimulation. Curr. Biol. 22 (4), R108–R111. https://doi.org/10.1016/j.cub.2012.01.013.

Cohen-Kadosh, K., Lisk, S., Lau, J.Y.F., 2016. The ethics of (neuro) feeding back to the developing brain. AJOB Neurosci. 7 (2), 132–133. https://doi.org/10.1080/21507740.2016.1189979.

Cortese, A., Amano, K., Koizumi, A., Kawato, M., Lau, H., 2016. Multivoxel neurofeedback selectively modulates confidence without changing perceptual performance. Nat. Commun. 7, 1–18. https://doi.org/10.1038/ncomms13669.

Cortese, A., Amano, K., Koizumi, A., Lau, H., Kawato, M., 2017. Decoded fMRI neurofeedback can induce bidirectional confidence changes within single participants. NeuroImage 149 (February), 323–337. https://doi.org/10.1016/j.neuroimage.2017.01.069.

deBettencourt, M.T., Norman, K.A., 2016. Neuroscience: incepting associations. Curr. Biol. 26 (14), R673–R675. https://doi.org/10.1016/j.cub.2016.05.041.

DeBettencourt, M.T., Cohen, J.D., Lee, R.F., Norman, K.A., Turk-Browne, N.B., 2015. Closed-loop training of attention with real-time brain imaging. Nat. Neurosci. 18 (3), 470–478. https://doi.org/10.1038/nn.3940.

Doruk Camsari, D., Kirkovski, M., Croarkin, P.E., 2018. Therapeutic applications of noninvasive neuromodulation in children and adolescents. Psychiatr. Clin. N. Am. 41 (3), 465–477. https://doi.org/10.1016/j.psc.2018.05.003.

Erler, A., 2011. Does memory modification threaten our authenticity? Neuroethics 4 (3), 235–249. https://doi.org/10.1007/s12152-010-9090-4.

Geraerts, E., Bernstein, D.M., Merckelbach, H., Linders, C., Raymaekers, L., Loftus, E.F., 2008. Lasting false beliefs and their behavioral consequences. Psychol. Sci. 19 (8), 749–753. https://doi.org/10.1111/j.1467-9280.2008.02151.x.

Hameed, M.Q., Dhamne, S.C., Gersner, R., Kaye, H.L., Oberman, L.M., Pascual-Leone, A., Rotenberg, A., 2017. Transcranial magnetic and direct current stimulation in children. Curr. Neurol. Neurosci. Rep. 17 (2), 1–25. https://doi.org/10.1007/s11910-017-0719-0.

Horstkötter, D., 2016. The ethics of novel Neurotechnologies: focus on research ethics and on moral values. AJOB Neurosci. 7 (2), 123–125. https://doi.org/10.1080/21507740.2016.1172135.

Ienca, M., Andorno, R., 2017. Towards new human rights in the age of neuroscience and neurotechnology. Life Sci. Soc. Policy 13 (1), 5. https://doi.org/10.1186/s40504-017-0050-1.

Ilieva, I., Hook, C., Farah, M., 2015. Prescription stimulants' effects on healthy inhibitory control, working memory, and episodic memory: a meta-analysis Irena. J. Cogn. Neurosci., 1–21. https://doi.org/10.1162/jocn.

Keynan, J.N., Meir-Hasson, Y., Gilam, G., Cohen, A., Jackont, G., Kinreich, S., et al., 2016. Limbic activity modulation guided by functional magnetic resonance imaging–inspired electroencephalography improves implicit emotion regulation. Biol. Psychiatry 80 (6), 490–496. https://doi.org/10.1016/j.biopsych.2015.12.024.

Keynan, J.N., Cohen, A., Jackont, G., Green, N., Goldway, N., Davidov, A., et al., 2019. Electrical fingerprint of the amygdala guides neurofeedback training for stress resilience. Nat. Hum. Behav. 3 (1), 63–73. https://doi.org/10.1038/s41562-018-0484-3.

Kimmel, H.D., 1986. The myth and the symbol of biofeedback. Int. J. Psychophysiol. 3 (3), 211–218. https://doi.org/10.1016/0167-8760(86)90029-2.

Klein, E., Goering, S., Gagne, J., Shea, C.V., Franklin, R., Zorowitz, S., et al., 2016. Brain-computer interface-based control of closed-loop brain stimulation: attitudes and ethical considerations. Brain Comput. Interfaces 3 (3), 140–148. https://doi.org/10.1080/2326263X.2016.1207497.

Lavazza, A., 2018. Freedom of thought and mental integrity: the moral requirements for any neural prosthesis. Front. Neurosci. 12, 1–10. https://doi.org/10.3389/fnins.2018.00082.

Linden, D., 2014. Brain Control: Developments in Therapy and Implications for Society, first ed. Palgrave Macmillan, New York, https://doi.org/10.1057/9781137335333.

Loftus, E.F., 2005. Planting misinformation in the human mind: a 30-year investigation of the malleability of memory. Learn. Mem. 12, 361–366. https://doi.org/10.1101/lm.94705.

Maier, L.J., Ferris, J.A., Winstock, A.R., 2018. Pharmacological cognitive enhancement among non-ADHD individuals—a cross-sectional study in 15 countries. Int. J. Drug Policy 58 (May), 104–112. https://doi.org/10.1016/j.drugpo.2018.05.009.

Maslen, H., Earp, B.D., Kadosh, R.C., Savulescu, J., 2014. Brain stimulation for treatment and enhancement in children: an ethical analysis. Front. Hum. Neurosci. 8, 1–5. https://doi.org/10.3389/fnhum.2014.00953.

Medaglia, J.D., Yaden, D., Helion, C., Haslam, M., 2019. Moral attitudes and willingness to induce cognitive enhancement and repair with brain stimulation. Brain Stimul. 12 (1), 44–53. https://doi.org/10.1016/j.brs.2018.09.014.Moral.

Megumi, F., Yamashita, A., Kawato, M., Imamizu, H., 2015. Functional MRI neurofeedback training on connectivity between two regions induces long-lasting changes in intrinsic functional network. Front. Hum. Neurosci. 9, 160. https://doi.org/10.3389/fnhum.2015.00160.

Meir-Hasson, Y., Kinreich, S., Podlipsky, I., Hendler, T., Intrator, N., 2014. An EEG finger-print of fMRI deep regional activation. NeuroImage 102 (P1), 128–141. https://doi.org/10.1016/j.neuroimage.2013.11.004.

Meir-Hasson, Y., Keynan, J.N., Kinreich, S., Jackont, G., Cohen, A., Podlipsky-Klovatch, I., et al., 2016. One-class FMRI-inspired EEG model for self-regulation training. PLoS One 11 (5), 1–17. https://doi.org/10.1371/journal.pone.0154968.

Nakazawa, E., Yamamoto, K., Tachibana, K., Toda, S., Takimoto, Y., Akabayashi, A., 2016. Ethics of decoded neurofeedback in clinical research, treatment, and moral enhancement. AJOB Neurosci. 7 (2), 110–117. https://doi.org/10.1080/21507740.2016.1172134.

Paret, C., Goldway, N., Zich, C., Keynan, J.N., Hendler, T., Linden, D., Cohen Kadosh, K., 2019. Current progress in real-time functional magnetic resonance-based neurofeedback: methodological challenges and achievements. NeuroImage 202. https://doi.org/10.1016/j.neuroimage.2019.116107, 116107.

Partridge, B.J., Bell, S.K., Lucke, J.C., Yeates, S., Hall, W.D., 2011. Smart drugs "as common as coffee": media hype about neuroenhancement. PLoS One 6 (11). https://doi.org/10.1371/journal.pone.0028416.

President's Council of Bioethics, 2003. Beyond Therapy. Biotechnology and the Pursuit of Happiness. Dana Press, New York.

Ramot, M., Grossman, S., Friedman, D., Malach, R., 2016. Covert neurofeedback without awareness shapes cortical network spontaneous connectivity. Proc. Natl. Acad. Sci. U. S. A. 113 (17), E2413–E2420. https://doi.org/10.1073/pnas.1516857113.

Ramot, M., Kimmich, S., Gonzalez-Castillo, J., Roopchansingh, V., Popal, H., White, E., et al., 2017. Direct modulation of aberrant brain network connectivity through real-time NeuroFeedback. elife 6, 1–23. https://doi.org/10.7554/eLife.28974.

Rance, M., Walsh, C., Sukhodolsky, D.G., Pittman, B., Qiu, M., Kichuk, S.A., et al., 2018. Time course of clinical change following neurofeedback. NeuroImage 181 (May), 807–813. https://doi.org/10.1016/j.neuroimage.2018.05.001.

Robineau, F., Meskaldji, D.E., Koush, Y., Rieger, S.W., Mermoud, C., Morgenthaler, S., et al., 2017. Maintenance of voluntary self-regulation learned through real-time fMRI neurofeedback. Front. Hum. Neurosci. 11 (March), 1–8. https://doi.org/10.3389/fnhum.2017.00131.

Ruiz, S., Lee, S., Soekadar, S.R., Caria, A., Veit, R., Kircher, T., et al., 2013. Acquired self-control of insula cortex modulates emotion recognition and brain network connectivity in schizophrenia. Hum. Brain Mapp. https://doi.org/10.1002/hbm.21427.

Sadato, N., Morita, K., Kasai, K., Fukushi, T., Nakamura, K., Nakazawa, E., et al., 2019. Neuroethical issues of the brain/MINDS project of Japan. Neuron 101 (3), 385–389. https://doi.org/10.1016/j.neuron.2019.01.006.

Schermer, M., 2015. Ethics of pharmacological mood enhancement. In: Handbook of Neuroethics, pp. 1178–1189, https://doi.org/10.1007/978-94-007-4707-4.

Sententia, W., 2006. Neuroethical considerations: cognitive liberty and converging technologies for improving human cognition. Ann. N. Y. Acad. Sci. 1013 (1), 221–228. https://doi.org/10.1196/annals.1305.014.

Sepulveda, P., Sitaram, R., Rana, M., Montalba, C., Tejos, C., Ruiz, S., 2016. How feedback, motor imagery, and reward influence brain self-regulation using real-time fMRI. Hum. Brain Mapp. https://doi.org/10.1002/hbm.23228.

Shibata, K., Watanabe, T., Sasaki, Y., Kawato, M., 2011. Perceptual learning incepted by decoded fMRI neurofeedback without stimulus presentation. Science 334 (6061), 1413–1415. https://doi.org/10.1126/science.1212003.

Shibata, K., Watanabe, T., Kawato, M., Sasaki, Y., 2016. Differential activation patterns in the same brain region led to opposite emotional states. PLoS Biol. 14 (9), 1–27. https://doi.org/10.1371/journal.pbio.1002546.

Shibata, K., Lisi, G., Cortese, A., Watanabe, T., Sasaki, Y., Kawato, M., 2019. Toward a comprehensive understanding of the neural mechanisms of decoded neurofeedback. NeuroImage 188 (July 2018), 539–556. https://doi.org/10.1016/j.neuroimage.2018.12.022.

Snowball, A., Tachtsidis, I., Popescu, T., Thompson, J., Delazer, M., Zamarian, L., et al., 2013. Long-term enhancement of brain function and cognition using cognitive training and brain stimulation. Curr. Biol. 23 (11), 987–992. https://doi.org/10.1016/j.cub.2013.04.045.

Taschereau-Dumouchel, V., Cortese, A., Chiba, T., Knotts, J.D., Kawato, M., Lau, H., 2018a. Towards an unconscious neural reinforcement intervention for common fears. Proc. Natl. Acad. Sci. 115 (13), 3470–3475. https://doi.org/10.1073/pnas.1721572115.

Taschereau-Dumouchel, V., Liu, K.Y., Lau, H., 2018b. Unconscious psychological treatments for physiological survival circuits. Curr. Opin. Behav. Sci. 24, 62–68. https://doi.org/10.1016/j.cobeha.2018.04.010.

Thibault, R.T., MacPherson, A., Lifshitz, M., Roth, R.R., Raz, A., 2018. Neurofeedback with fMRI: a critical systematic review. NeuroImage 172 (September 2017), 786–807. https://doi.org/10.1016/j.neuroimage.2017.12.071.

Watanabe, T., Sasaki, Y., Shibata, K., Kawato, M., 2017. Advances in fMRI real-time neurofeedback. Trends Cogn. Sci. 21 (12), 997–1010. https://doi.org/10.1016/j.tics.2017.09.010.

Westbrook, A., van den Bosch, R., Määttä, J.I., Hofmans, L., Papadopetraki, D., Cools, R., Frank, M.J., 2020. Dopamine promotes cognitive effort by biasing the benefits versus costs of cognitive work. Science 367 (6484), 1362–1366. https://doi.org/10.1126/SCIENCE.AAZ5891.

Westphal, A., Chow, T., Ngoy, C., Zuo, X., Liao, V., Storozuk, L., et al., 2019. Anodal Transcranial direct current stimulation to the left rostrolateral prefrontal cortex selectively improves source memory retrieval. J. Cogn. Neurosci., 1–12. https://doi.org/10.1162/jocn.

Wexler, A., Thibault, R., 2019. Mind-Reading or misleading? Assessing direct-to-consumer electroencephalography (EEG) devices marketed for wellness and their ethical and regulatory implications. J. Cogn. Enhanc. 3 (1), 131–137. https://doi.org/10.1007/s41465-018-0091-2.

Young, K.D., Siegle, G.J., Zotev, V., Phillips, R., Misaki, M., Yuan, H., et al., 2017. Randomized clinical trial of real-time fMRI amygdala neurofeedbackfor major depressive disorder: effects on symptoms and autobiographical memory recall. Am. J. Psychiatr. 174 (8), 748–755. https://doi.org/10.1176/appi.ajp.2017.16060637.

Yuste, R., Goering, S., Agüeray Arcas, B., Bi, G., Carmena, J.M., Carter, A., et al., 2017. Four ethical priorities for neurotechnologies and AI. Nature 551 (7679), 159–163. https://doi.org/10.1038/551159a.

Zahn, R., Weingartner, J.H., Basilio, R., Bado, P., Mattos, P., Sato, J.R., et al., 2019. Blame-rebalance fMRI neurofeedback in major depressive disorder: a randomised proof-of-concept trial. NeuroImage: Clinical 24 (August), 101992. https://doi.org/10.1016/j.nicl.2019.101992.

Zuk, P., Torgerson, L., Sierra-Mercado, D., Lazaro-Munoz, G., 2018. Neuroethics of neuromodulation: an update. Curr. Opin. Biomed. Eng. 8, 45–59. https://doi.org/10.1016/j.cobme.2018.10.003.

Zweerings, J., Hummel, B., Keller, M., Zvyagintsev, M., Schneider, F., Klasen, M., Mathiak, K., 2019. Neurofeedback of core language network nodes modulates connectivity with the default-mode network: a double-blind fMRI neurofeedback study on auditory verbal hallucinations. NeuroImage 189 (January), 533–542. https://doi.org/10.1016/j.neuroimage.2019.01.058.

CHAPTER 15

Resource reference for fMRI neurofeedback researchers

James S. Sulzer

Department of Mechanical Engineering, University of Texas at Austin, Austin, TX, United States

1 Resources for rtfMRI neurofeedback

Neurofeedback is a relatively small field; as a result it relies on the resourcefulness and ingenuity of the researchers to create tools. Over recent years, a number of resources have become available for new and advanced neurofeedback researchers courtesy of the scientific community. These resources include neurofeedback software, databases, websites, and an email list. This chapter tabulates these resources as a reference for the reader. This reference is intended to point the researcher to different resources, but does not provide a subjective evaluation of these resources. Links are included to both source code and further information where necessary. Links to publications on these resources or to those using these resources are also included. We do not include clinical trial resources, as they are beyond the scope of this chapter, but researchers planning to run clinical trials may want to visit the CONSORT website before beginning their study (consort-statement.org) and should consider registering in advance on a recognized clinical trial registry such as clinicaltrials.gov.

fMRI Neurofeedback. https://doi.org/10.1016/B978-0-12-822421-2.00018-1

Websites	Features
neurofeedback-research.org	Links to software, images, and metaanalysis initiative
rtfin.org	Links to literature, resources, and events

Email list	Features	Subscribe
rtfin@utlists.utexas.edu	• Job announcements • Technical questions • Events • Resources	utlists.utexas.edu/sympa/subscribe/rtfin

Neurofeedback software	Features	Links	Publication
AFNI Real-Time Interface	• Python-based interface for AFNI's real-time code as standalone library • Compatibility with Windows, OS X, and Linux • Provides template experiment using PsychoPy • Requires AFNI installation	Code: github.com/roopchansinghv/afni-real-time-interface-in-python Info: pypi.org/project/afniRTI/	
BART	• Open-source • Capable of traditional and adaptive neurofeedback	Code: github.com/bart-group/BART	
Bimodal/Flexible VR Neurofeedback	• VR environment written in C# and unity • Compatible with any data/analysis • Training two neural patterns independently or in parallel • Bimodal neurofeedback (e.g., fMRI with EEG)	Code: github.com/LAM-UPC/Flexible_VR_neurofeedback_v5.0	doi.org/10.5281/zenodo.3256442
Bioimage Suite	• Written in C++/TCL • Uses GPU acceleration • Connectome-based neurofeedback	Info: medicine.yale.edu/bioimaging/suite/	sciencedirect.com/science/article/pii/S1053811920301713 link.springer.com/article/10.1007%2Fs12021-013-9176-3

BrainIAK	• Cloud-based, open-source • Interface written in Python • Can be configured to run from cloud, cluster, or control room	Code: github.com/brainiak/rt-cloud Tutorial: github.com/brainiak/brainiak-aperture	osf.io/db2ev
DecNef	• Based on basic Matlab and SPM • Decoded neurofeedback • Plug-and-play but modifiable • Accommodates continuous or dichotomous target constructs	Info: bicr.atr.jp/decnefpro/software/	academic.oup.com/scan/advance-article/doi/10.1093/scan/nsaa063/5828926
FieldTrip	• Matlab-based scripts that run real-time on Siemens scanners • Requires FieldTrip running on another machine in network	Info: fieldtriptoolbox.org/development/realtime/fmri/	
fMRwhy	• Matlab- and SPM12-based toolbox • BIDS-compatible workflows • fMRI quality checking and preprocessing • Real-time multiecho fMRI analysis	Code: github.com/jsheunis/fMRwhy	
FRIEND	• Written in C++ • Standalone ROI, connectivity, and decoded neurofeedback • Uses FSL-based functions	Code: nitrc.org/projects/friend/	frontiersin.org/articles/10.3389/fnbeh.2015.00003/full
Multipurpose VR Biofeedback	• Open-source, written in C# and unity • VR environment for feedback • Compatible with any data/analysis	Code: github.com/LAM-UPC/VR_multipurpose_v1.0	doi.org/10.1093/brain/awaa011
OpenNFT	• Open-source, Python, and Matlab-based • Platform independent, compatible with most scanners • ROI, connectivity, DCM, and decoded neurofeedback capability • Real-time quality assessment	Code: github.com/OpenNFT/OpenNFT Info: opennft.org	sciencedirect.com/science/article/pii/S1053811917305050 sciencedirect.com/science/article/pii/S2352340917303517
Personode	• Open-source MATLAB-based toolbox • Uses resting-state data to obtain subject-specific ROI • Helps classification of group-specific ICA maps into canonical resting-state networks	Code: github.com/gustavopamplona/Personode	link.springer.com/article/10.1007/s12021-019-09449-4

Continued

Neurofeedback software	Features	Links	Publication
Pyneal	• Open-source, Python-based • Supports fully customizable analyses by the user • Can accommodate different scanners	Code: github.com/jeffmacinnes/pyneal	frontiersin.org/articles/10.3389/fnins.2020.00900/full
Real-Time Quality Control Toolbox	• Open-source; written in Matlab and Bash • Real-time preprocessing • Real-time QC metric display (FD, Global Z-score, tSNR, Grayplot)	Code: github.com/rtQC-group/rtQC	zenodo.org/record/3239084#-X-LA2thKiUl
Scan Session Tool	• Open-source, written in Python • (f)MRI scan session documentation and automatized data archiving • Save session protocol and raw data into unified hierarchical folder structure • Cross-platform • Special support for Turbo-BrainVoyager	Info: fladd.github.io/ScanSessionTool	
scanSTAT	• Freeware for Mac • Allows real-time viewing of medical images	Info: brainmapping.org/scanSTAT/	
Turbo BrainVoyager (TBV)	• Commercial software from Brain Innovation • Offers an open C++ plugin interface for custom analysis steps • ROI, connectivity, and multivariate capability • Compatible with most scanners	Info: brainvoyager.com/products/turbobrainvoyager.html	
TBV Thermometer	• Open-source, Matlab-based • ROI and connectivity-based feedback • Works with TBV	Code: github.com/CIBIT-ICNAS/TBV_Thermometer	doi.org/10.1371/journal.pone.0155961

Experimental Paradigm Creation	Features	Links	Publication
Expyriment	• Open-source, written in Python • Library for cognitive and neuroscientific experiments • Design and conduct timing-critical experiments • Cross-platform • Plugins available for interfacing with TBV	Info: expyriment.org	doi.org/10.3758/s13428-013-0390-6
Pyparadigm	• Simple, declarative image/screen composition • Handles keyboard and mouse input • Based on and interoperable with pygame • Does not interfere with programming style	Info: pyparadigm.readthedocs.io/en/latest/	frontiersin.org/articles/10.3389/fninf.2019.00059/full

Databases	Features	Links	Publication
ATR Dataset	• One database, five DecNef studies • Targets different psychological constructs and ROIs but with the same neurofeedback design • Contains more than 60 subjects, each with at least three training sessions • Decoder construction data are also available	Info: https://bicr-resource.atr.jp/drmd/	nature.com/articles/s41597-021-00845-7
Empenn Datasets	• Two NF datasets (XP1/XP2) using motor imagery task • XP1—10 subjects, XP2—20 subjects, all healthy • Using different feedback (unimodal, bimodal 1D, or bimodal 2D) of simultaneous EEG-fMRI training • Data available in BIDS format	XP1: openneuro.org/datasets/ds002336d XP2: openneuro.org/datasets/ds002338	nature.com/articles/s41597-020-0498-3

Continued

Databases	Features	Links	Publication
Neurofeedback Methods Database	• Interactive metaanalysis of 128 neurofeedback studies • Analyzes type of feedback, scanner, preprocessing techniques	Info: rtfmri-methods.herokuapp.com/	onlinelibrary.wiley.com/doi/full/10.1002/hbm.25010
Real-Time Multiecho fMRI Database	• Contains resting-state and task data from 28 healthy volunteers • BIDS-compliant	Info: rt-me-fmri.herokuapp.com/	biorxiv.org/content/10.1101/2020.12.07.414490v1 biorxiv.org/content/10.1101/2020.12.07.414490v1
Rockland Database	• Anonymized cognitive, behavioral, genetics, and neuroimaging data from over 1000 subjects • Covers ages 6–85 years old • Resting-state fMRI, DTI, structural images	Info: http://fcon_1000.projects.nitrc.org/indi/enhanced/	frontiersin.org/articles/10.3389/fnins.2012.00152/full

Index

Note: Page numbers followed by *f* indicate figures, *t* indicate tables, and *b* indicate boxes.

early *vs.* higher visual areas, 97–98
fusiform face area (FFA), 95–97
higher-order visual areas, 94–97
parahippocampal place area (PPA), 95–97

ventral pathway, 94–95
visual motion imagery strategies, 95
Visual sensitivity, 89
Volitional regulation, of midbrain, 138

W
WiiFit protocol, 253

Y
Y-BOCS, 219
Yoked sham, 69

Printed in the United States
by Baker & Taylor Publisher Services